I0828512

HISTORIC PHOTOS OF
GRAND RAPIDS

TEXT AND CAPTIONS BY KAROLEE R. HAZLEWOOD

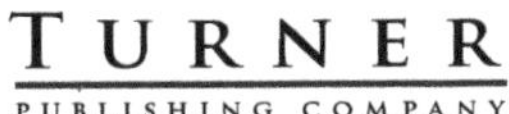

Harvesting and hauling cut logs was once accomplished without the aid of steam-powered or motorized machinery.

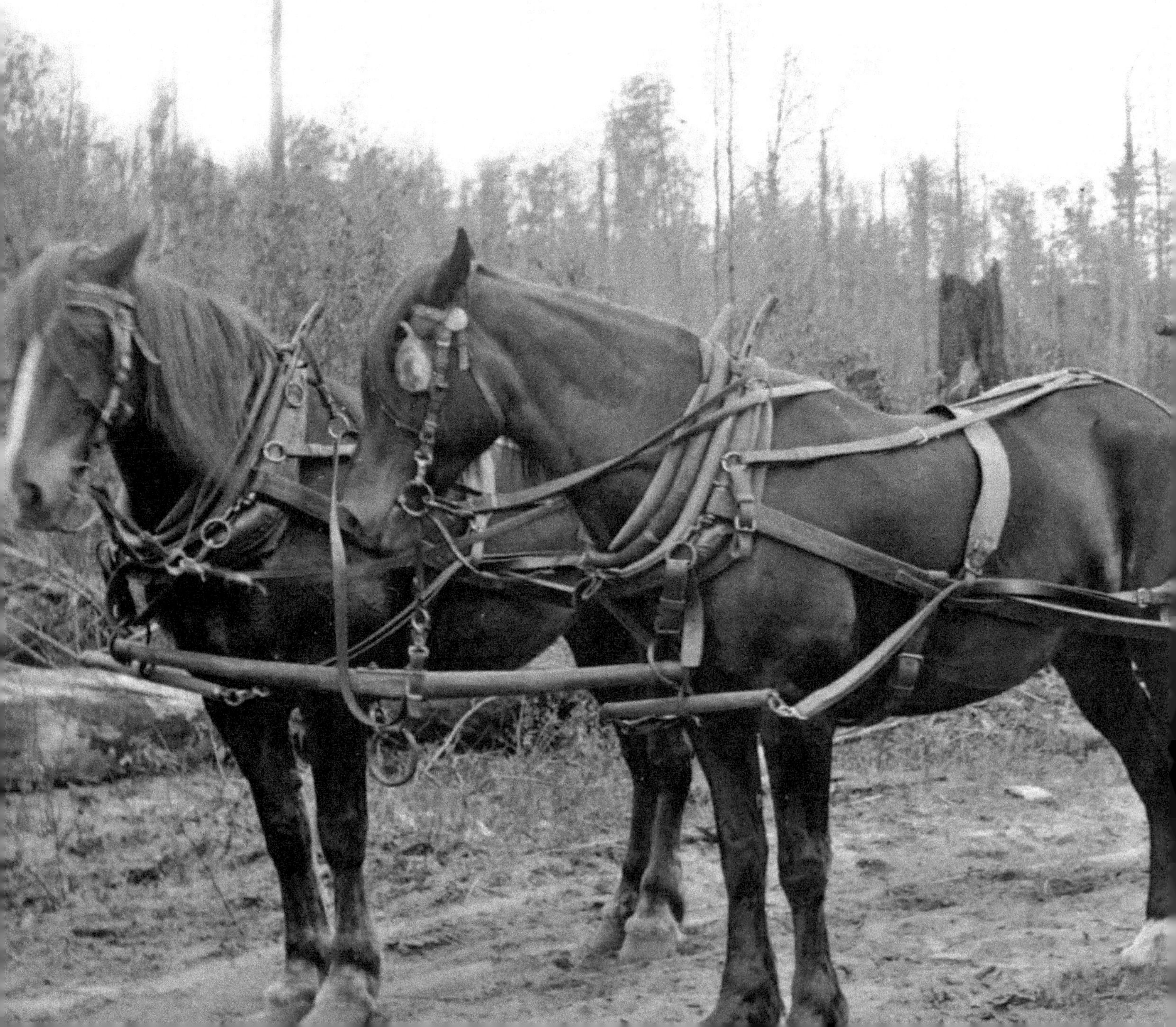

HISTORIC PHOTOS OF GRAND RAPIDS

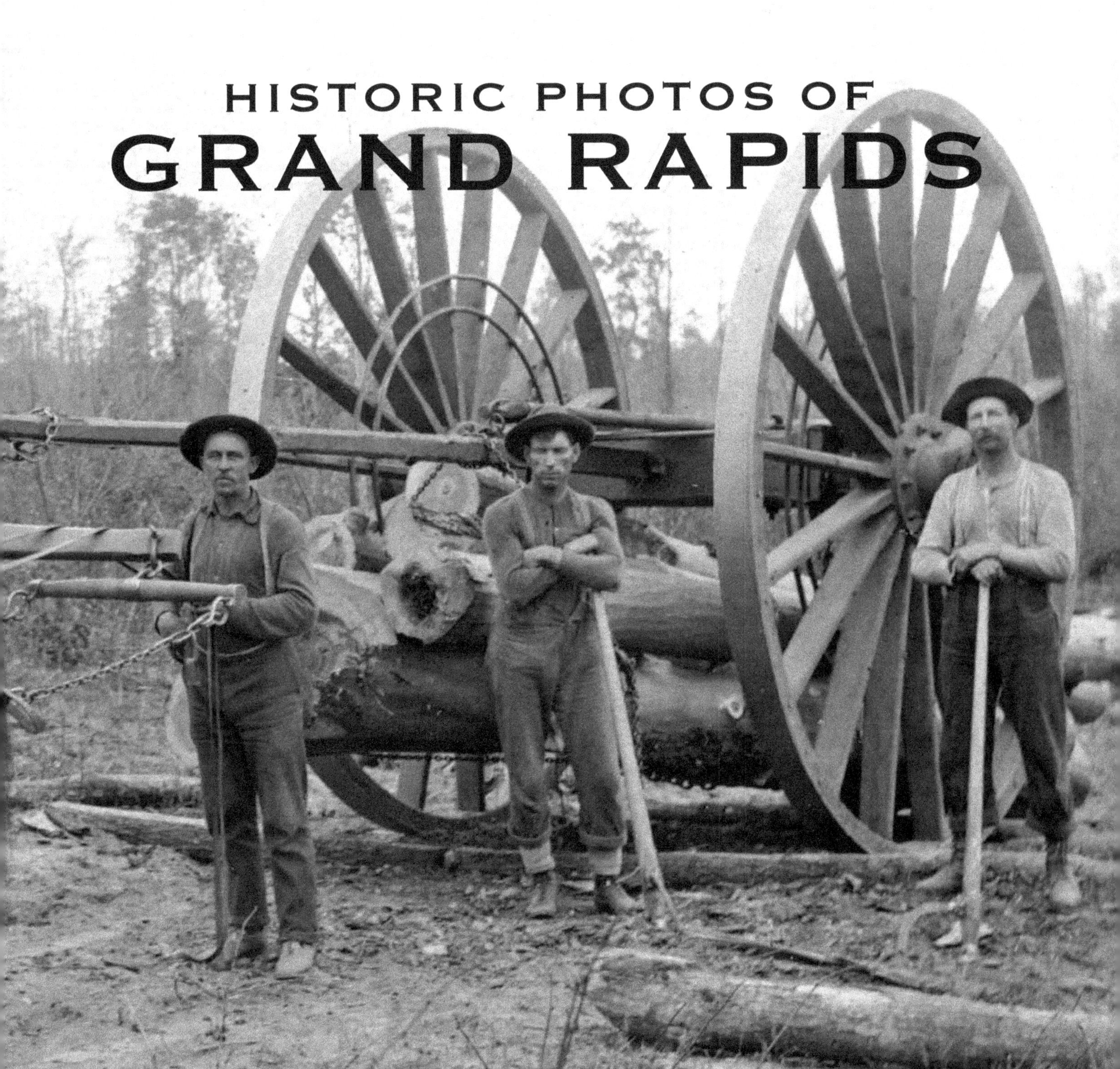

Turner Publishing Company
www.turnerpublishing.com

Historic Photos of Grand Rapids

Library of Congress Control Number: 2008901862

ISBN-13: 978-1-59652-473-6

Printed in the United States of America

ISBN 978-1-68442-028-5 (hc)

Contents

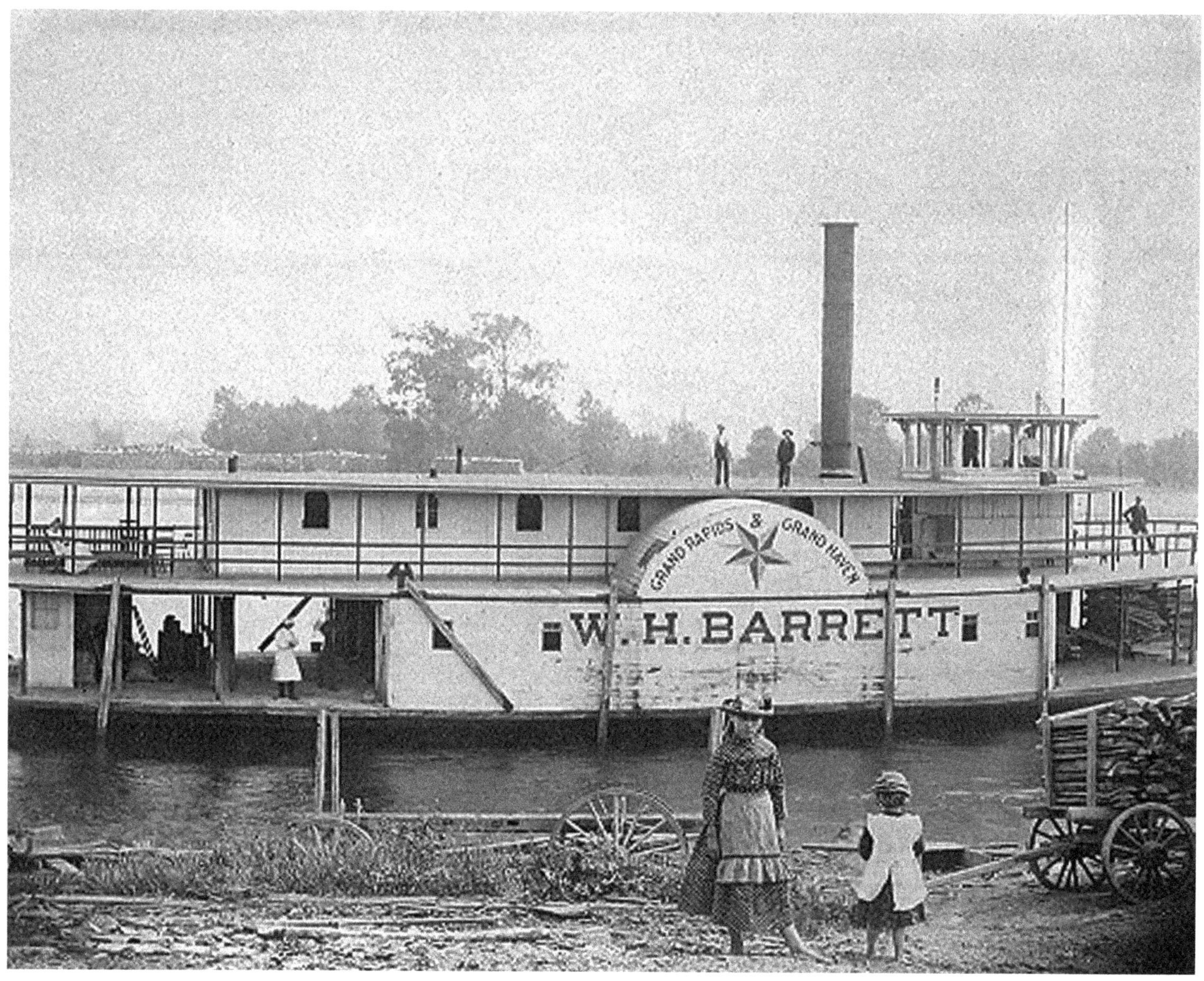

The wood-fueled steamer, *W. H. Barrett,* ran between Grand Rapids and Grand Haven on the Grand River. Steamboat *Barrett* was built in 1874 and ran until 1894. It was designed and built by John Muir for the Ganoe Company.

Acknowledgments

This volume, *Historic Photos of Grand Rapids,* is the result of the cooperation and efforts of many individuals and organizations. It is with great thanks that we acknowledge the valuable contribution of the Grand Rapids History and Special Collections Department of the Grand Rapids Public Library for their generous support.

Preface

Grand Rapids has thousands of historic photographs that reside in archives, both locally and nationally. This book began with the observation that, while those photographs are of great interest to many, they are not easily accessible. During a time when Grand Rapids is looking ahead and evaluating its future course, many people are asking, How do we treat the past? These decisions affect every aspect of the city—architecture, public spaces, commerce, infrastructure—and these, in turn, affect the way that people live their lives. This book seeks to provide easy access to a valuable, objective look into the history of this great city.

The power of photographs is that they are less subjective than words in their treatment of history. Although the photographer can make decisions regarding subject matter and how to capture and present it, photographs do not provide the breadth of interpretation that text does. For this reason, they offer an original, untainted perspective that allows the viewer to interpret and observe.

This project represents countless hours of review and research. The researchers and writer have reviewed thousands of photographs in numerous archives. We greatly appreciate the generous assistance of the individuals and organizations listed in the acknowledgments of this work, without whom this project could not have been completed.

The goal in publishing this work is to provide broader access to this set of extraordinary photographs that seek to inspire, provide perspective, and evoke insight that might assist people who are responsible for determining Grand Rapids' future. In addition, the book seeks to preserve the past with adequate respect and reverence.

With the exception of touching up imperfections caused by the damage of time and cropping where necessary, no other changes have been made. The focus and clarity of many images is limited to the technology and the ability of the photographer at the time they were taken.

The work is divided into eras. Beginning with some of the earliest-known photographs of Grand Rapids, the first section records photographs through the end of the nineteenth century. The second section spans the beginning of the twentieth century through World War I. Section Three moves through the era between the great wars. The last section covers the World War II era to recent times.

In each of these sections we have made an effort to capture various aspects of life through our selection of photographs. People, commerce, transportation, infrastructure, religious institutions, and educational institutions have been included to provide a broad perspective.

We encourage readers to reflect as they go walking in Grand Rapids, strolling through the city, its parks, and its neighborhoods. It is the publisher's hope that in utilizing this work, longtime residents will learn something new and that new residents will gain a perspective on where the city has been, so that each can contribute to its future.

—Todd Bottorff, Publisher

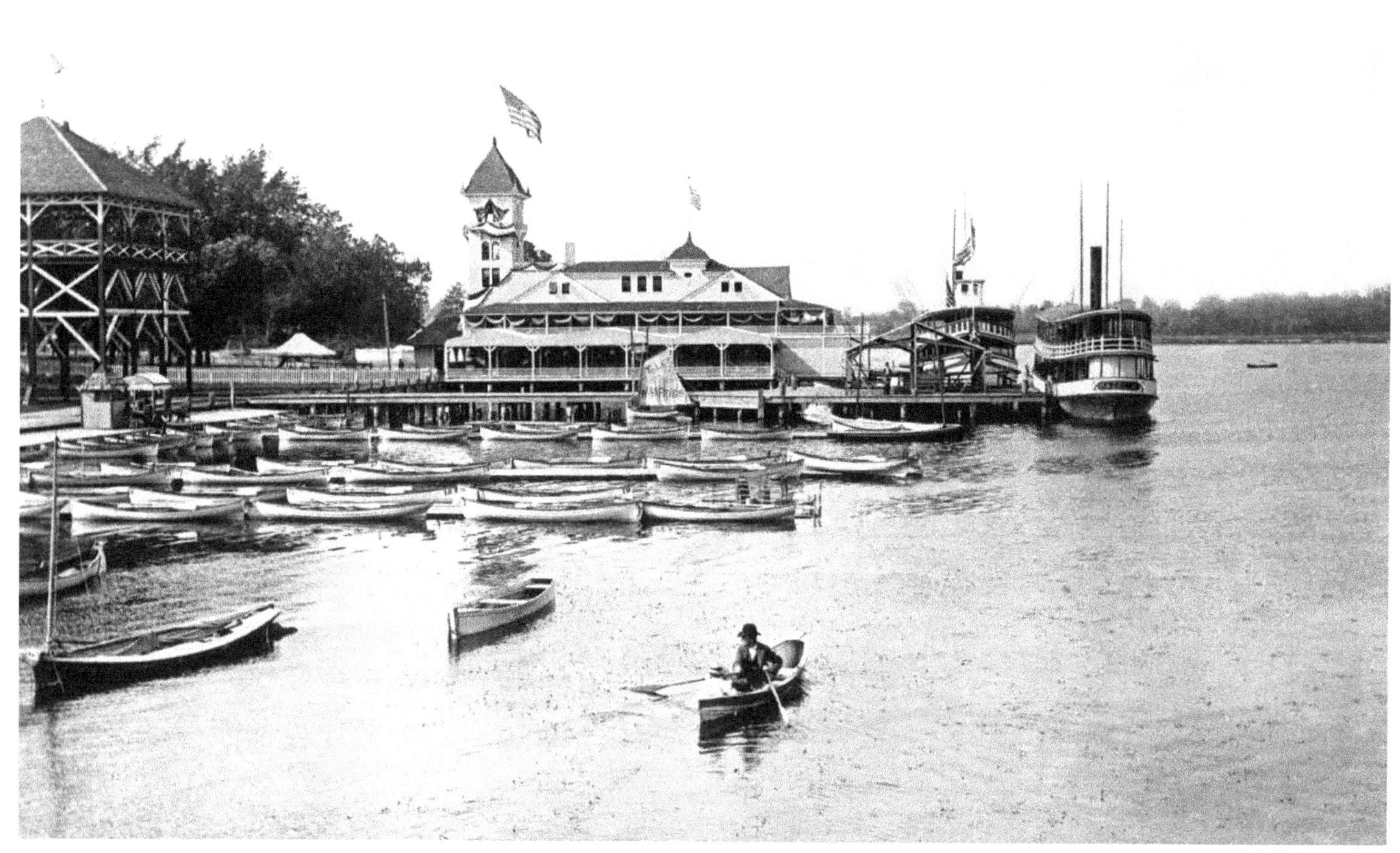

A view of Reed's Lake facing north.

The Birth of a City

(1850–1899)

The city of Grand Rapids was named after the Grand River, the longest river in the state, running into Lake Michigan and directly through the city. The city itself was chartered in 1850, but its story began much earlier. Frenchman Louis Campau started trading posts along principal Indian routes in 1827 and was to become known as the "father" of the city. He is best known for buying and establishing the entire area that would eventually become "downtown Grand Rapids," paying the federal government $90 for it in 1831. That 72 acres of land was named the "Village of Grand Rapids."

The population rose from 2,686 in 1850 to 87,565 by 1900. The city had grown from an area of four sections to 16 square miles in less than half a century. With the influx of immigrants from around the world to work in the furniture industry, many denominations of churches were organized to provide comfort to the different nationalities of families. With such growth, many municipal services were added. Grand Rapids built its first fire house in 1855. The police department was organized in 1871, the same year the first school system was introduced. Electrical street lights were activated in 1881. Trains began running in 1858, followed closely by the street railway cars in 1865. The first Post Office was also established at that time.

Furniture factories sprang up after the Civil War when the area was booming. At the nation's centennial celebration in Philadelphia in 1876, Grand Rapids became recognized as the leader in the production of fine and artistic furniture. The first furniture exhibition in Grand Rapids was held in 1878, attracting buyers from around the nation. The 1890 census, although it shows that furniture manufacturing offered the largest number of jobs, also shows 484 other factories in the city at the time. These included the logging industry (which fueled the furniture industry), and the production of cigars, band instruments, boats, and shoes, along with knitting companies, breweries, and carpet sweepers. All these factories brought buyers, visitors, and tourists who appreciated the recreational facilities, theaters, and hotel accommodations the city offered. Grand Rapids was also the favorite convention site in the state, for the same reasons.

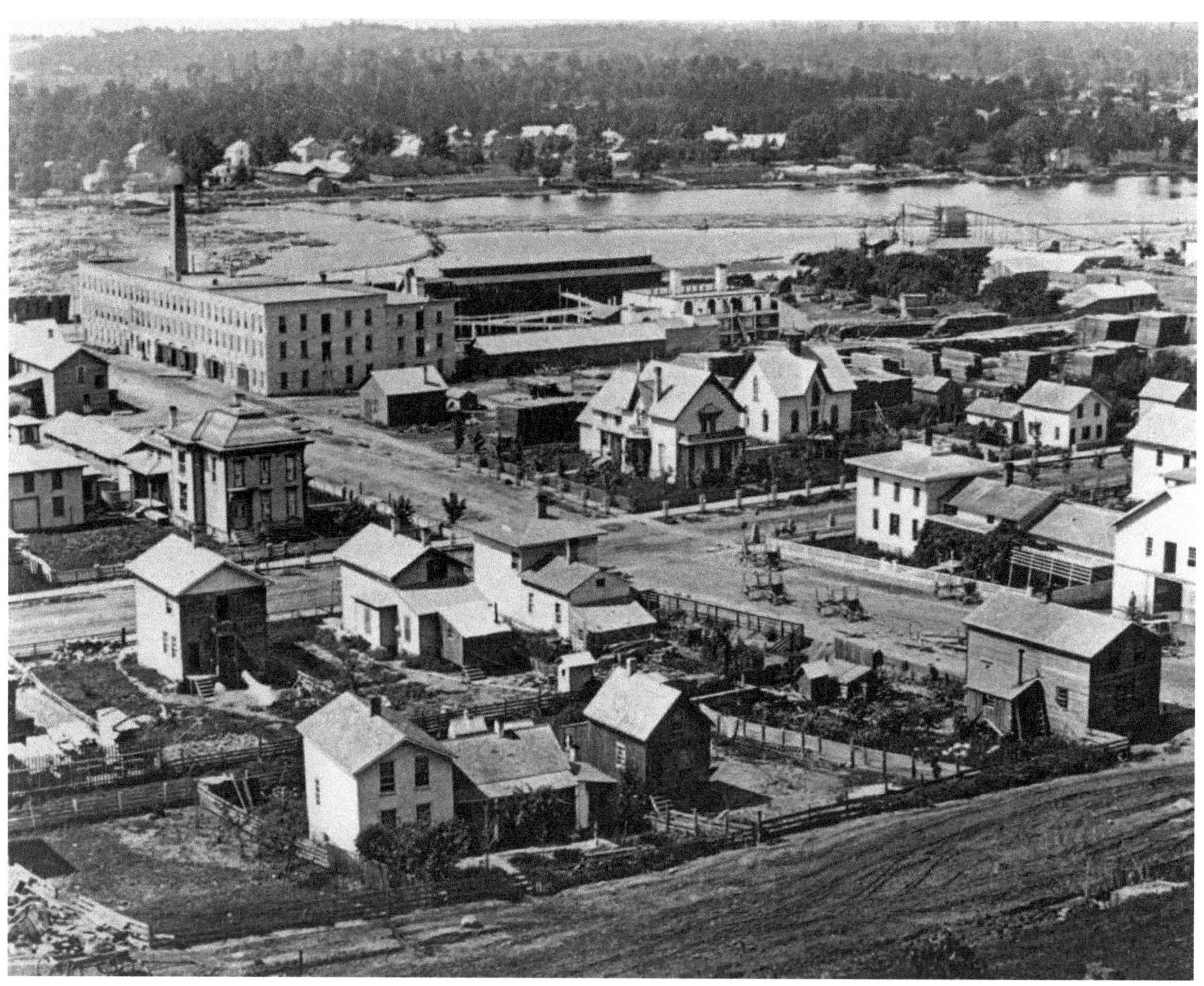

A view from the Sixth Street hill. The dam on the Grand River was built in 1849. C. C. Comstock's Tub and Pail Company is on the left. The Sixth Street bridge has not yet been built.

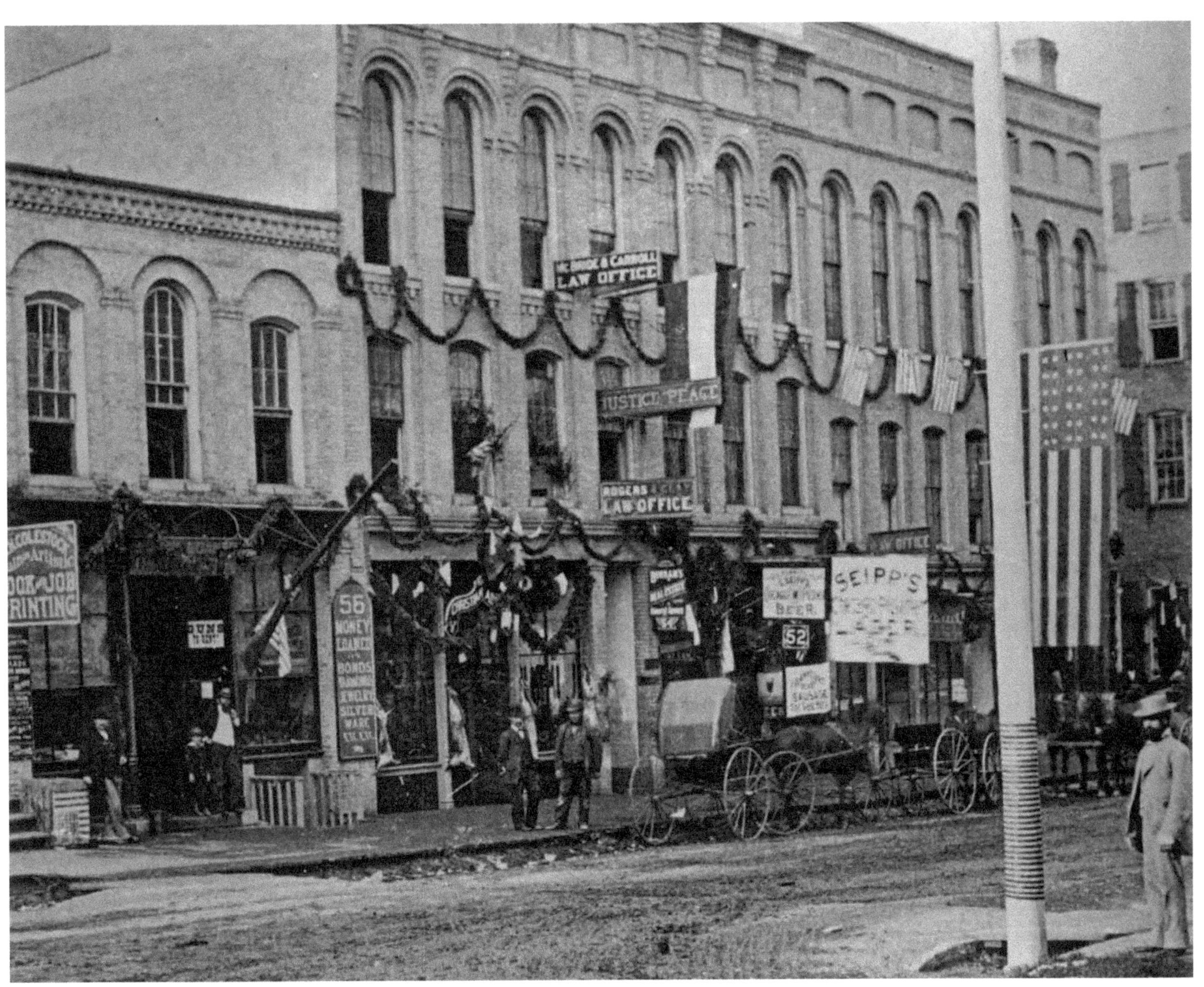

Lyon Street in 1876.

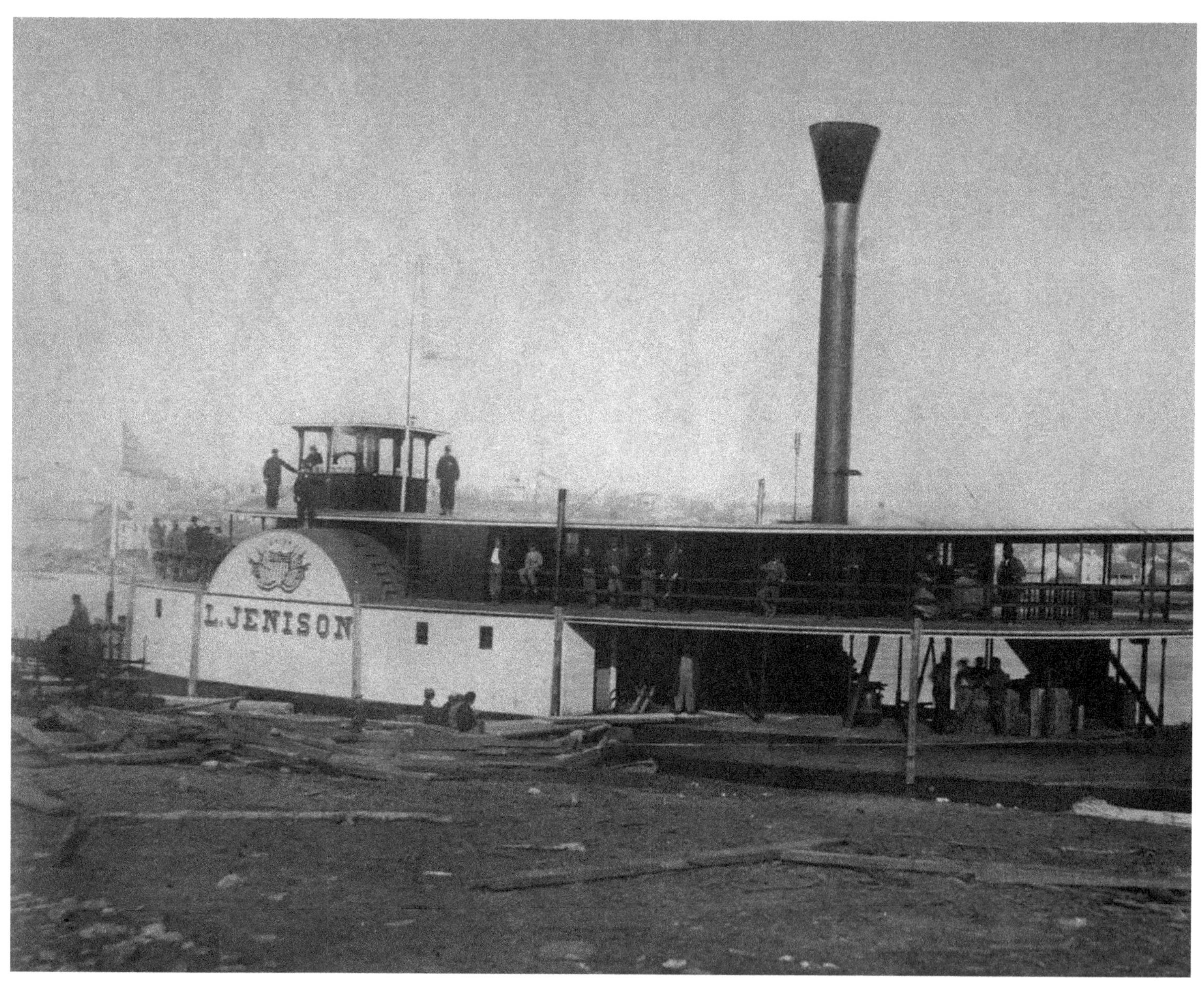

The *L. Jenison,* named for Lucius and Lyman Jenison, was built by Ganoe and Byron Ball in 1867. It ran up and down the Grand River for eight years. Like many steamboats, it perished in a fire.

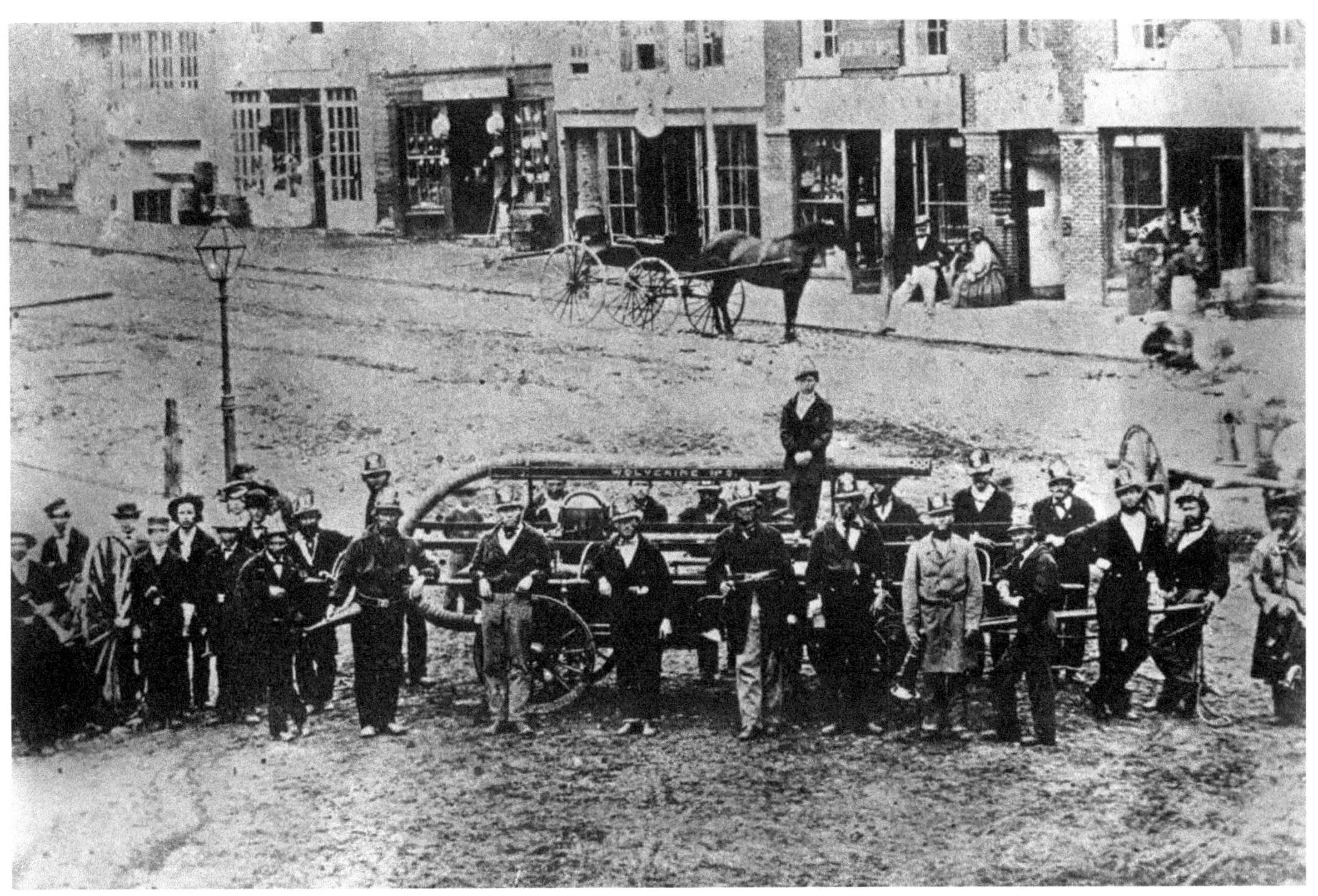

Fire companies were in existence by 1844, composed mainly of a few fire buckets. The hand fire-pump, shown here in 1860, was part of the Wolverine Fire Company #3.

St. Mark's Episcopal Church, located at the head of Pearl Street.

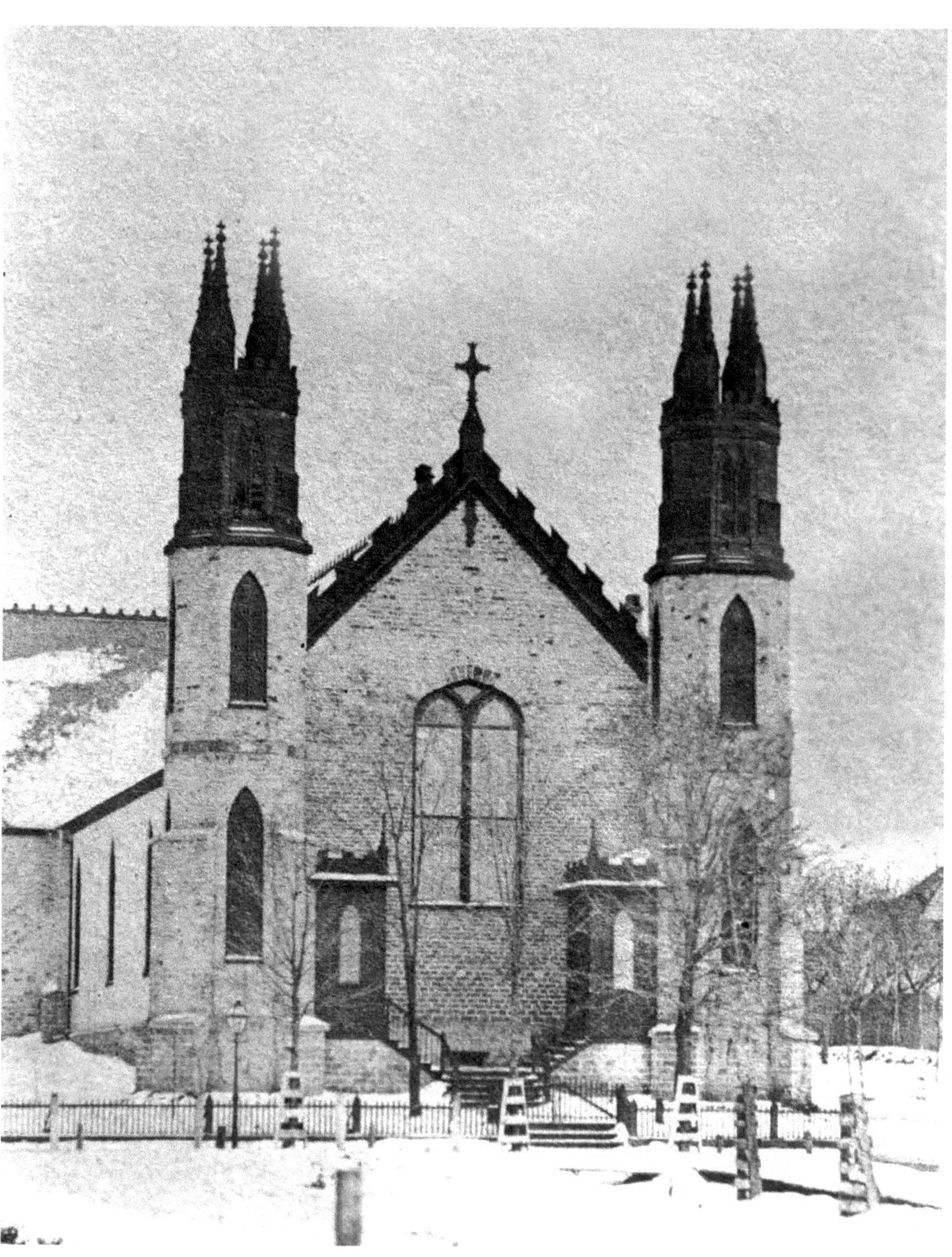

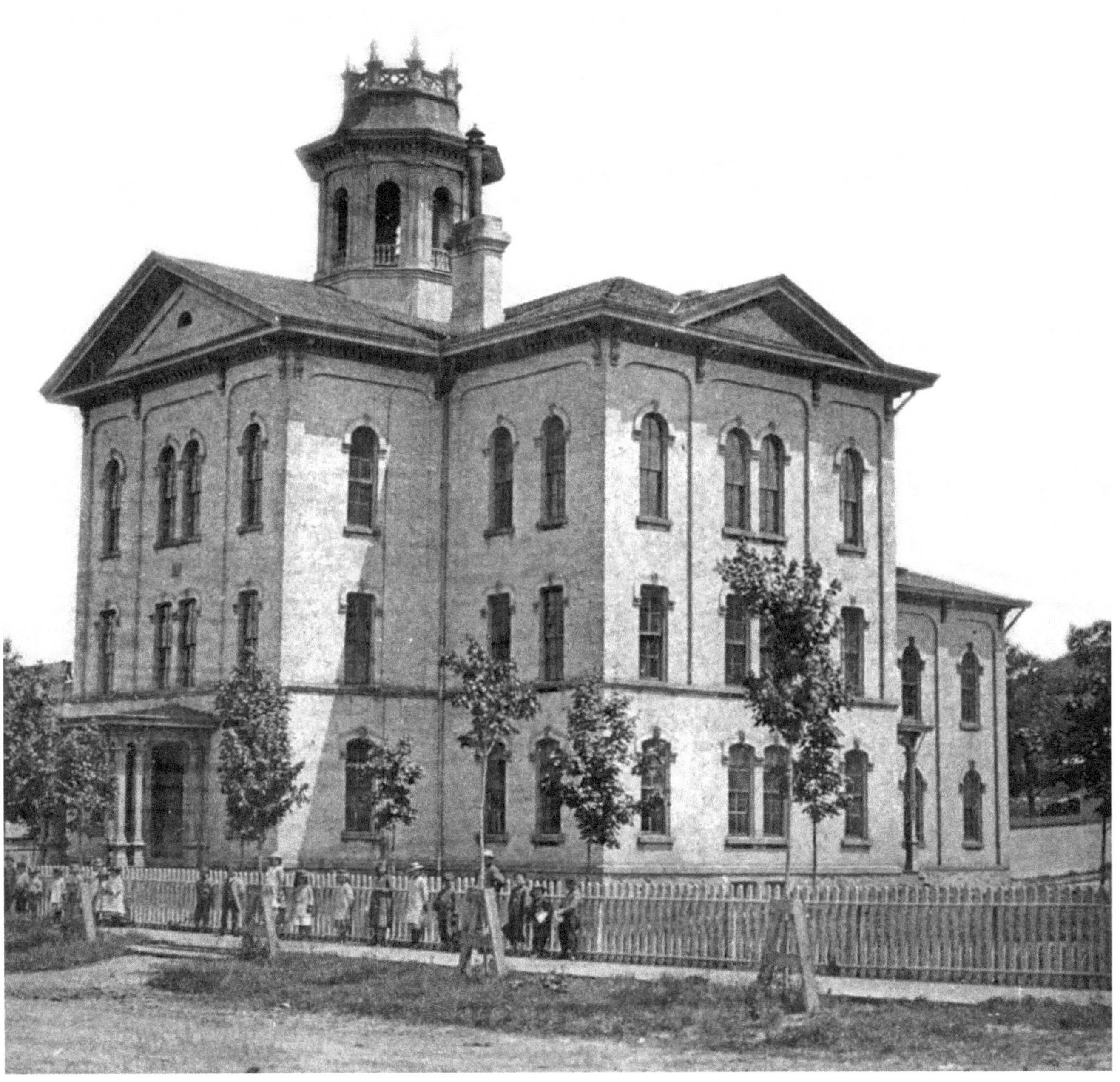

The North Ionia School was located on North Ionia Street between Walbridge and Coldbrook. Built in 1871 with room for 600 students, this was one of the original schools to become part of the city school system when it was organized that same year.

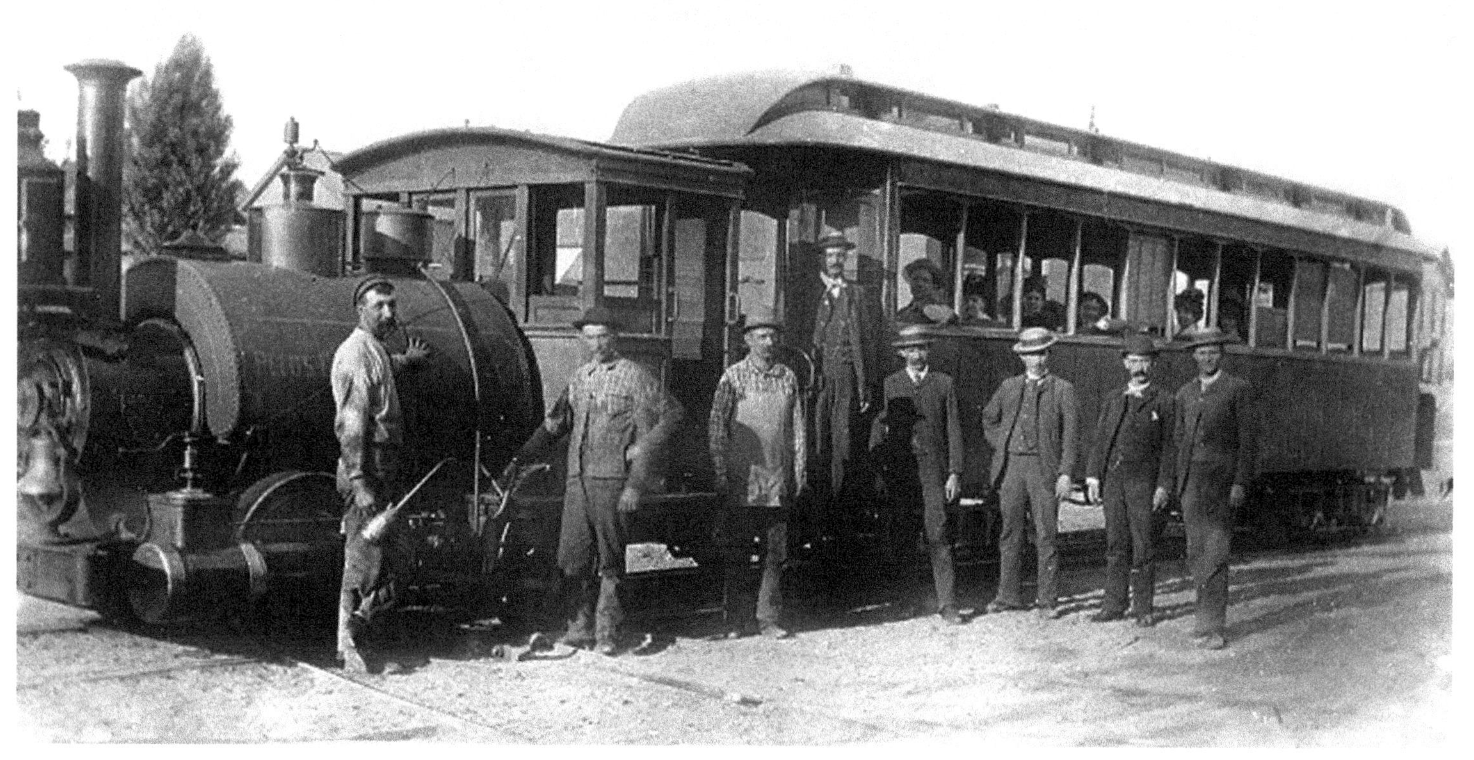

The Reed's Lake Street Railway Company ran from Sherman Street and Eastern Avenue, heading east on Sherman to Reed's Lake.

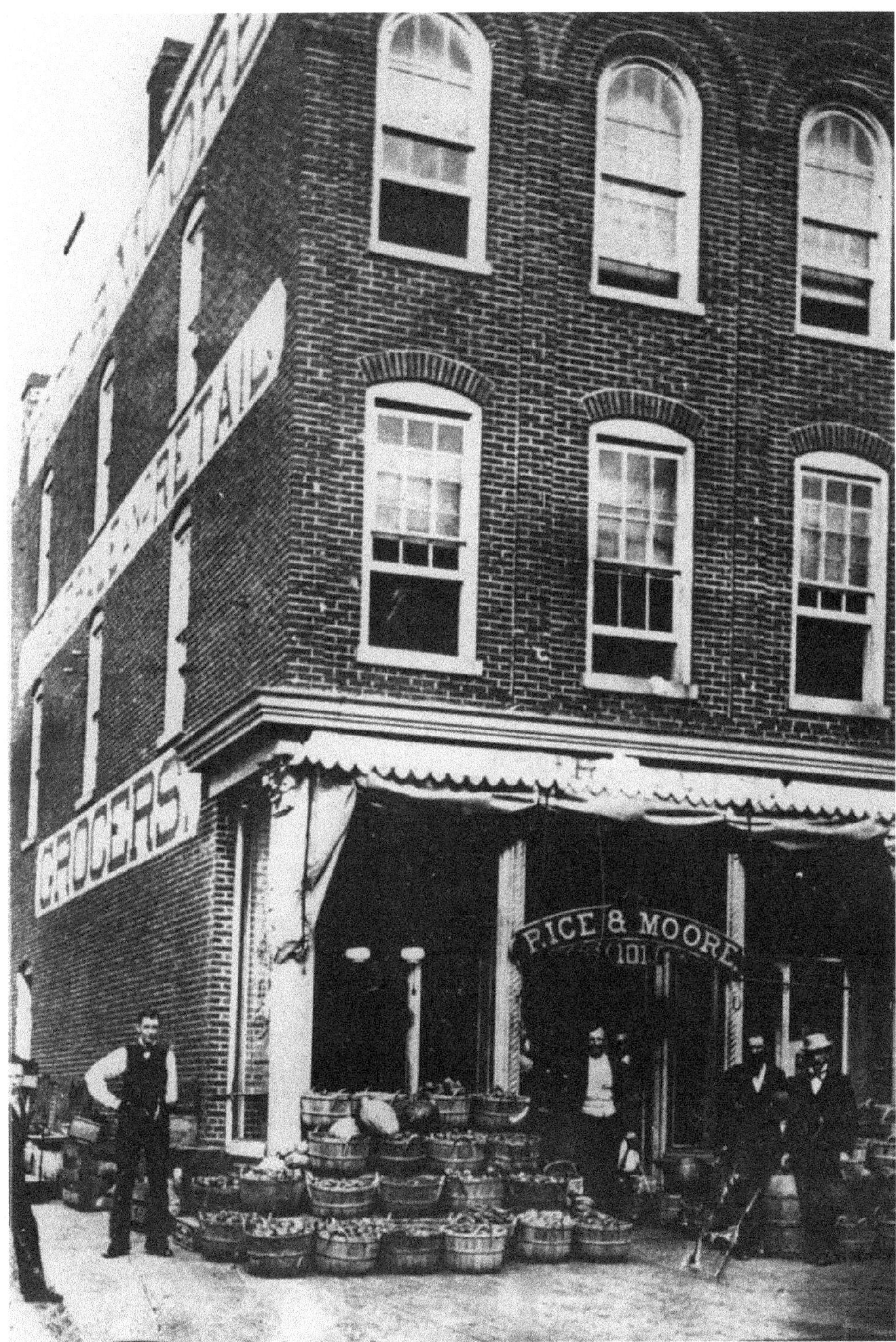

The first Police Headquarters was located on the second floor of Rice and Moore's Grocery on the southeast corner of Monroe and Ionia from 1871 to 1882, when the headquarters was moved to a larger facility on the corner of Lyon and Campau streets.

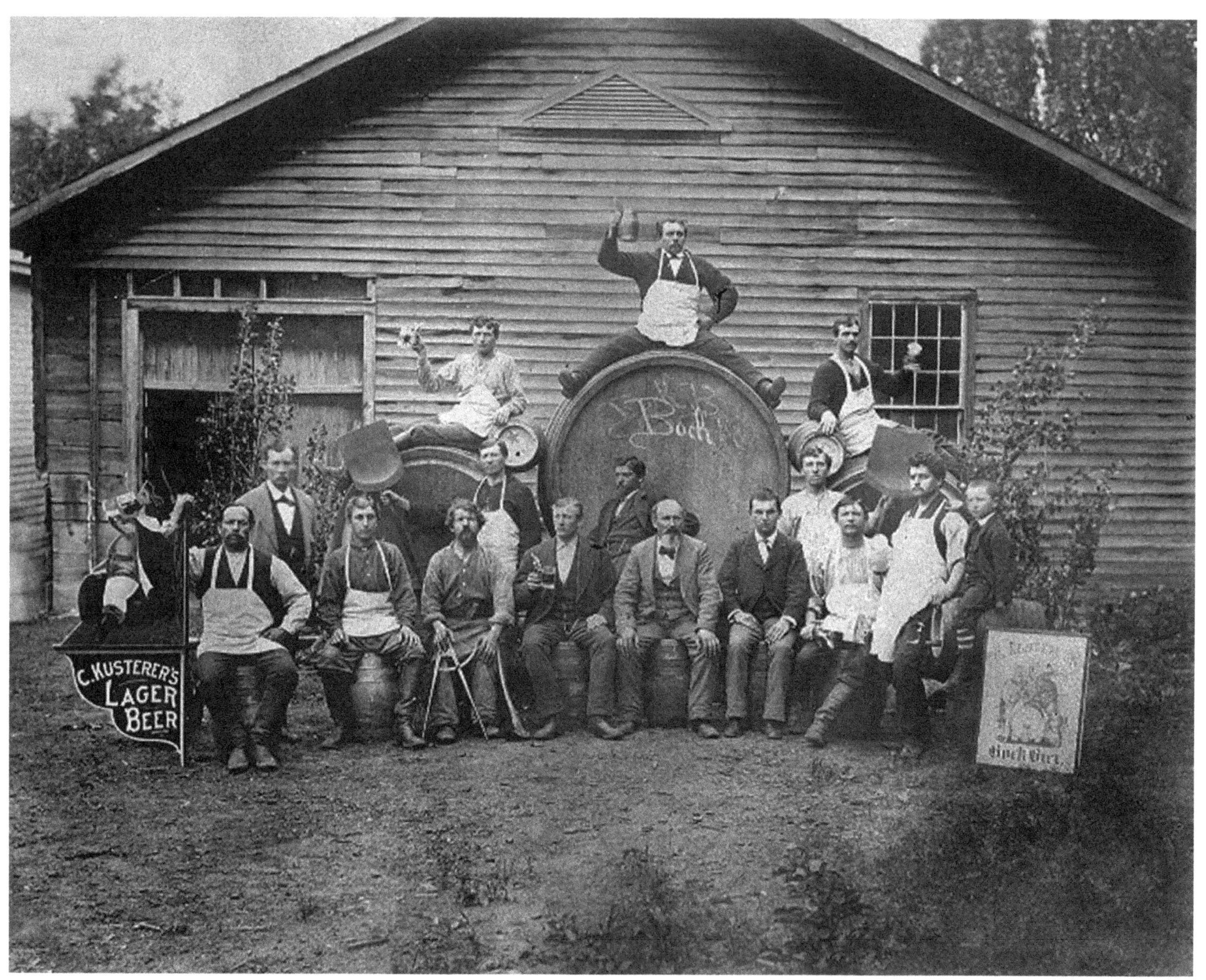

The northeast corner of Michigan Street and Ottawa Avenue was the home of C. Kusterer's Lager Beer and Kusterer's Cooper Shop. Employees pictured are (front row) Vincent Fox, Frank Wagner, George Koch, Adolph Goetz, Chris Kusterer, Chris Kusterer, Jr., Charles Merkle, Ed. Wagner, and Kid Kusterer. In the second row are an unidentified person, Adam Herl, Chris Wagner, and Aug. Kusterer. In the third row are John Hubel and another unidentified person. Seated atop the large keg is Ada Alberts.

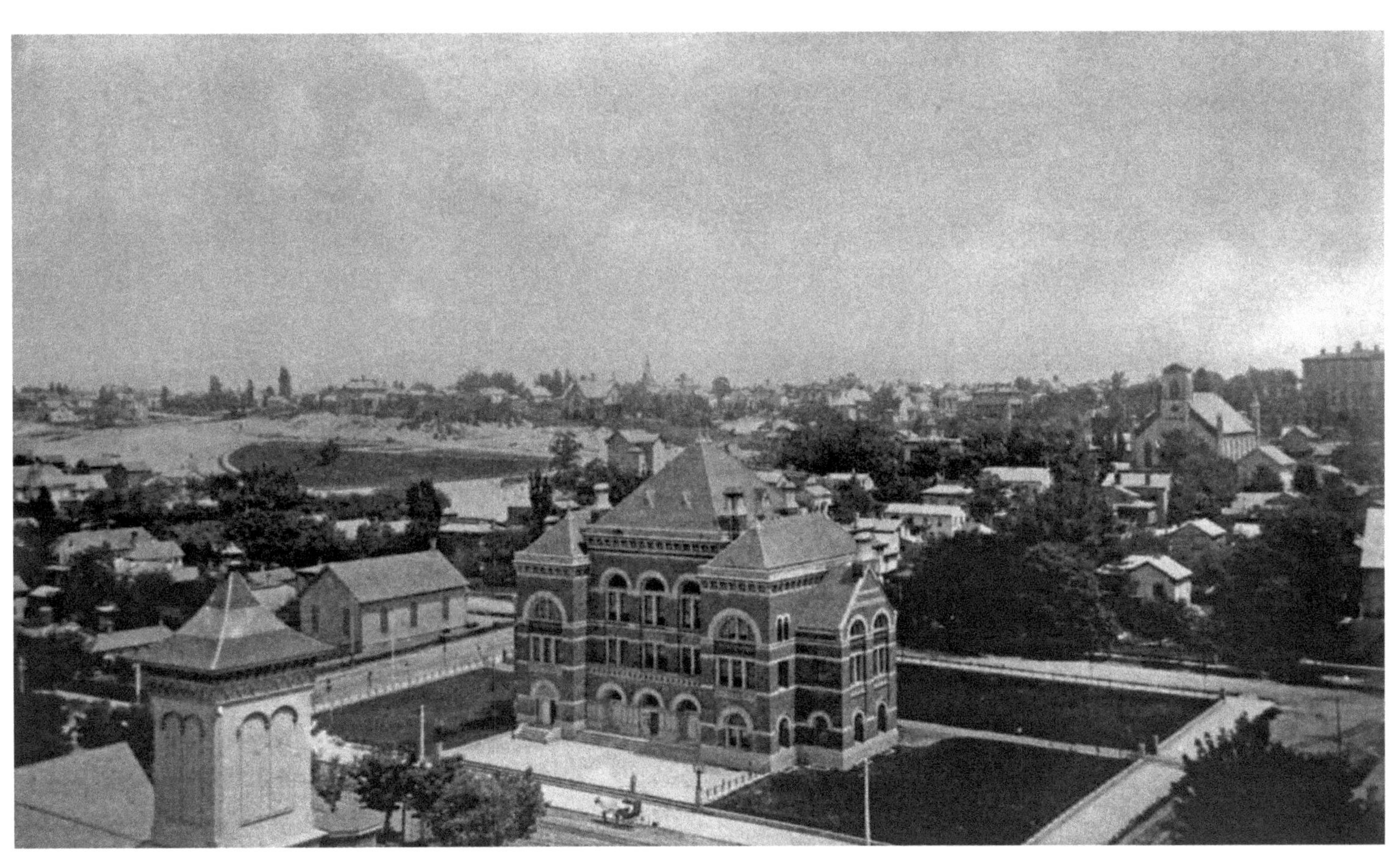

Downtown as it was beginning to grow. The Post Office is at center. The Swedenborgian, Universalist, and Second Reformed churches are visible, along with the old high school.

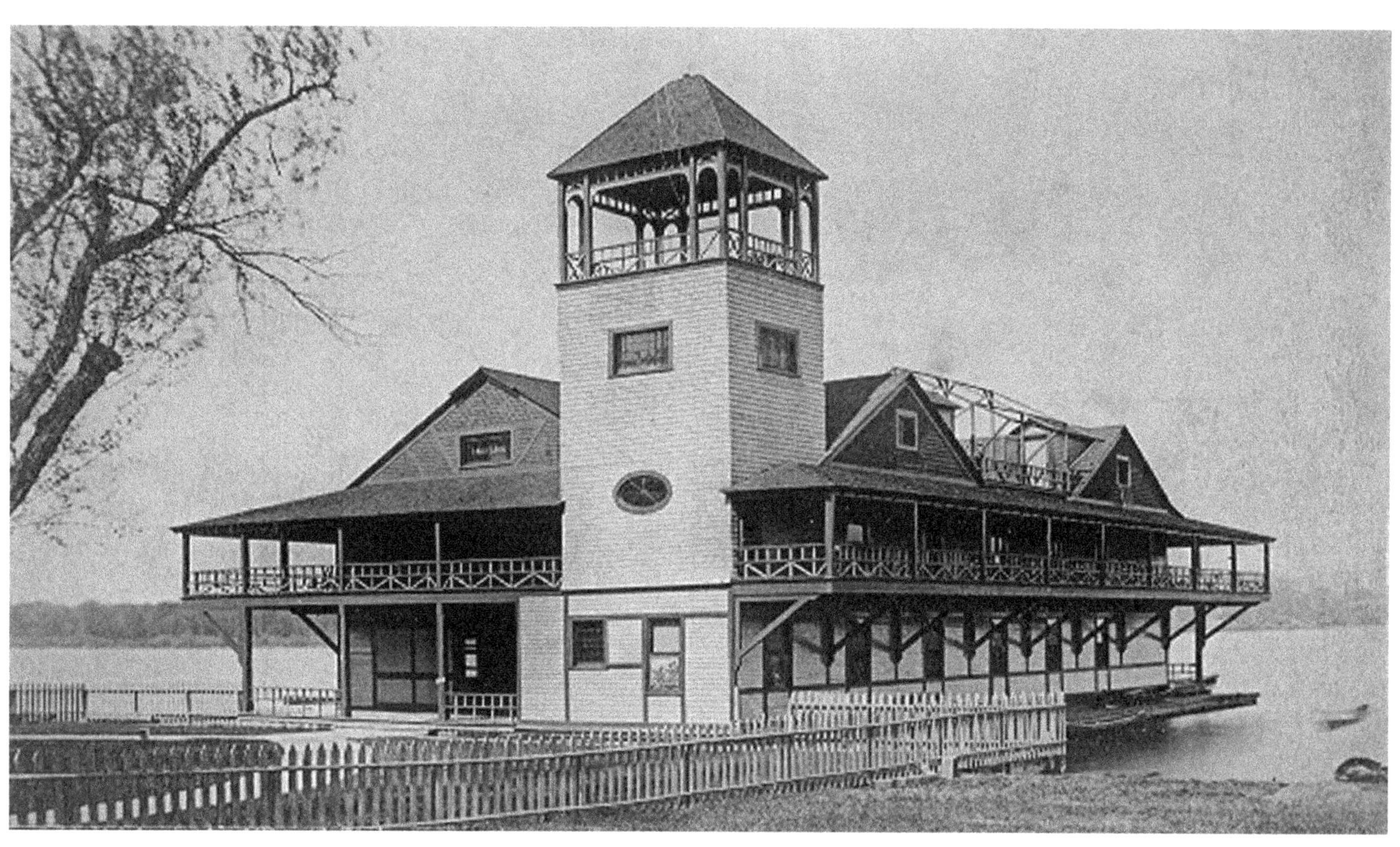

The first O-Wash-Ta-Nong Club House at Reed's Lake was erected in 1886. It was located at the north end of what is now John Collins Park.

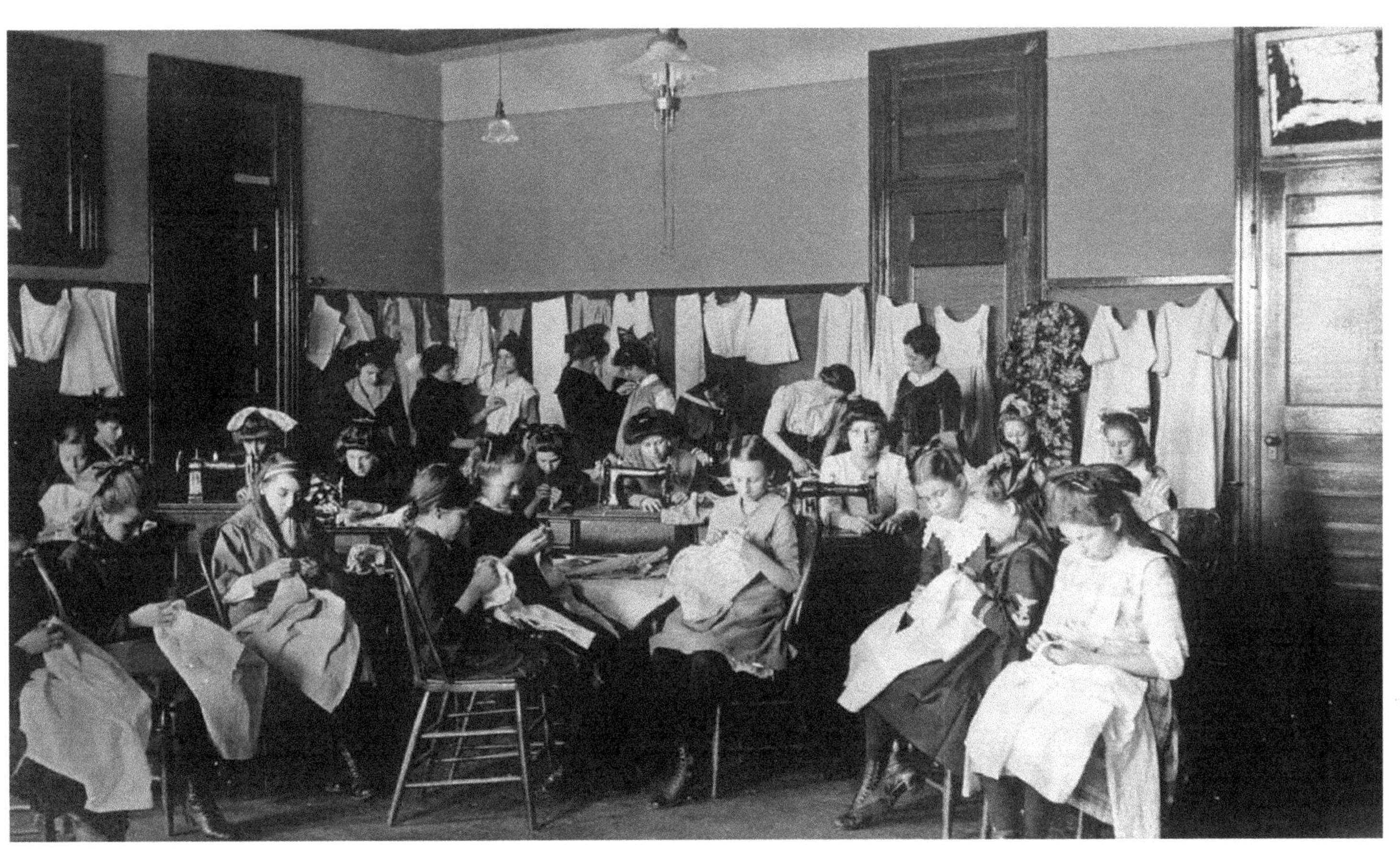

A sewing class at East Bridge Street School.

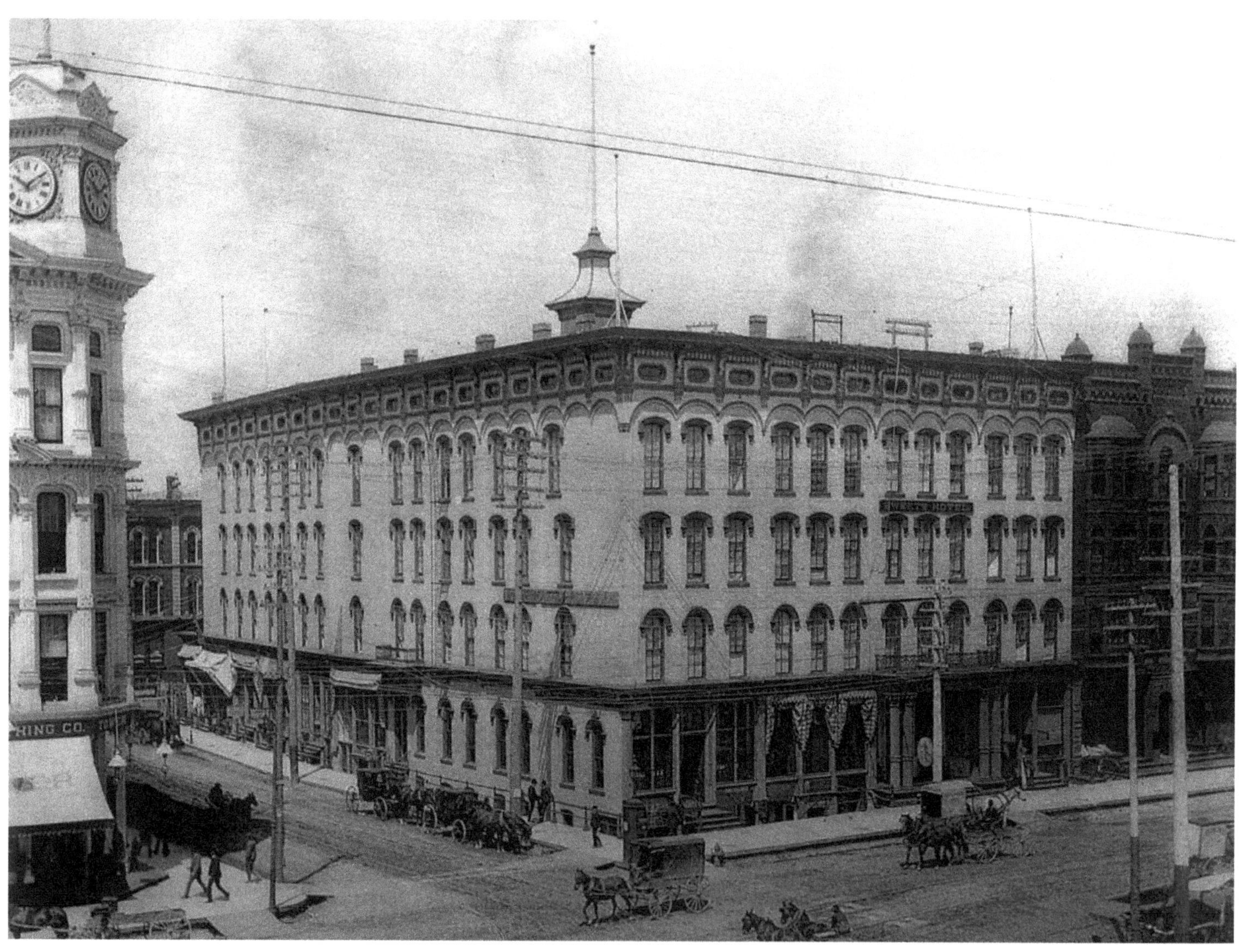

The Sweet's Hotel was built in 1868 by Martin L. Sweet. It was later renamed the Pantlind Hotel after J. Boyd Pantlind took over in 1902. It is currently part of the Amway Grand Plaza Hotel.

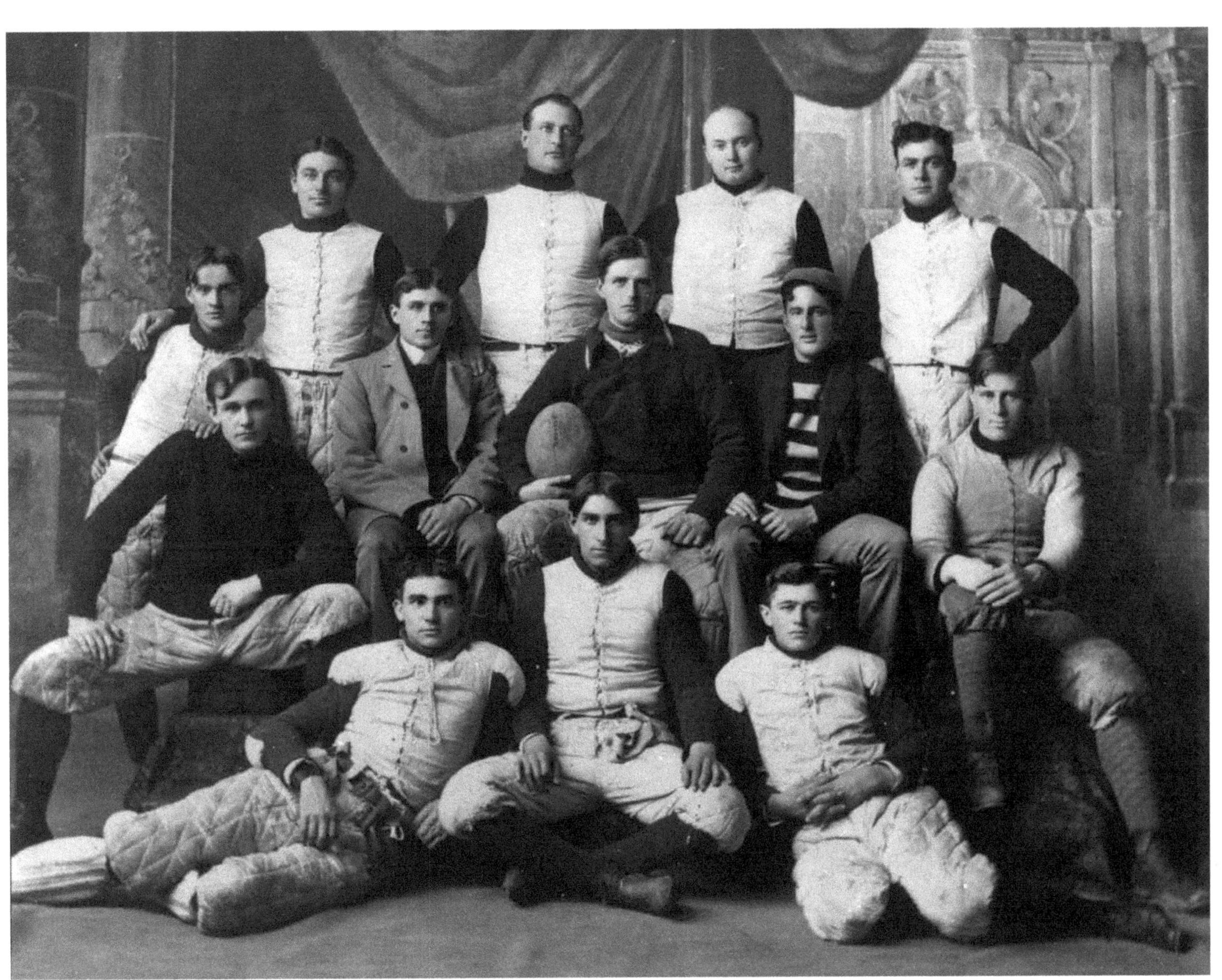

A local football team takes time out to pose for a group portrait.

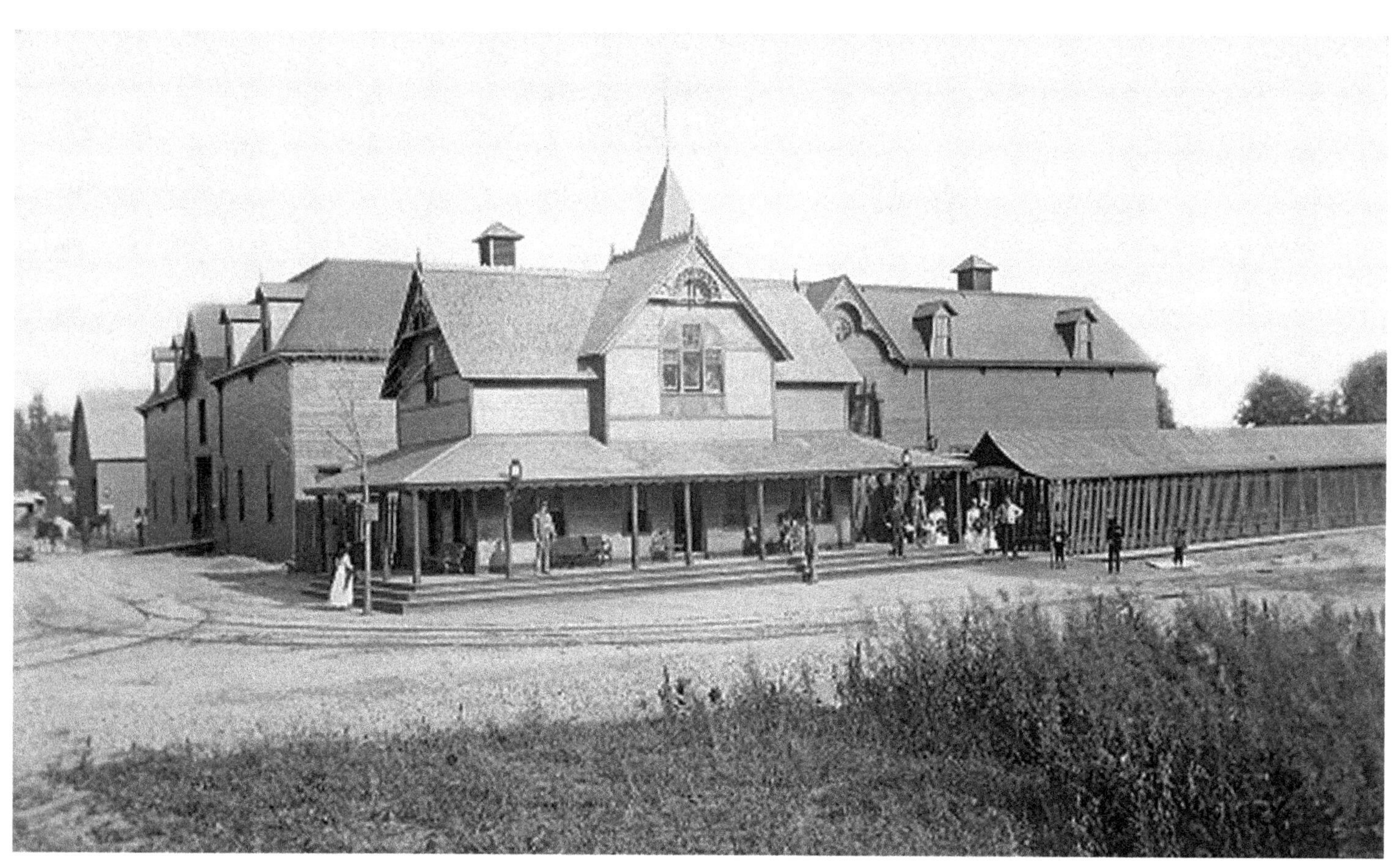

The station and streetcar barns on East Street, now Eastern Avenue, just south of Cherry Street.

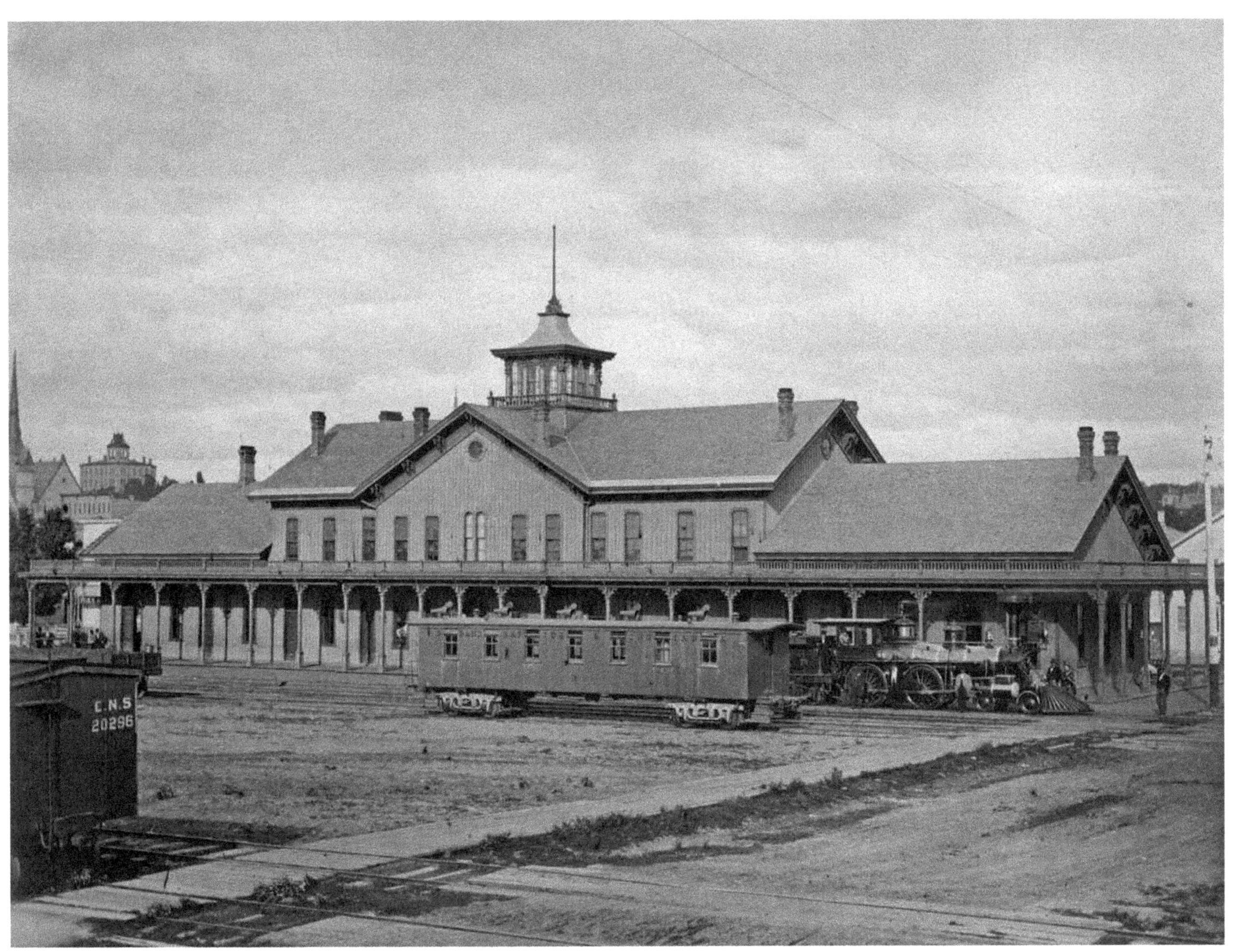

An early steam locomotive idles at the platform of the first Union Station. The Grand Rapids and Indiana Railroad ran to Kalamazoo and other cities to the south.

Catching the noon train at Union Depot. This image reveals the wood and iron spans of the train shed from track level. Engineers of the era competed to span ever-greater widths using single-gable arch designs.

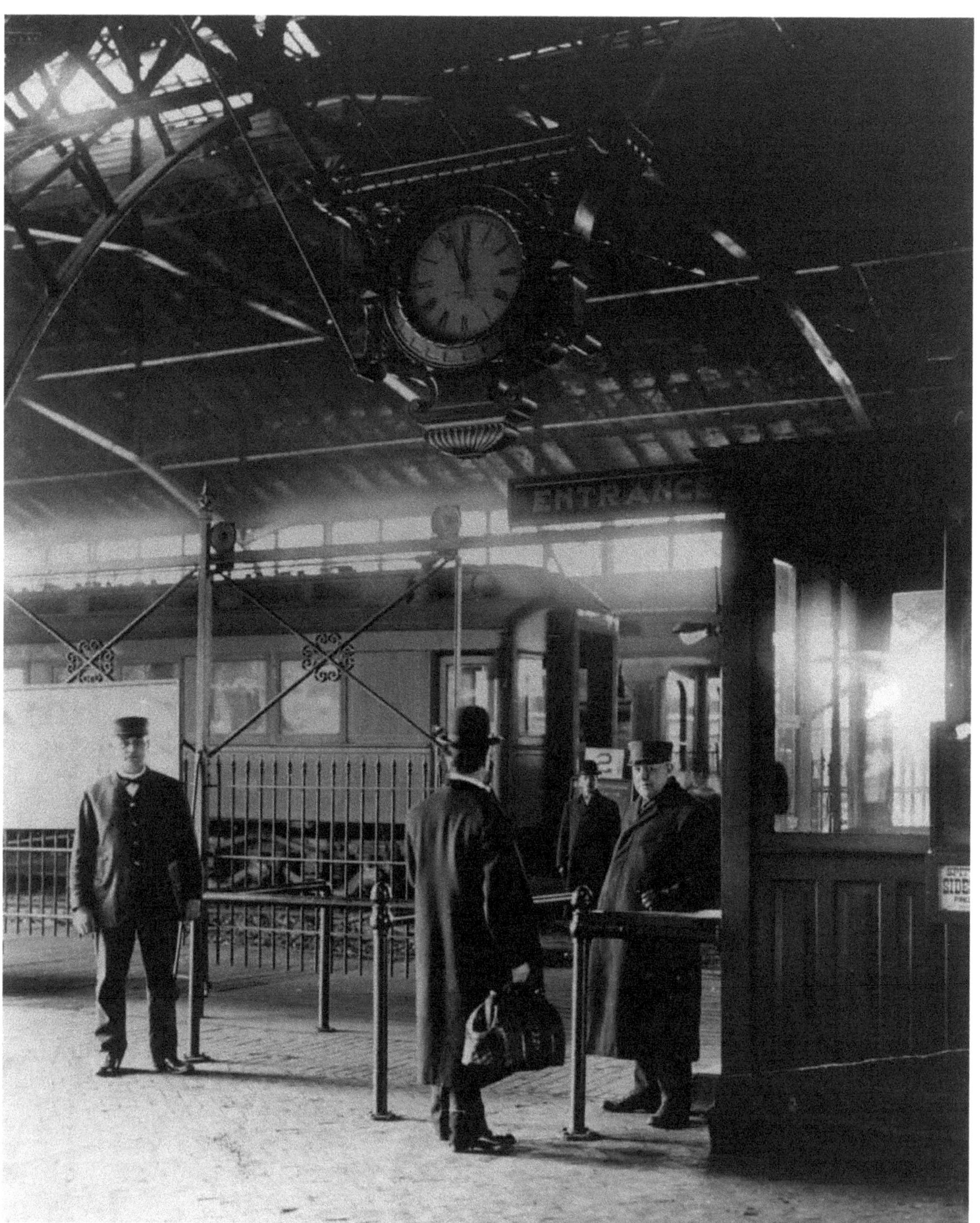

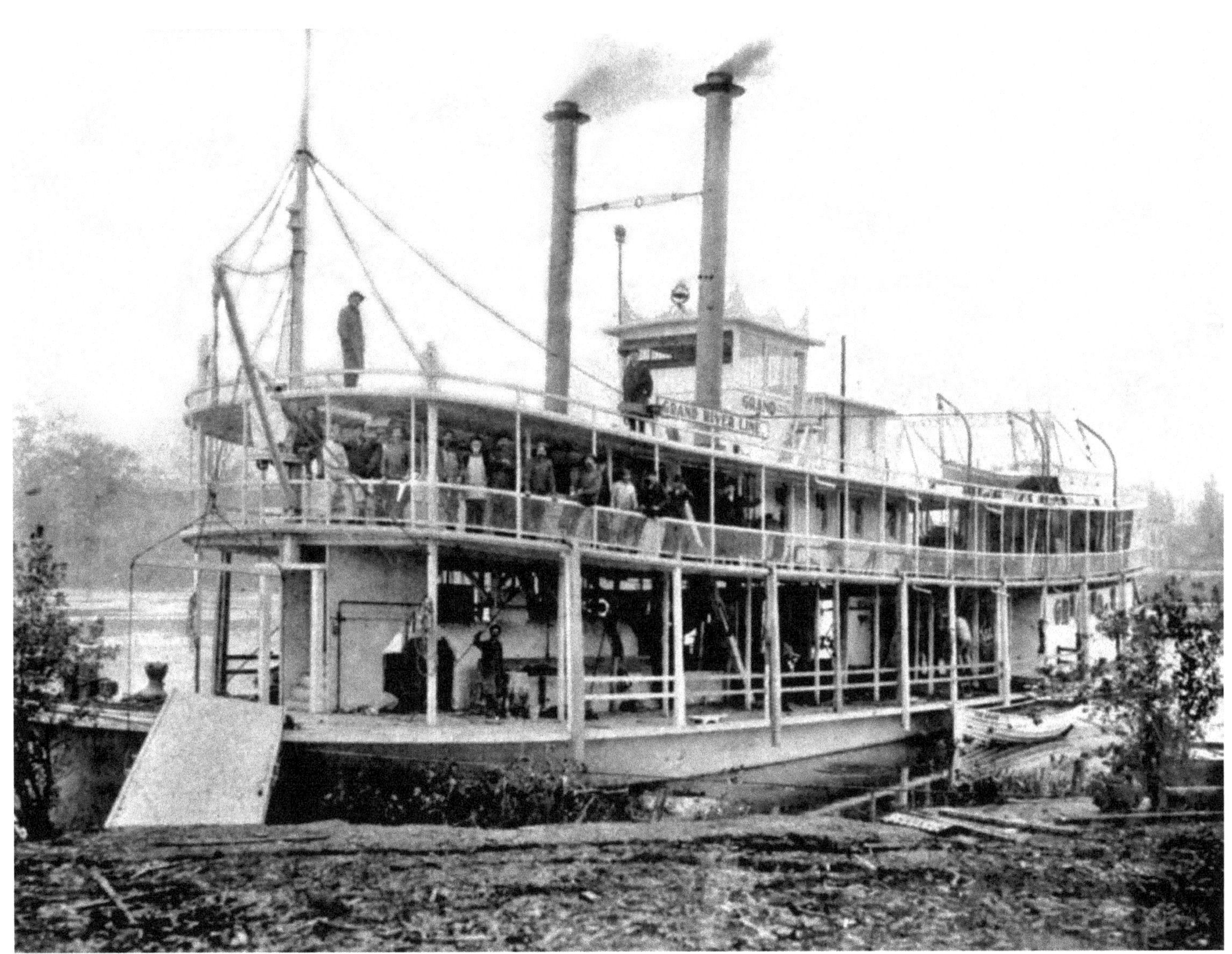

The *Grand* steamboat was part of the Grand River Line.

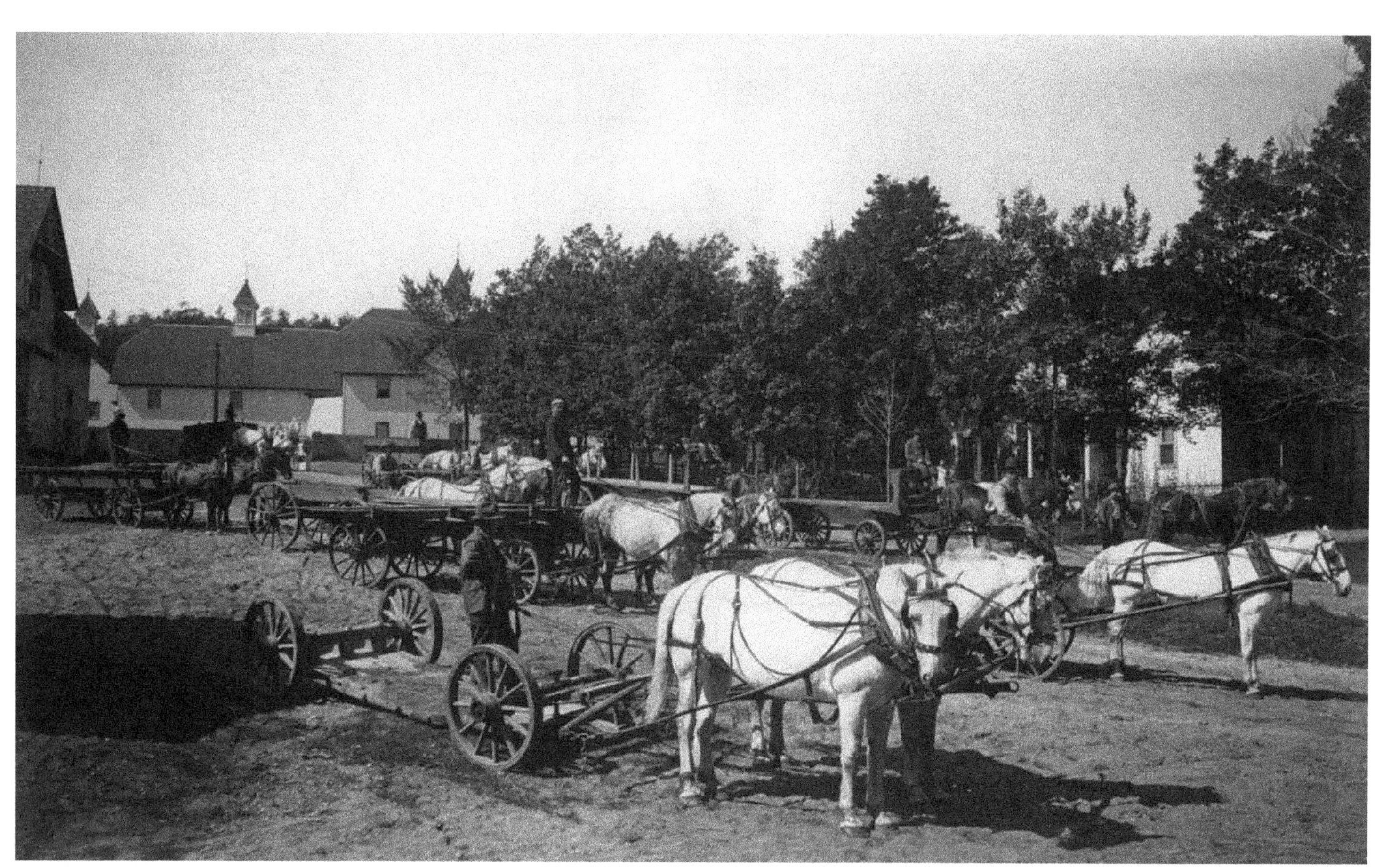

Teams pulling wagons leave for the fields and work.

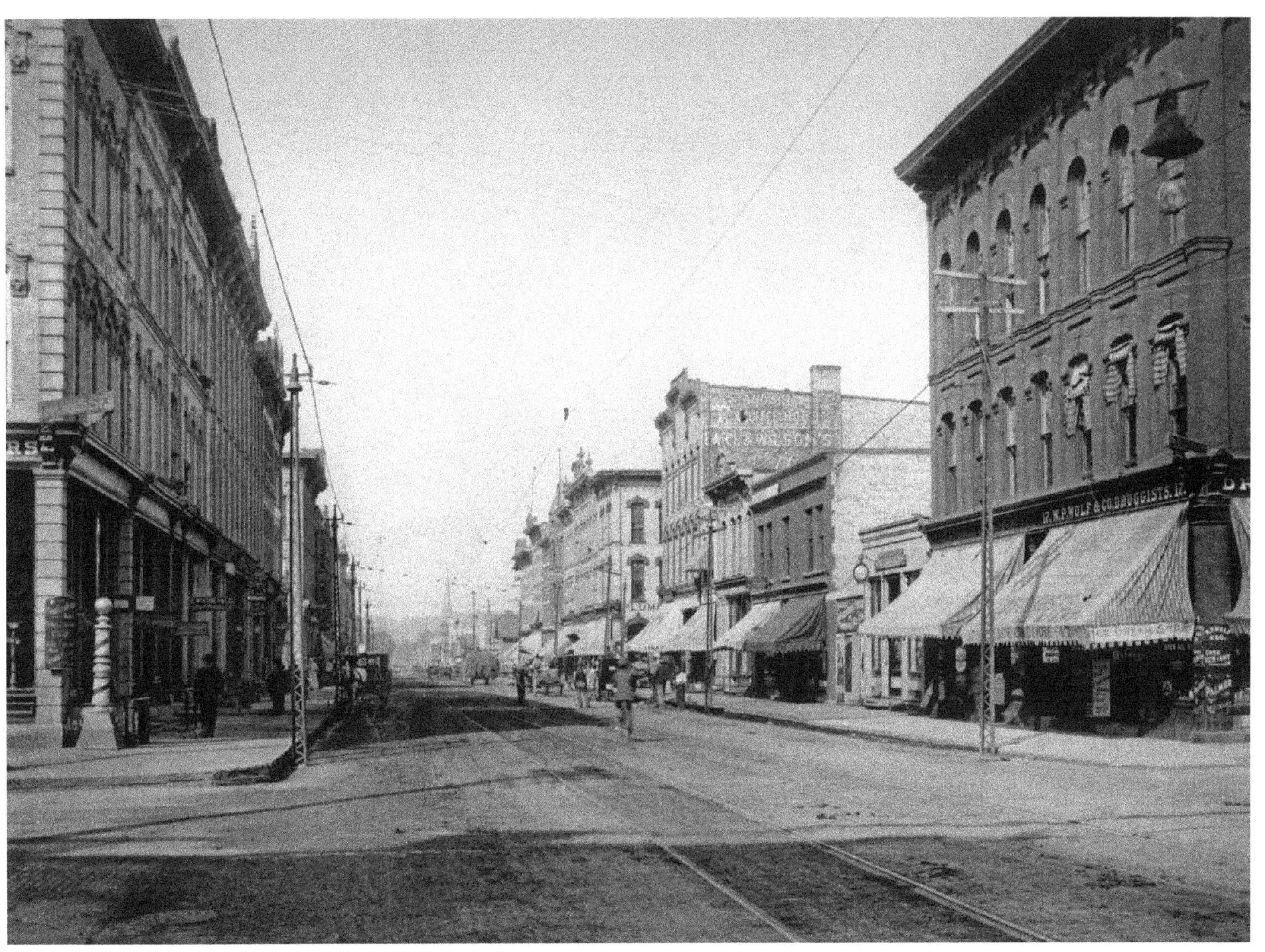

A view of West Bridge Street at Scribner. On the corner, ice cream sodas are available for a nickel at the W. P. Wolf drugstore, which advertises that it is open all night.

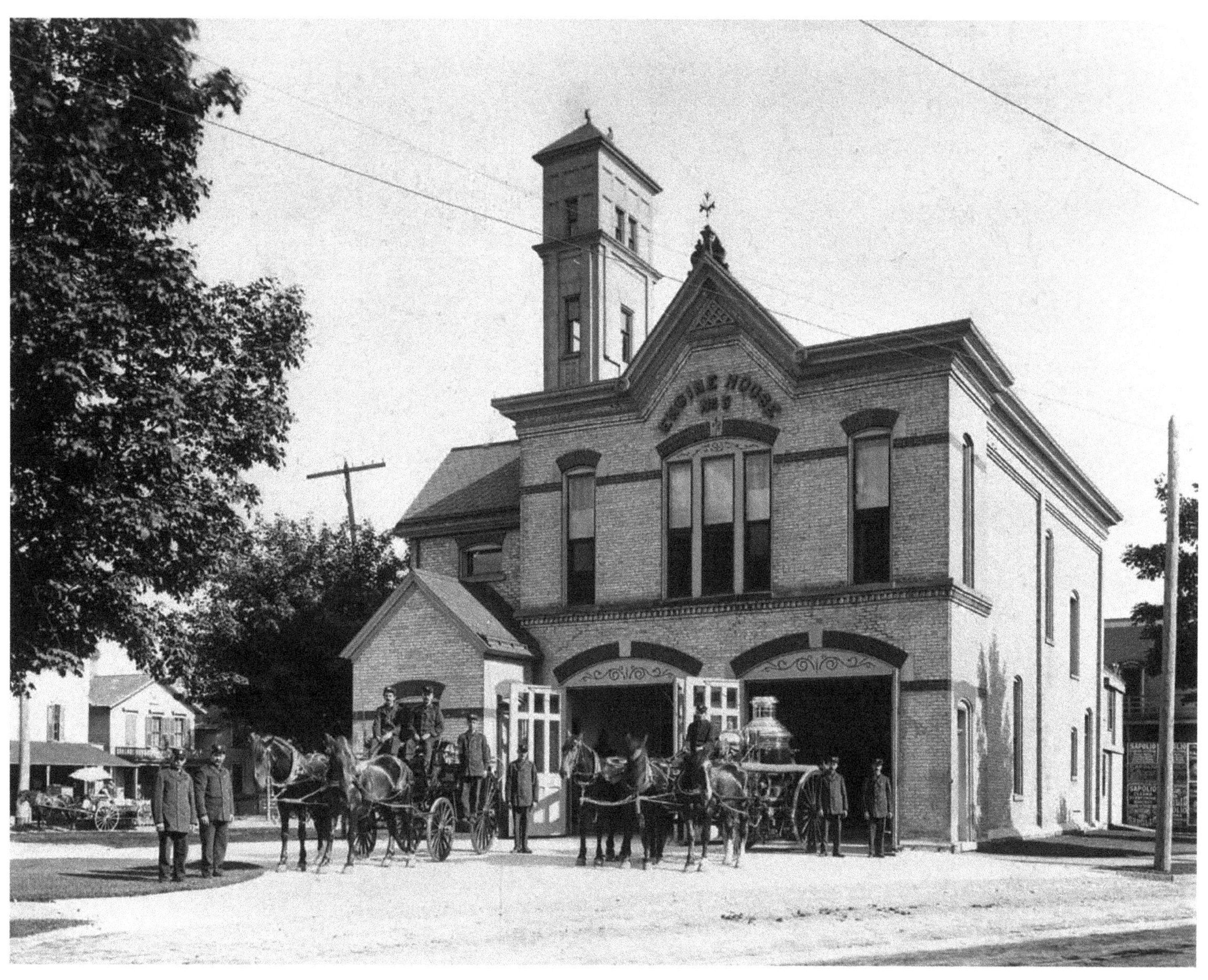

Engine House #6, at 312 Granville Avenue SW. Construction began in 1877 and the building was in service by 1879. This is the oldest building in Michigan still extant that was once used as a fire station.

Dawn of a New Century

(1900–1919)

As the new century dawned, Grand Rapids was still growing. As streetcars gave way to automobiles, the recreational opportunities available in Grand Rapids became abundant. John Ball Park (Ball had bequeathed 40 acres of land to the city upon his death in 1884) and Reed's Lake were favorite destinations for relaxation and entertainment. Sports played a vital role in the lives of the city's residents. Curling, a team game played on ice and known also as "ice chess," was especially popular.

Factories and retail stores multiplied. More than 60 local furniture factories produced fine, hand-crafted pieces for customers all over the nation. Farmers markets were popular, making fresh produce available to the city's residents. In 1904, the Ryerson Public Library, now the Grand Rapids Public Library, opened its doors. This literary mecca was a gift from Martin Ryerson. The city found much to celebrate in the early decades of the new century. Parades for Memorial Day, July 4th, and Labor Day were common, and the city observed its 60th anniversary, with weeklong festivities.

On Thursday, March 24, 1904, the Grand River began to overflow its banks and steadily rose until the following Monday, when it crested at more than two feet above the old high mark. Much of the city's west side was underwater.

The suffrage movement was moving forward. Women were campaigning to gain the right to vote. The state headquarters for the Michigan Equal Franchise Association was located in the McKay Tower.

As World War I began, Grand Rapids contributed to the war effort. Furniture factories banded together to produce airplanes and other materiel needed to pursue the war. Women did their part, working as nurses, in munitions factories, and using their domestic skills to make socks and other clothing for the soldiers.

President Gerald R. Ford was born about this time, and his family would soon move to Grand Rapids, which became his childhood home.

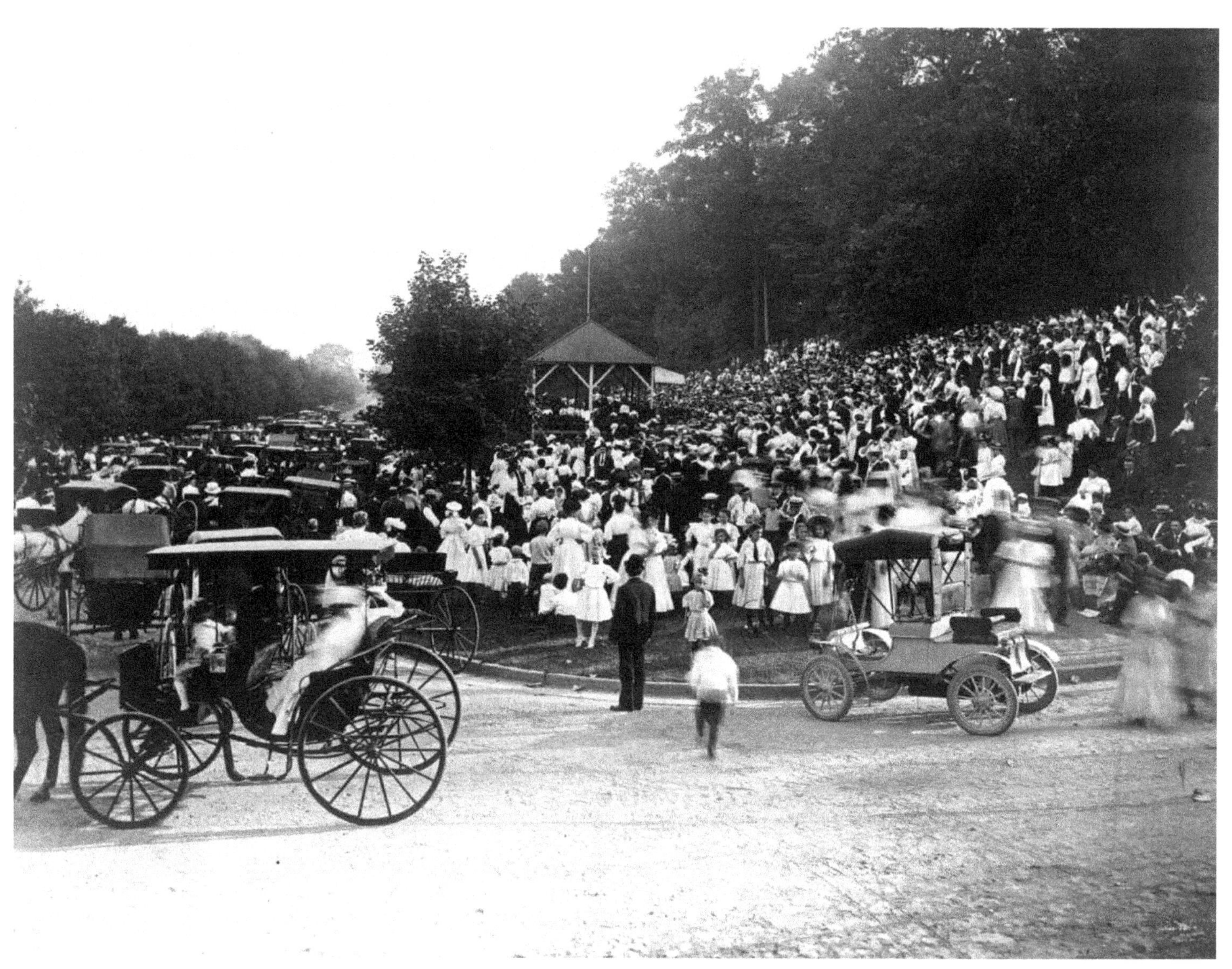

Citizens enjoy a concert at John Ball Park. John Ball had bequeathed the park's original 40 acres to the city in 1884. The park's zoo began in 1891 with a pair of rabbits.

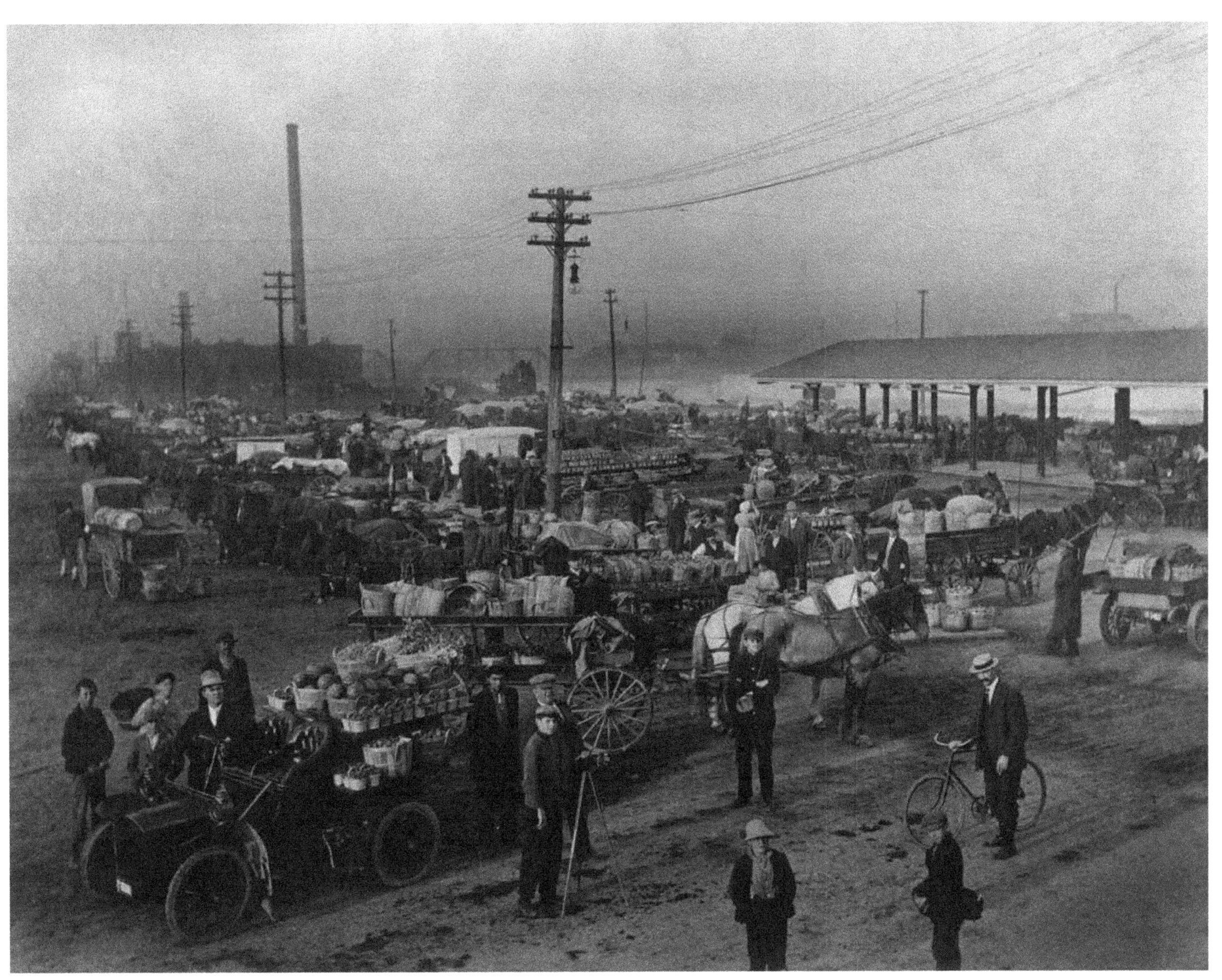

Farmers sell their wares at one of the city's markets. This one was located on Island Park. Wholesale markets like this one served the many grocery stores that existed in those days.

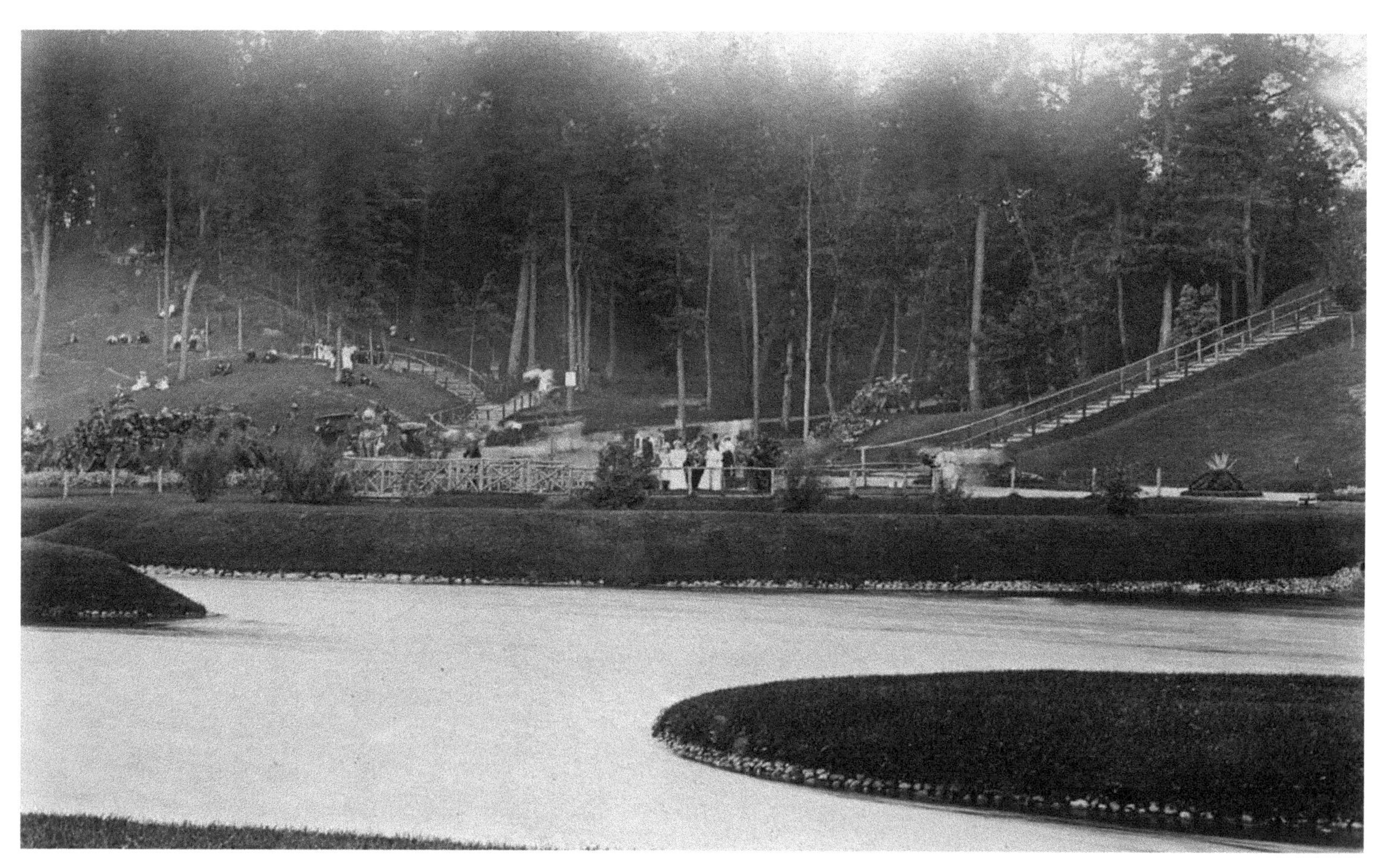

The ponds at John Ball Park as they appeared a century ago.

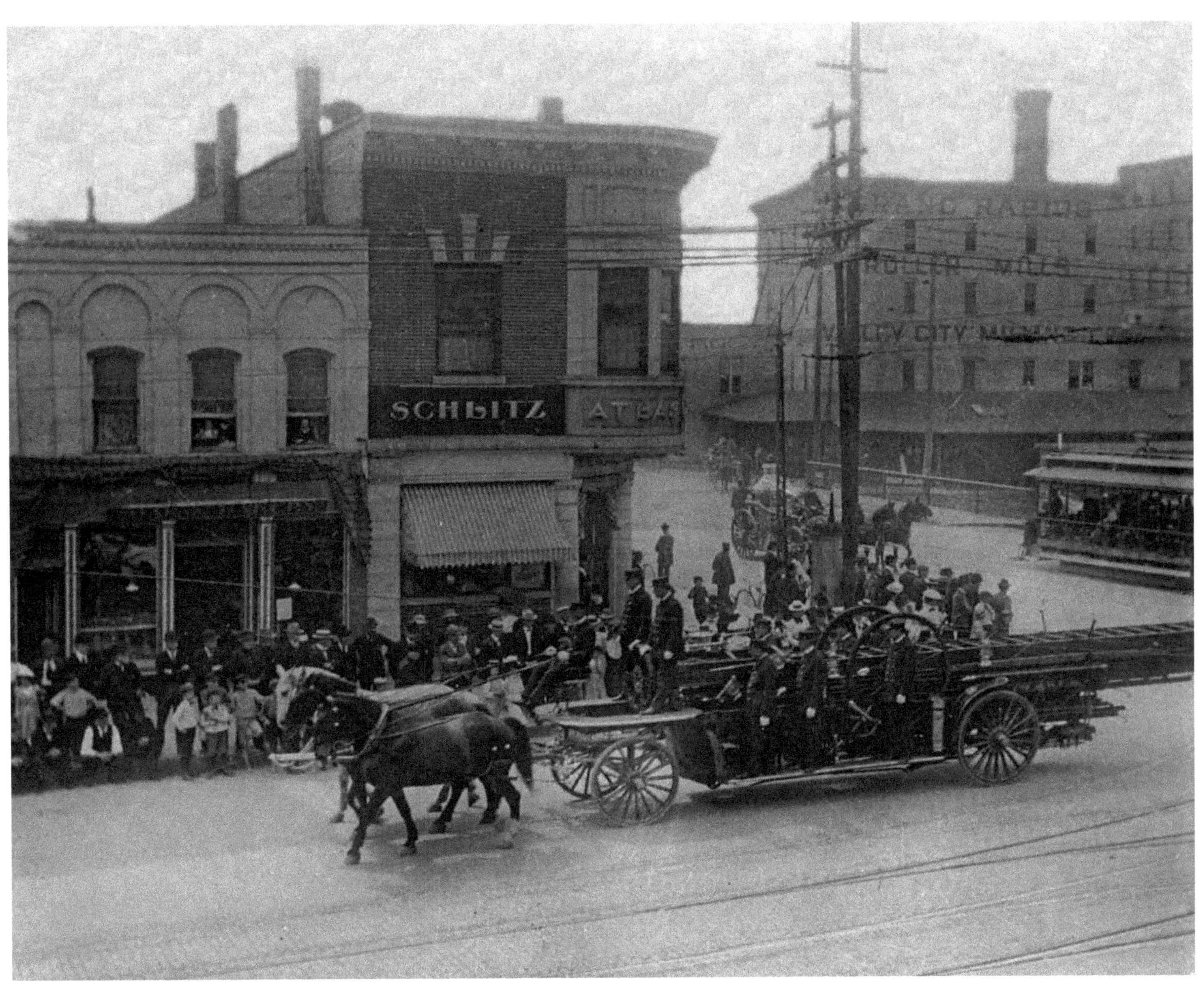

Monroe Avenue just south of Bridge Street, with Valley City Milling Company visible in the background. In the foreground is a three-horse team pulling a hook and ladder fire truck, which is followed by a three-horse steam pumper around the corner.

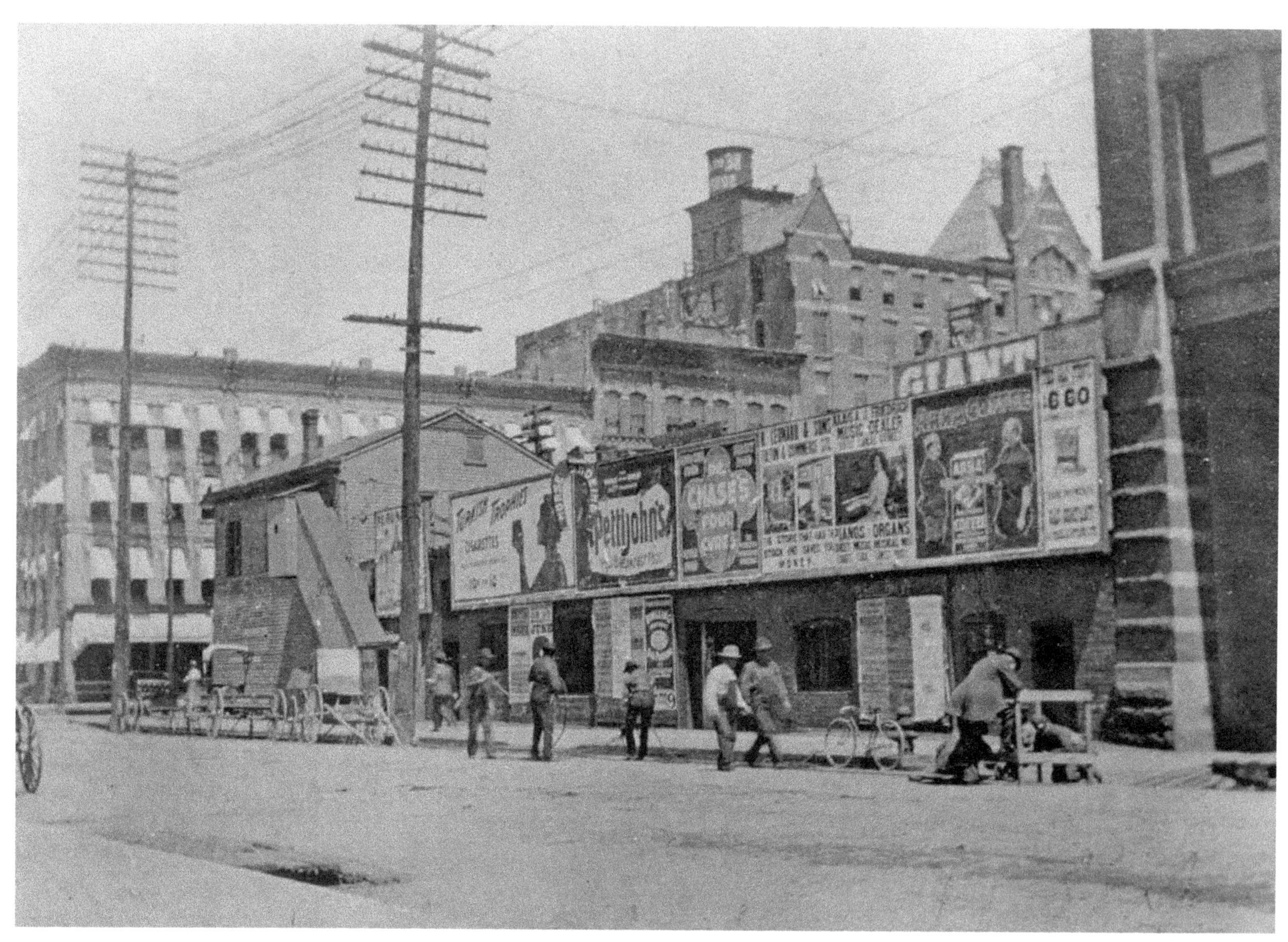

Advertisements abound along Louis Street. Tucked away among the ads is the Hooper Blacksmith Shop.

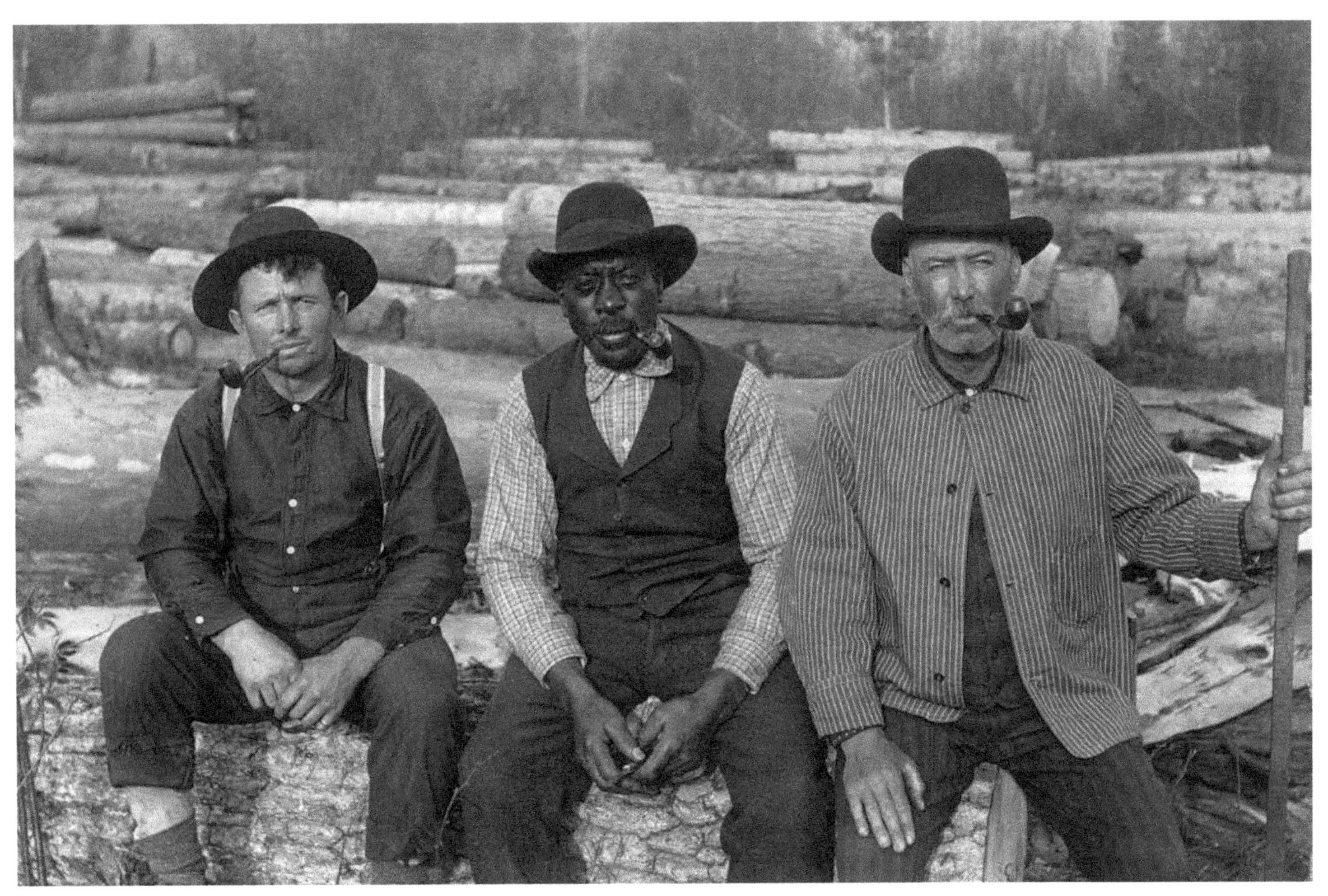

In the early days, many Grand Rapids area men chose lumberjacking as their occupation.

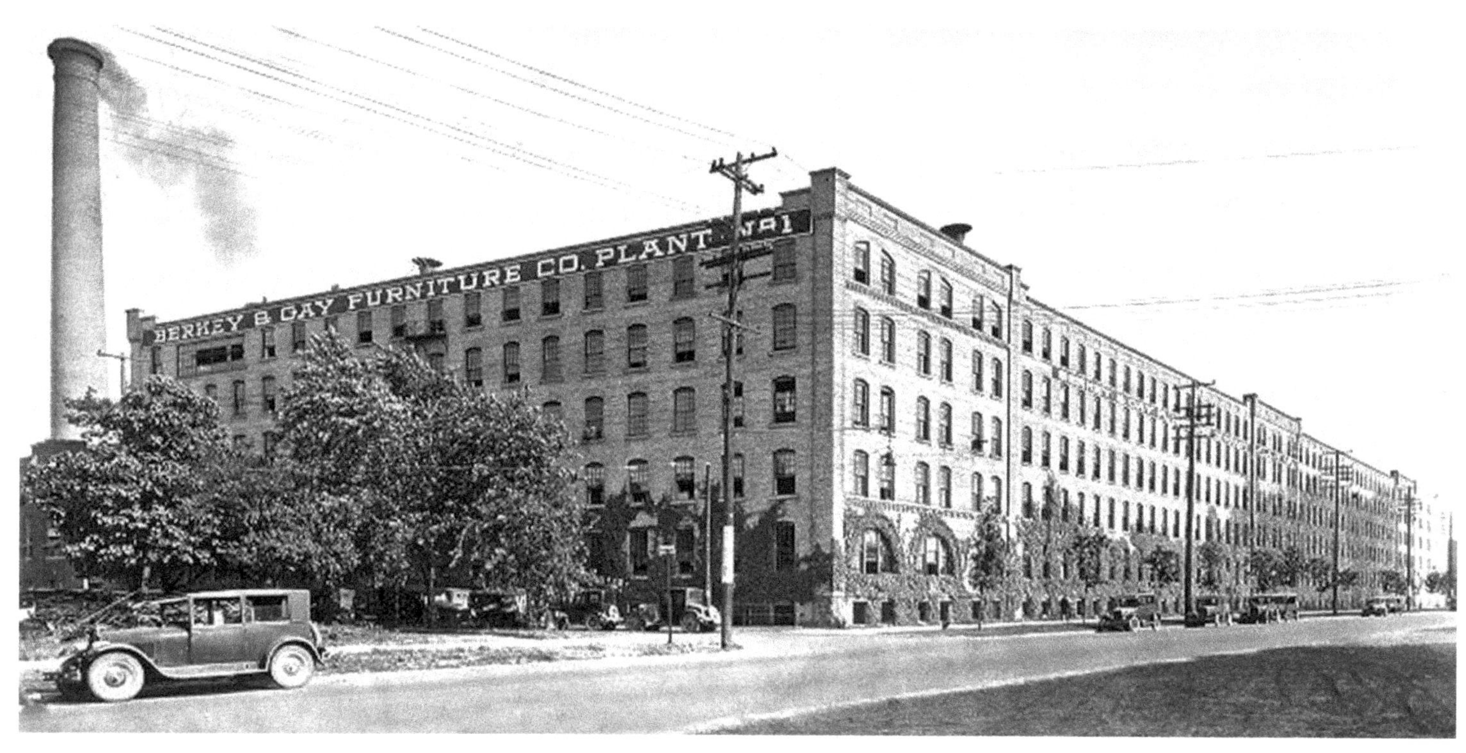

One of Grand Rapids' great furniture plants. Berkey & Gay Furniture Company Plant #1 was located on North Monroe.

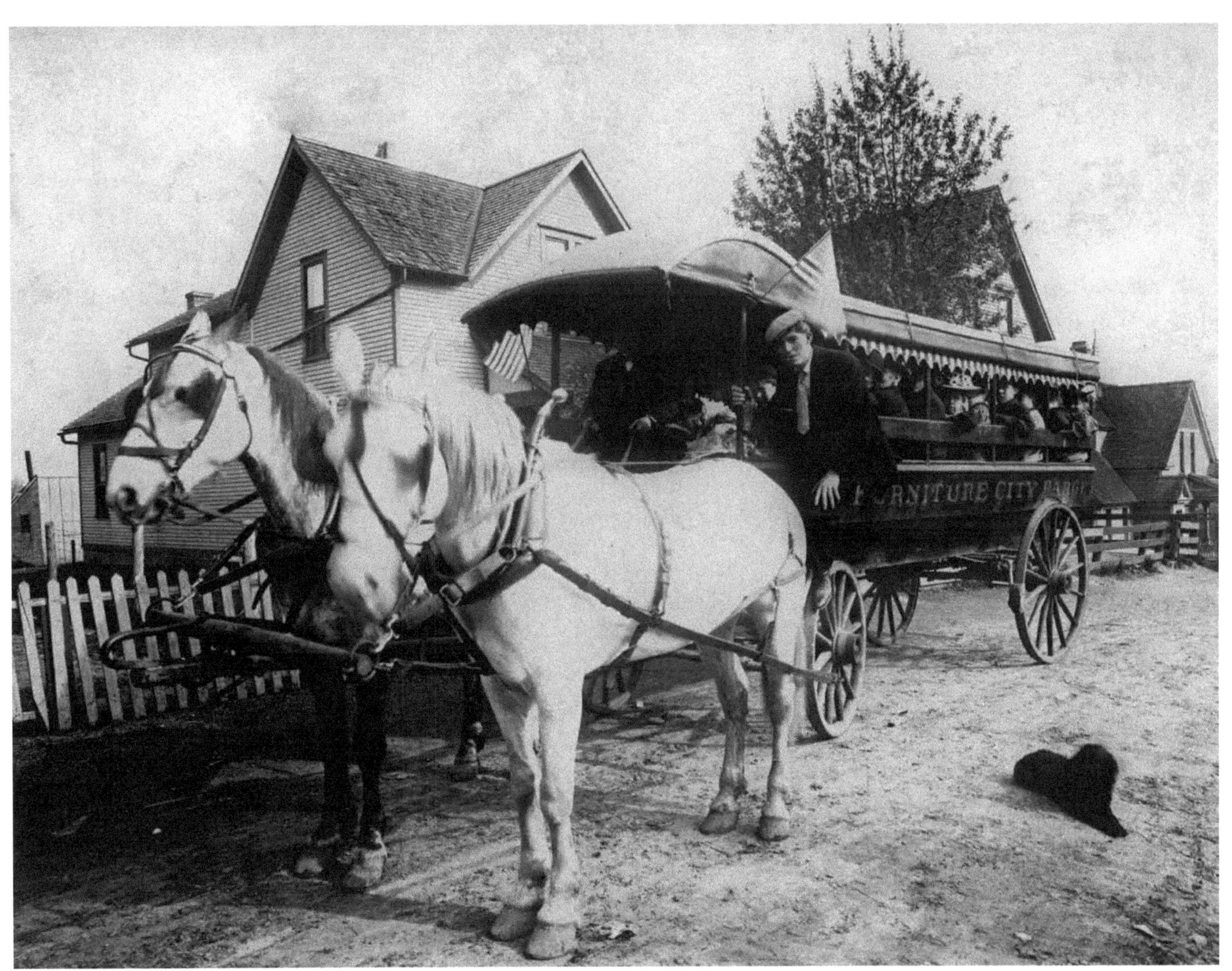

The Furniture City Barge provided transportation throughout the city.

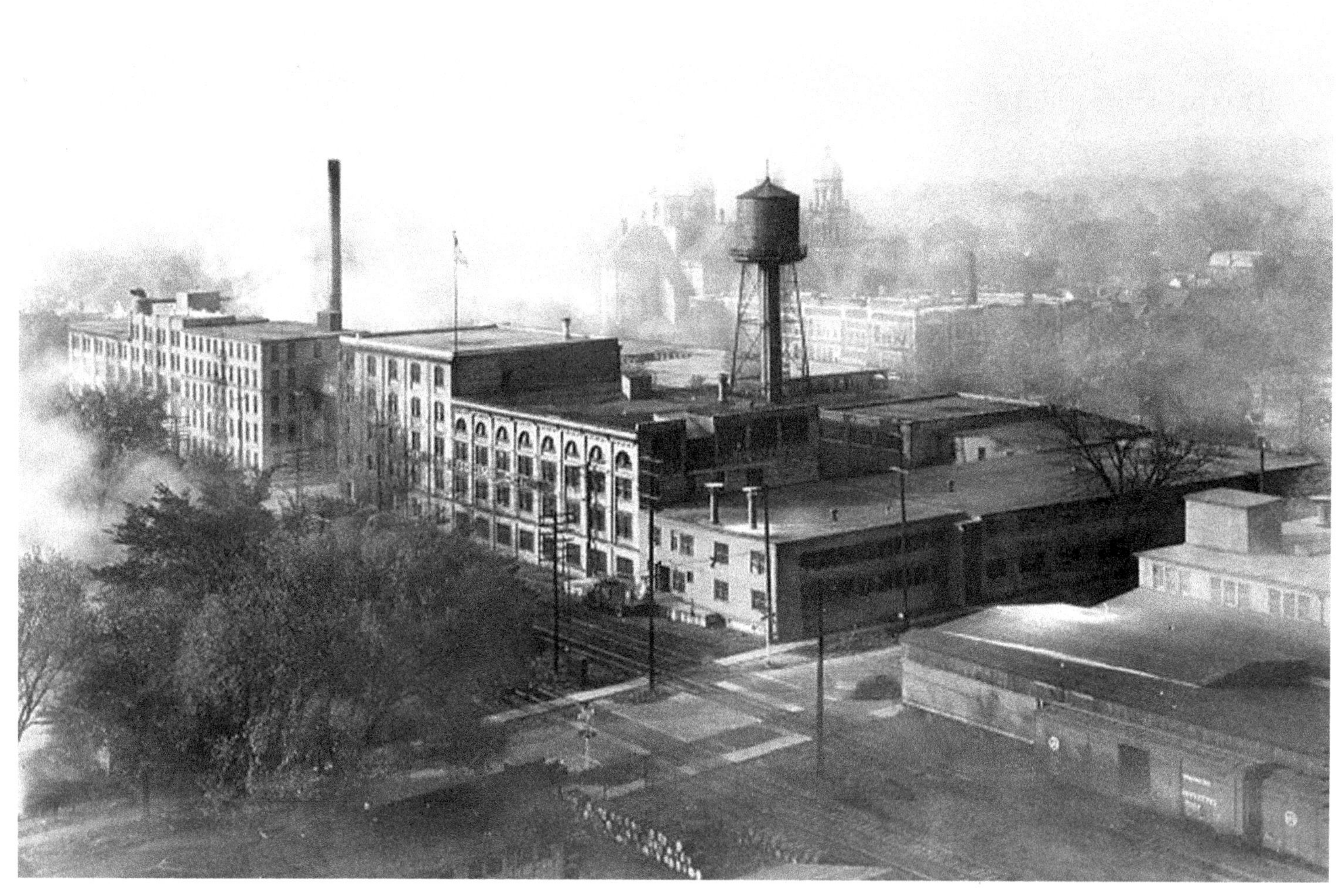

A bird's-eye view of the Widdicomb Furniture Company's Fifth Street plant.

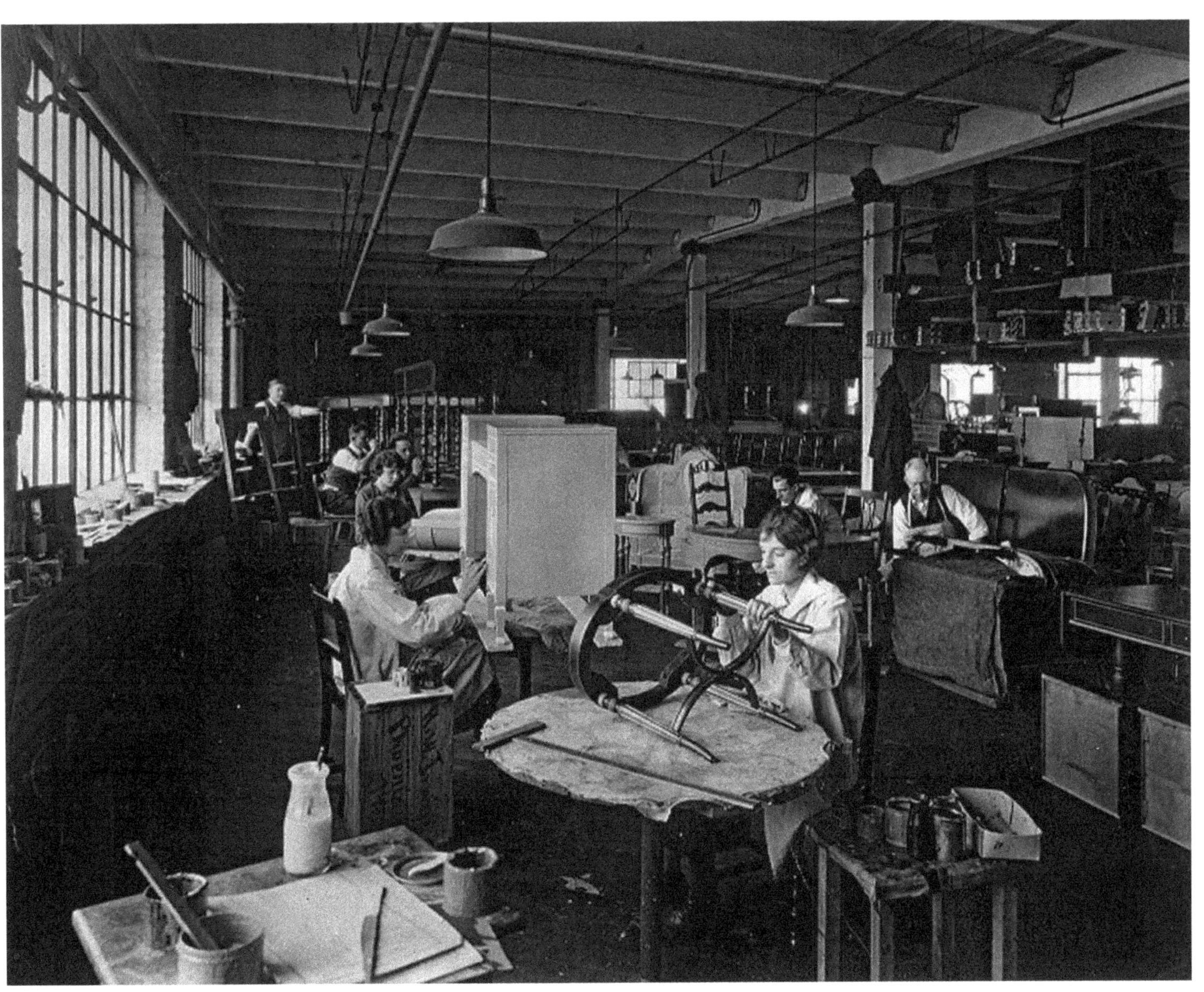

At the R. W. Irwin-Phoenix Furniture factory, employees put the finishing touches on furnishings ranging from dining-room tables to bedroom dressers.

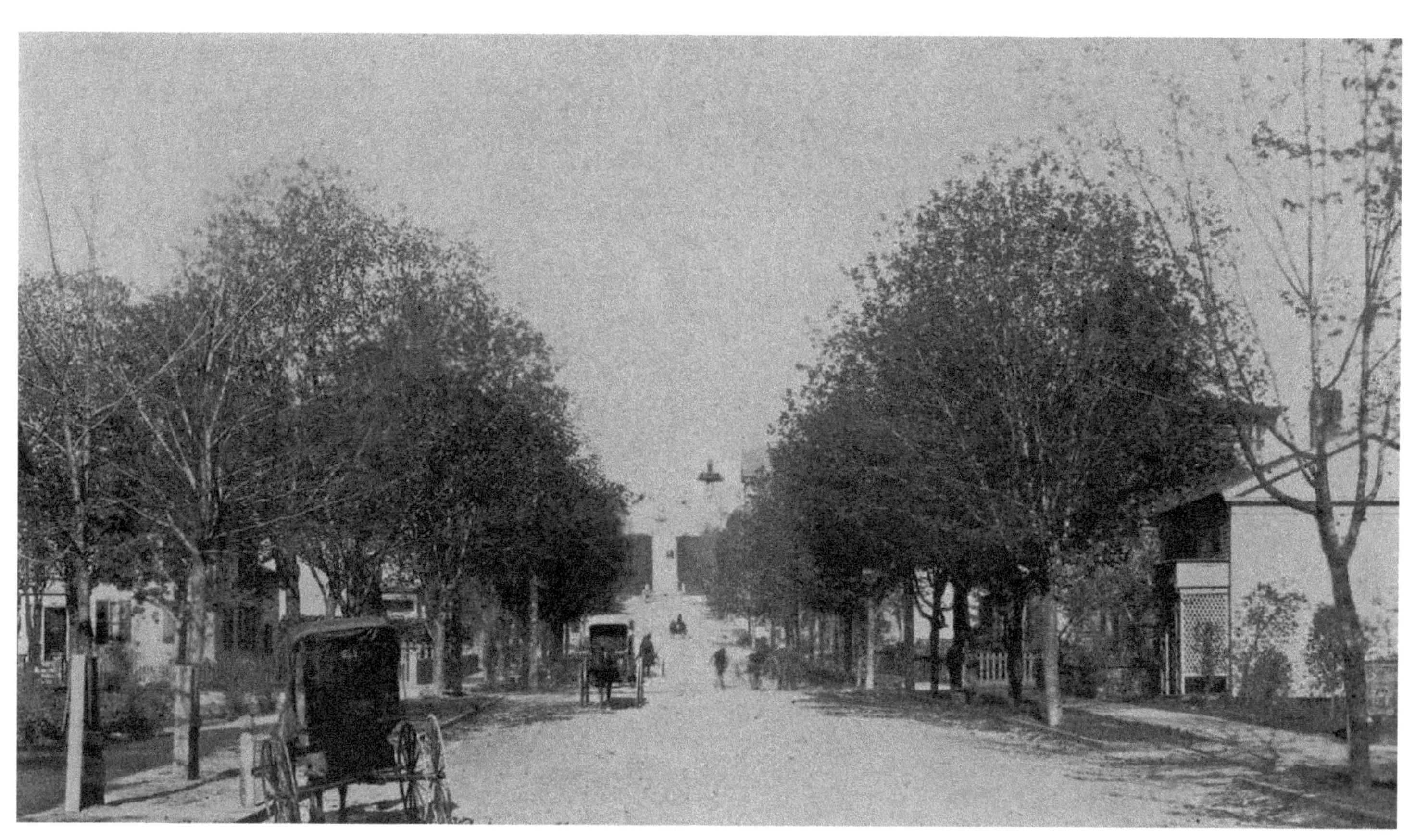

Crescent Street at Kent Street. Crescent Street Park is visible in the distance at the top of the hill.

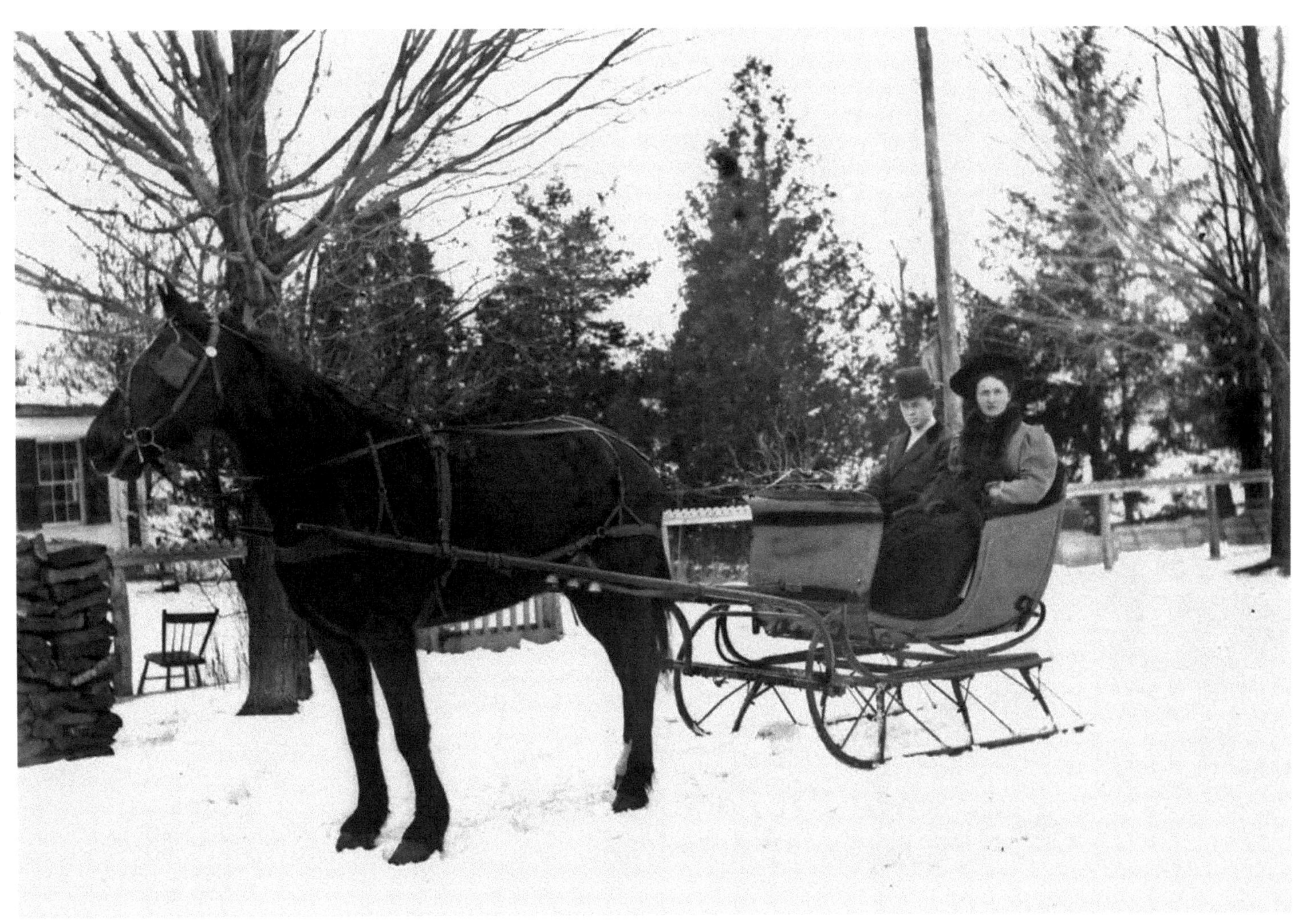

An area couple enjoys a winter sleigh ride.

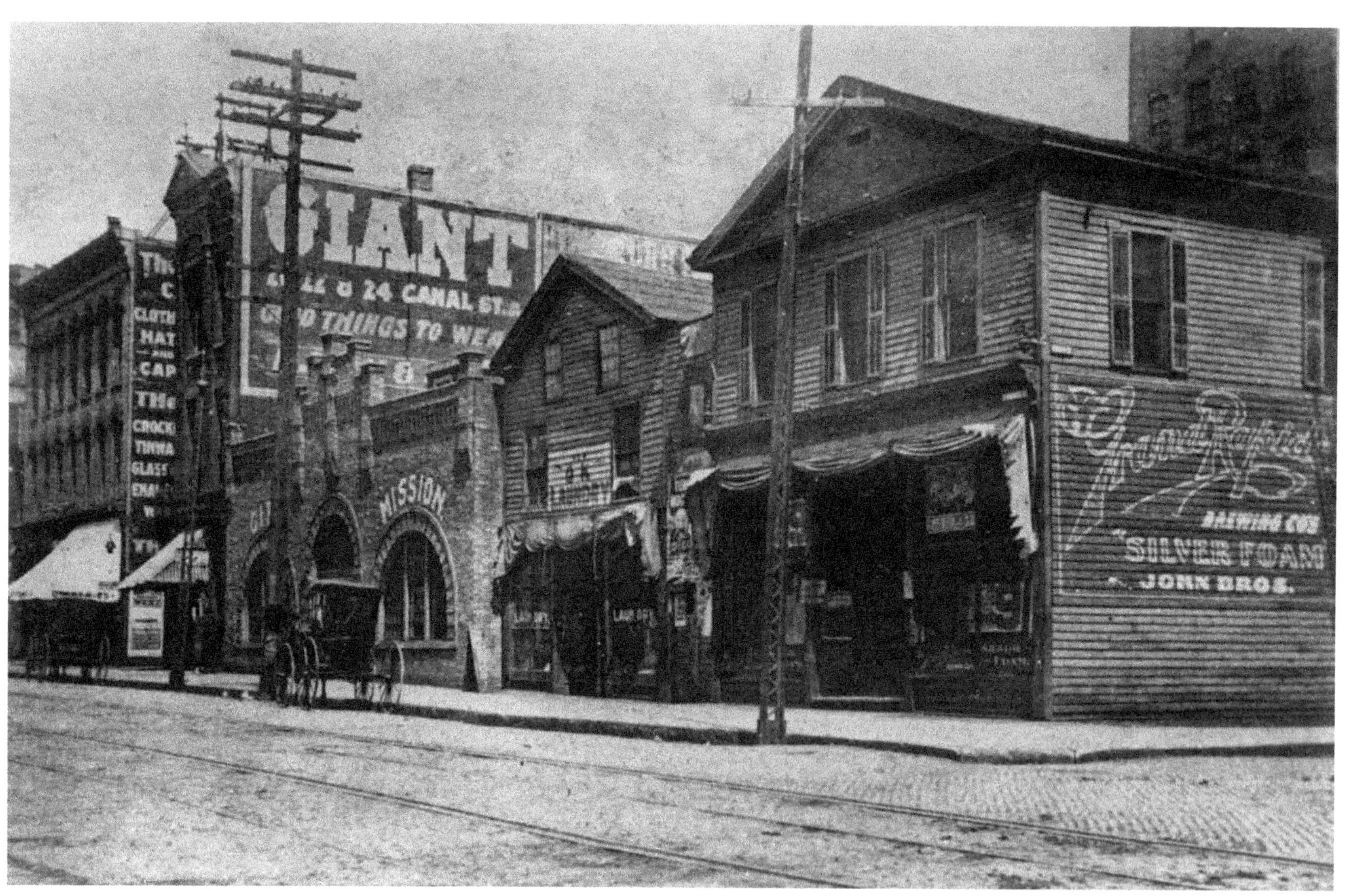

The City Mission and O K Laundry were among the many businesses at the corner of Market and Louis streets.

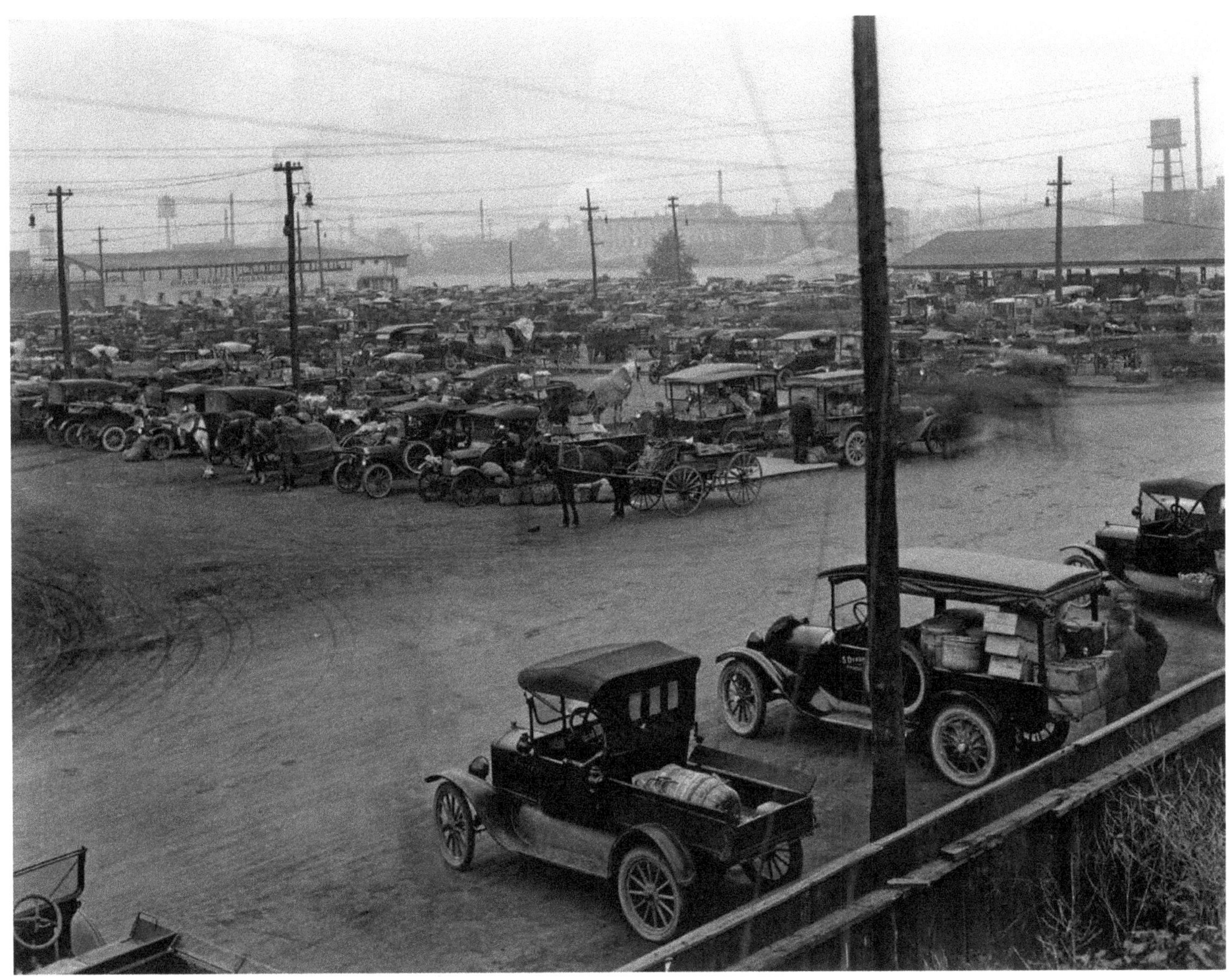

City Farm Market was located at Island Park. With the transition from horse-drawn wagons to motorized vehicles, the number of loads brought to market was on the increase. The Island Park baseball stadium is visible in the background.

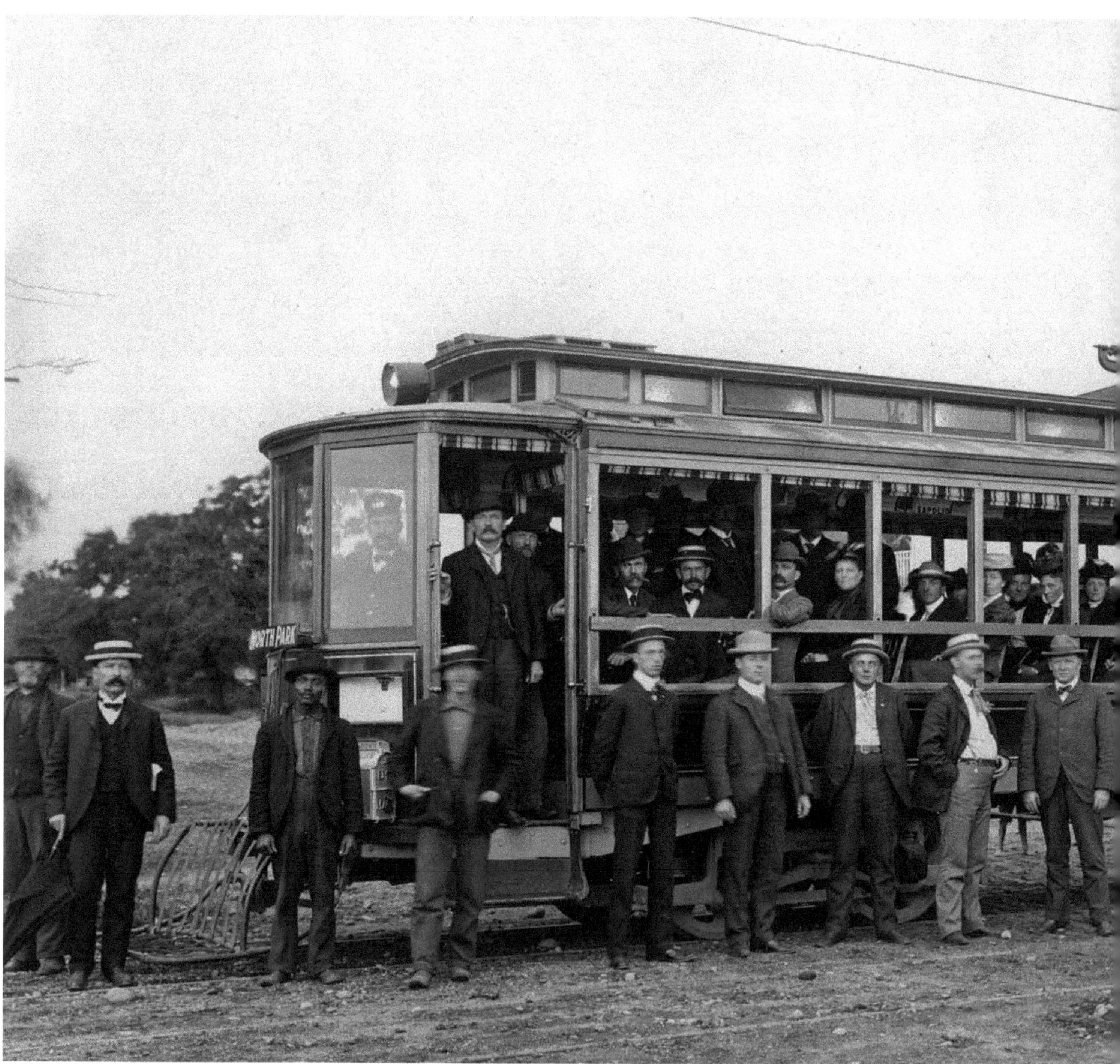
NORTH PARK

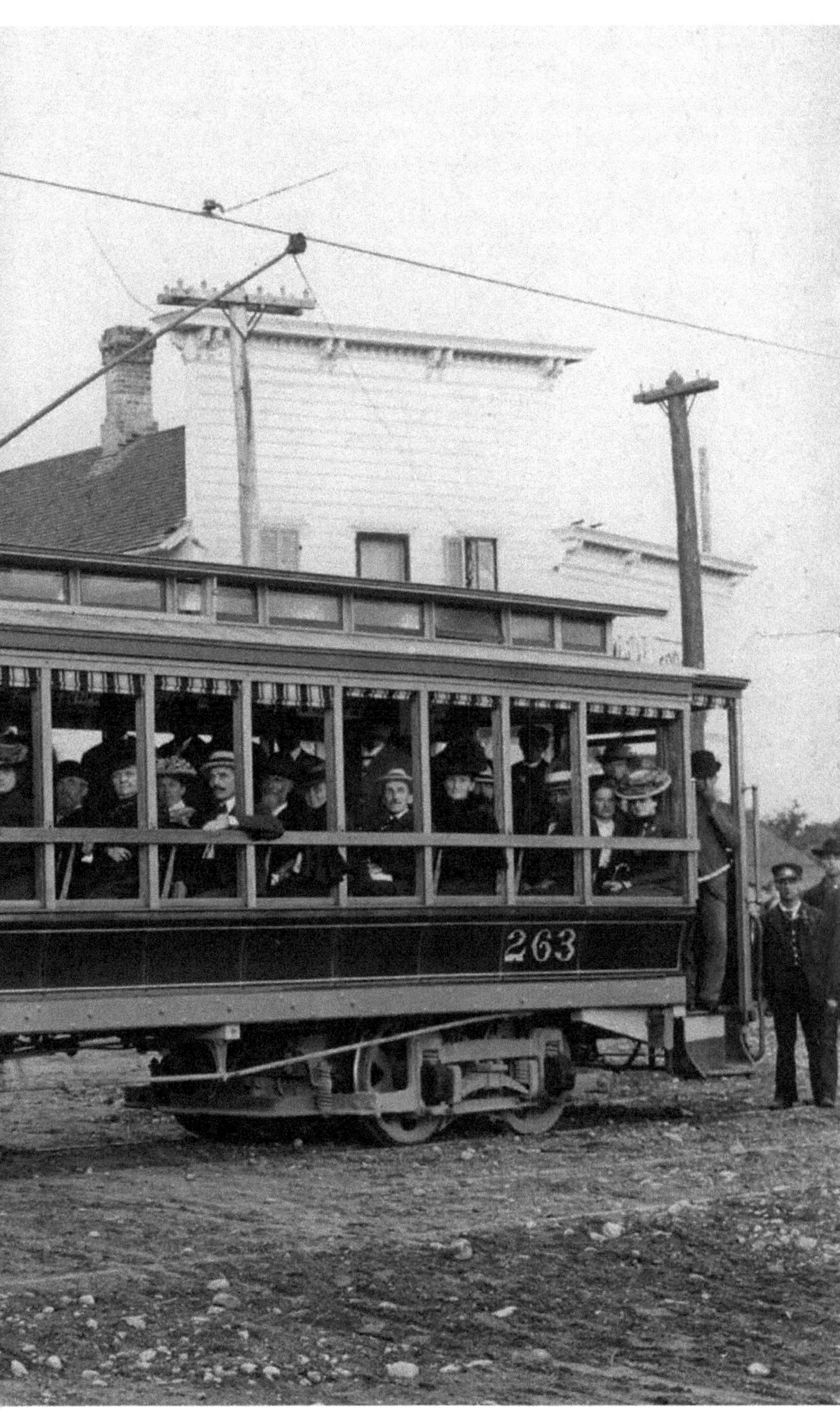

Electric streetcars were introduced in 1891 and rapidly replaced horse-drawn trolleys and cable cars.

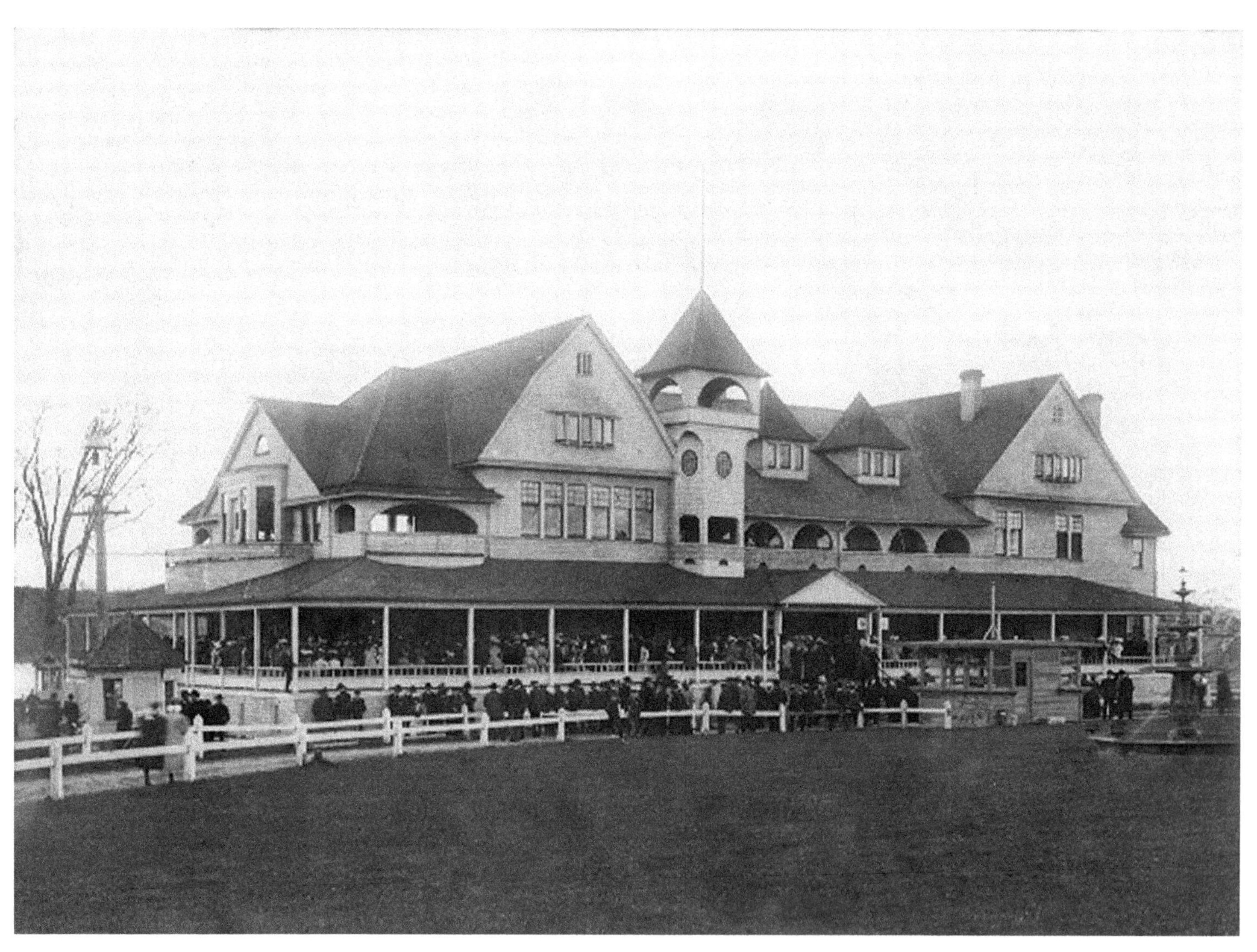

North Park Pavilion, north of the city limits on the Grand Rapids Street Railway line.

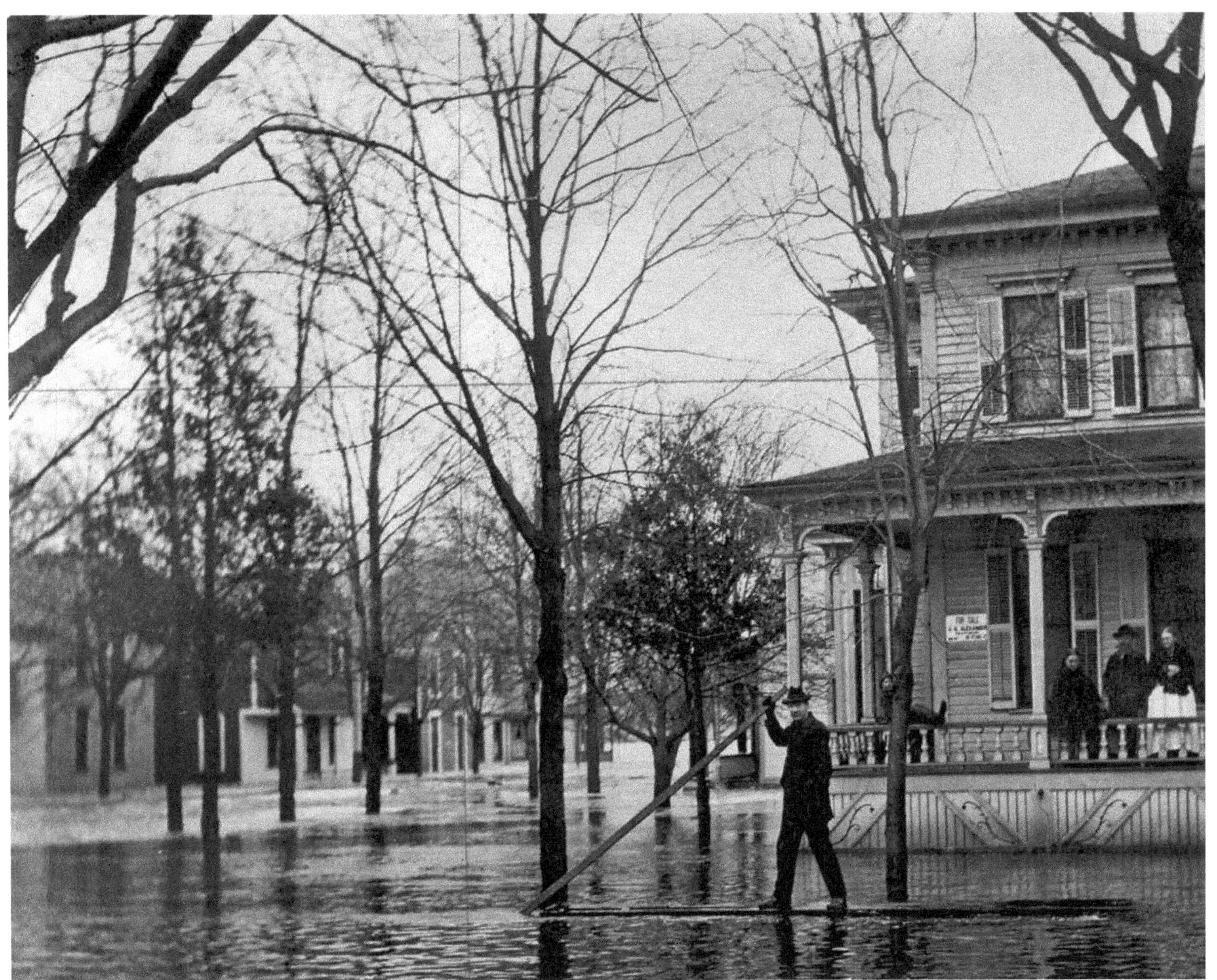

The Flood of March 1904 was the greatest and most destructive flood ever experienced in Grand Rapids. More than half the populated area on the west side of the Grand River was underwater. This view reveals the situation on Fourth Street between Turner and Broadway avenues.

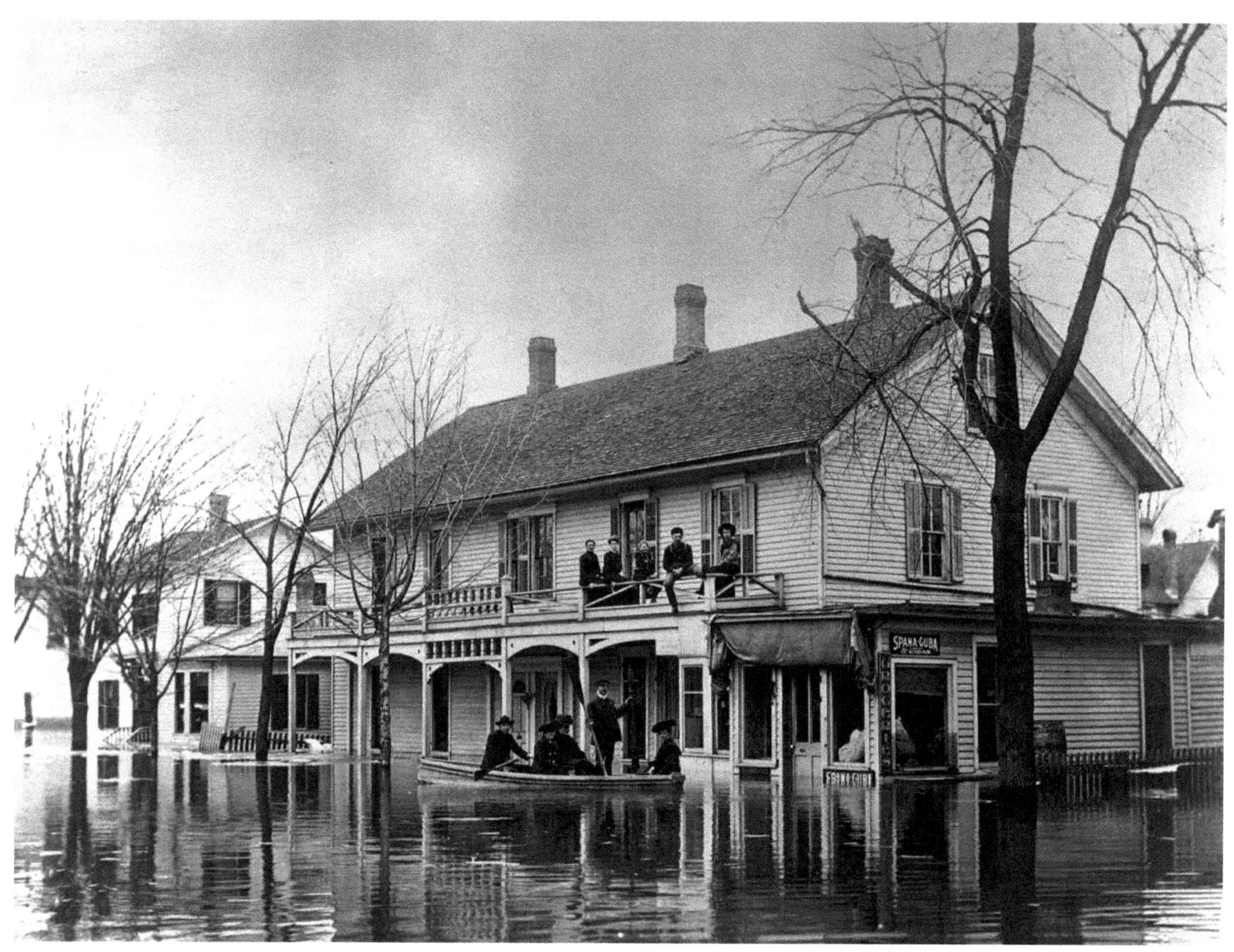

This view of the Flood of 1904 captures the area along Eighth Street and Turner Avenue. Determined not to let the rising waters dismay her spirit, the woman at porchtop center smiles for the camera.

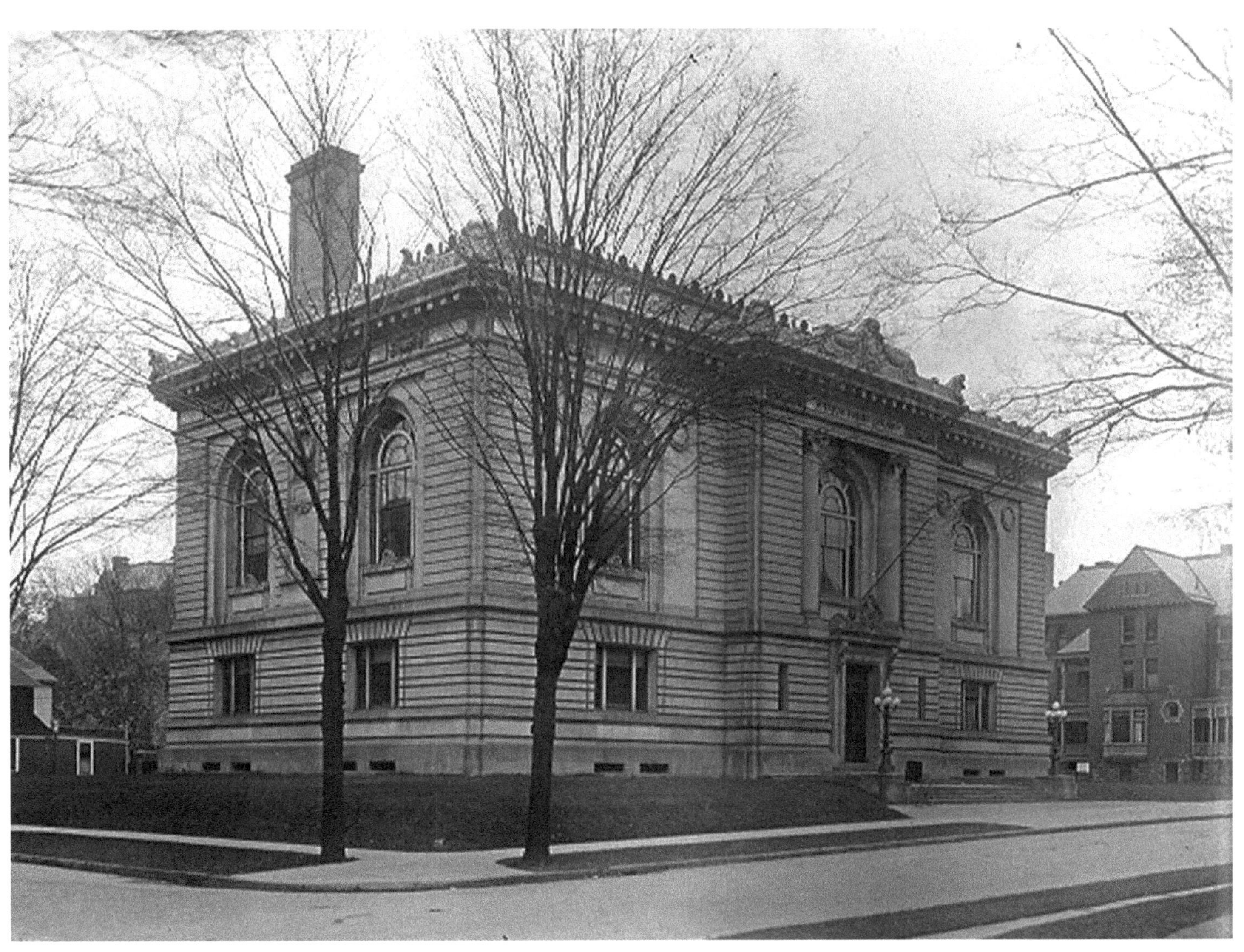

Ryerson Public Library, now known as the Grand Rapids Public Library, was built in 1904. The Library was a gift to the city by Martin Ryerson, a prominent Chicago industrialist who was born in Grand Rapids.

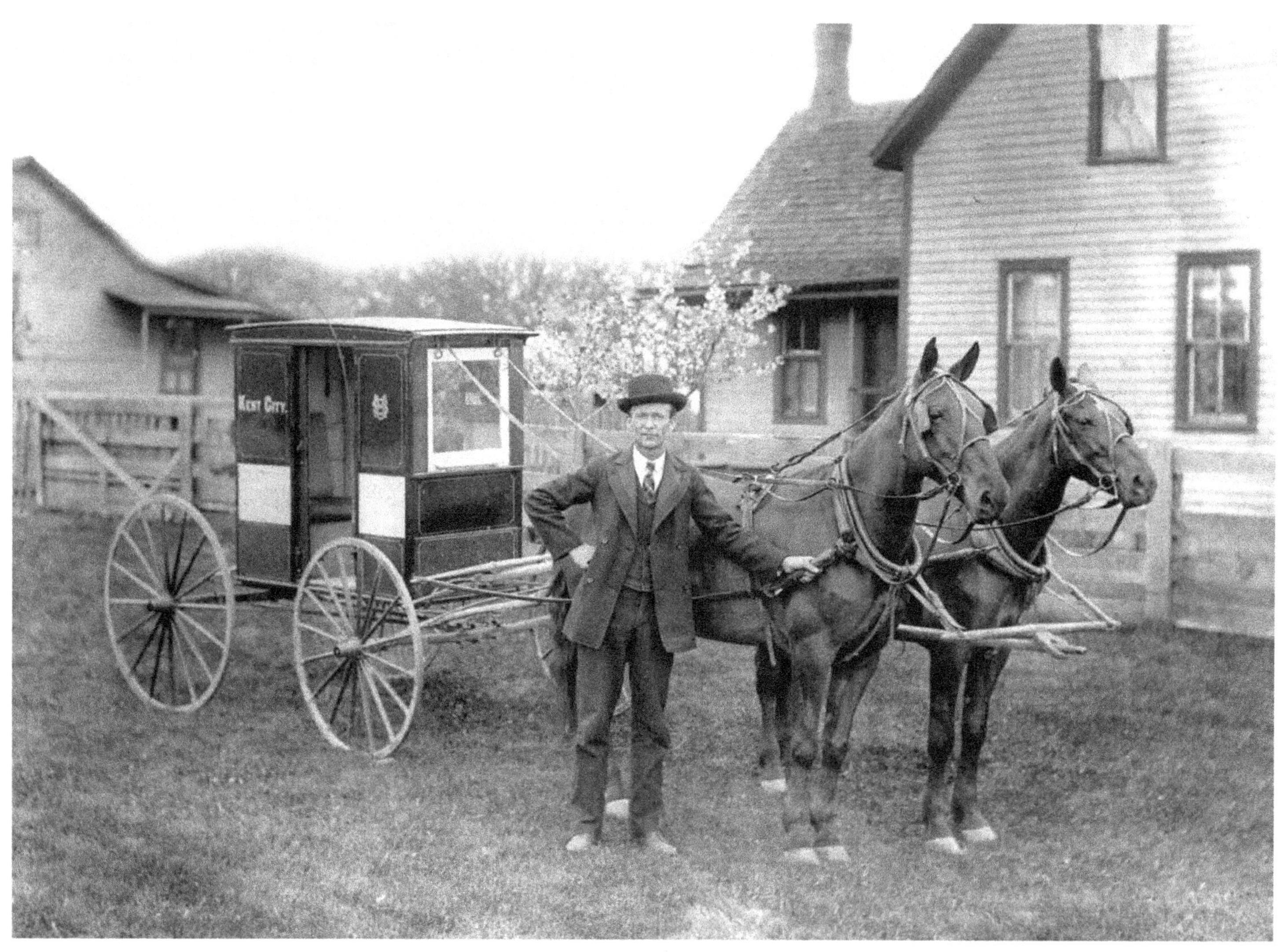

Outside the city limits, rural free delivery started as an experiment in 1886 and became official in 1902. This mail carrier from Kent City poses with his horses and buggy.

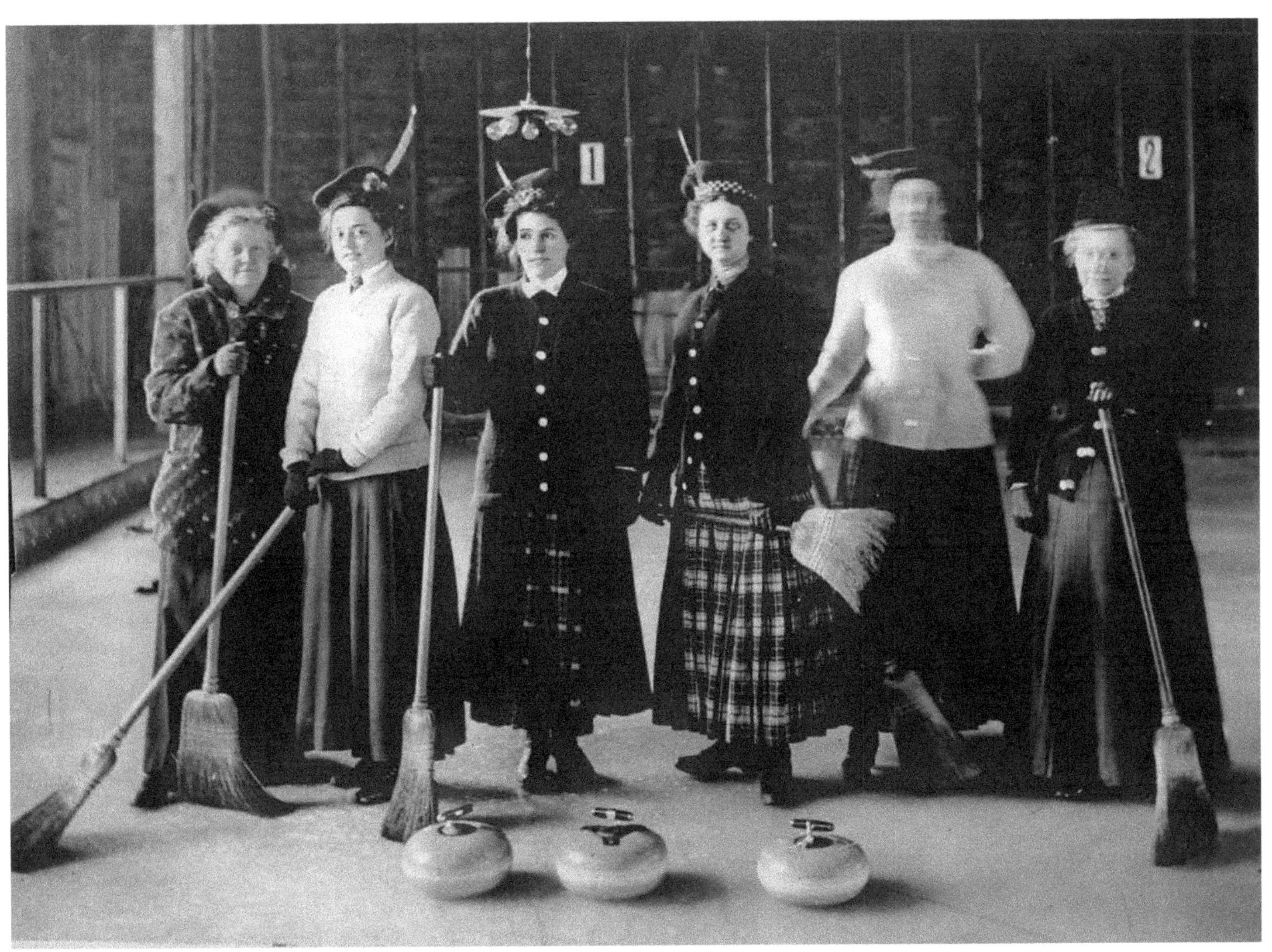

Curling is a team sport in which a large stone is pushed down the ice toward its target. Two sweepers with brooms accompanied each stone to help direct it to its target. In 1908, Grand Rapids was home to the first curling club composed entirely of women. From left to right are Mrs. John Brower, Miss Helen Barstow, Mrs. F. E. Hill, Mrs. Stuart Foote, Miss Rosetta Leitelt, and Mrs. H. B. Snyder.

The soda fountain at West's Drug Store, located at 8-10 Canal, which is today 184-186 Monroe, opposite the Pantlind Hotel. Doesn't that Pineapple Ice sound good?

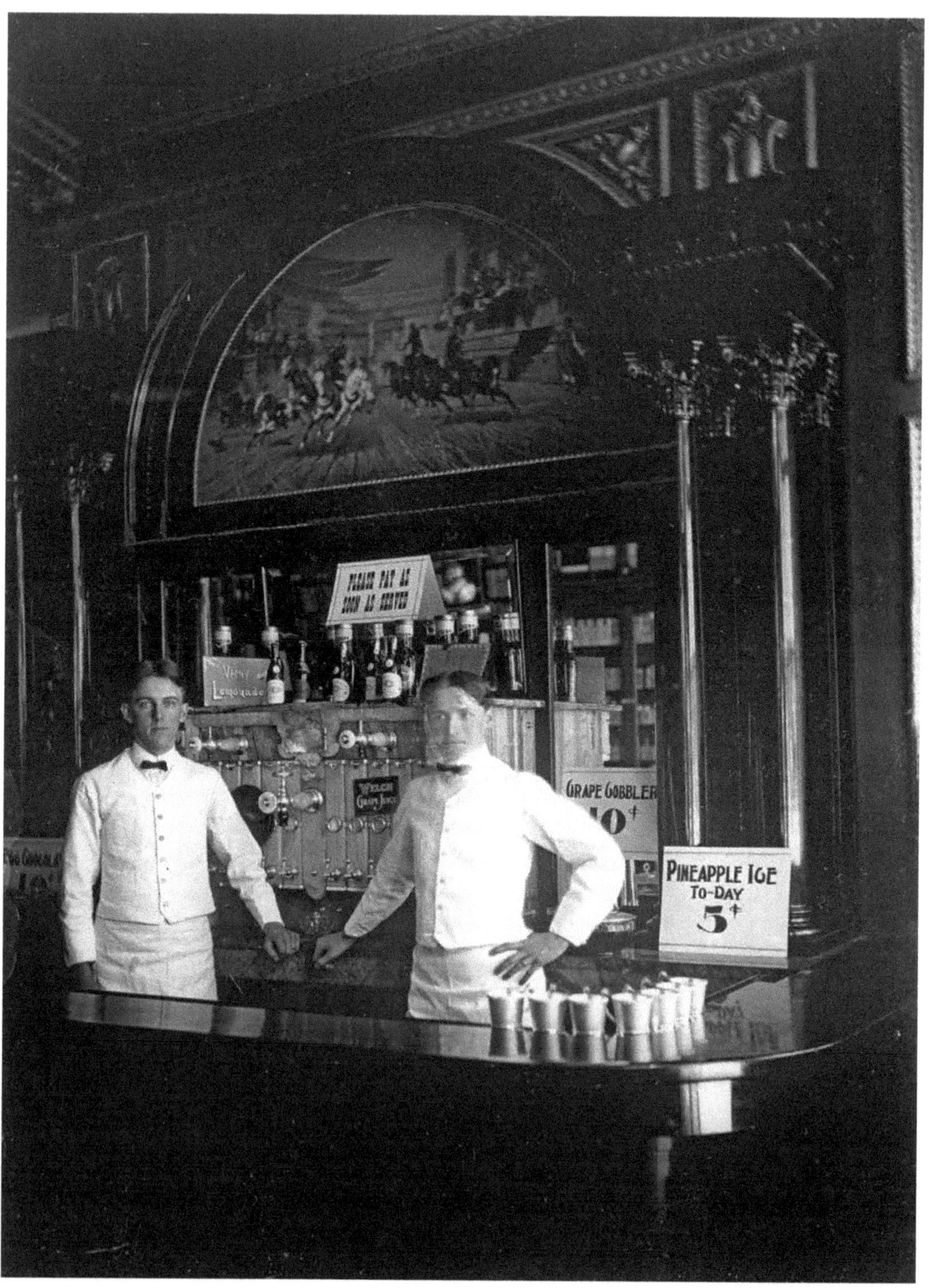

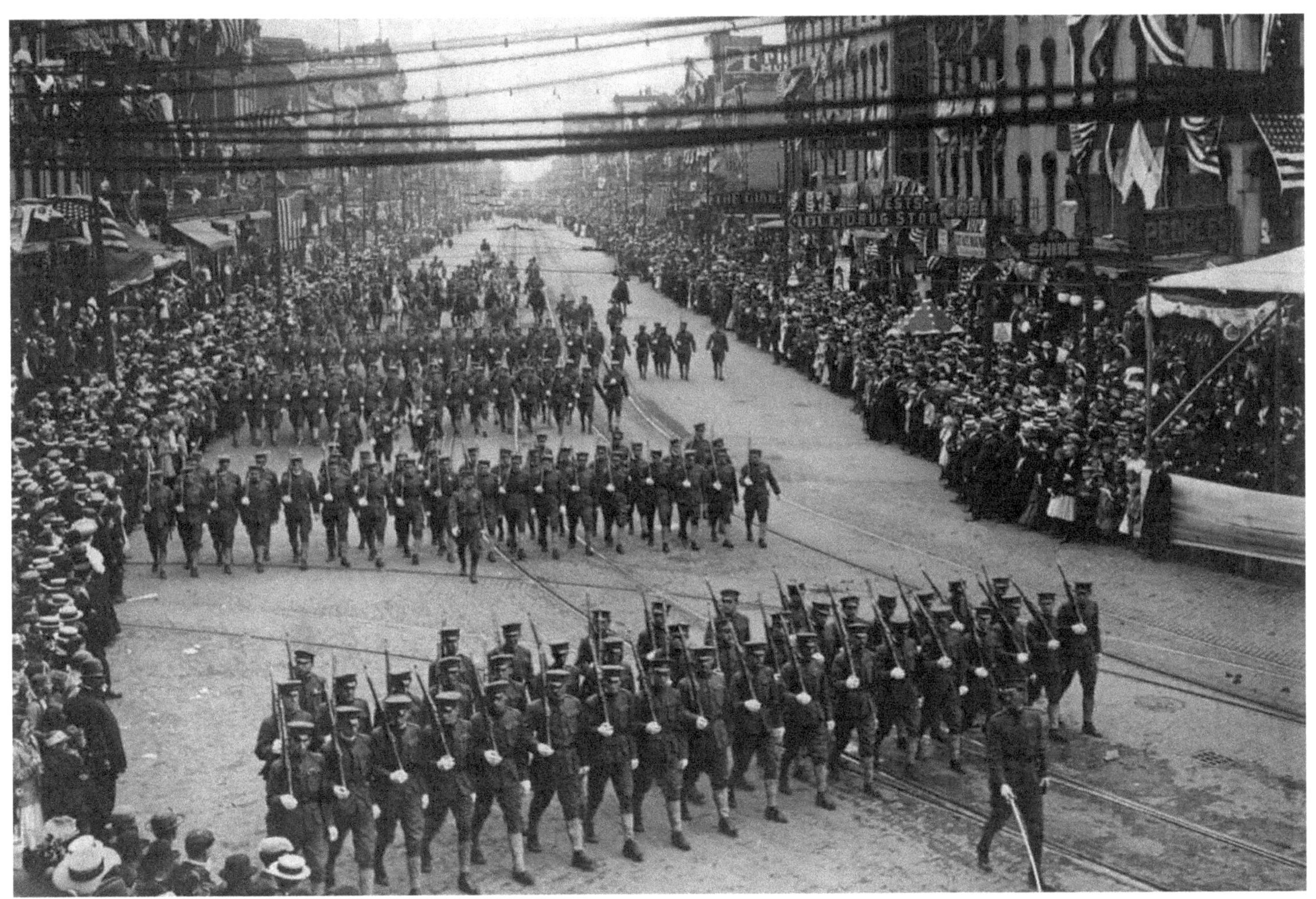

For the Homecoming Celebration in 1910, the entire city shut down to observe the festivities for five days. There were parades, pageants, fireworks, concerts, circus performances, and speeches galore. In this parade, soldiers demonstrate precision marching.

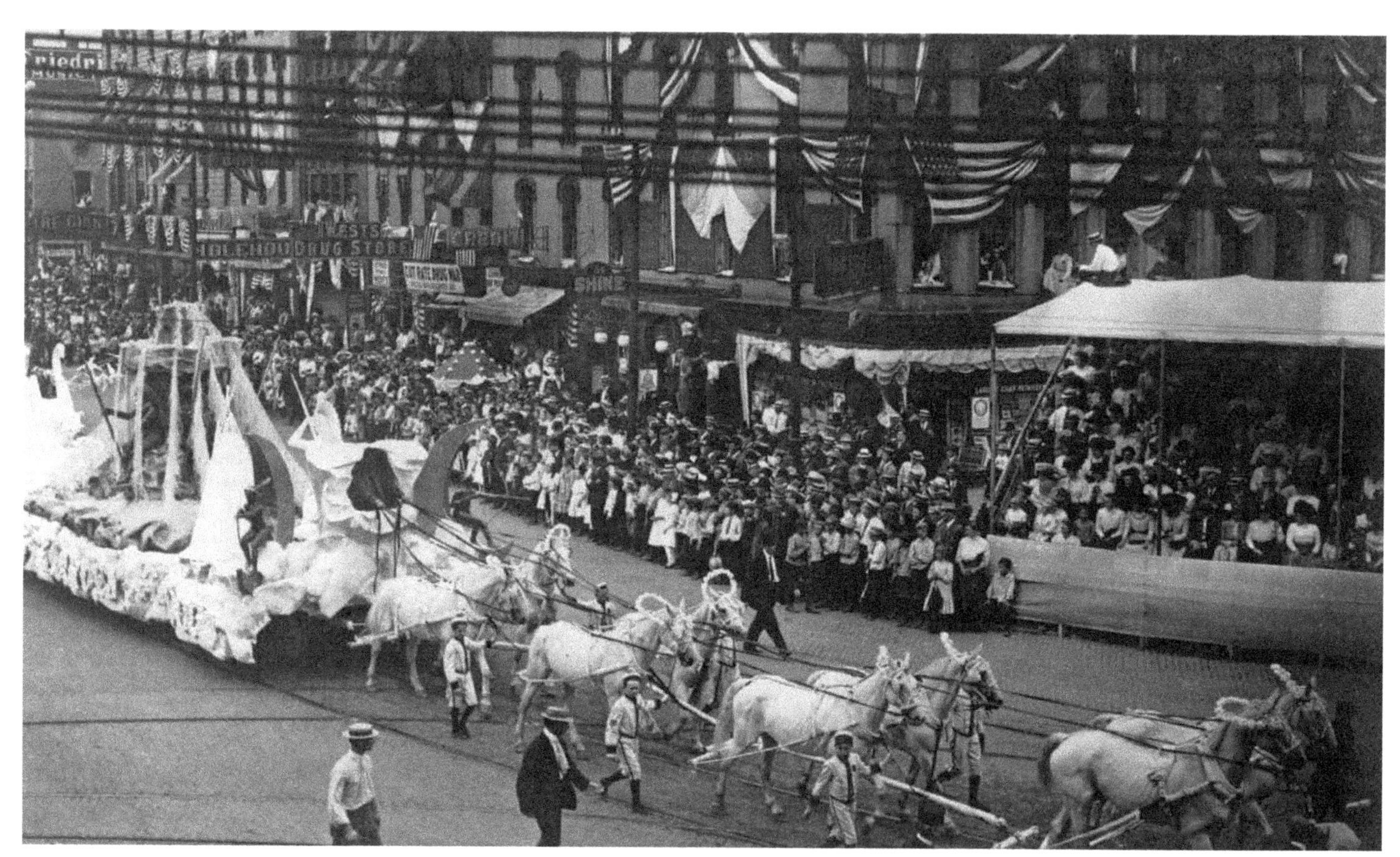

A horse-drawn float in a Homecoming Celebration parade.

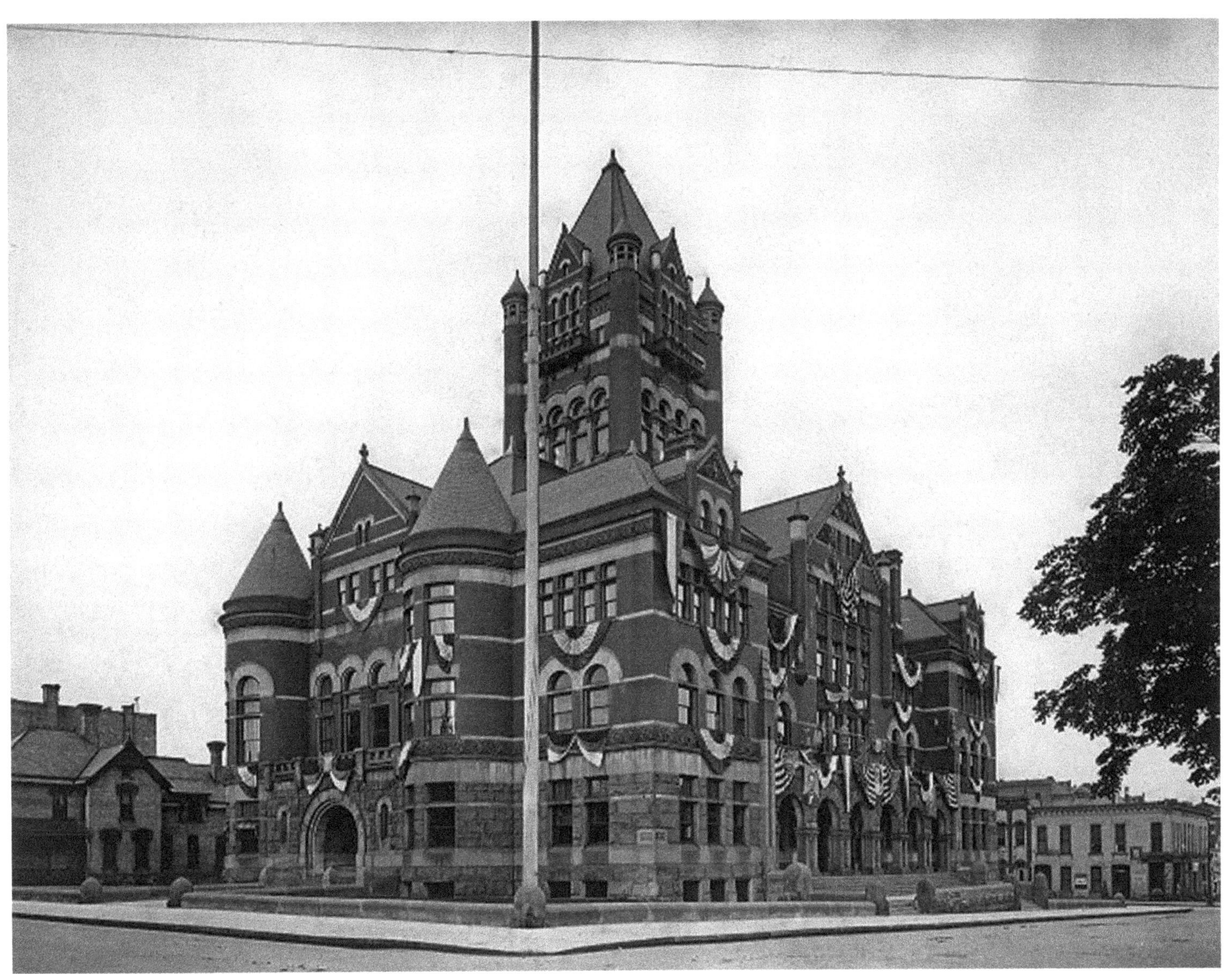

The cornerstone of the County Building was laid on July 4, 1889. Located on the corner of Ottawa Avenue and Crescent Street, it was razed during the urban renewal movement of the 1960s.

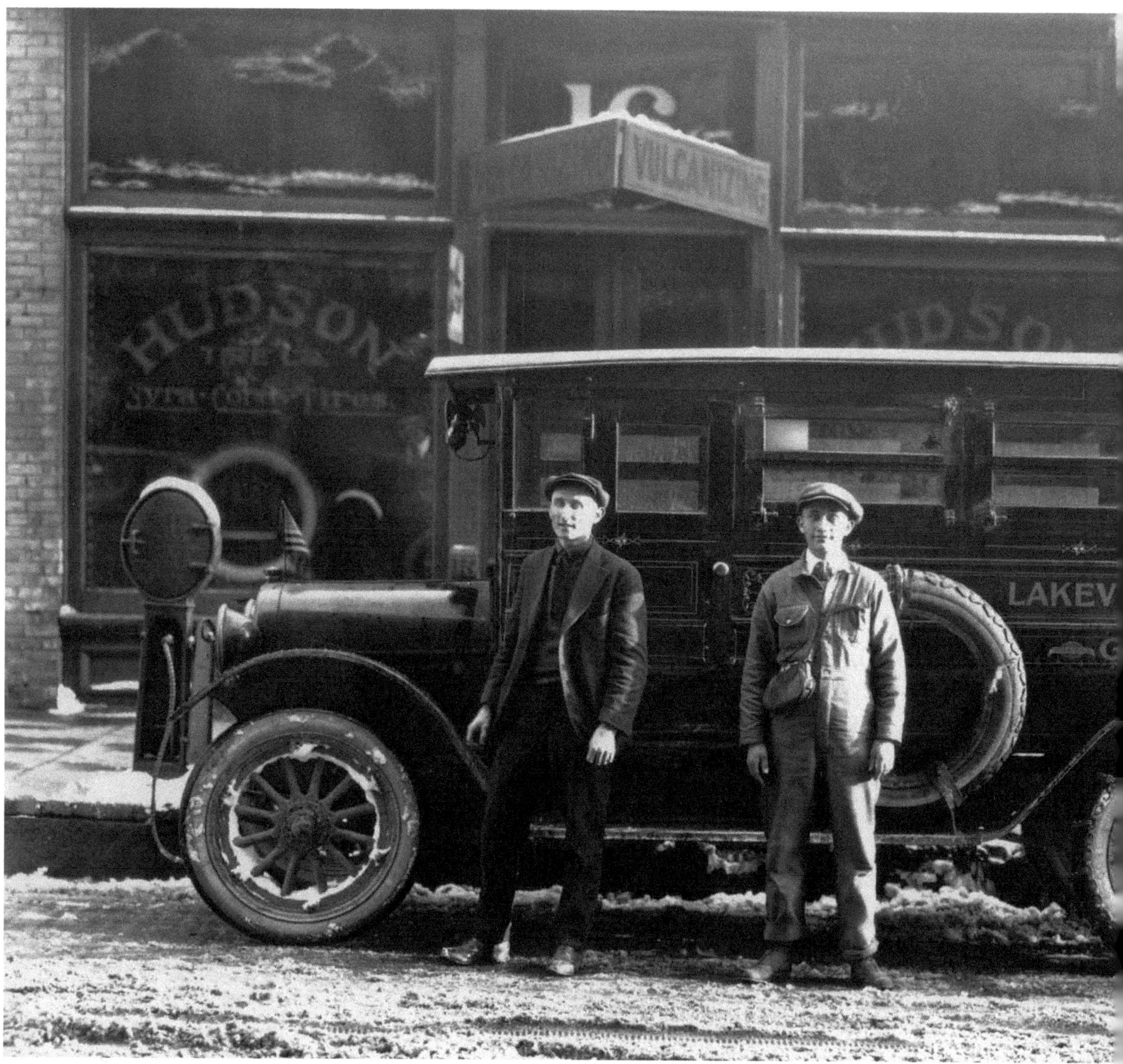
HUDSON
LAKEV

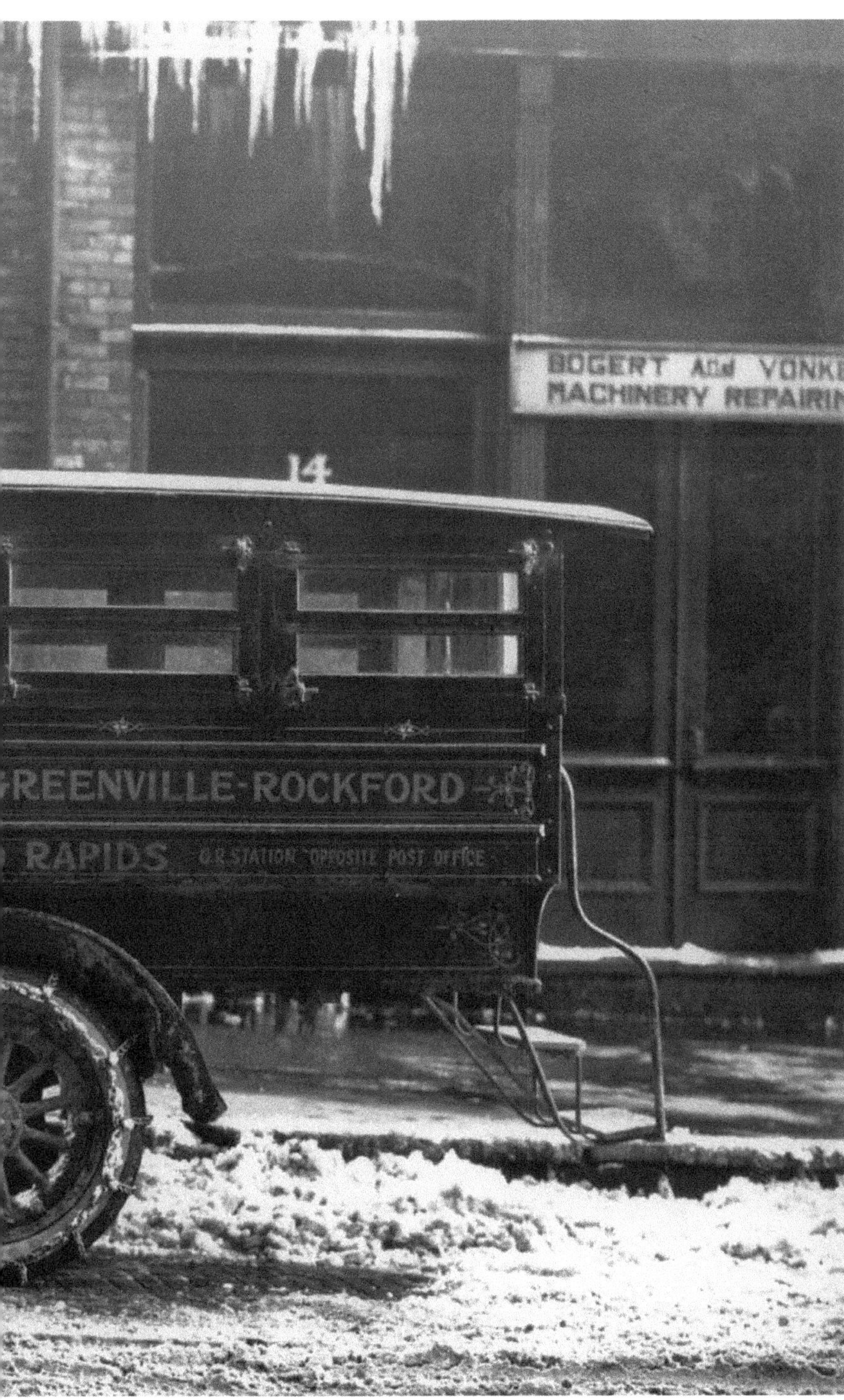

This bus line served the outlying areas of Lakeview, Greenville, and Rockford. The Grand Rapids station was located opposite the post office.

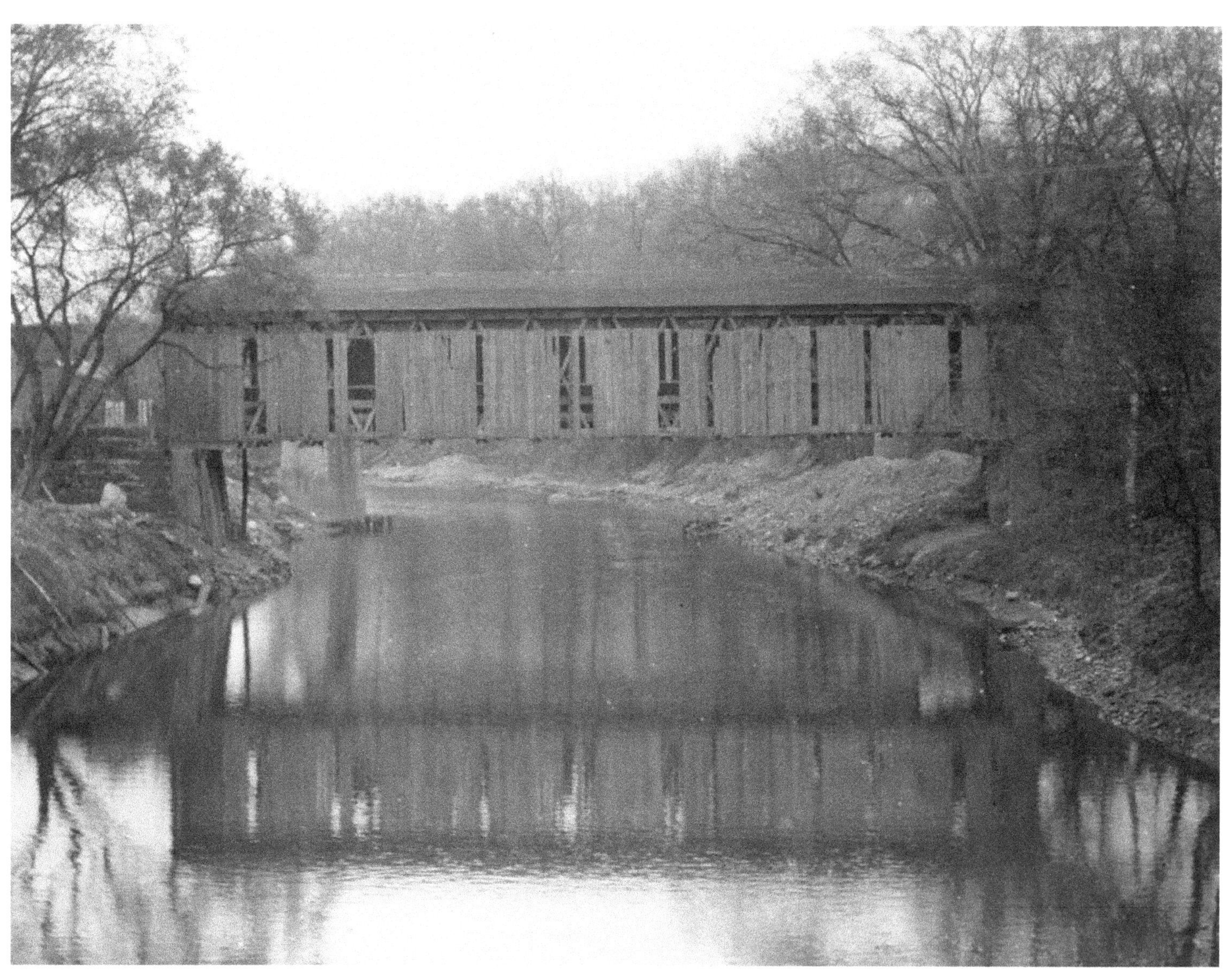

The Ada Covered Bridge was erected in 1867 across the Thornapple River, just south of where the Thornapple enters the Grand River. It was destroyed by fire after repairs were made in 1979. A replica pedestrian bridge now stands in its place.

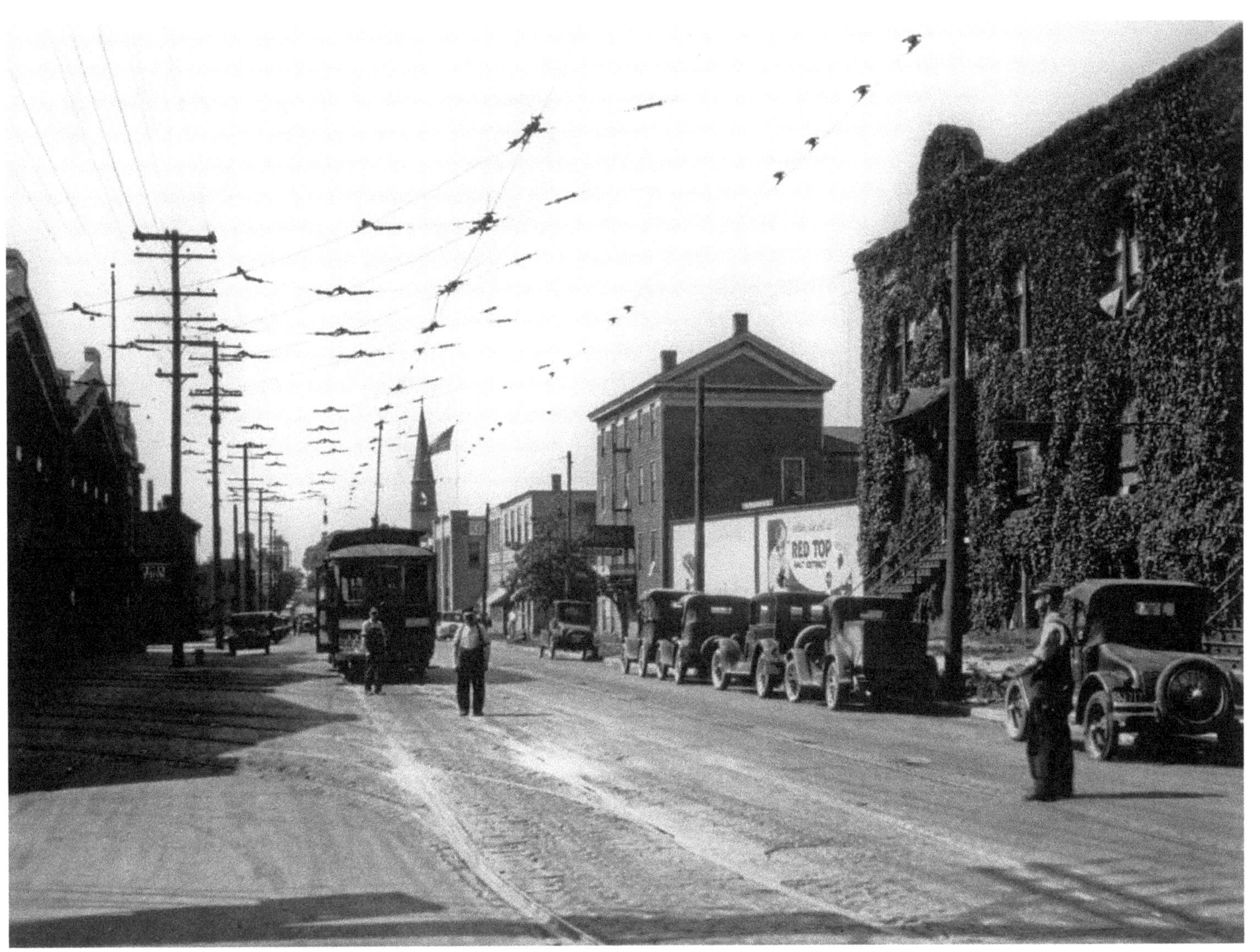

Early in the twentieth century, mobility was on the increase. Both streetcars and automobiles are seen plying the streets of Grand Rapids in this image.

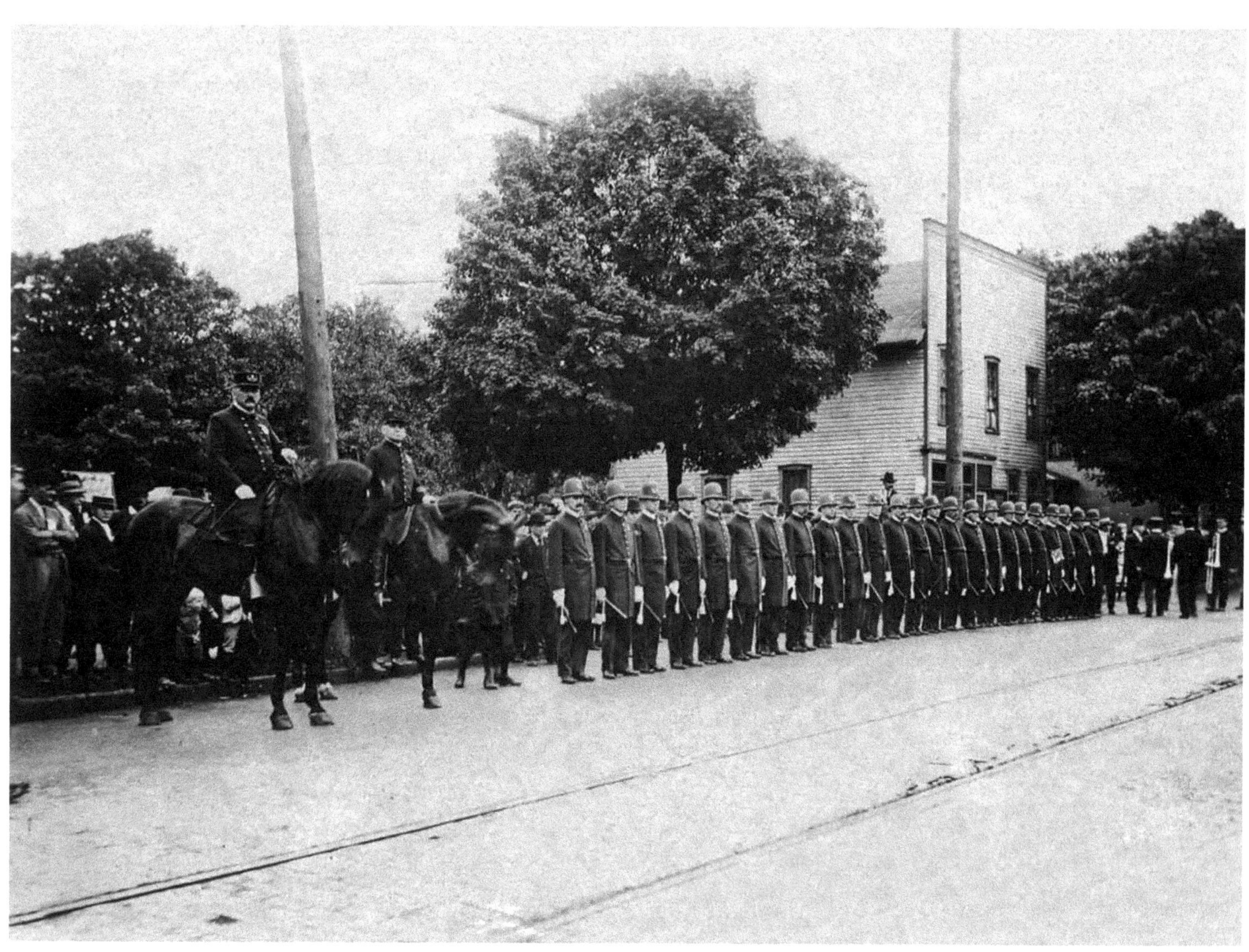

The Grand Rapids Police Department lines up in 1910.

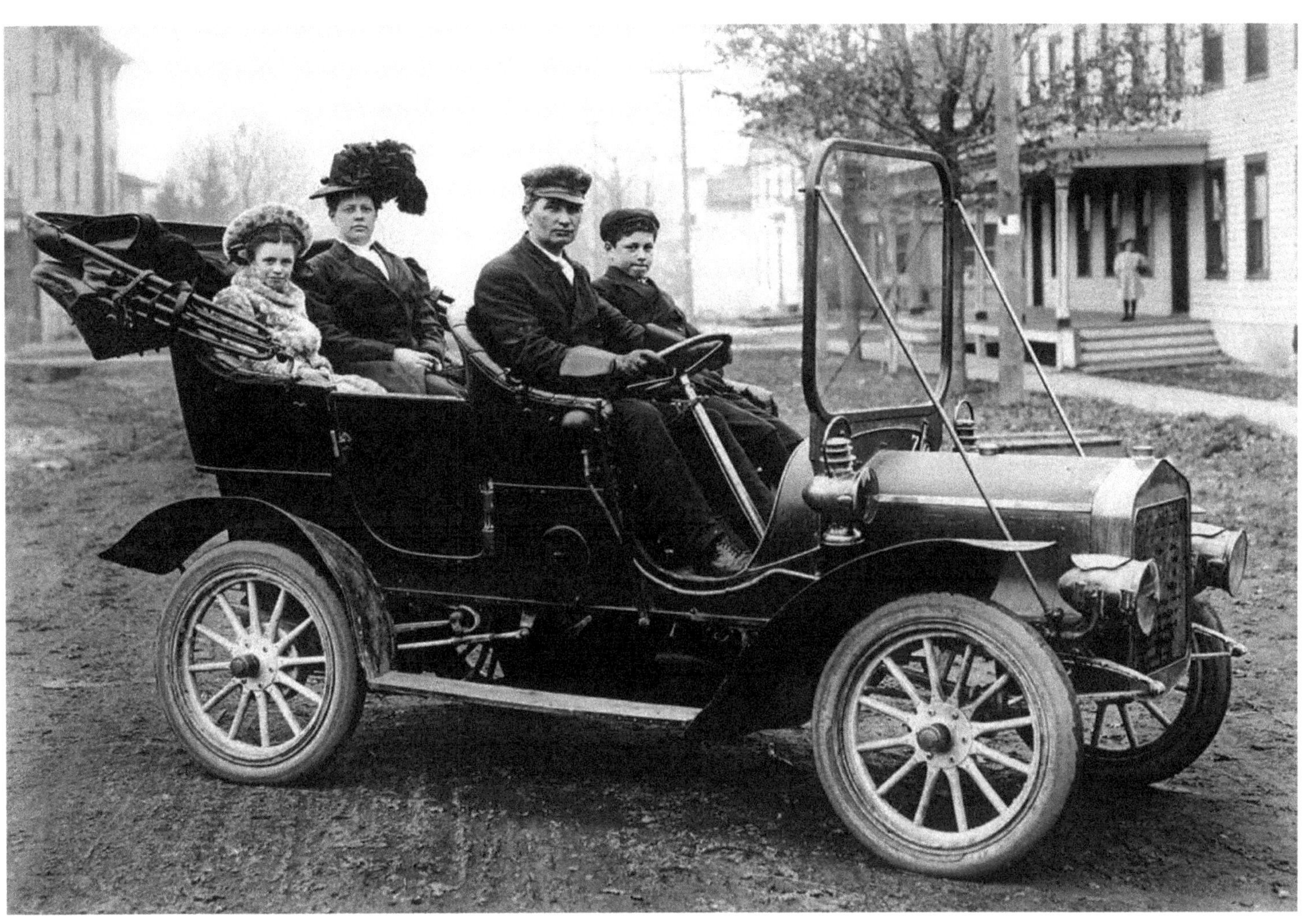

Austin Automobile Company was in business from 1901 to 1921. The company was founded by James and Walter Austin. They built large, expensive touring cars like the one seen here.

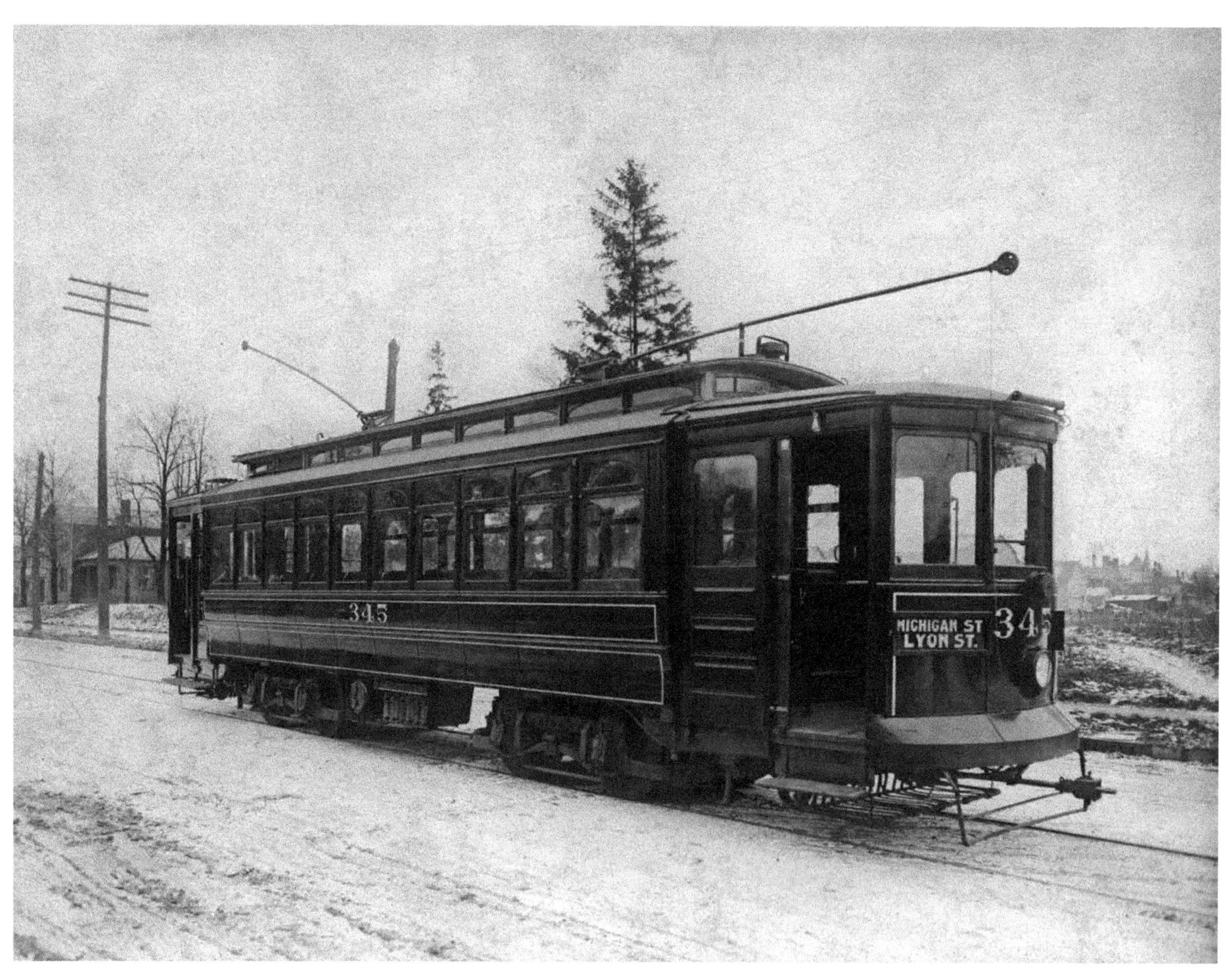

Pictured on a snowy day is one of ten streetcars purchased in 1912. Streetcar #345 ran the Michigan-Lyon streets route.

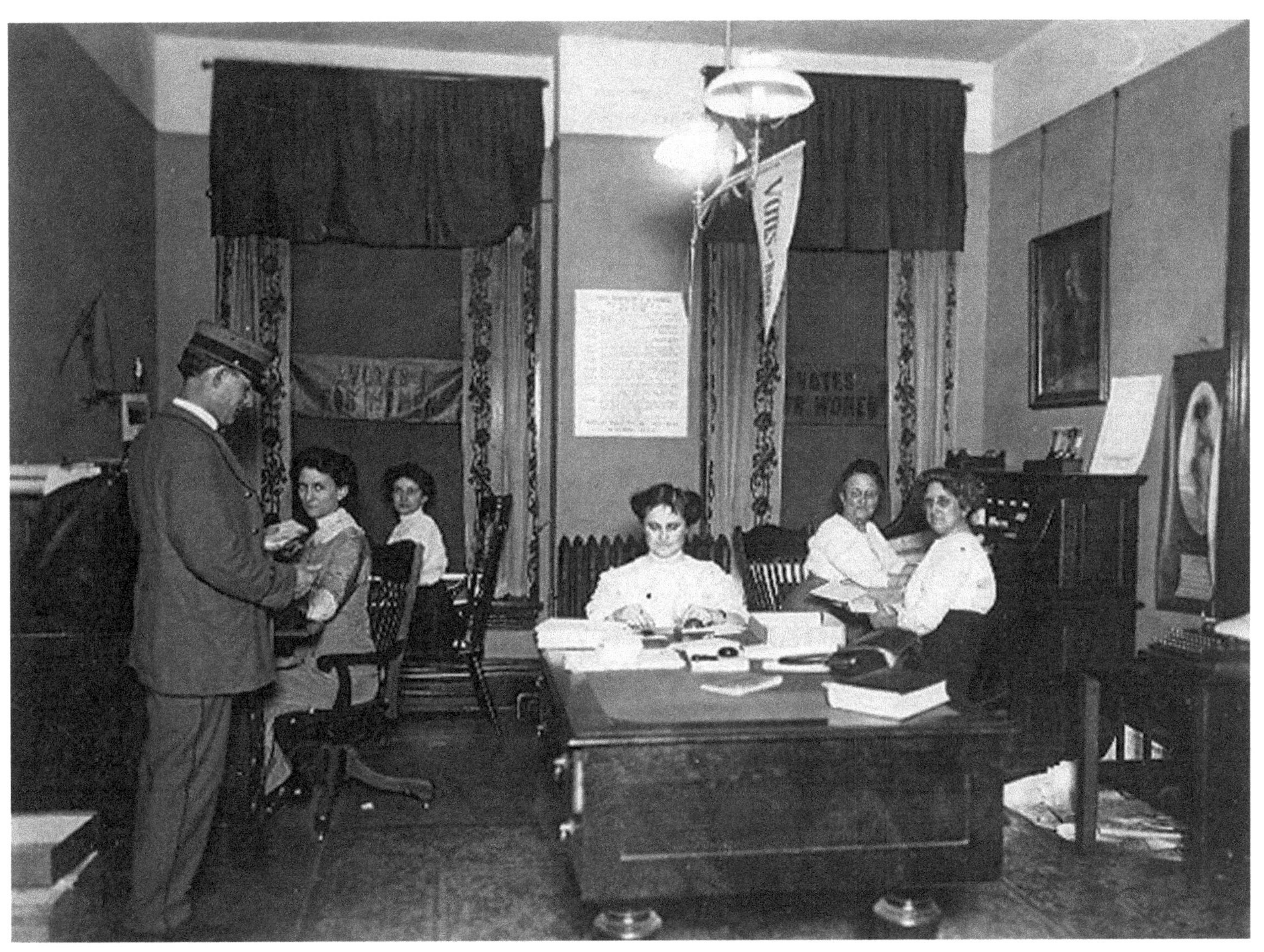

The Michigan Women's Suffrage Campaign Headquarters, located in the Fourth National Bank Building, was a busy place. In the photograph are Mrs. Lois Jones, Mrs. Fred Rowe, Mrs. C. B. Hamilton, Mrs. W. F. Blake, and Mrs. Huntley Russell.

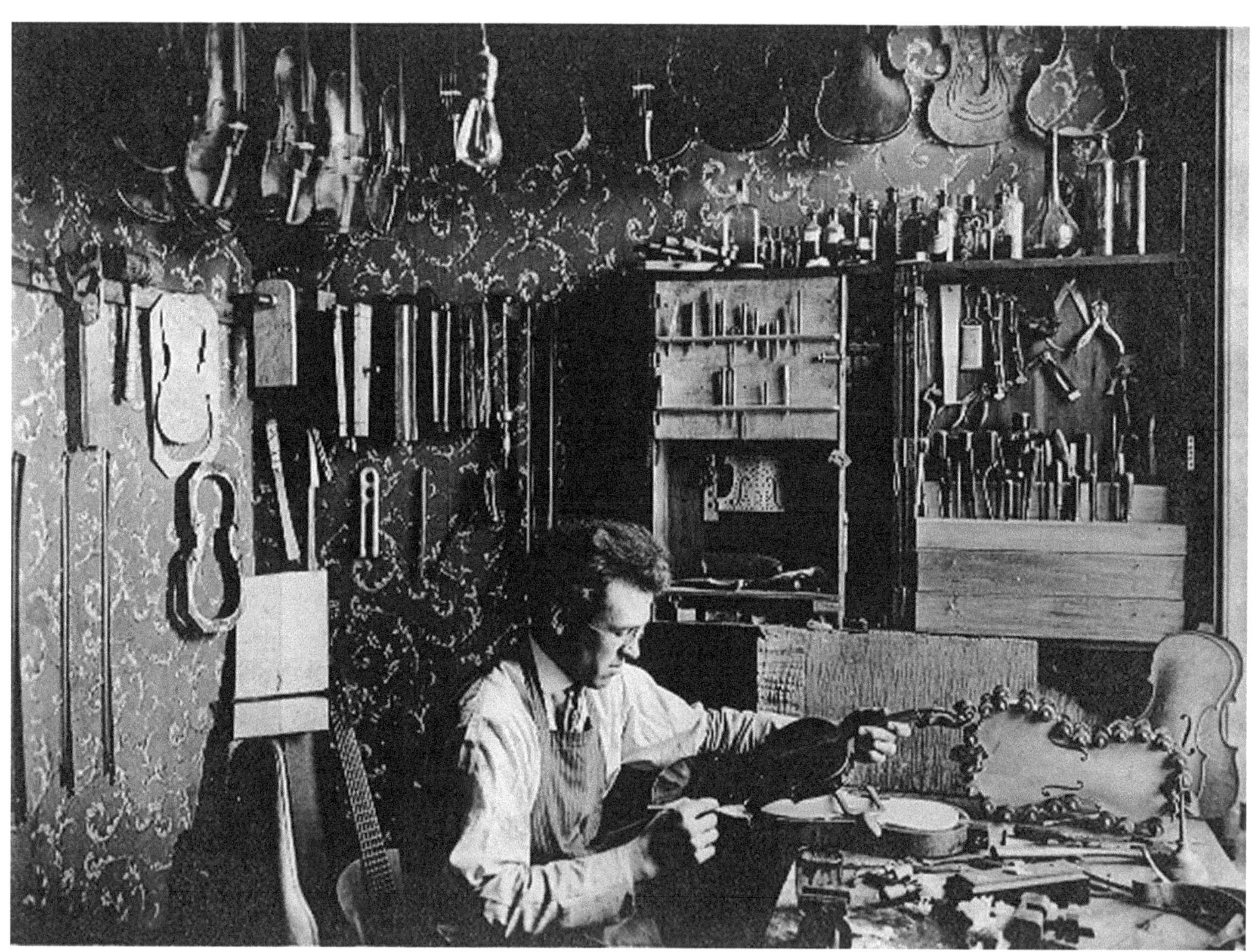

An interior view of Killinger's Instrument Repair Shop. Killinger was a violin maker and repaired all kinds of stringed instruments.

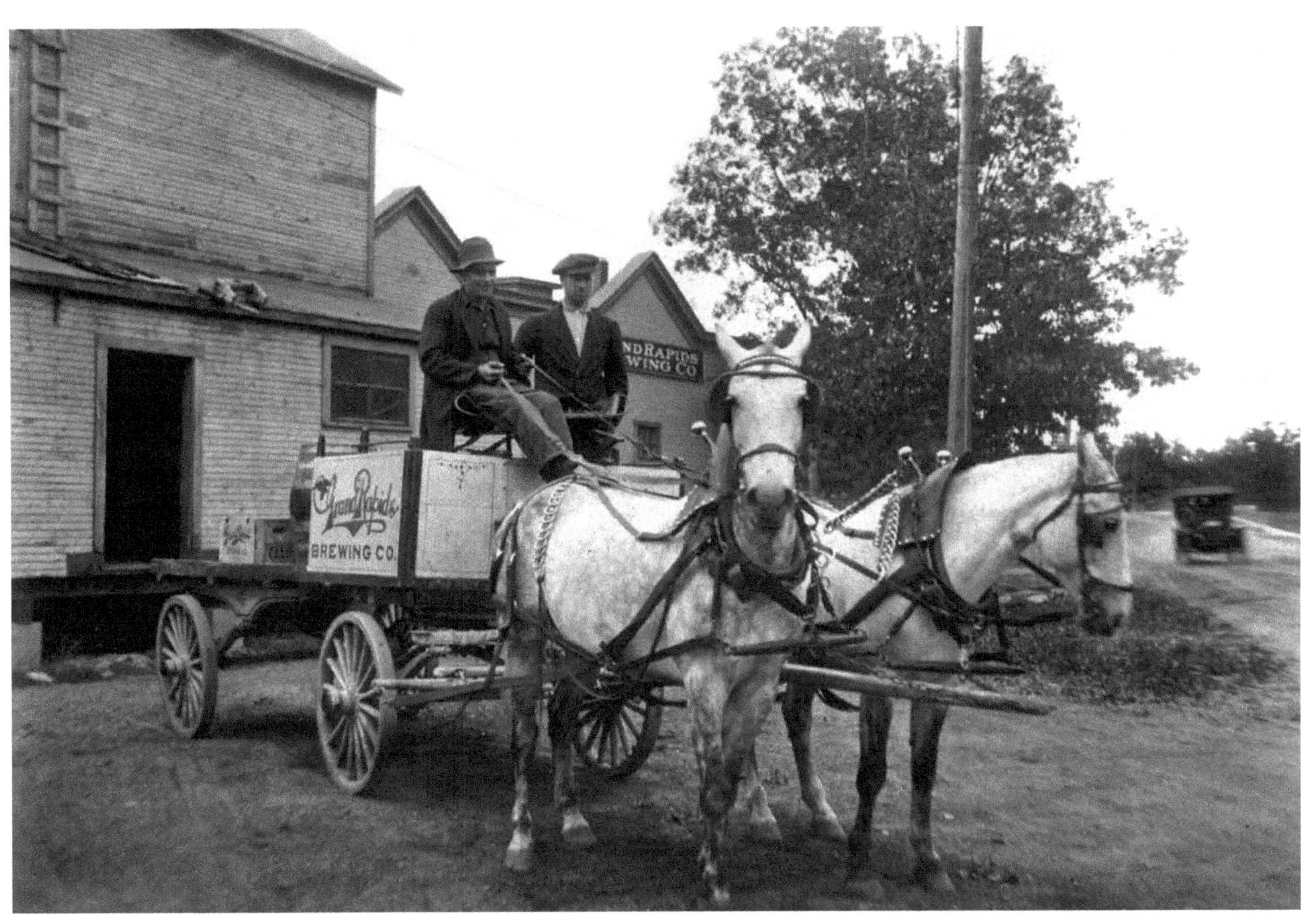

Making a delivery of Silver Foam beer, for which the Grand Rapids Brewing Company was known.

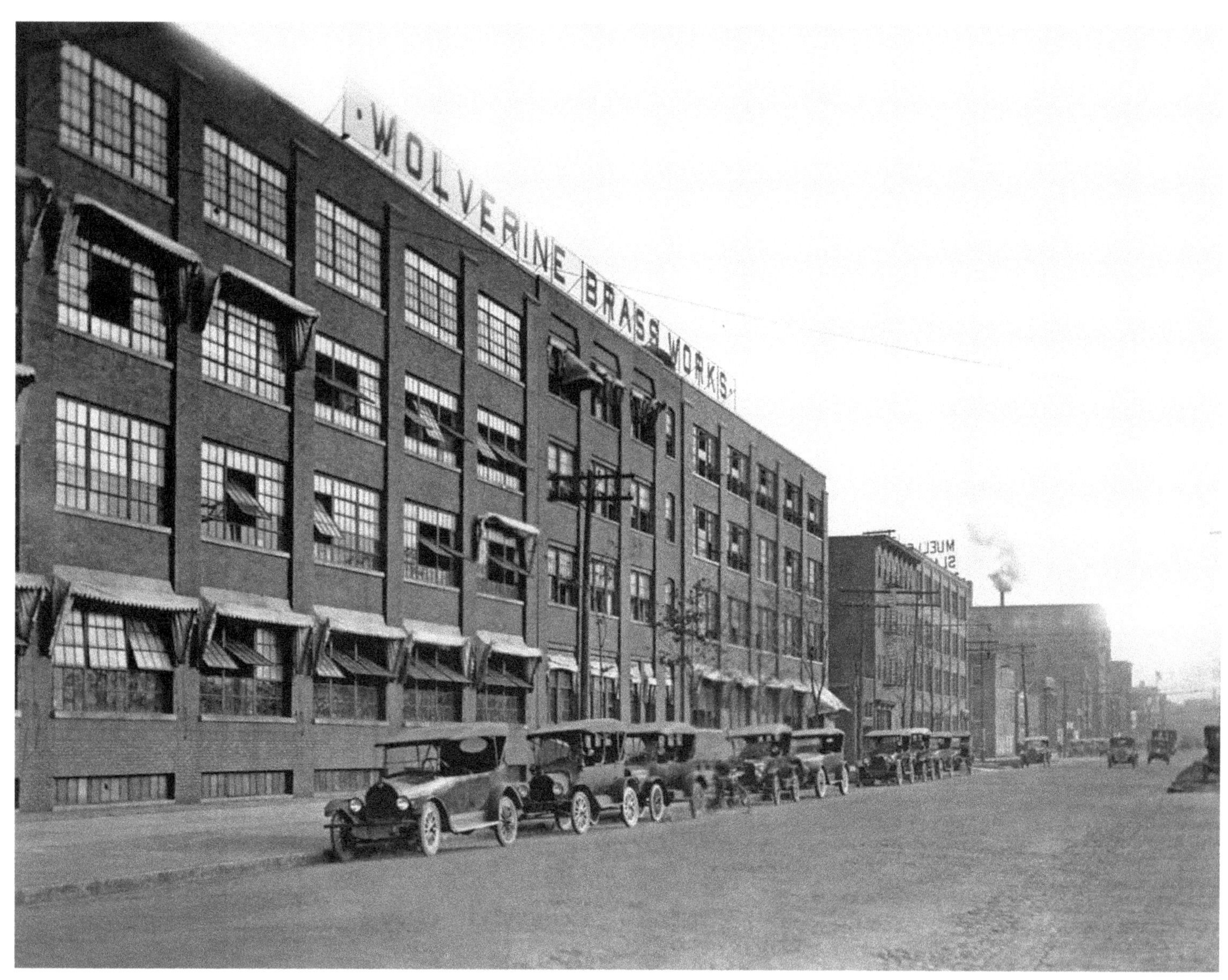

The Wolverine Brass Works building is located at 620-648 Monroe Avenue NW. The company was founded in 1896 by L. A. Cornelius. Its first product was a brass clamp designed to hold a porcelain basin to a lavatory top.

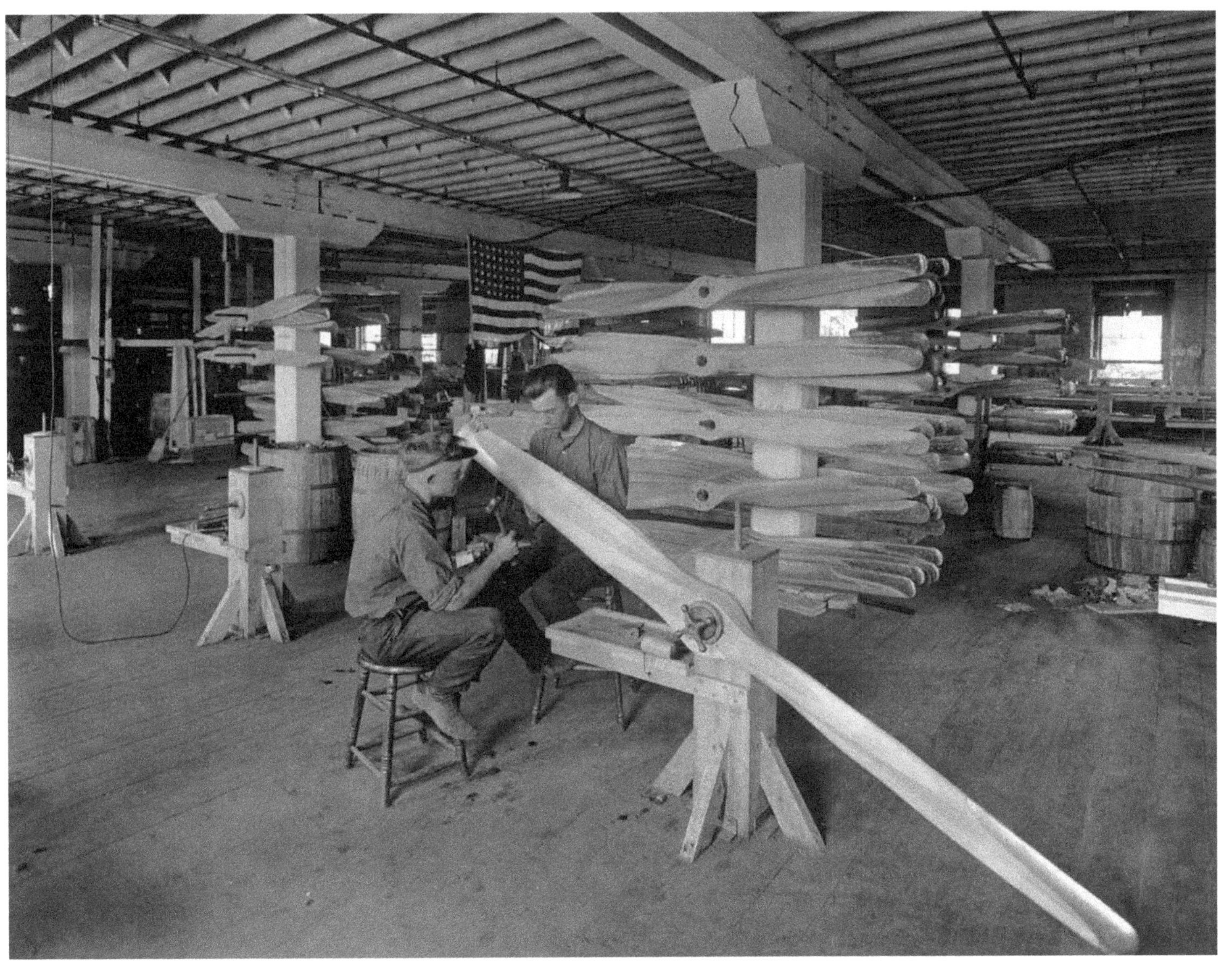

The Grand Rapids Airplane Company, comprising several area furniture factories, manufactured wooden airplane propellers during World War I for the war effort. These men are putting metal tips on the propellers at the Phoenix Furniture Company.

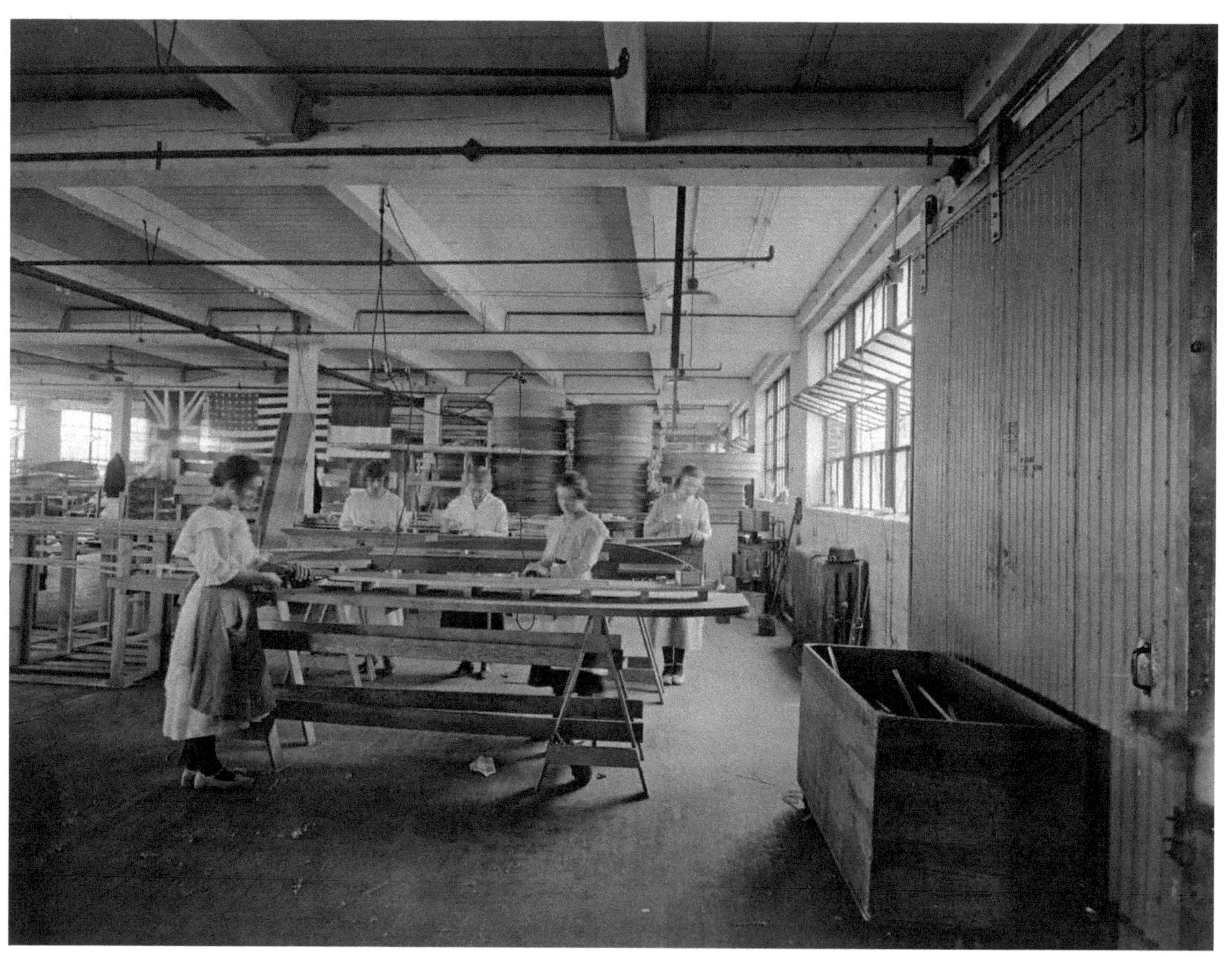

Around 1918, workers at the Grand Rapids Airplane Company assemble the parts that will become aircraft for the war effort.

Between the Wars

(1920–1939)

Prohibition rallied area proponents of social reform and closed local bars and saloons for nearly fifteen years, throughout the 1920s and early 1930s. However, the endeavor proved unsuccessful.

Architecture was of everlasting interest as the downtown skyline continued to change. Landmark buildings were not destined to be permanent features. Whether it was new construction, additions or renovations, or unfortunate explosions, the skyline was shifting. Locals took pride in the appearance of many buildings under construction, as the city successfully competed with comparably sized cities throughout the United States.

Grand Rapids has always enjoyed recreation—in particular, sailing and boating in the summer, snowmobiling and skiing in the winter. Reed's Lake, in the elegant East Grand Rapids neighborhood, has been one such destination for enjoyment. In the 1920s and 1930s, the growing popularity of motion pictures also led to several theaters being built in the area.

The YMCA (Young Men's Christian Association) played an important part in the city's growth. They offered citizenship classes, intramural sporting events, and family-oriented activities at the various factories.

Industry and transportation continued to expand. Grand Rapids businessmen sent the first shipment of furniture by airplane to the J. L. Hudson Company of Detroit, delivered by the plane *Miss Grand Rapids*. The Kent County Airport was making expansion plans. Automobiles were being produced by DeVaux-Hall, and both streetcars and automobiles were sharing the crowded, brick-laid streets.

The Depression of the 1930s left its mark on Grand Rapids. The city manager, George Welsh, chose to deal with it in a very resourceful manner. He created the scrip labor program. Residents worked for scrip, which they could spend in the city-owned stores. The Civic Auditorium and Richmond Pool were built by scrip laborers. City streets and sewers were also built. During the winters, the laborers cleaned the streets and sidewalks.

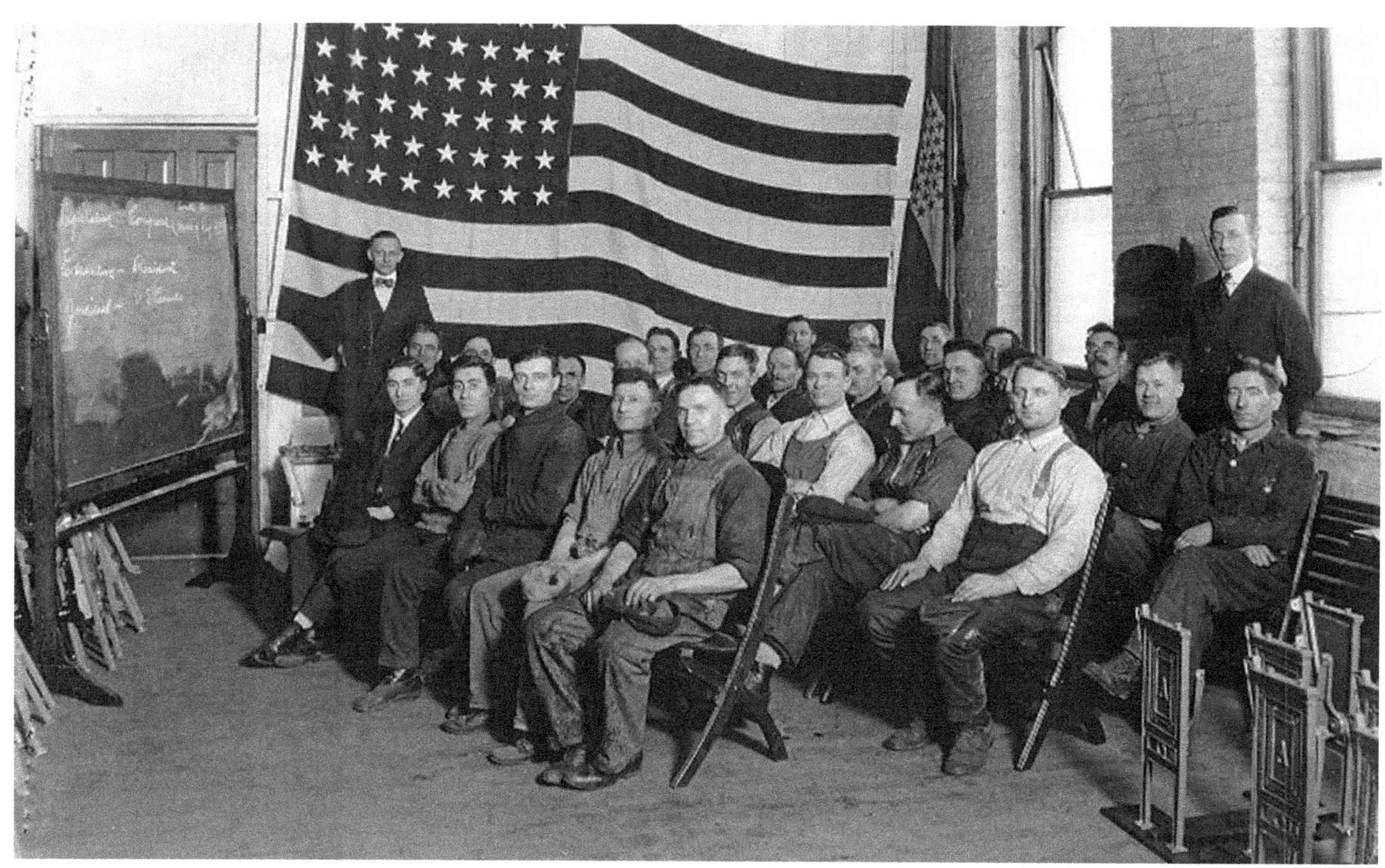

The YMCA (Young Men's Christian Association) Industrial Services regularly held citizenship classes like this one at American Seating Company.

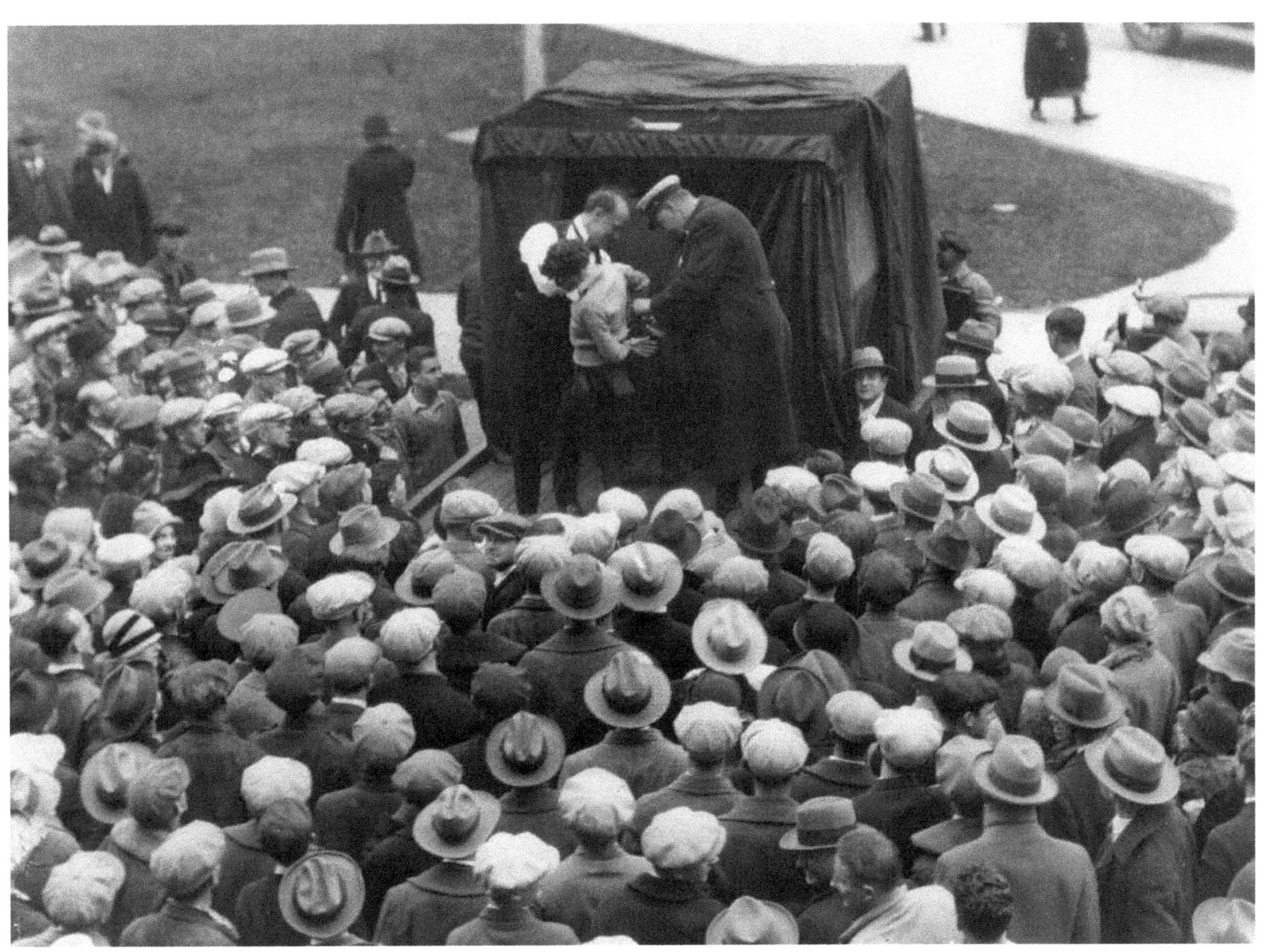

Harry Houdini provided a free exhibition in front of the Grand Rapids Herald building in 1920. Thousands watched as the master escape artist performed.

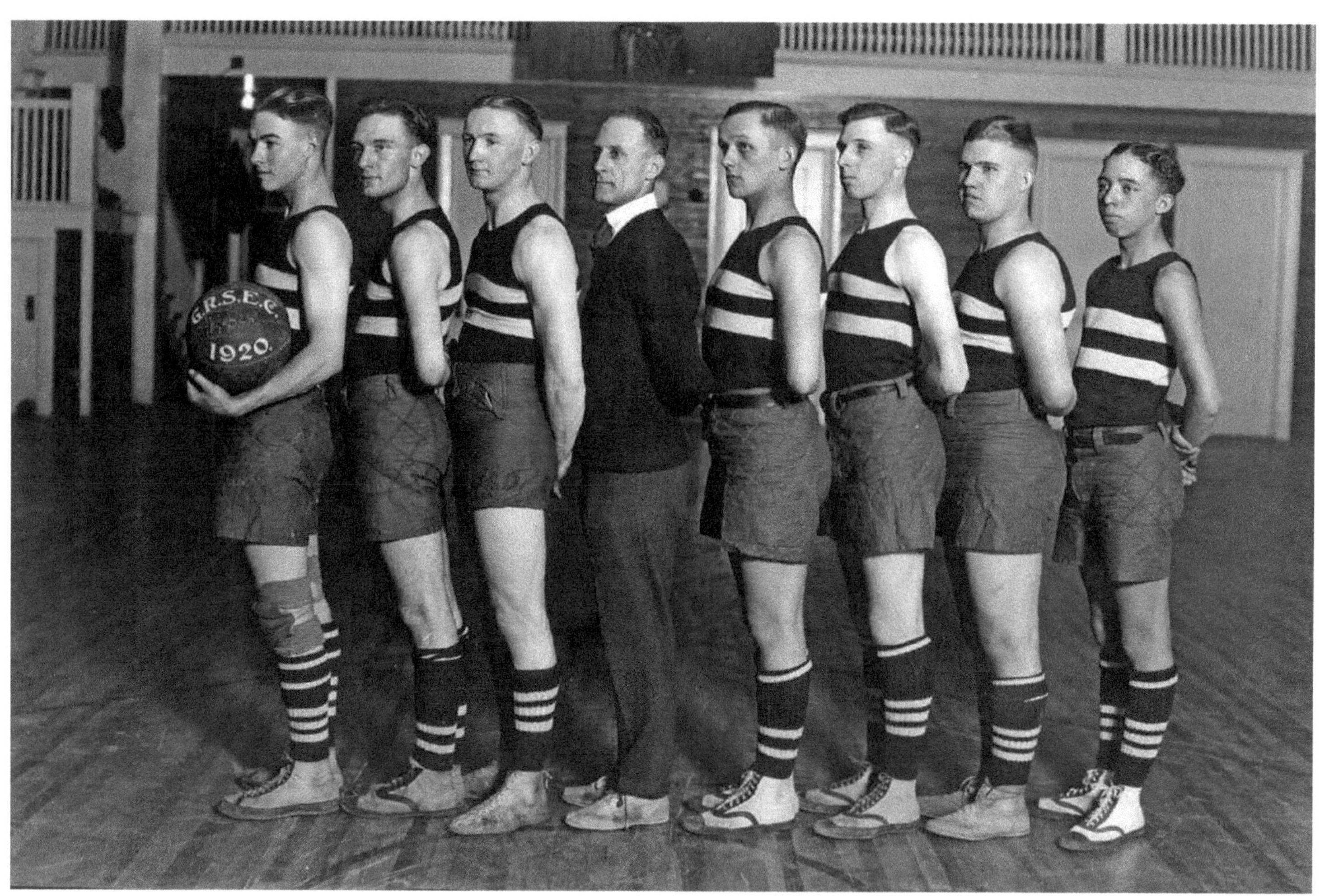

The Grand Rapids School Equipment Company basketball team poses for a group portrait in 1920. Company teams were organized by the YMCA Industrial Services.

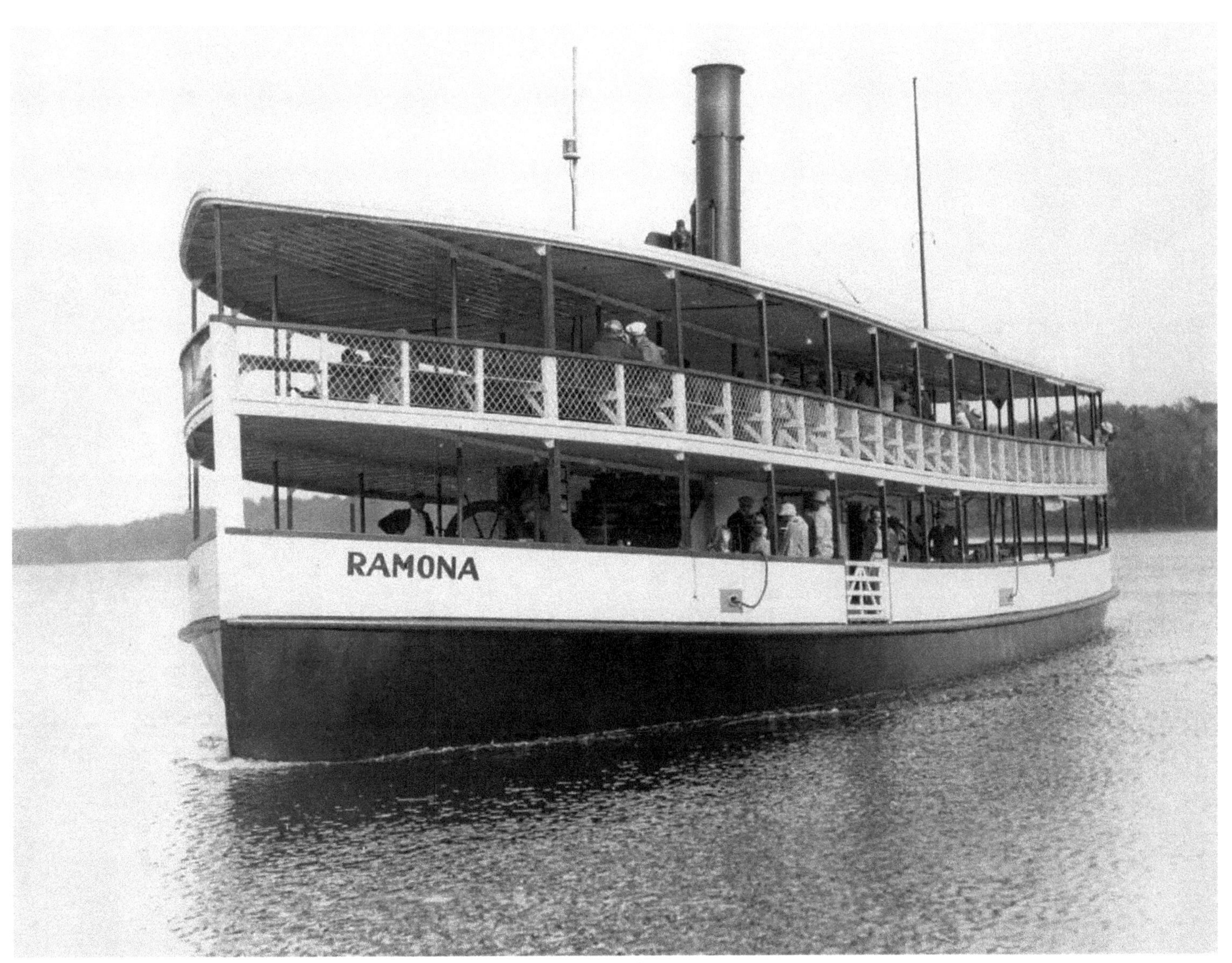

The *Ramona* steamship, filled with passengers, plies Reed's Lake.

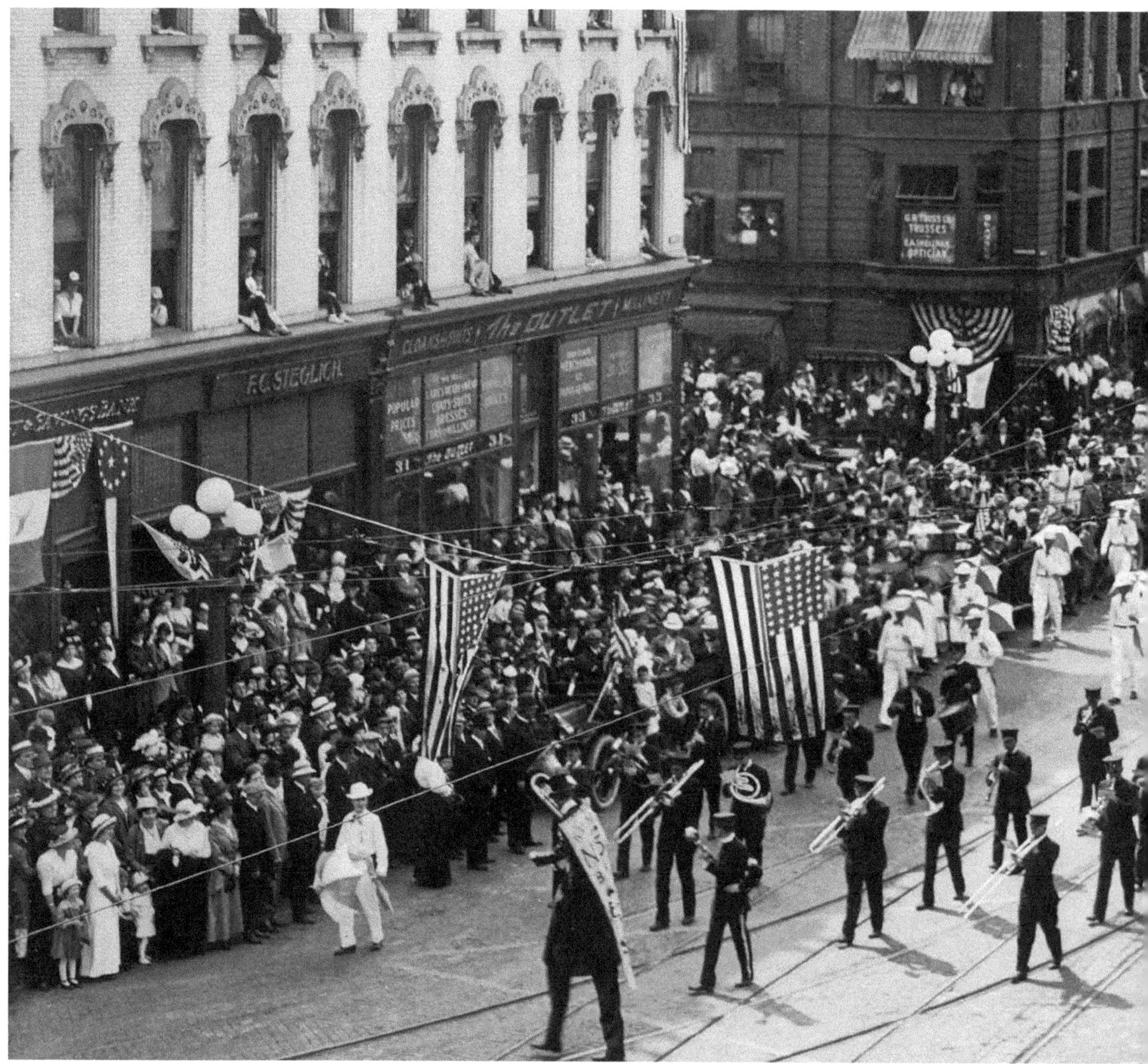

F.C. STEGLICH
The OUTLET
POPULAR PRICES

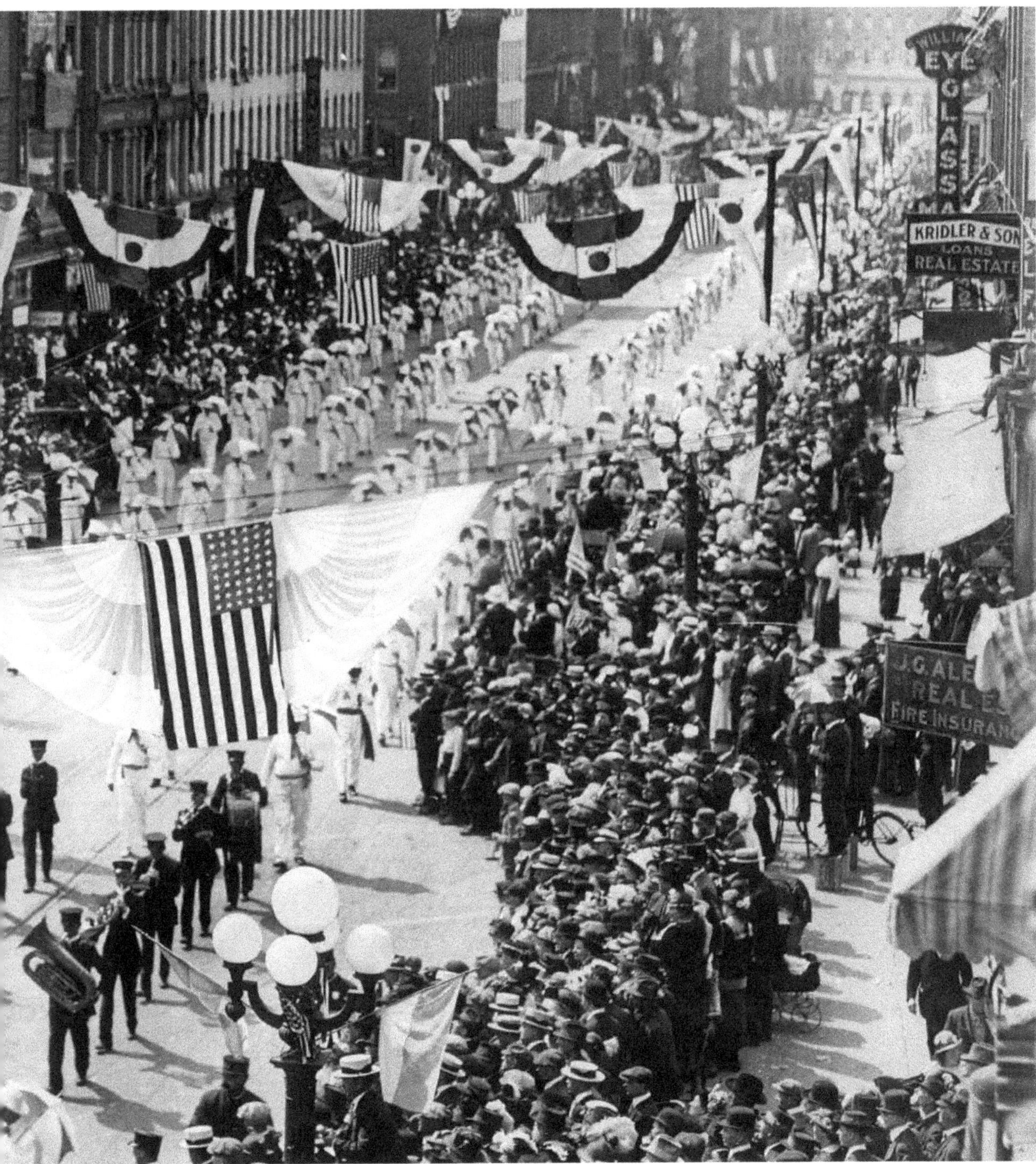

People love a parade. The Benevolent and Protective Order of Elks parade was attended by thousands.

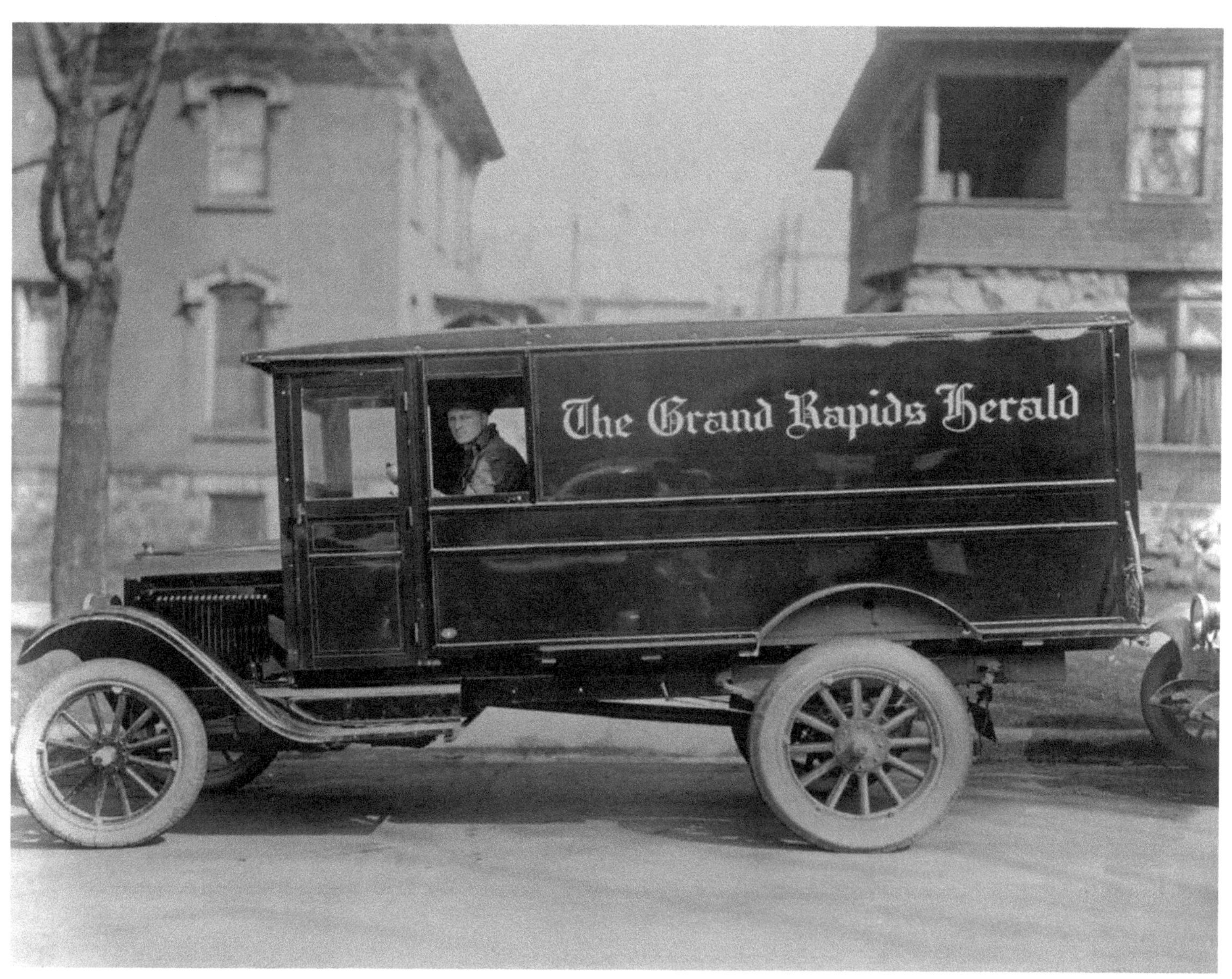

A *Grand Rapids Herald* delivery truck. The newspaper was in operation from 1892 to 1959.

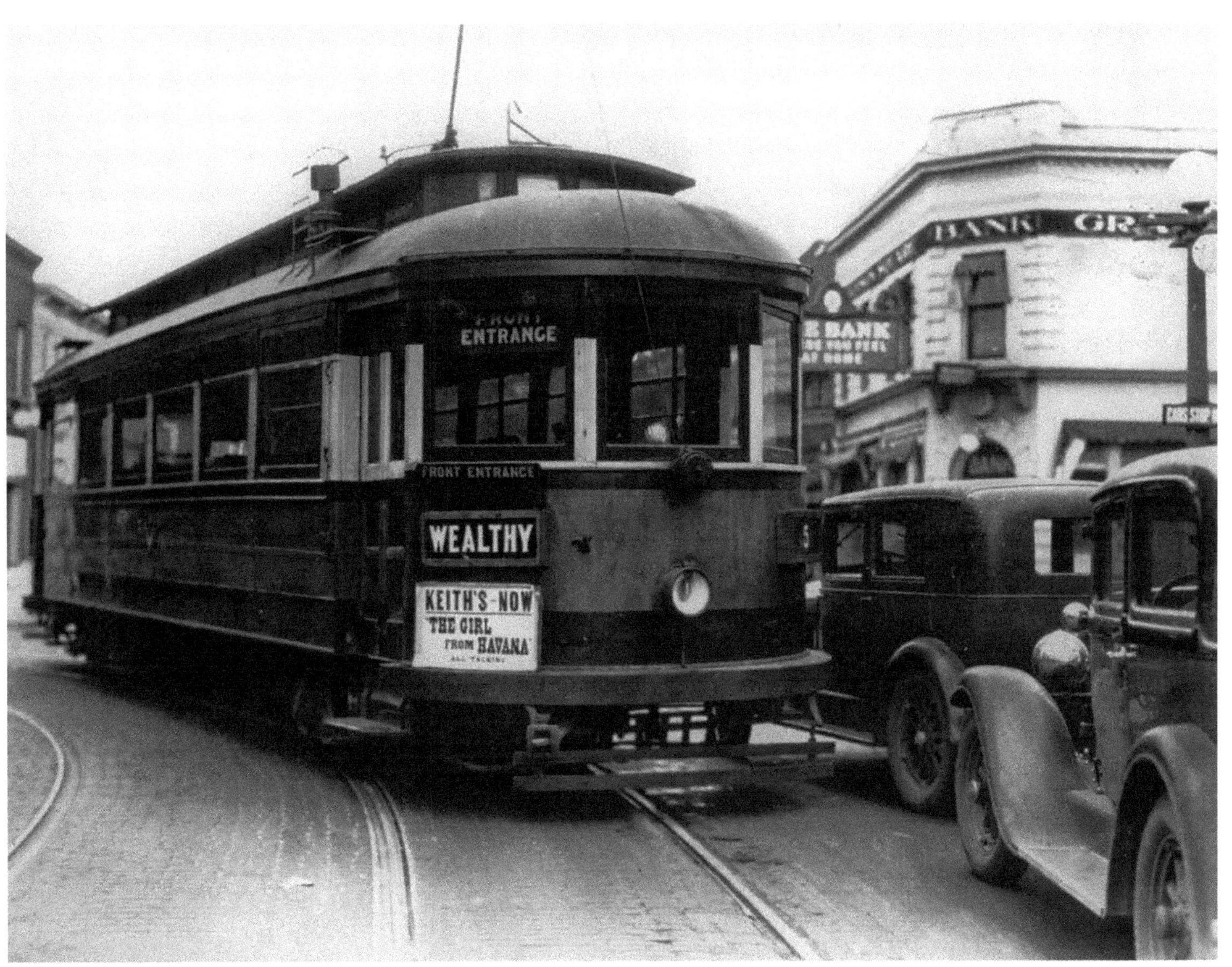

Around 1929, it isn't clear whether the automobiles or the streetcar is winning the battle on this crowded street.

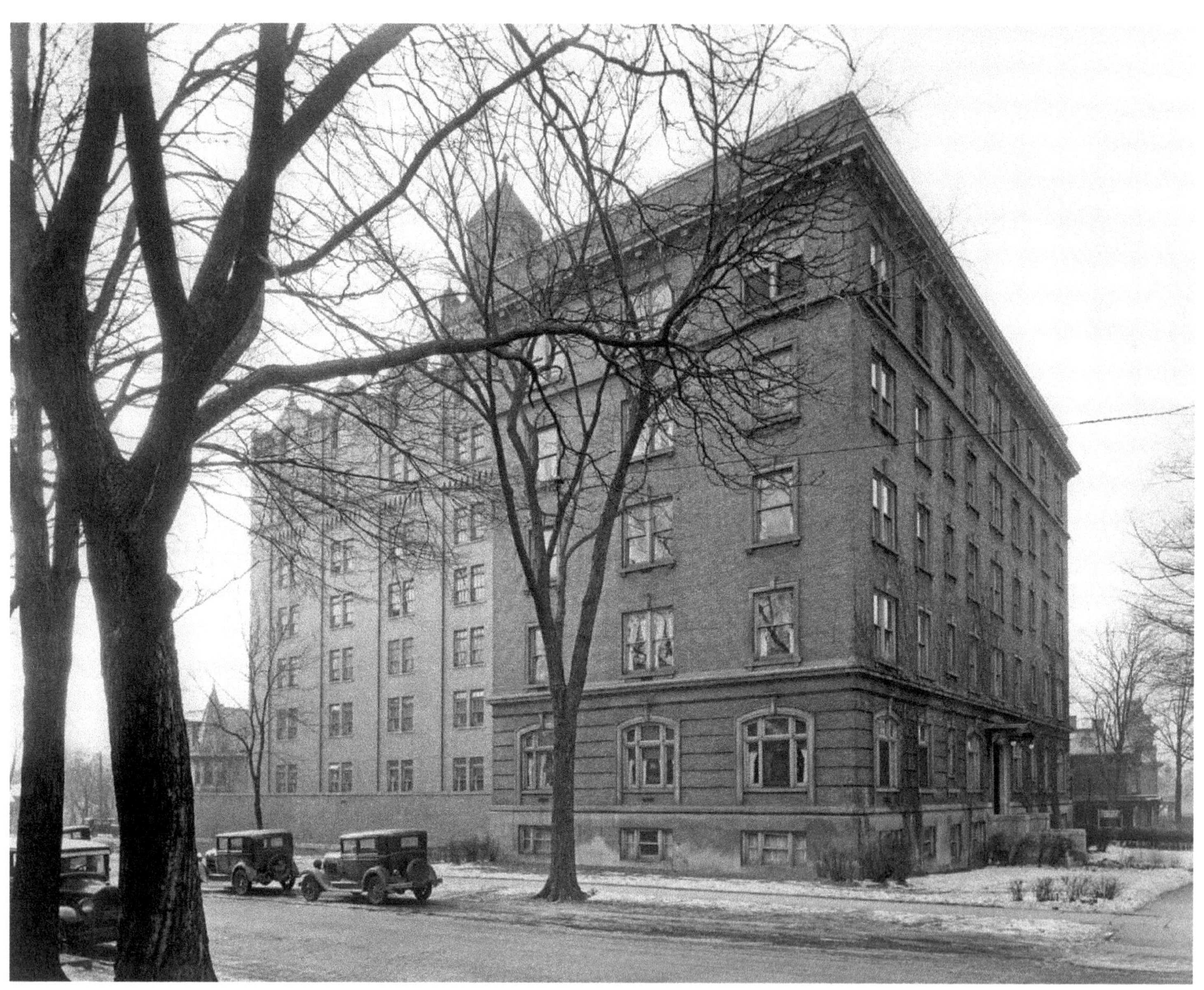

Saint Mary's Hospital, now Saint Mary's Mercy Medical Center. This view shows the old McAuley Building, which was torn down in 2001, as the Saint Mary's complex grew.

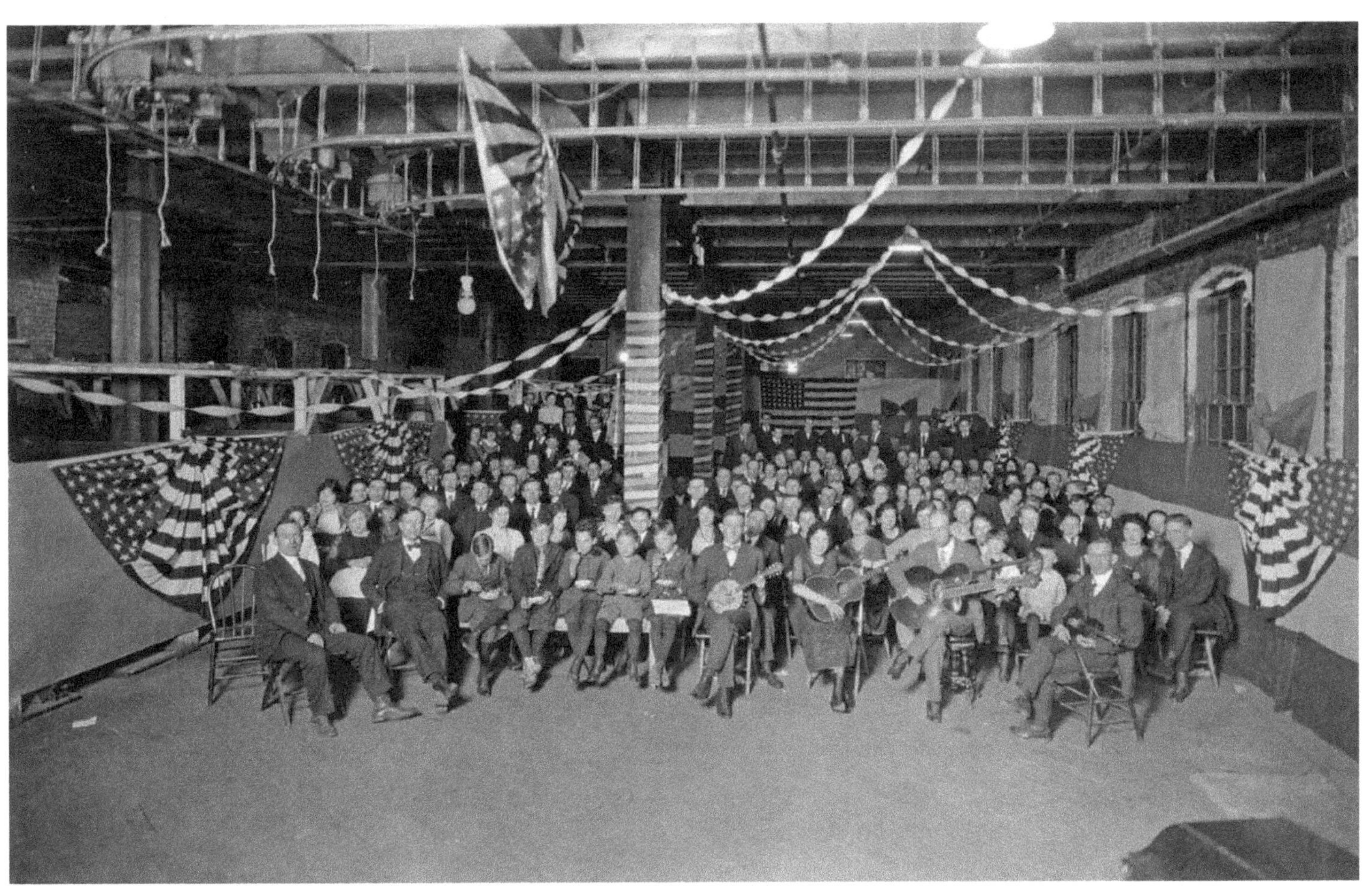

The Hart Plate Mirror Company employees and their families enjoy an indoor picnic sponsored by the YMCA Industrial Services.

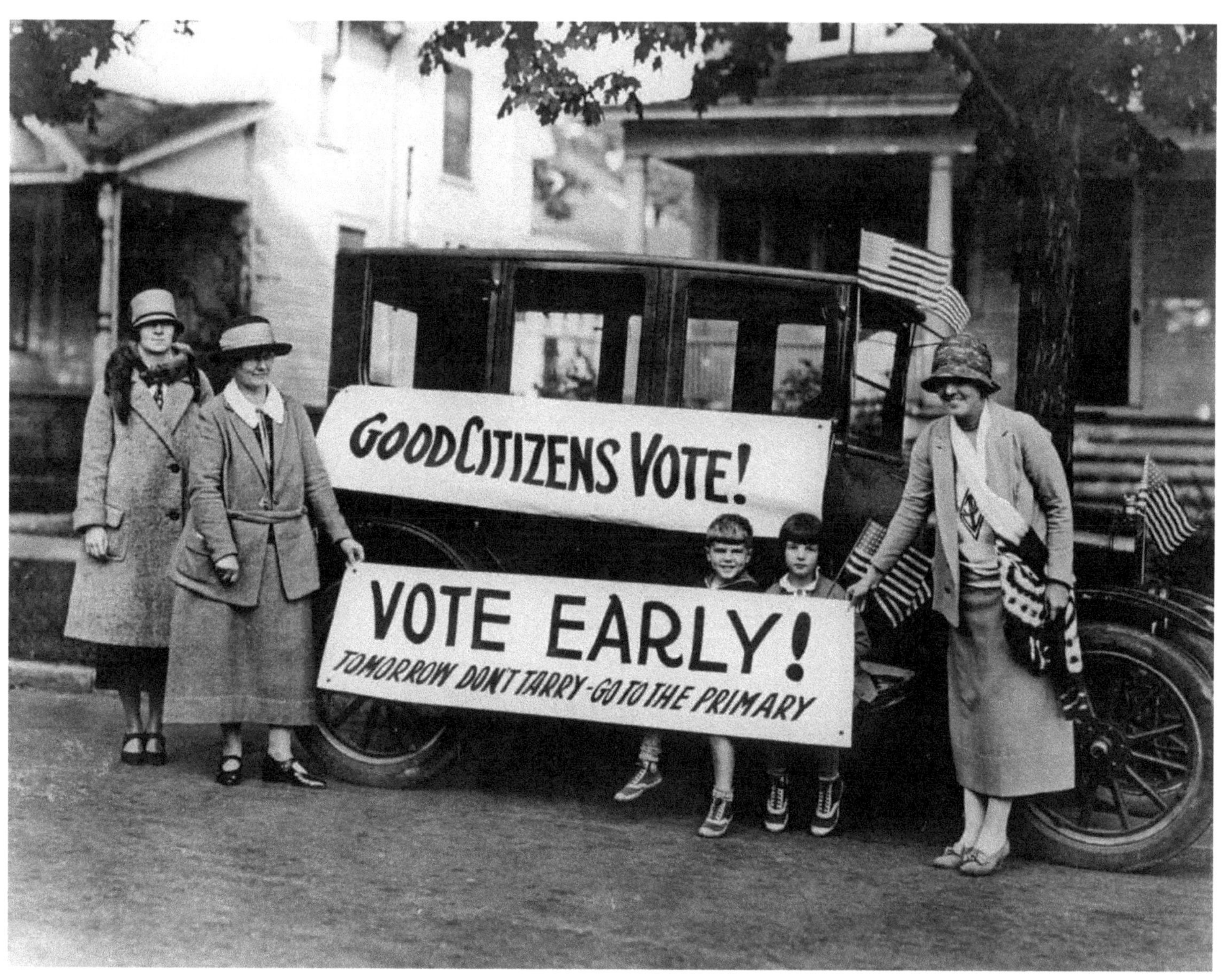

Members of the Grand Rapids League of Women Voters hold signs promoting voting in the 1924 primary election. David and Mary Amberg sit next to their mother, Mrs. Julius H. Amberg. On the left side is Miss Florence Shelley and Miss Grace Van Hoesen.

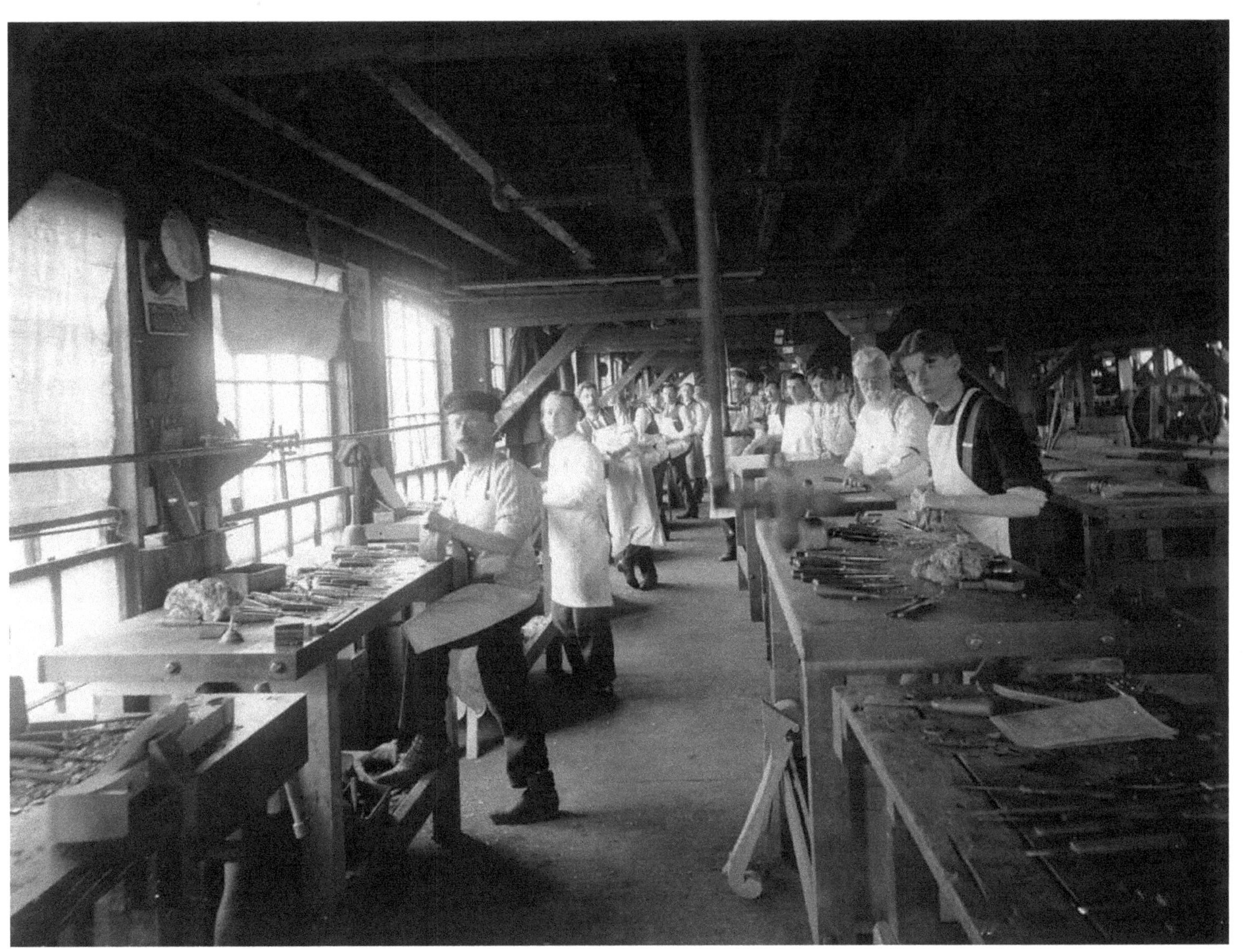

An interior view of the Robert W. Irwin Furniture factory, located at 432 Monroe NW. The company was in operation from 1919 to 1953.

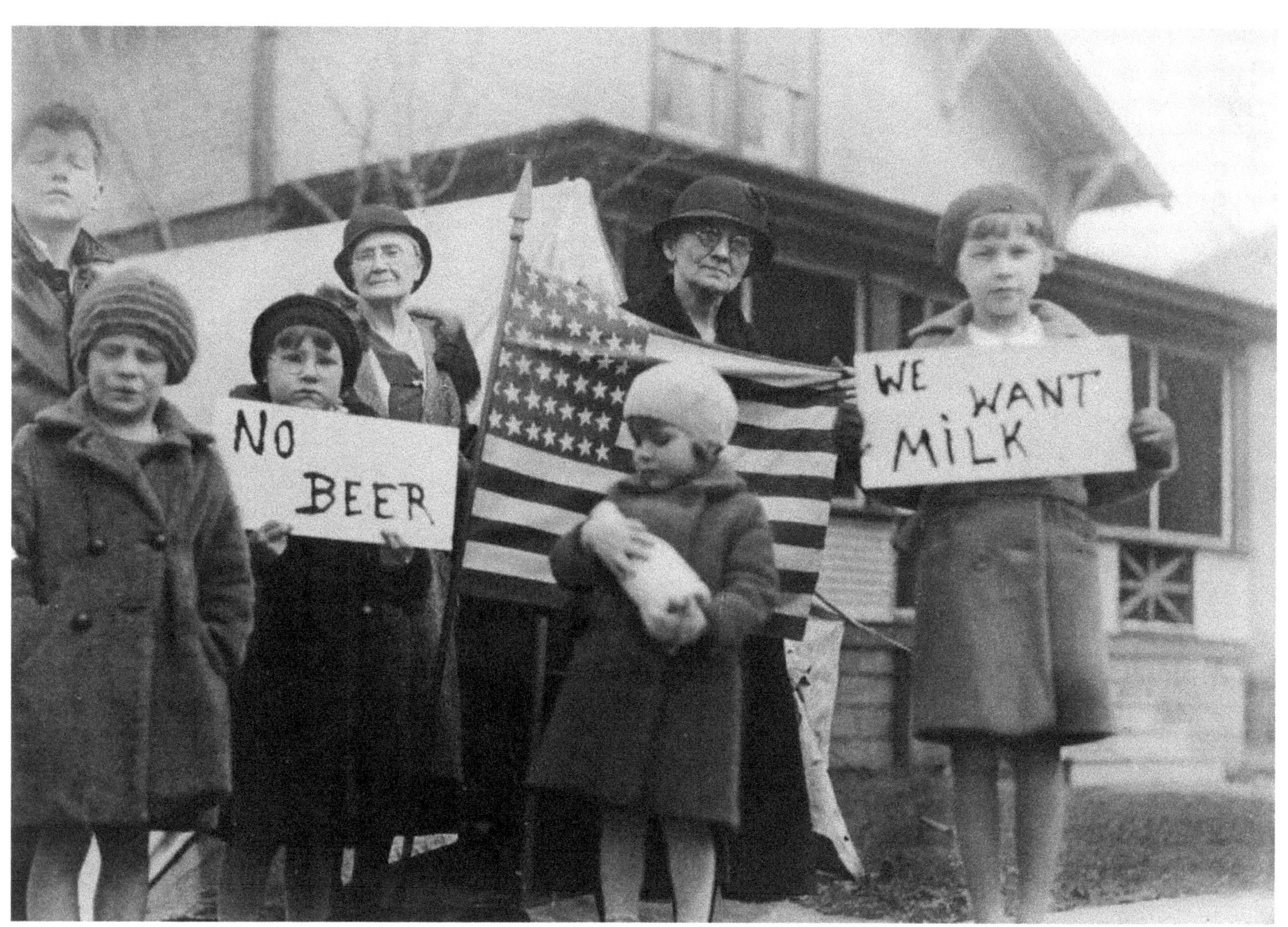

Area residents in support of Prohibition.

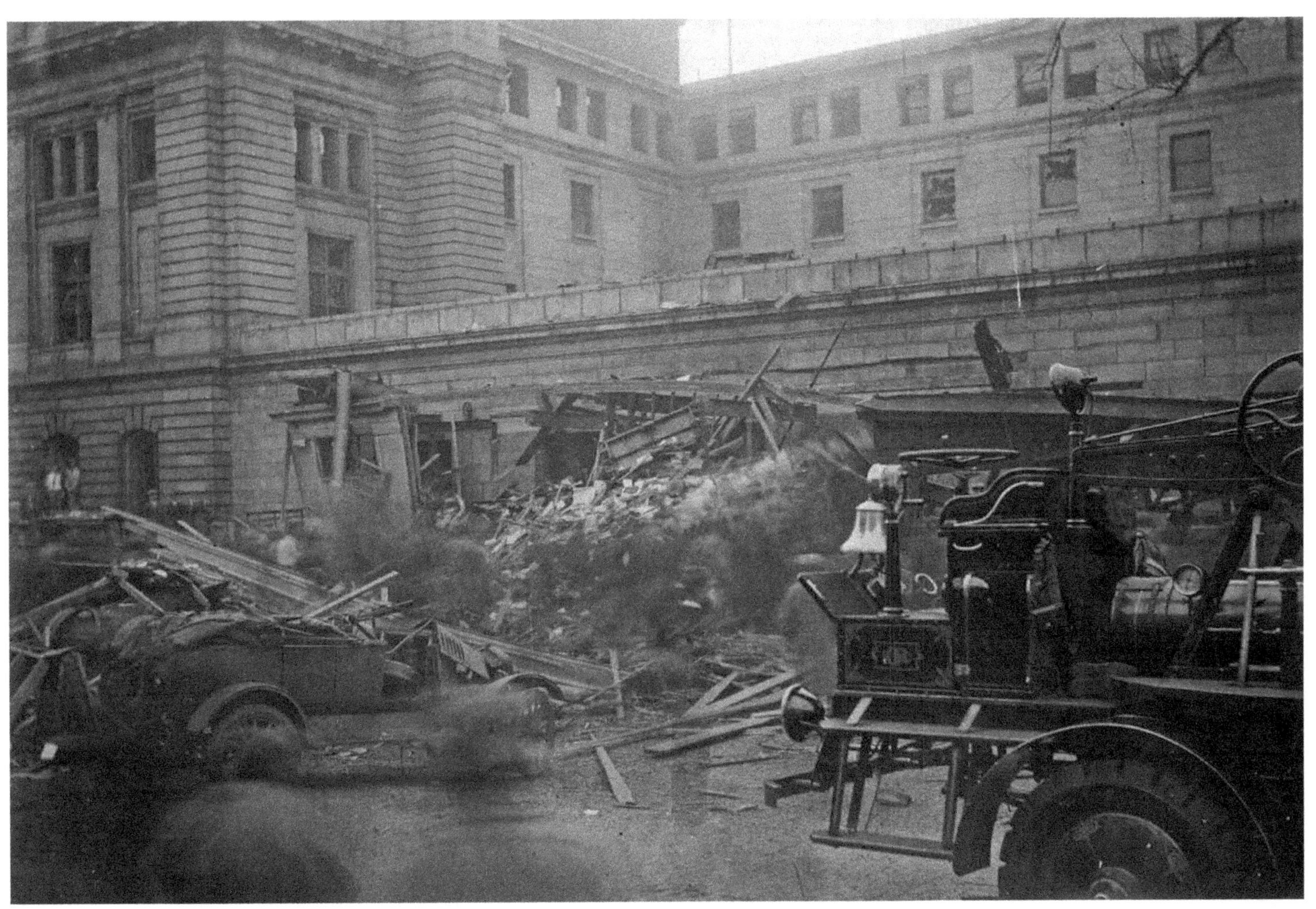

An explosion ripped through the Post Office on November 11, 1924. An investigation concluded that the explosion was caused by ignition of illuminating gas escaping from a broken main on Division Avenue. Three persons were killed and more than twelve injured.

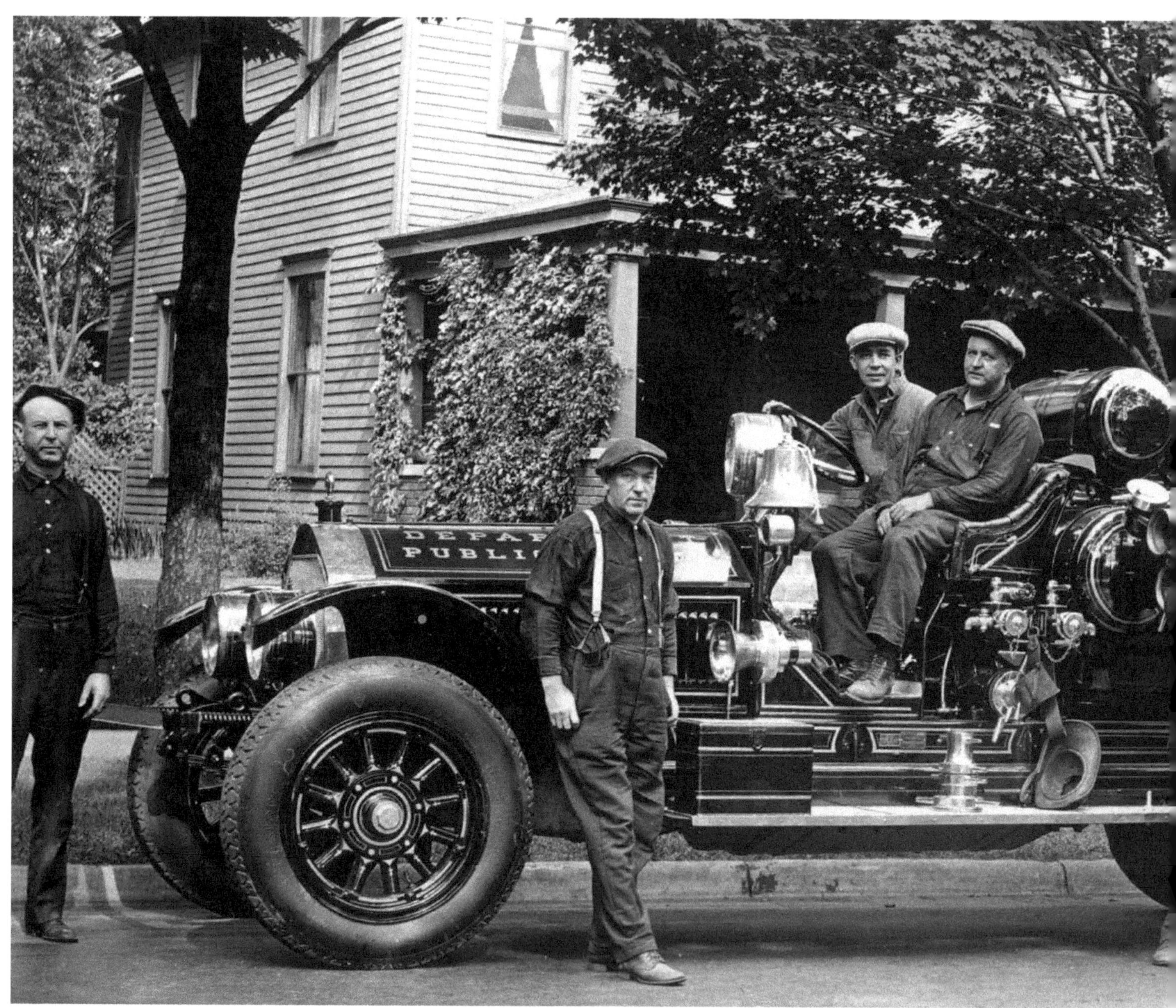
DEPAR
PUBLI

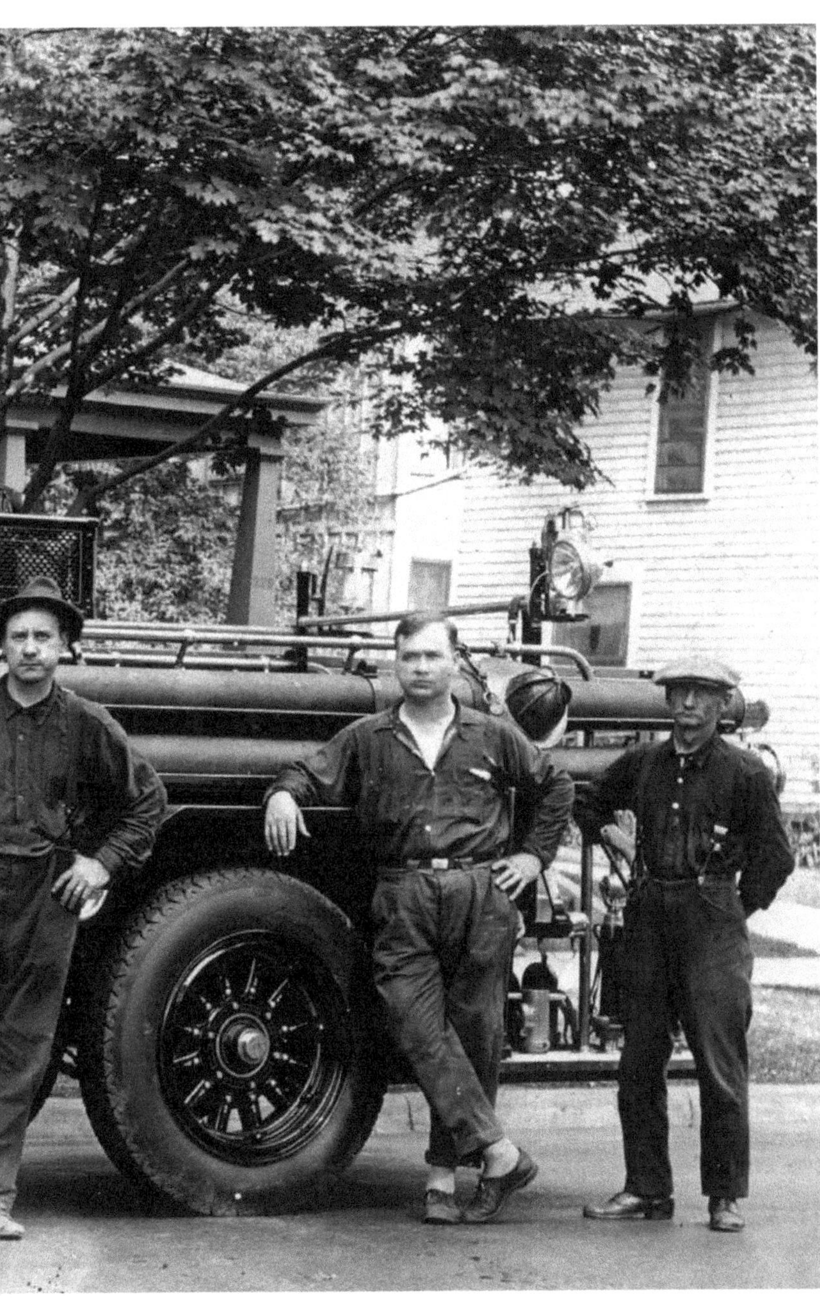

A Grand Rapids Fire Department crew poses with fire truck in 1926.

Two "Polar Bears" at the Grand Rapids Airport in 1927. These veterans had been part of a contingent of troops nicknamed Polar Bears, many of them from Michigan, sent on a mission to Russia during World War I.

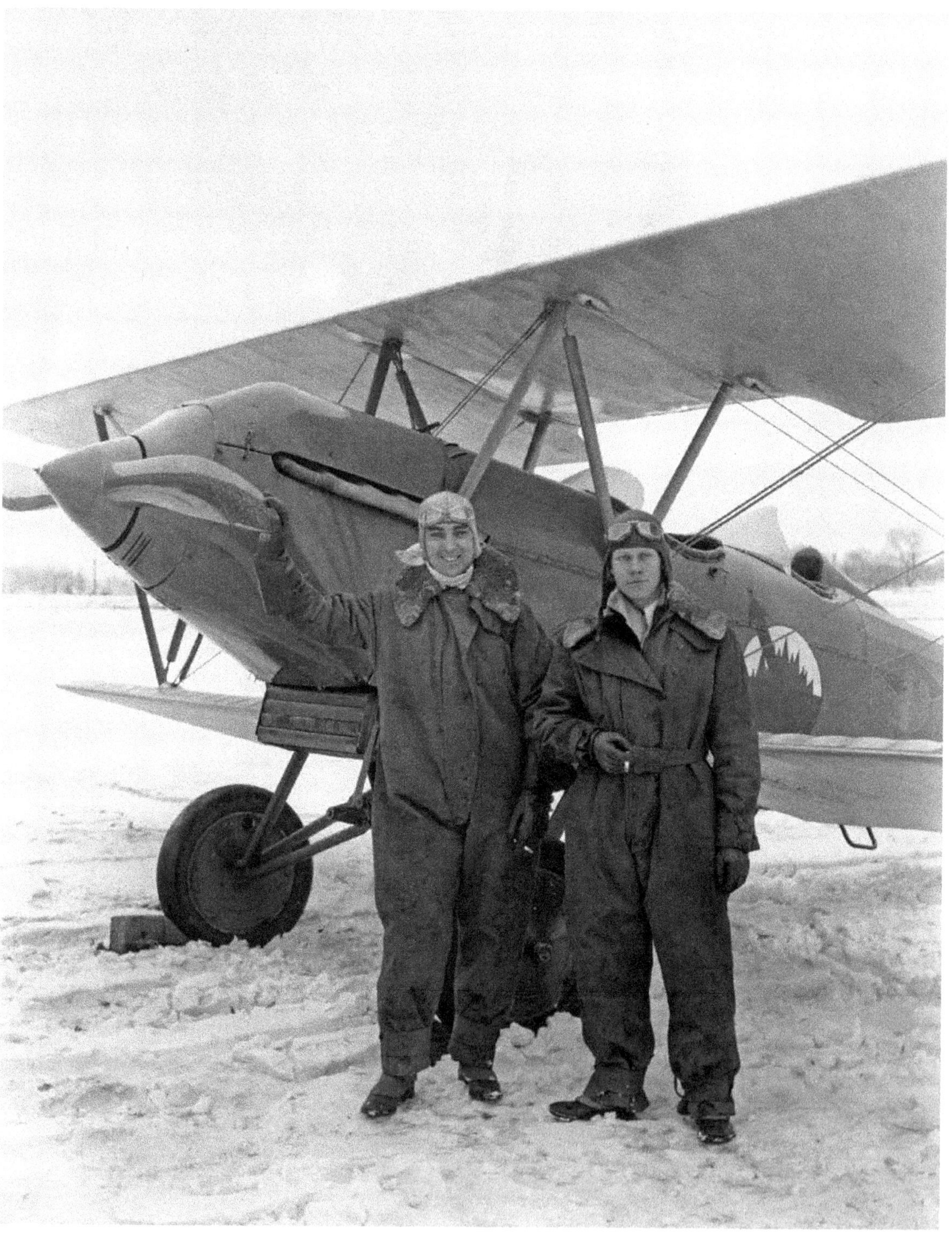

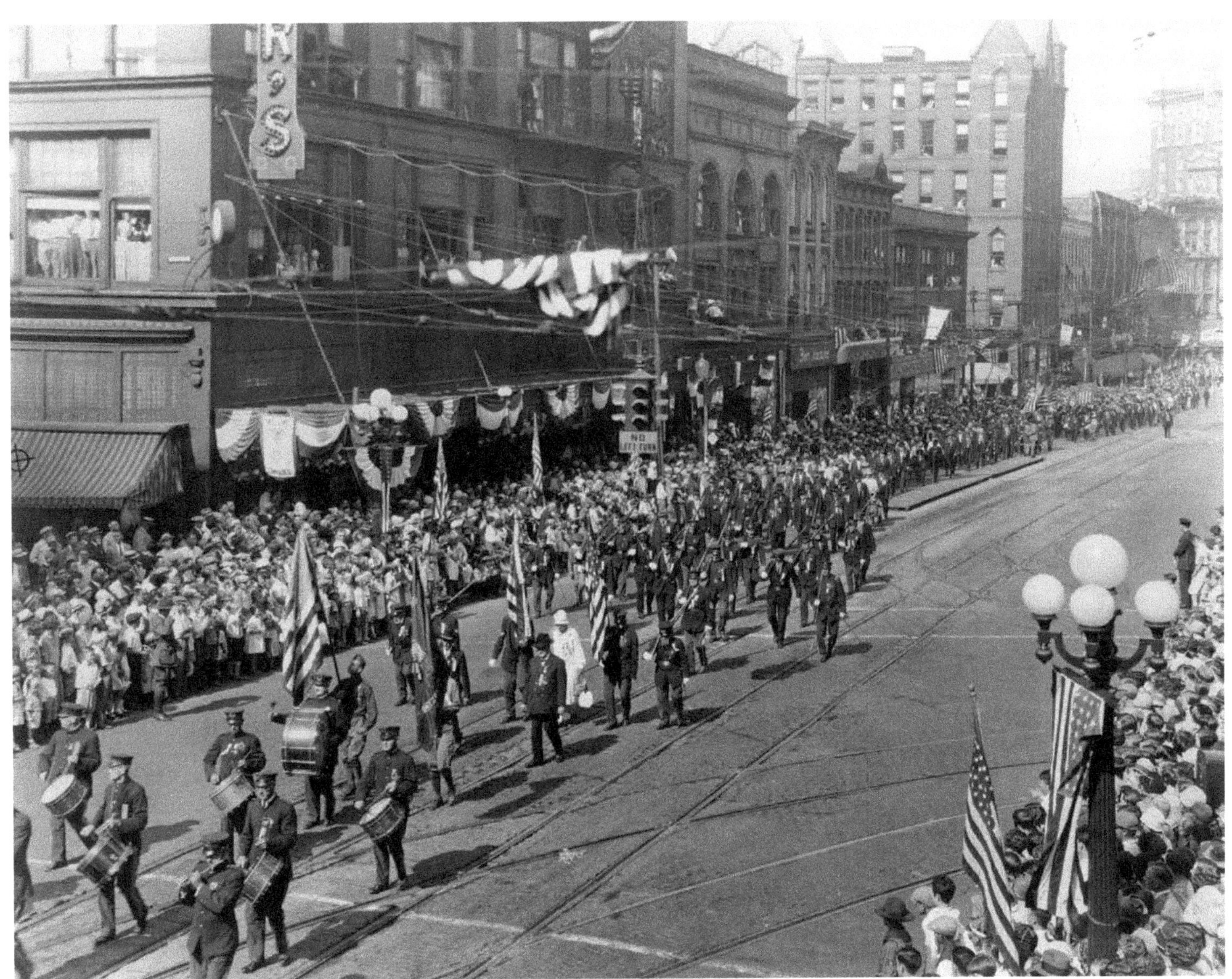

Citizens turn out to show their support of area veterans during this veterans' parade.

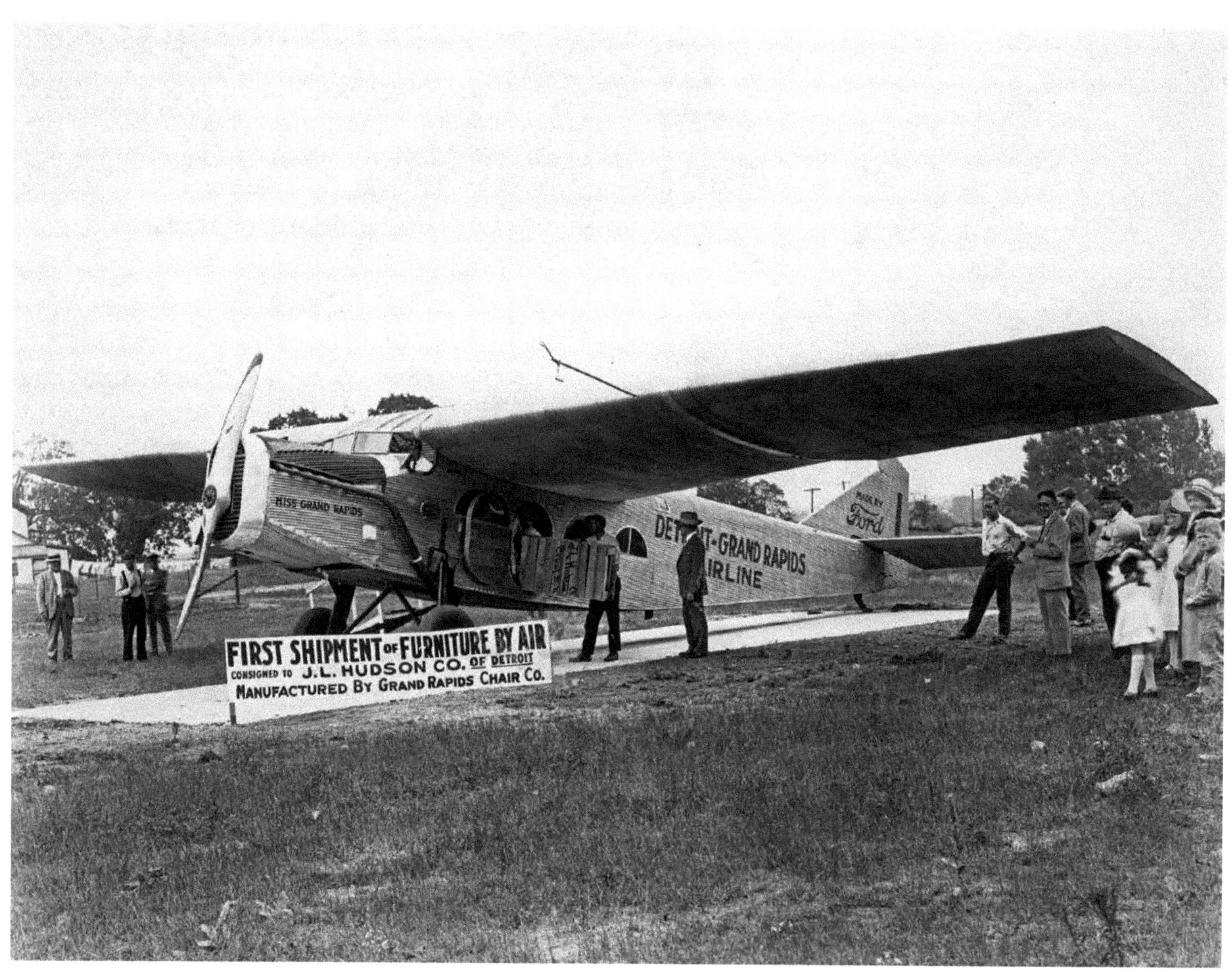

The first shipment of furniture by air from Grand Rapids to Detroit on the Ford-Stout airplane *Miss Grand Rapids.* This shipment was bound for the J. L. Hudson Company.

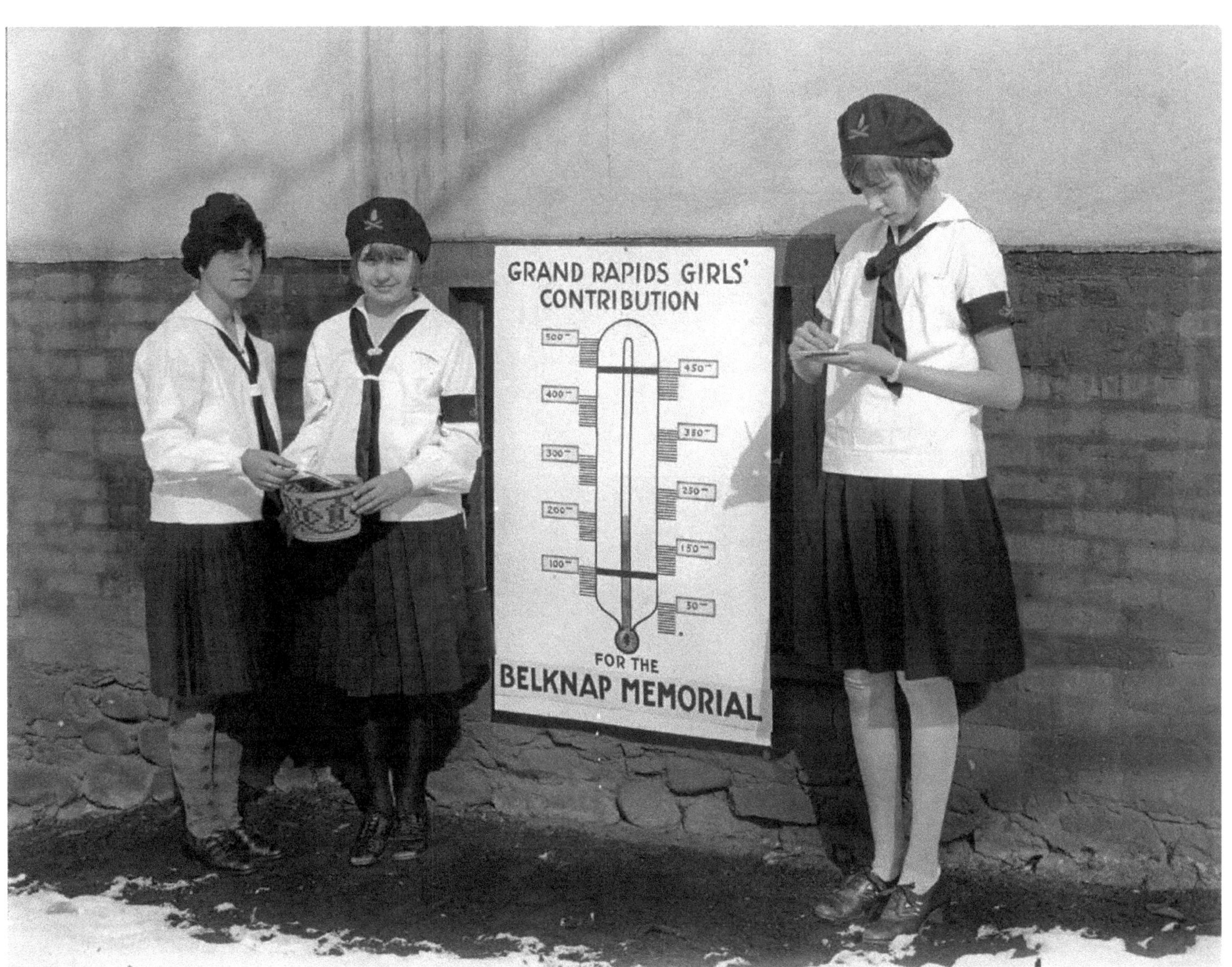

Grand Rapids Girl Scouts collect contributions for the Charles Belknap Memorial.

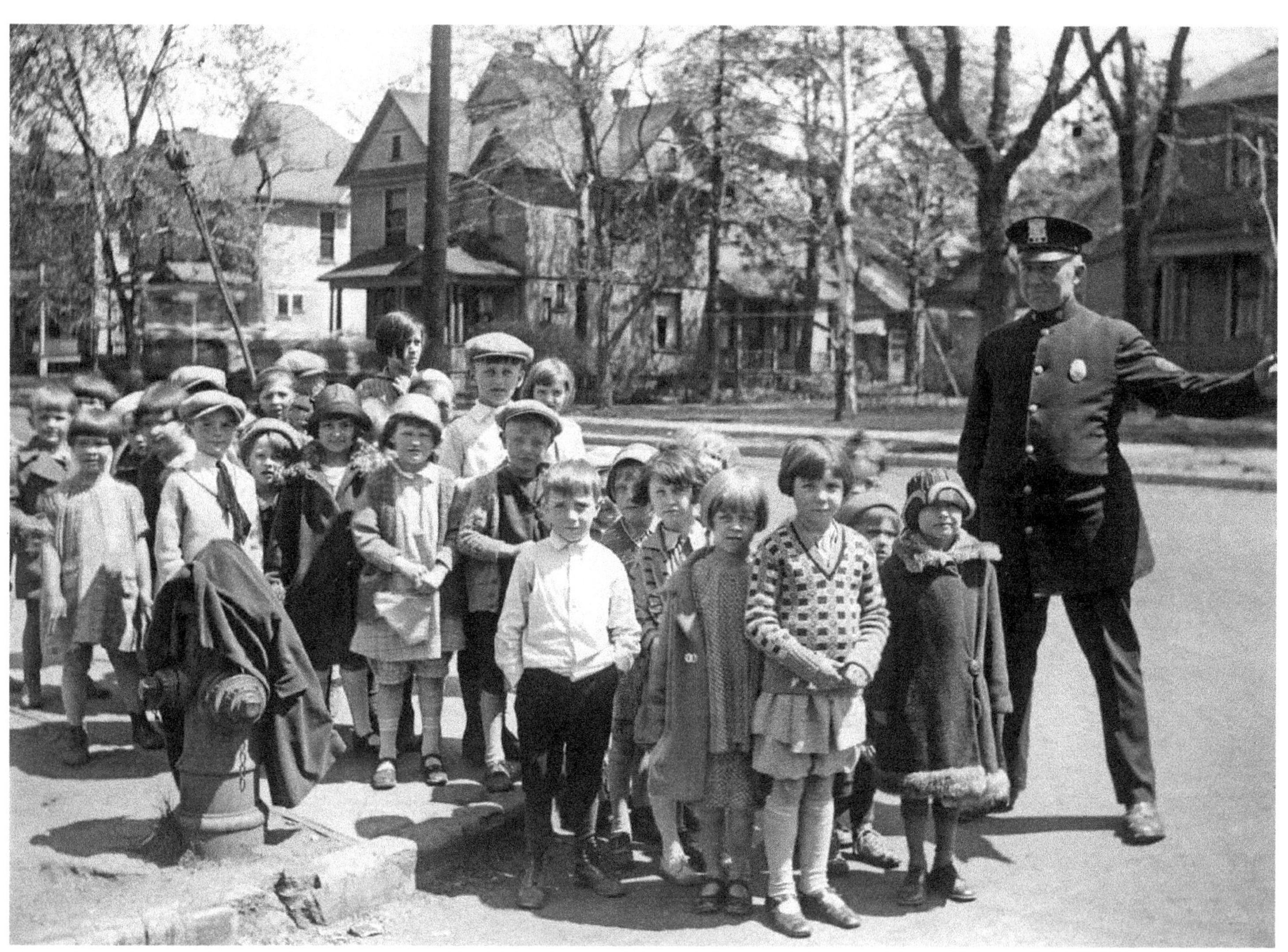

Officer John J. Lemke escorts a group of schoolchildren safely across the street near Congress School.

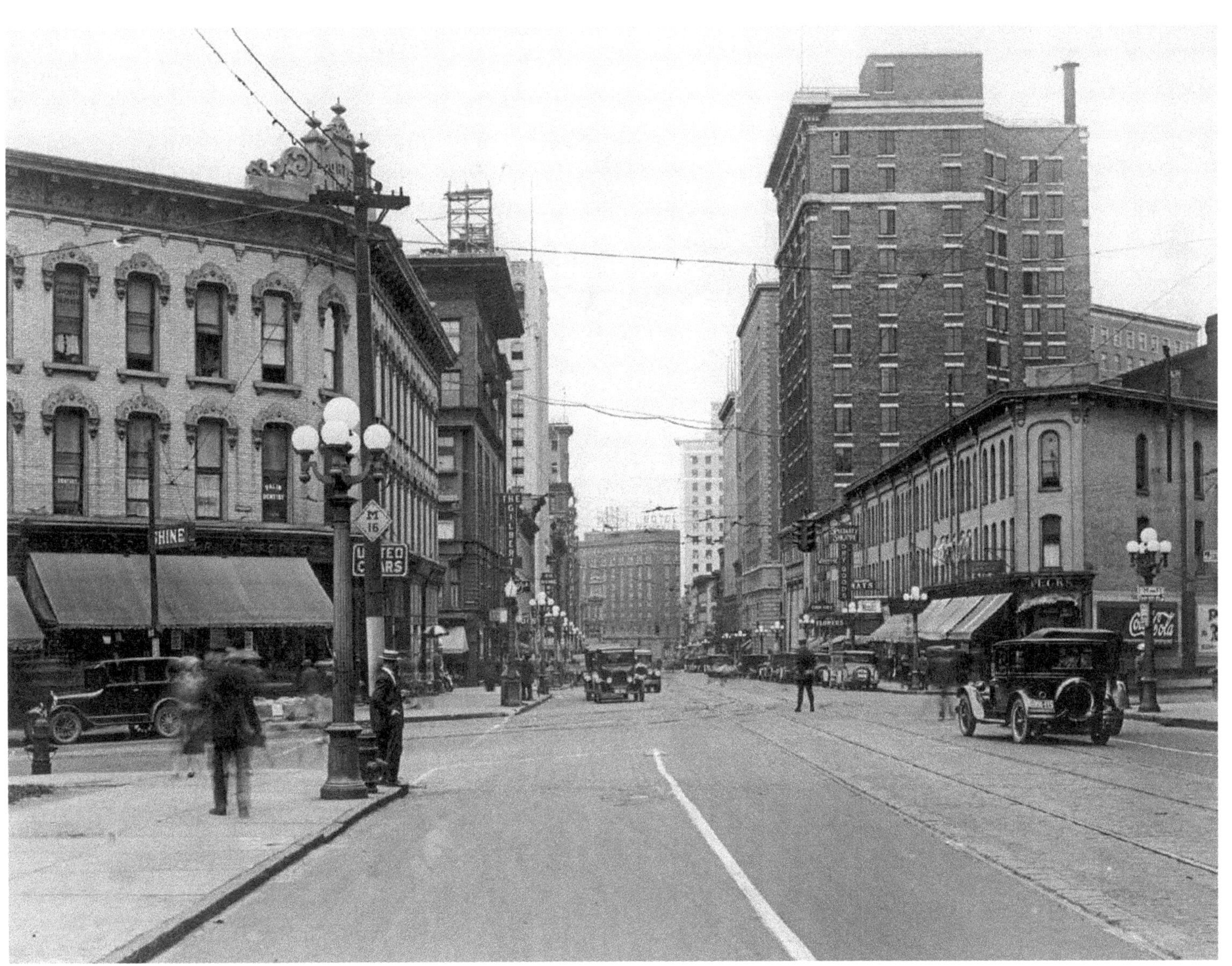

Monroe Avenue at Division, facing west.

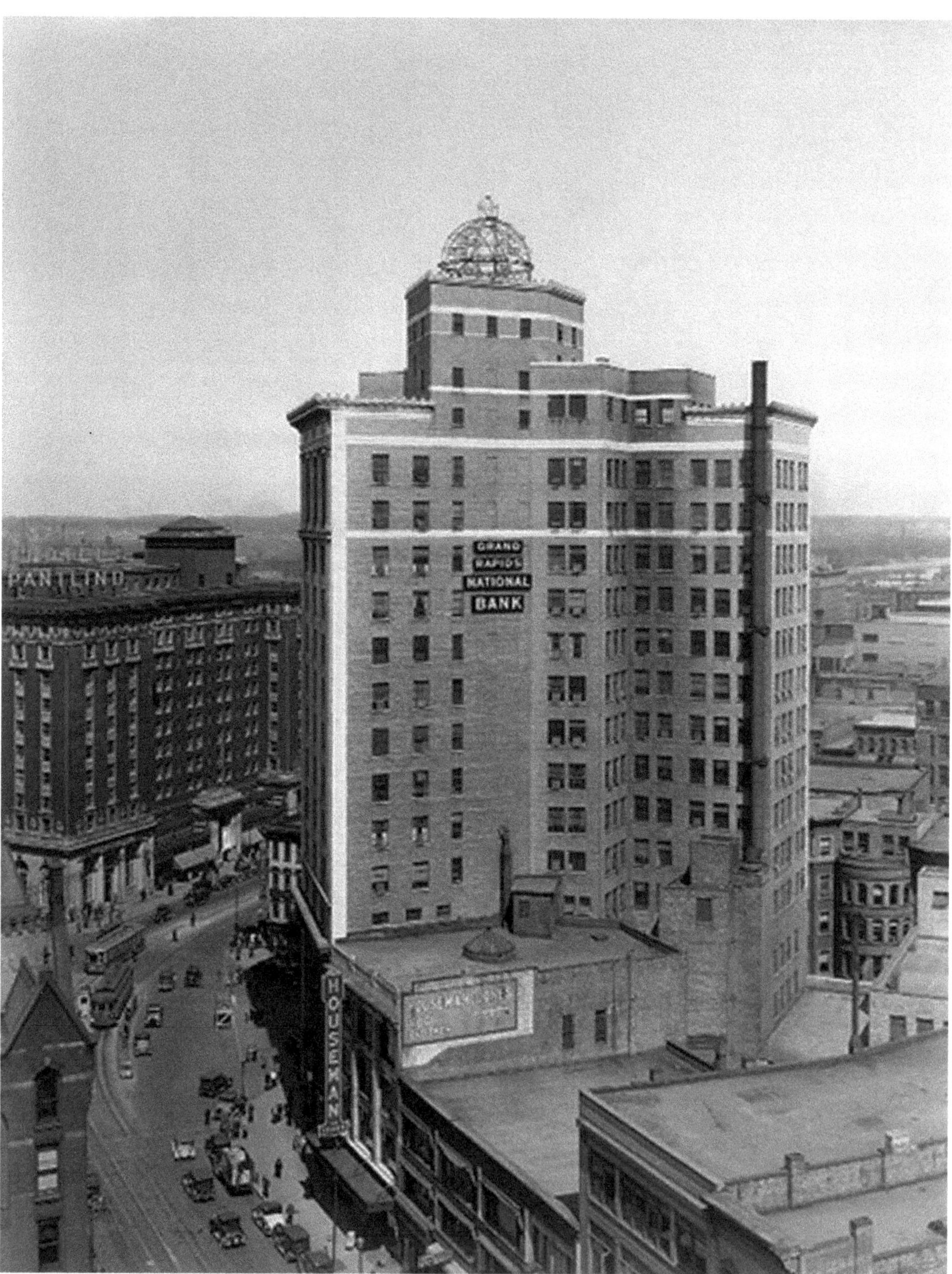

A bird's-eye view of the Grand Rapids National Bank, now known as the McKay Tower. It was built in 1915-16, and the upper floors were added in 1926-27.

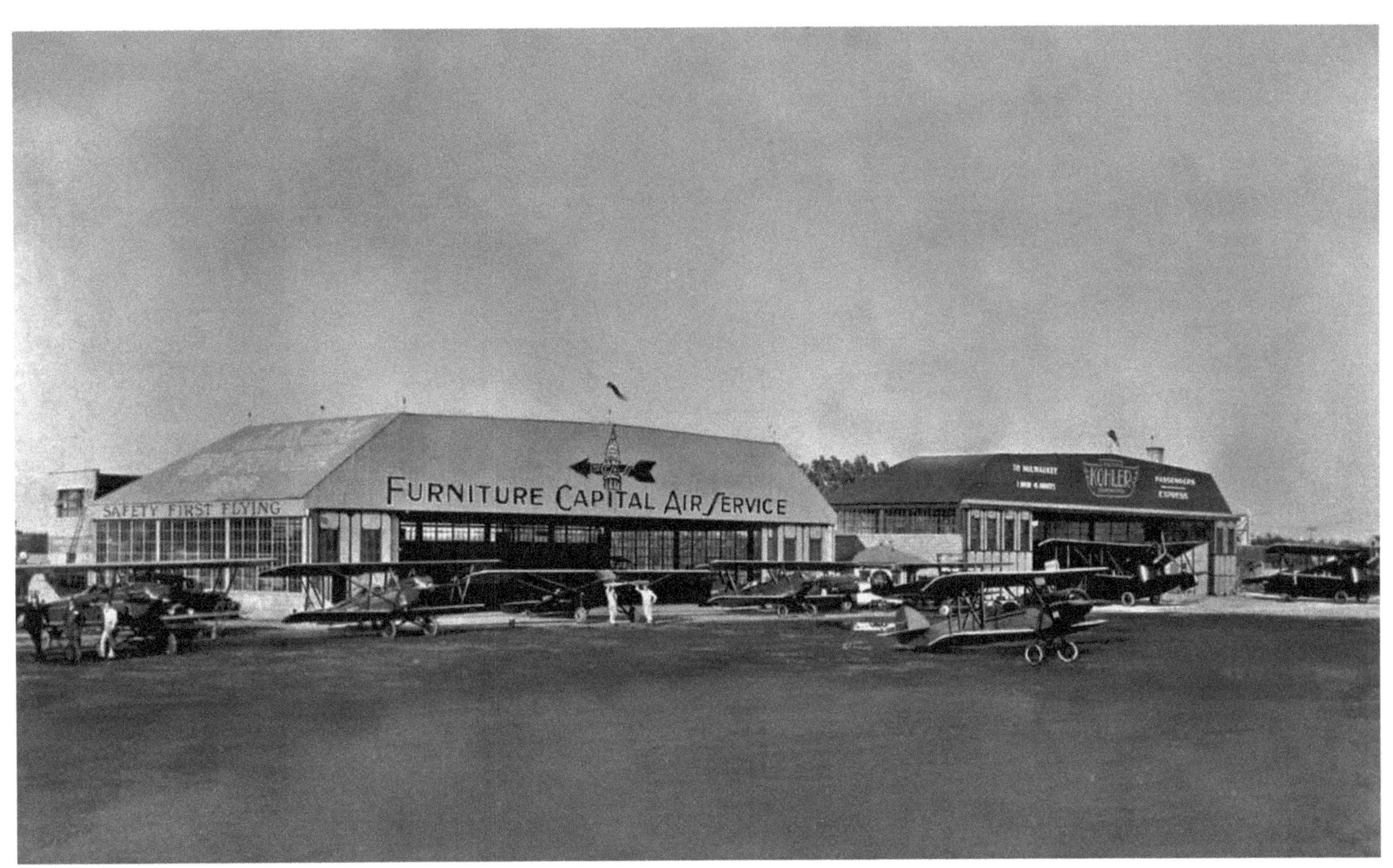

Furniture Capital Air Service and Kohler Air at Grand Rapids Airport.

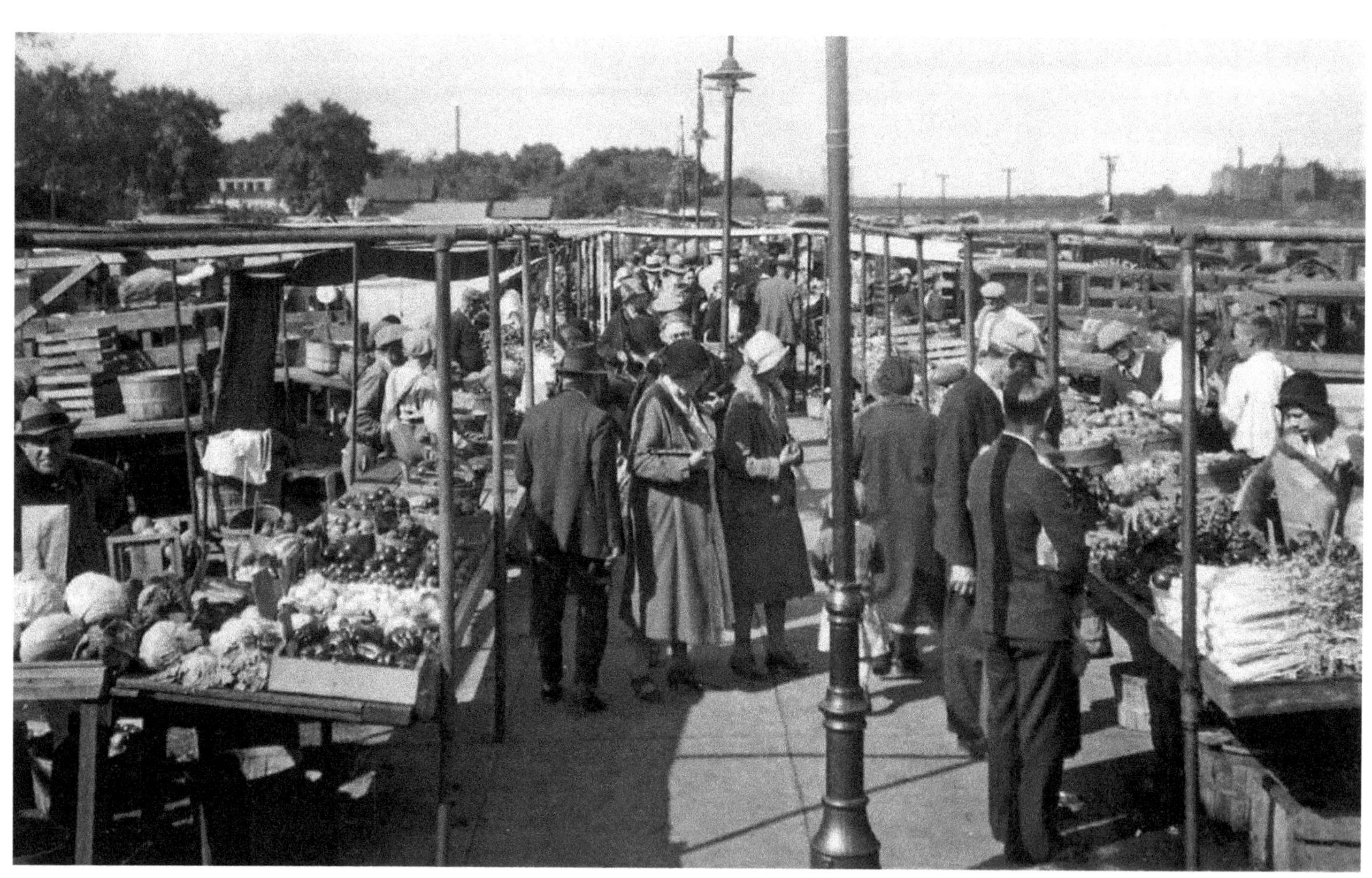

Leonard Street Produce Market was the most prosperous of the three markets in the days revisited here. At one time, 560 loads had come into the market, more loads than stalls.

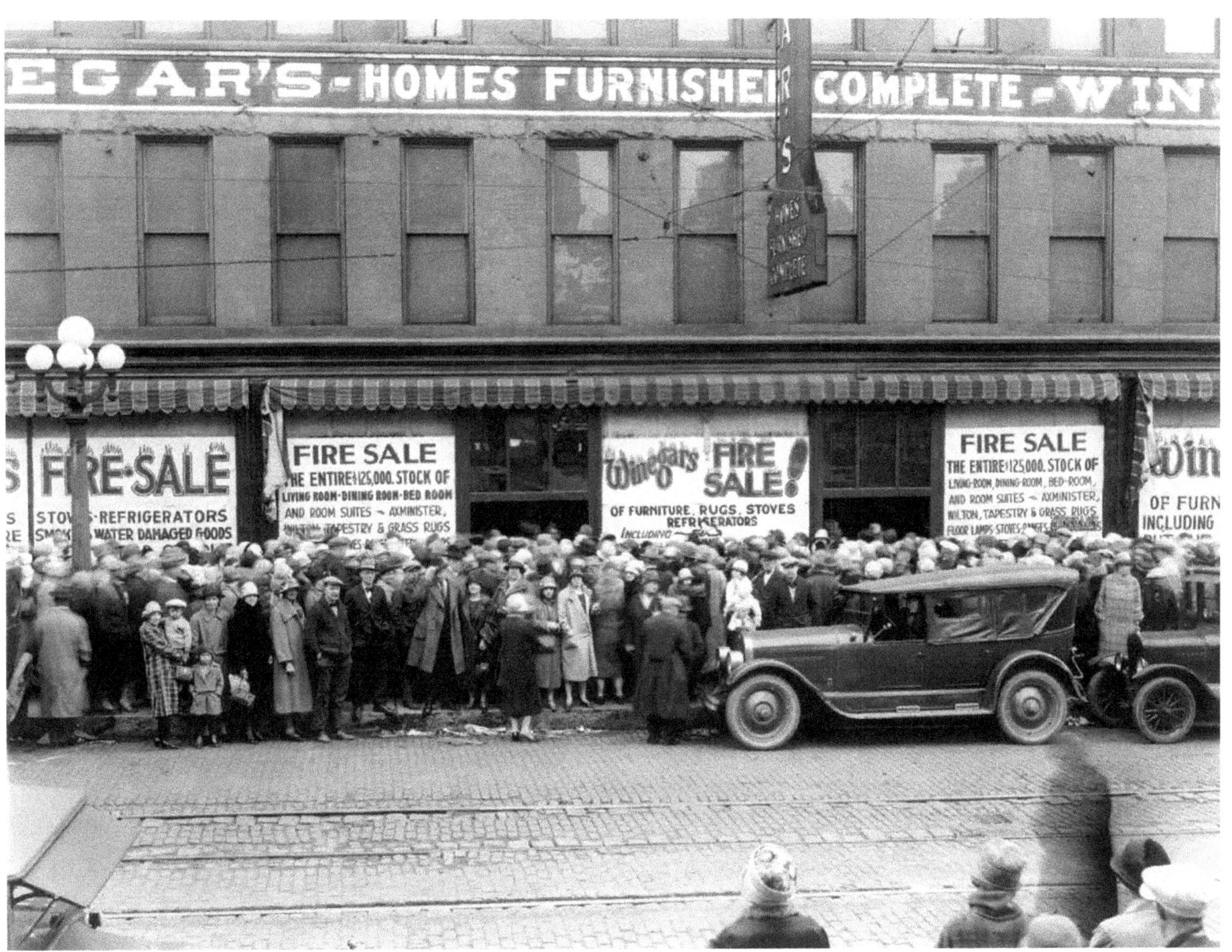

A crowd of people stands outside Winegar Furniture Store at 201-207 South Division Street. Winegar's was holding a "Fire Sale"—with the entire stock of furniture, rugs, and appliances at reduced prices.

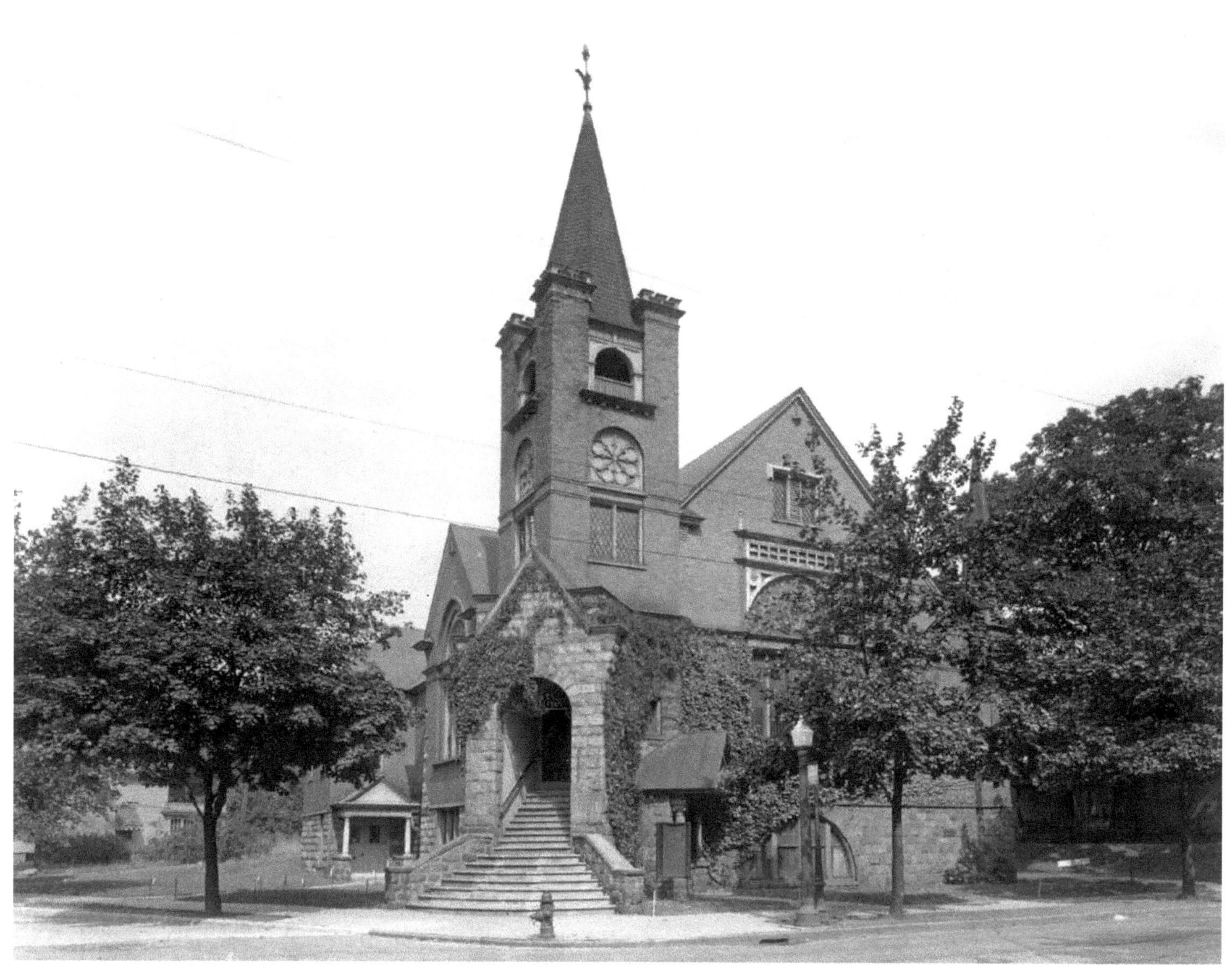

The Second Congregational Church, located at 1331 Plainfield Avenue NE, was built in 1874 and held services regularly until 1950.

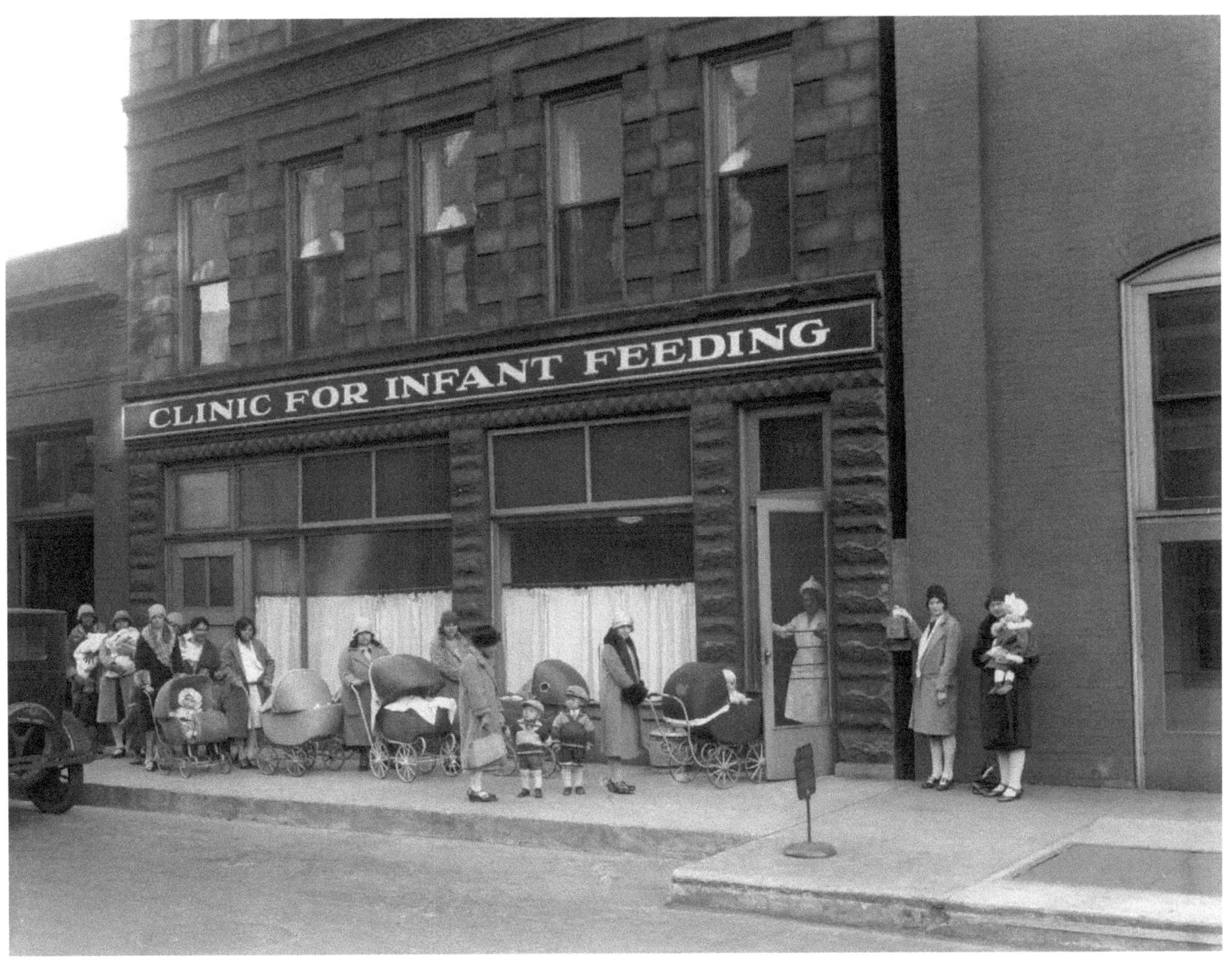

Concerned about the city's high rate of infant mortality in the early years of the twentieth century, socially conscious women formed seven infant clinics, such as this one at 112 Louis NW, to instruct new mothers in the care of their babies.

The Civil War Monument was constructed and dedicated in 1885. The dedication featured a two-mile parade through downtown Grand Rapids, which drew crowds of more than 3,000 veterans and 30,000 spectators. The monument's original white bronze developed a Confederate gray patina, which caused a local uproar that led to the painting of the monument a Union blue. The Civil War Monument was restored in 2006.

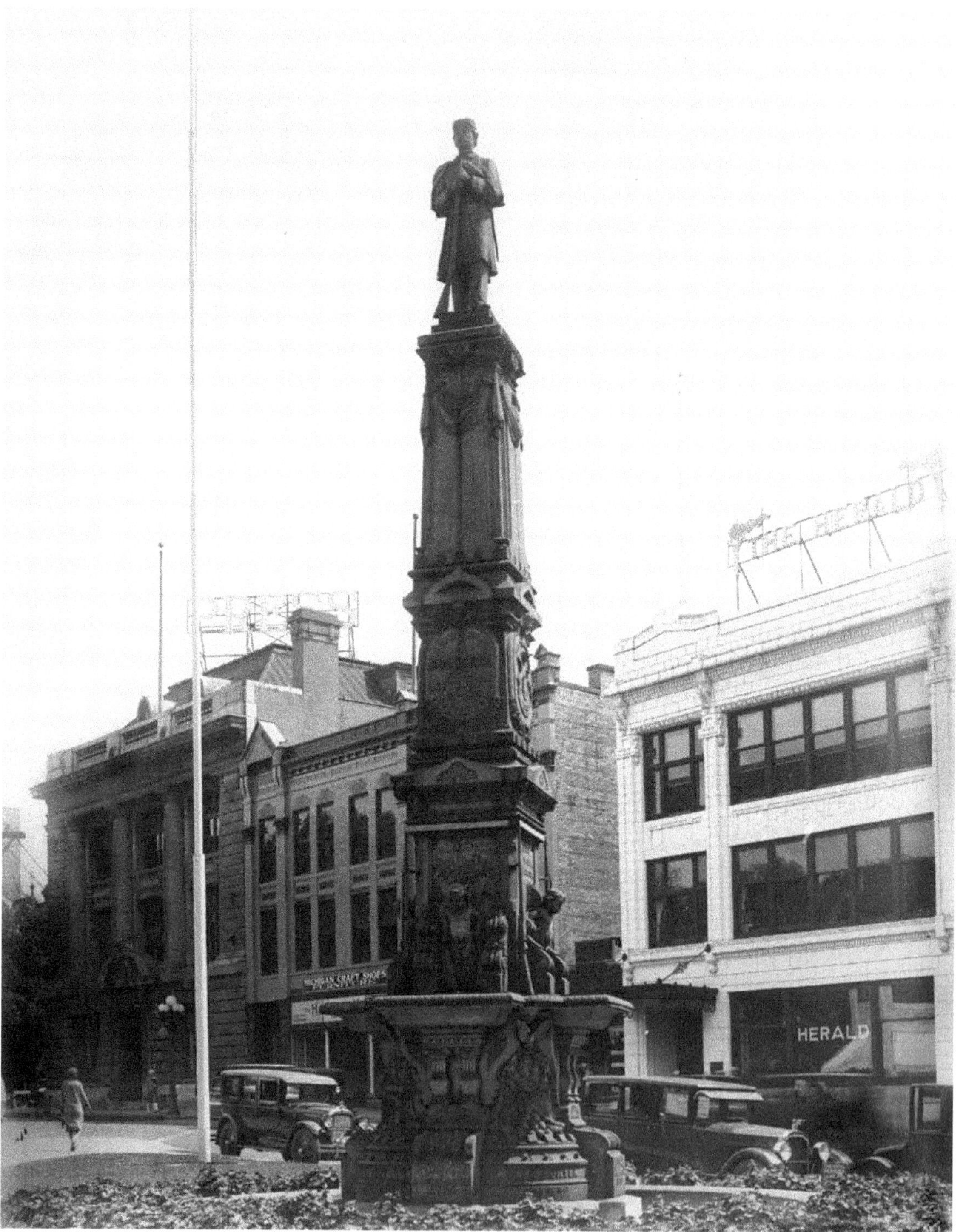

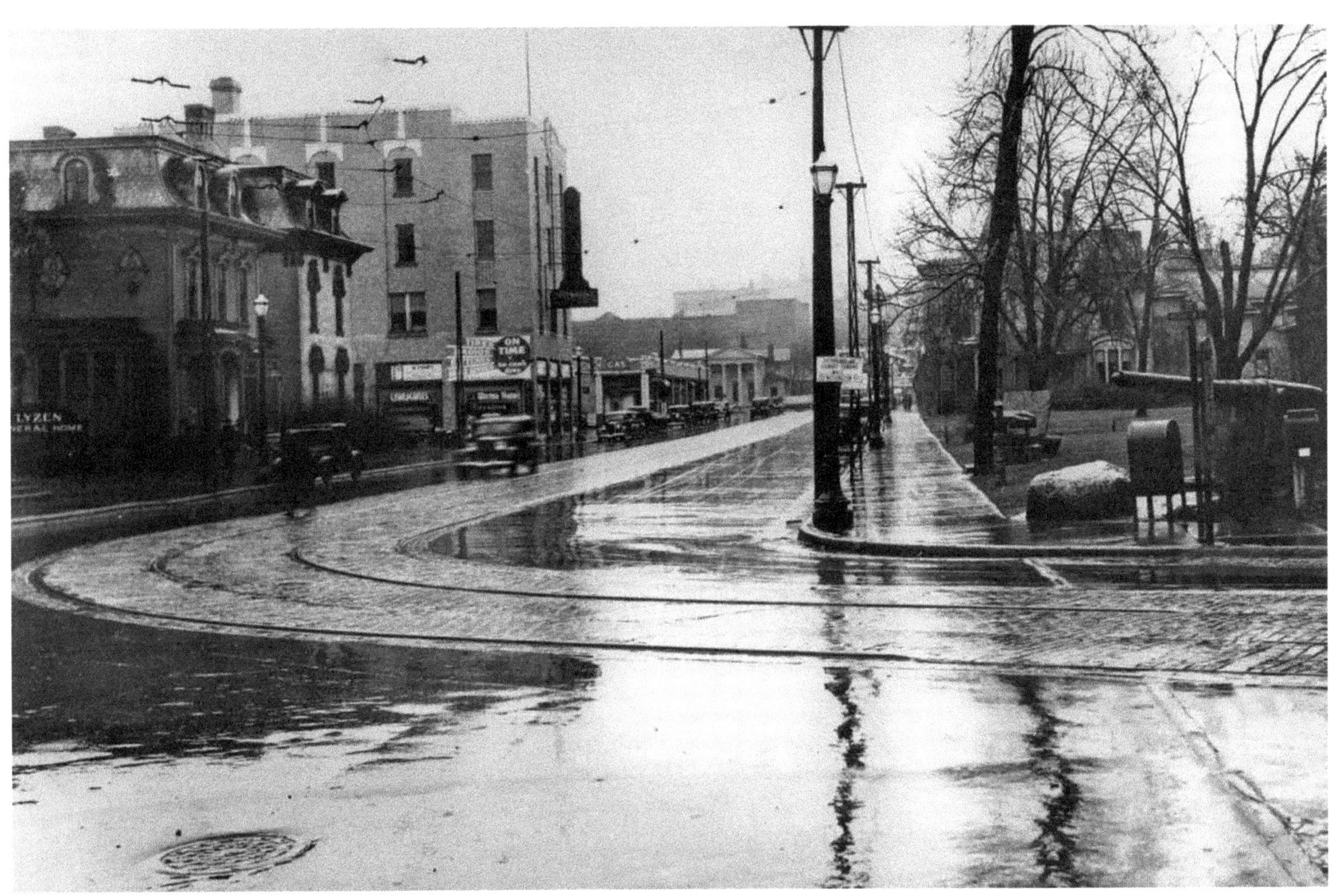

A view facing north on Jefferson Avenue toward Fulton Street.

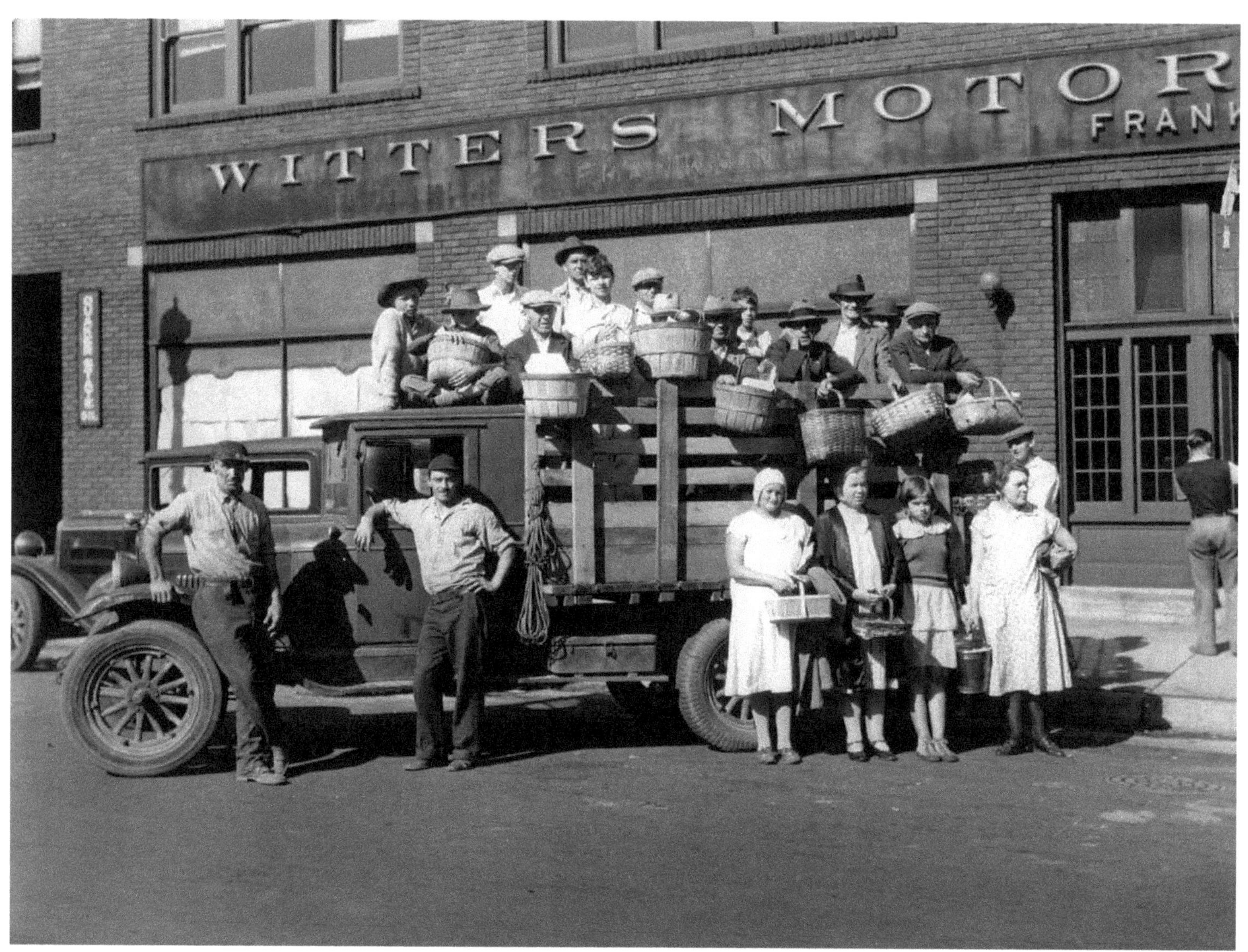

During the years of the Great Depression, City Manager George Welsh instituted a scrip wage system and set up a municipal food store. As many as sixty work projects were underway at the same time. Playgrounds and parks were reconditioned. Flood-inducing obstructions in the river were removed. Streets were graded and repaired. This image shows berry pickers leaving for the fields, another work project that was part of the program.

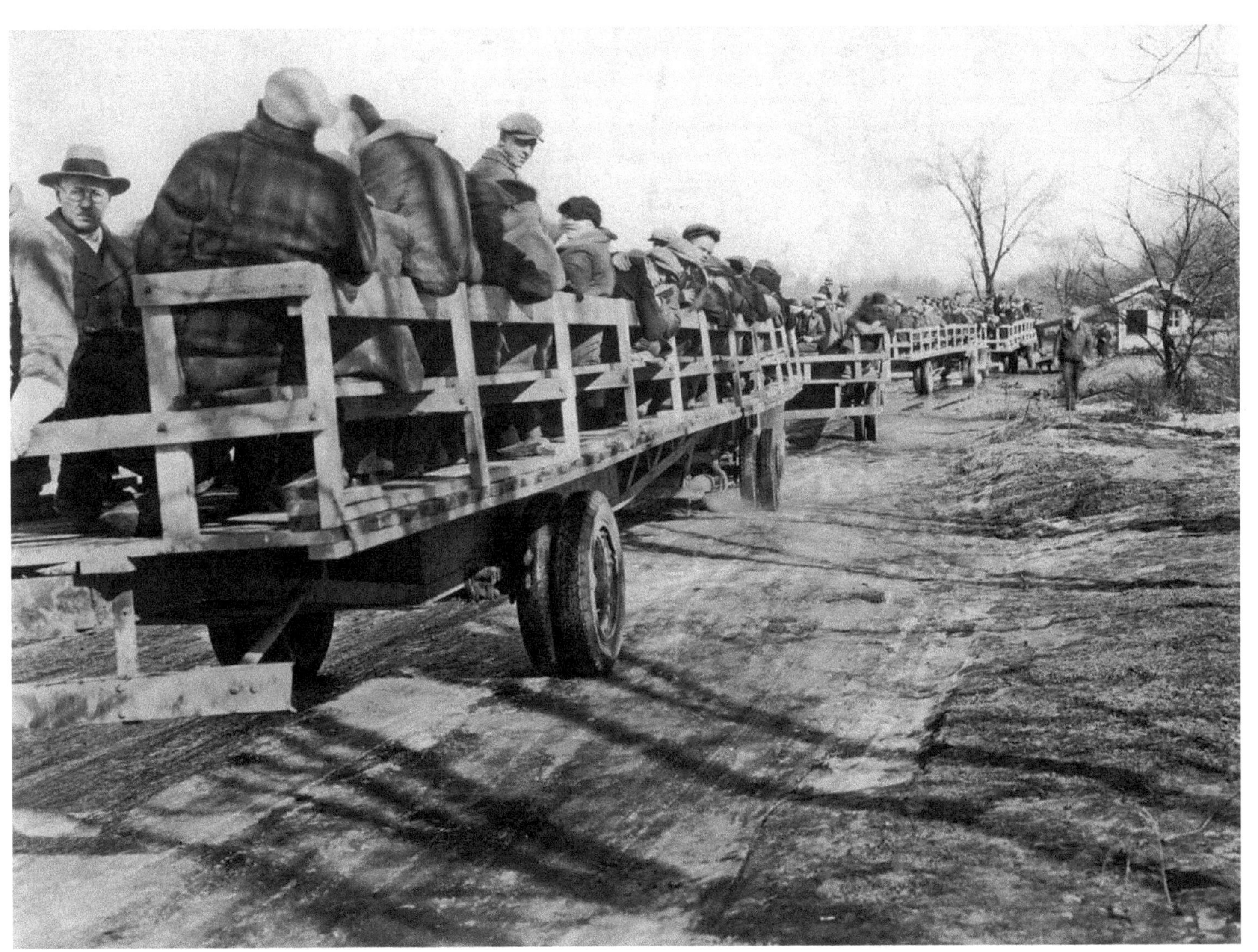

These scrip laborers are ready to depart for the various work-projects job sites.

These scrip laborers are laying pipe at Front Avenue and Third Street in 1931.

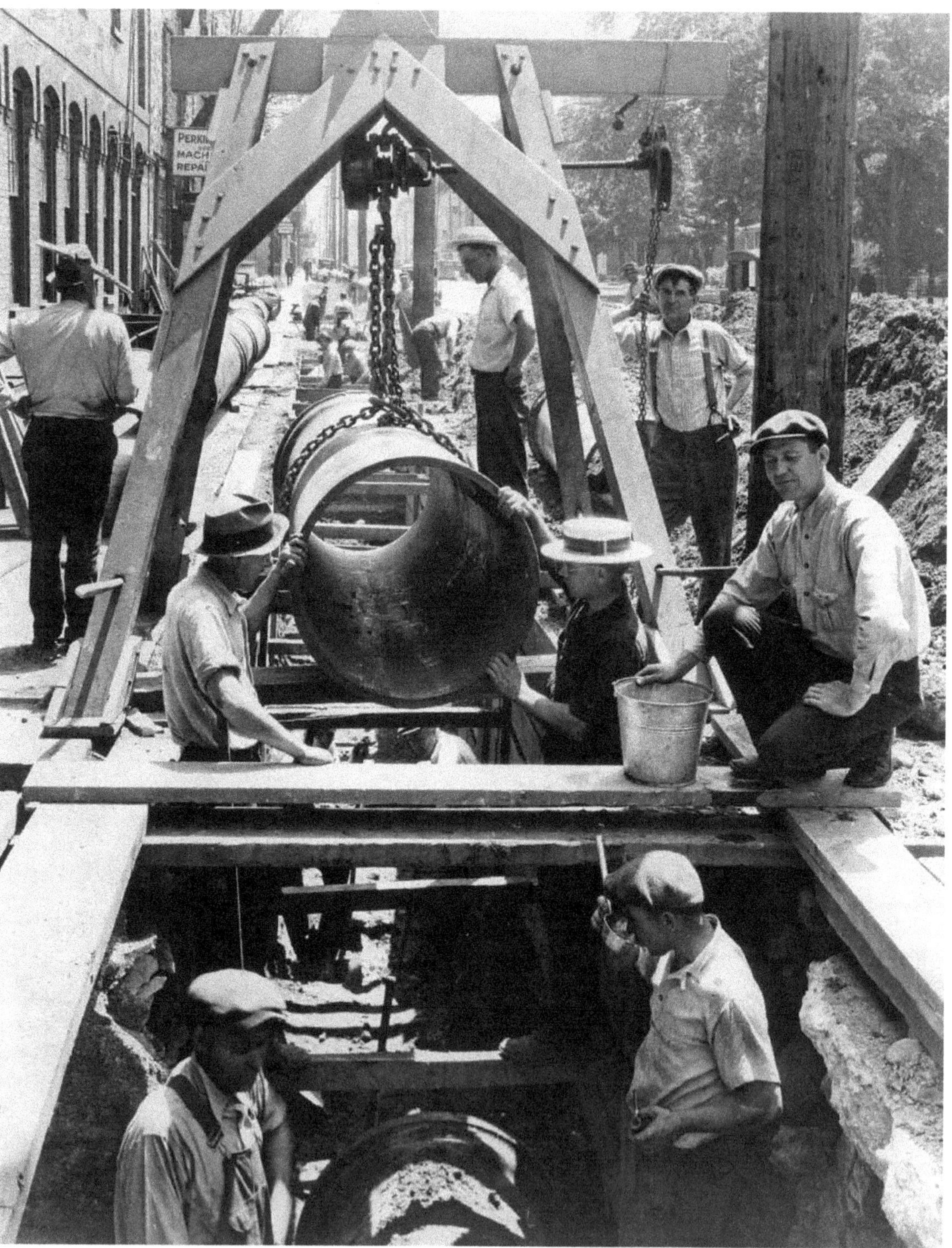

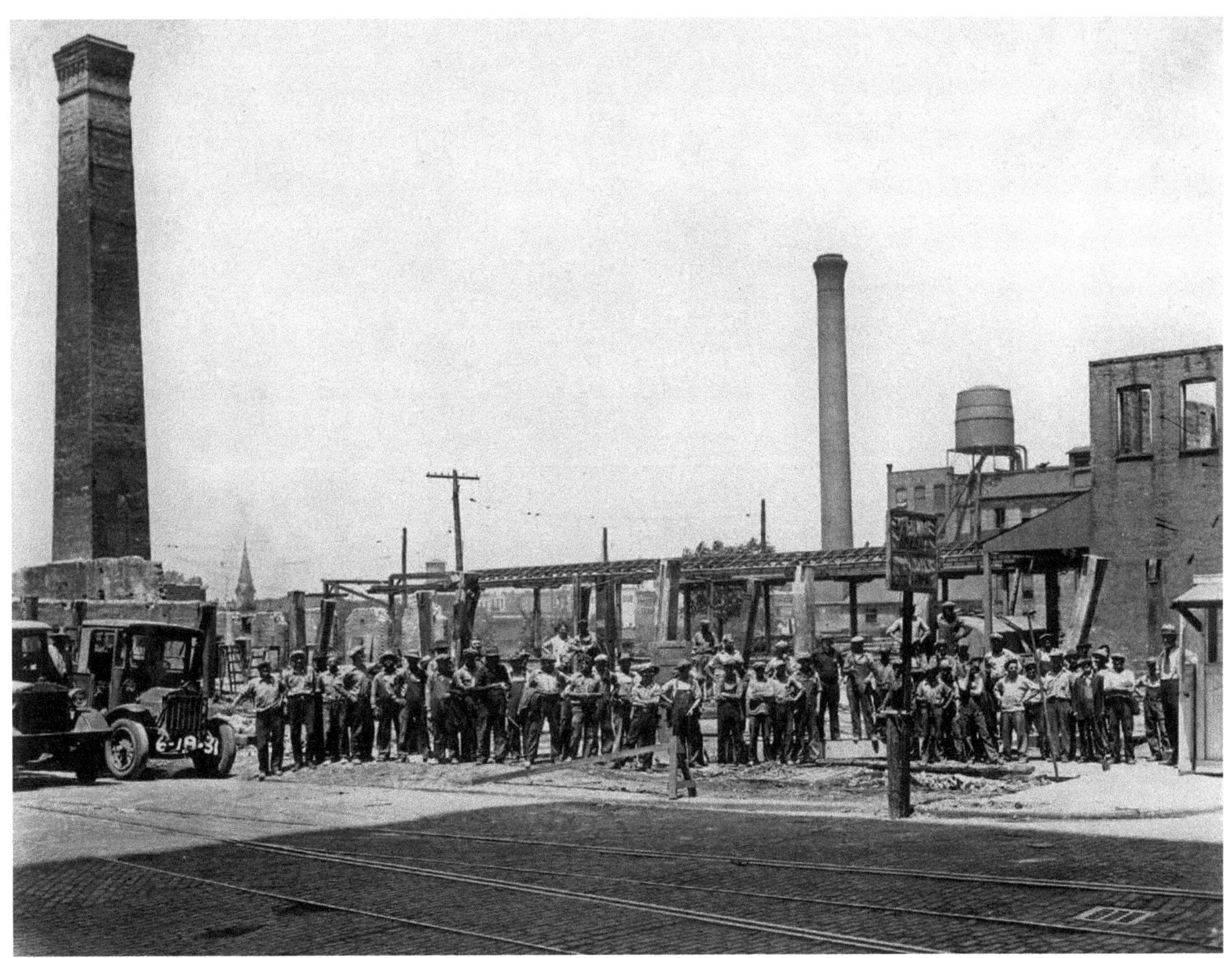

Scrip laborers line up for work at an area job site.

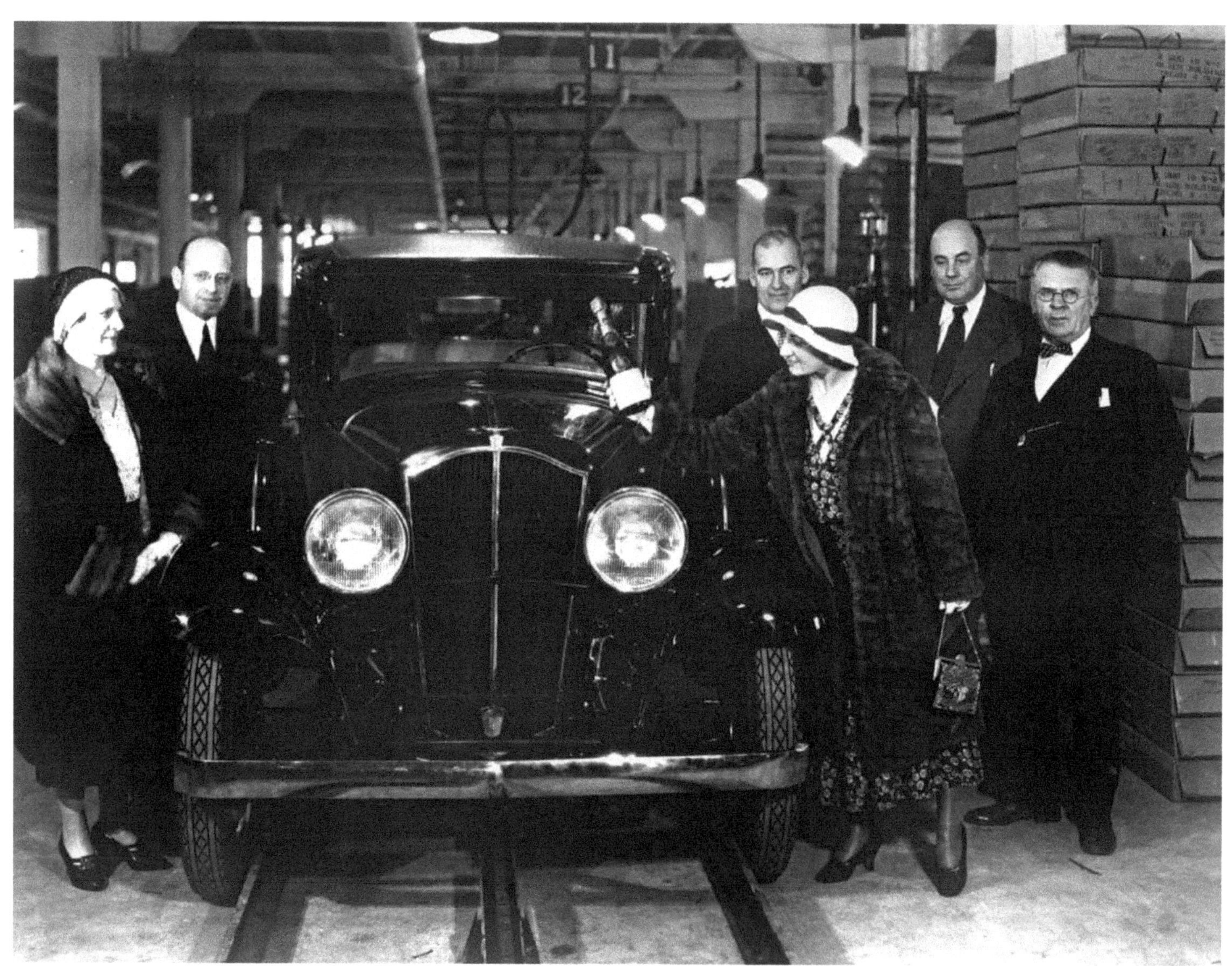

A DeVaux automobile is christened as it comes off the production line.

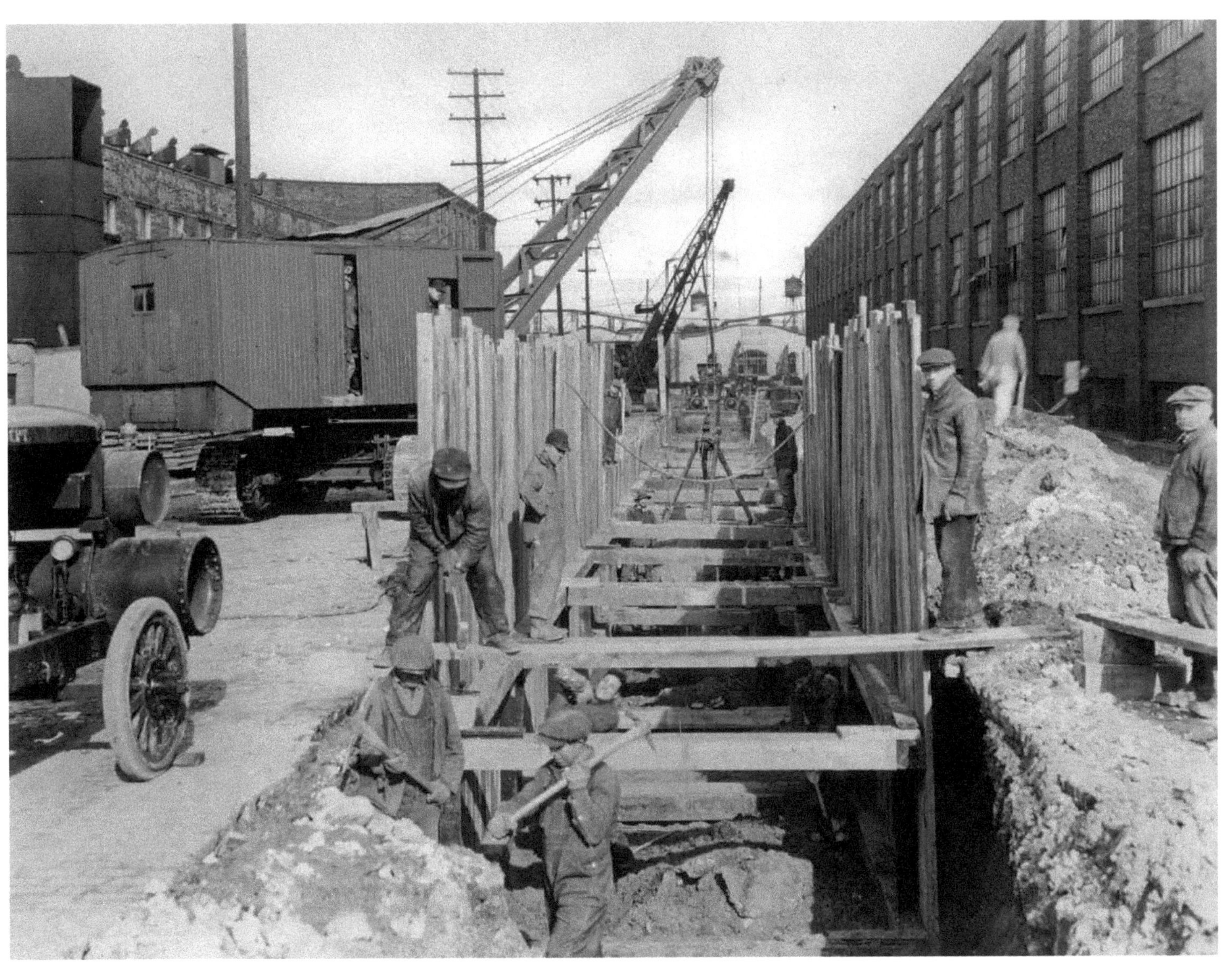

Scrip laborers worked in all parts of the city. These men are working on Godfrey Avenue.

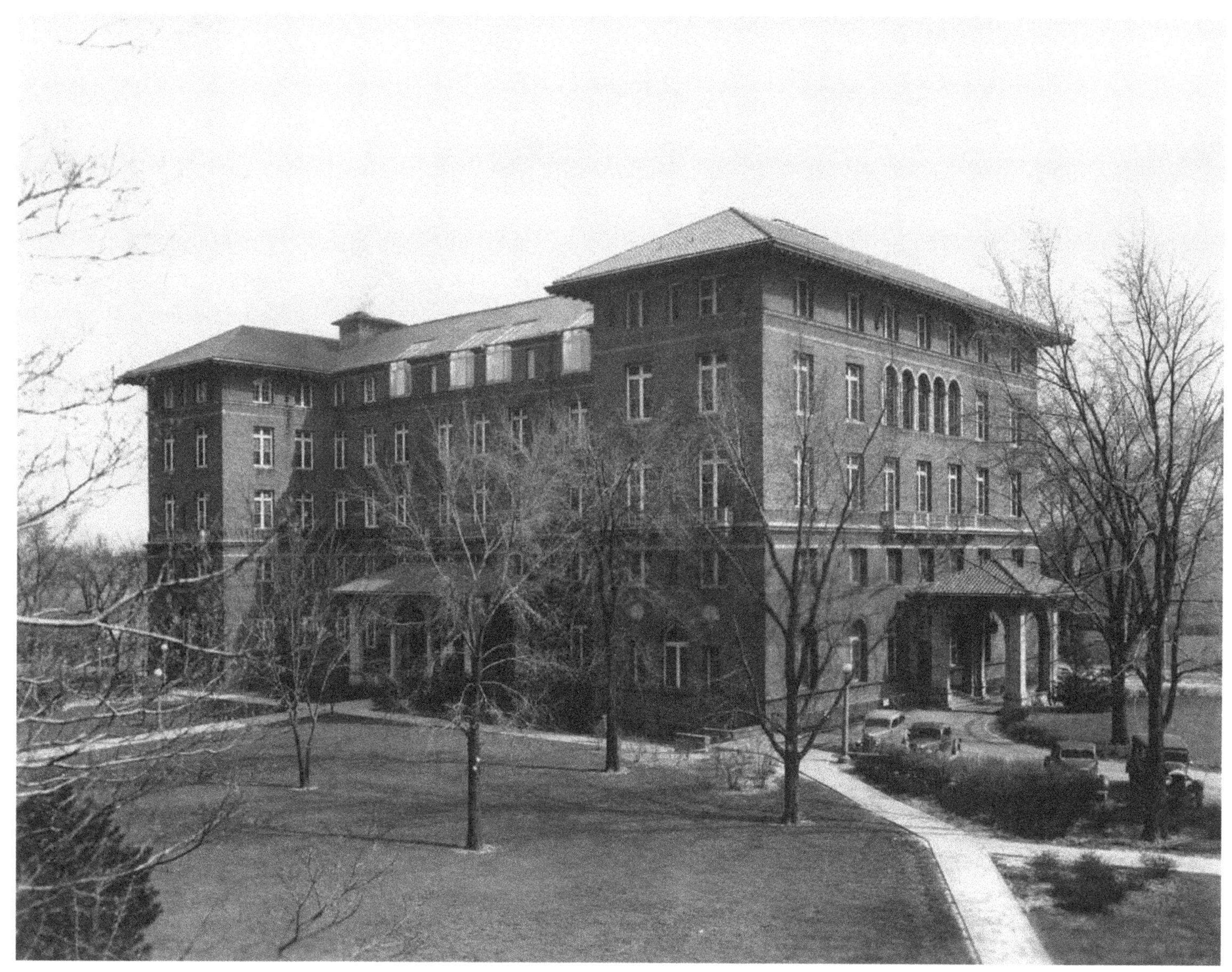

Blodgett Hospital, now known as Spectrum Health-Blodgett Campus, at Plymouth and Wealthy SE. John Blodgett, Sr., and his wife, Minnie Cumnock Blodgett, donated land and funds in 1914 for construction of the hospital.

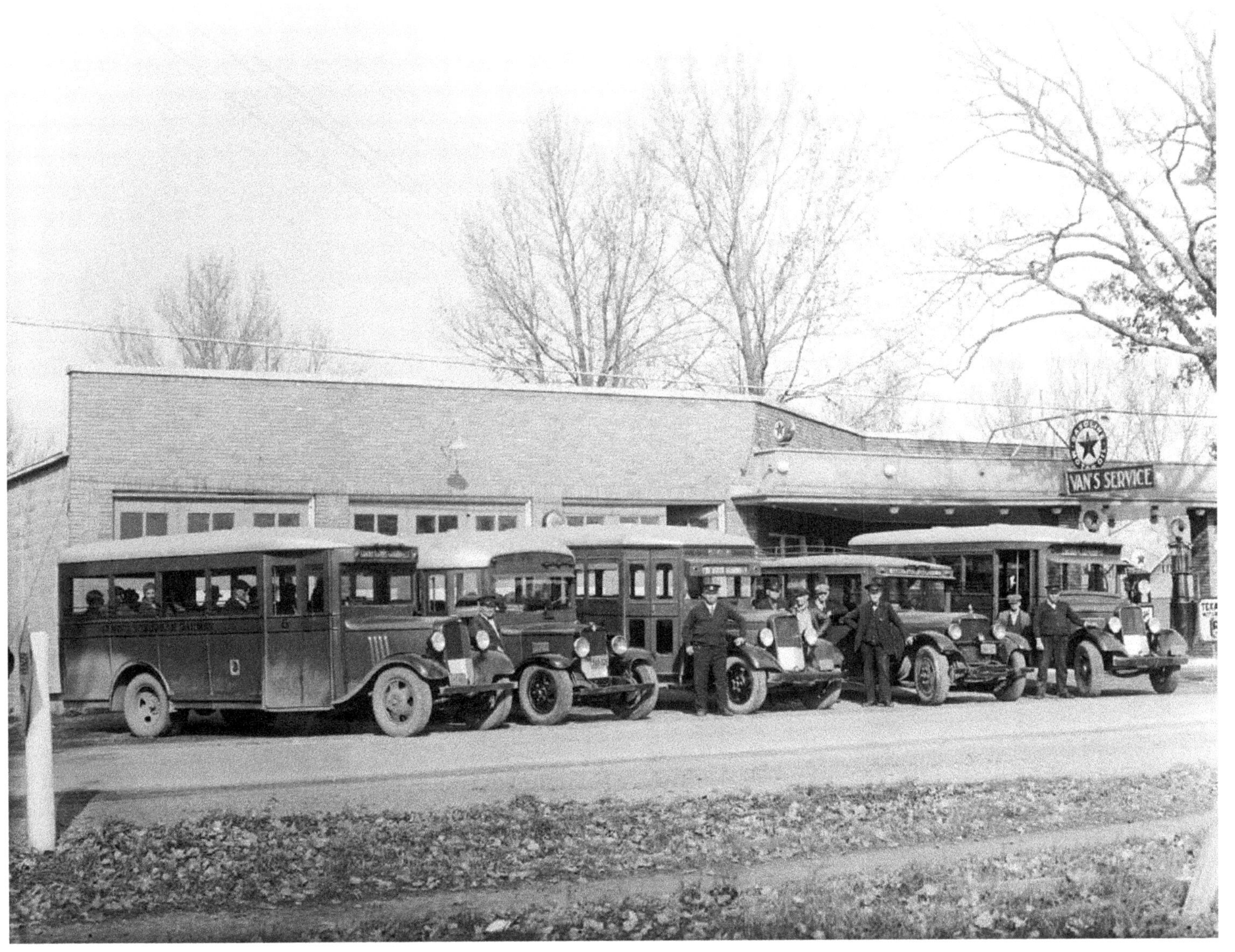

United Suburban Railway Bus Line served transportation needs from Grand Rapids to Grandville. Stations were located on Louis, Market, Ottawa, and West Washington streets.

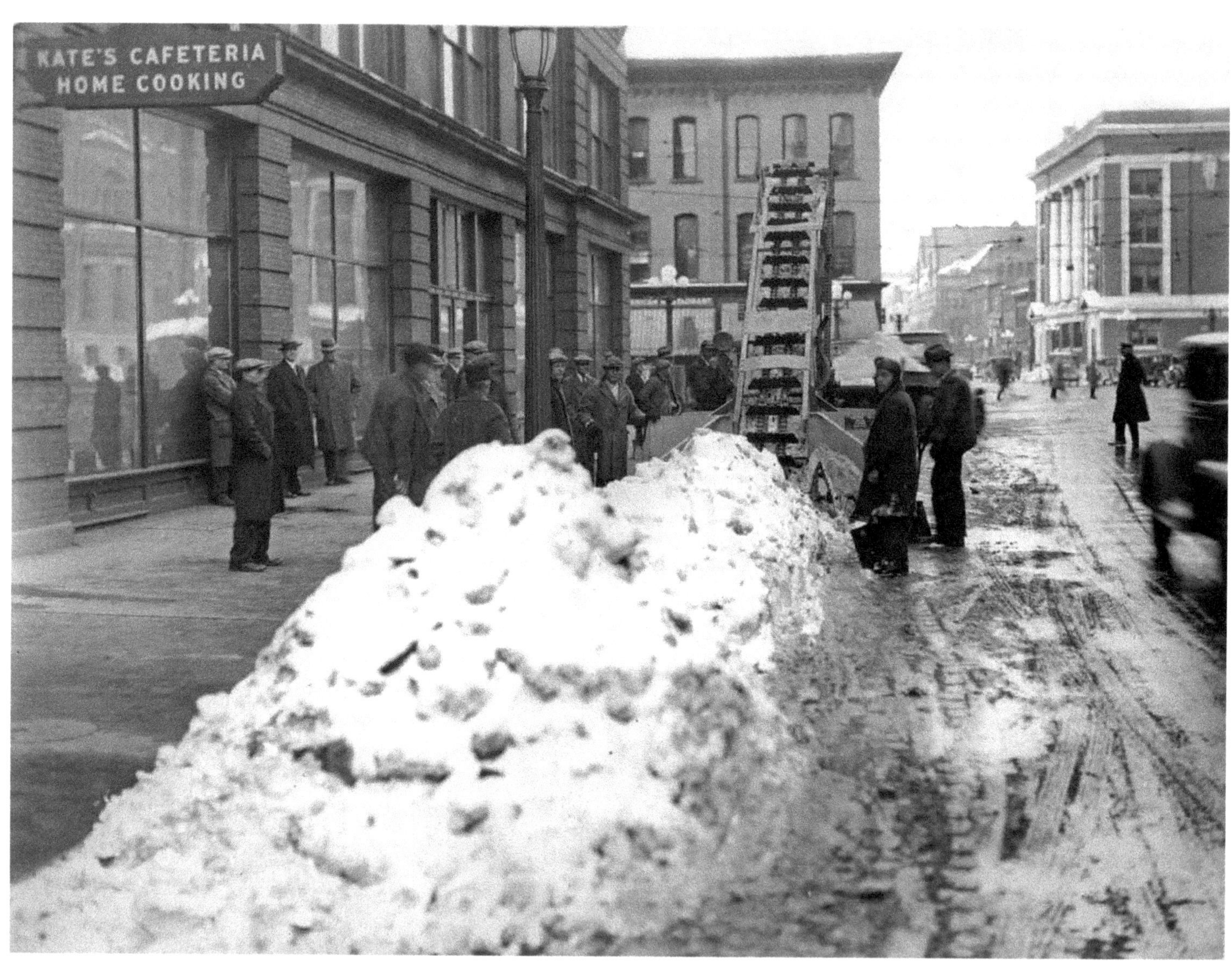

Scrip workers helped keep the city's streets and sidewalks clear of snow and ice. Shown here, an elevator is being operated to load mounds of snow onto a waiting dump truck.

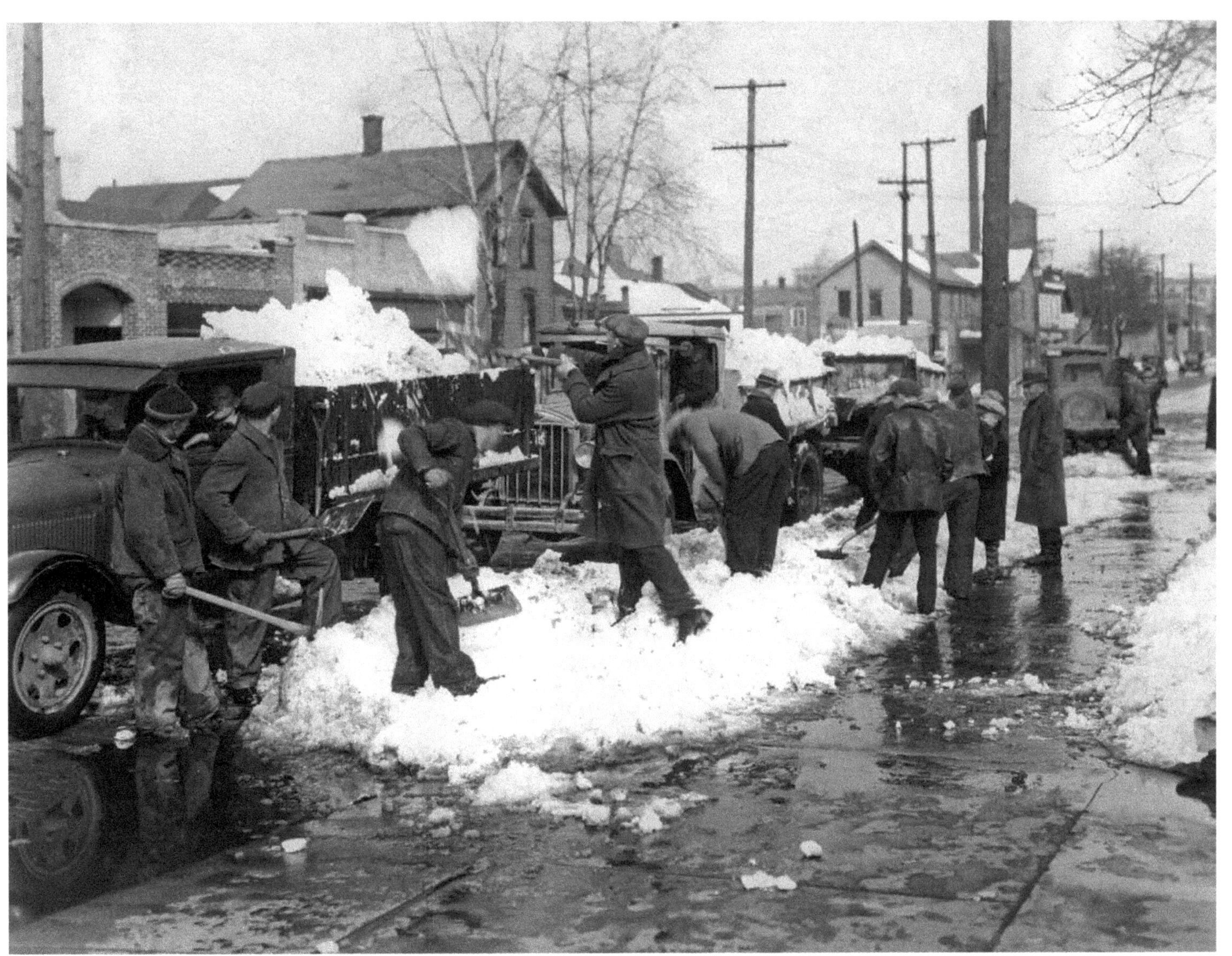

Many hands made the job of snow removal much less burdensome.

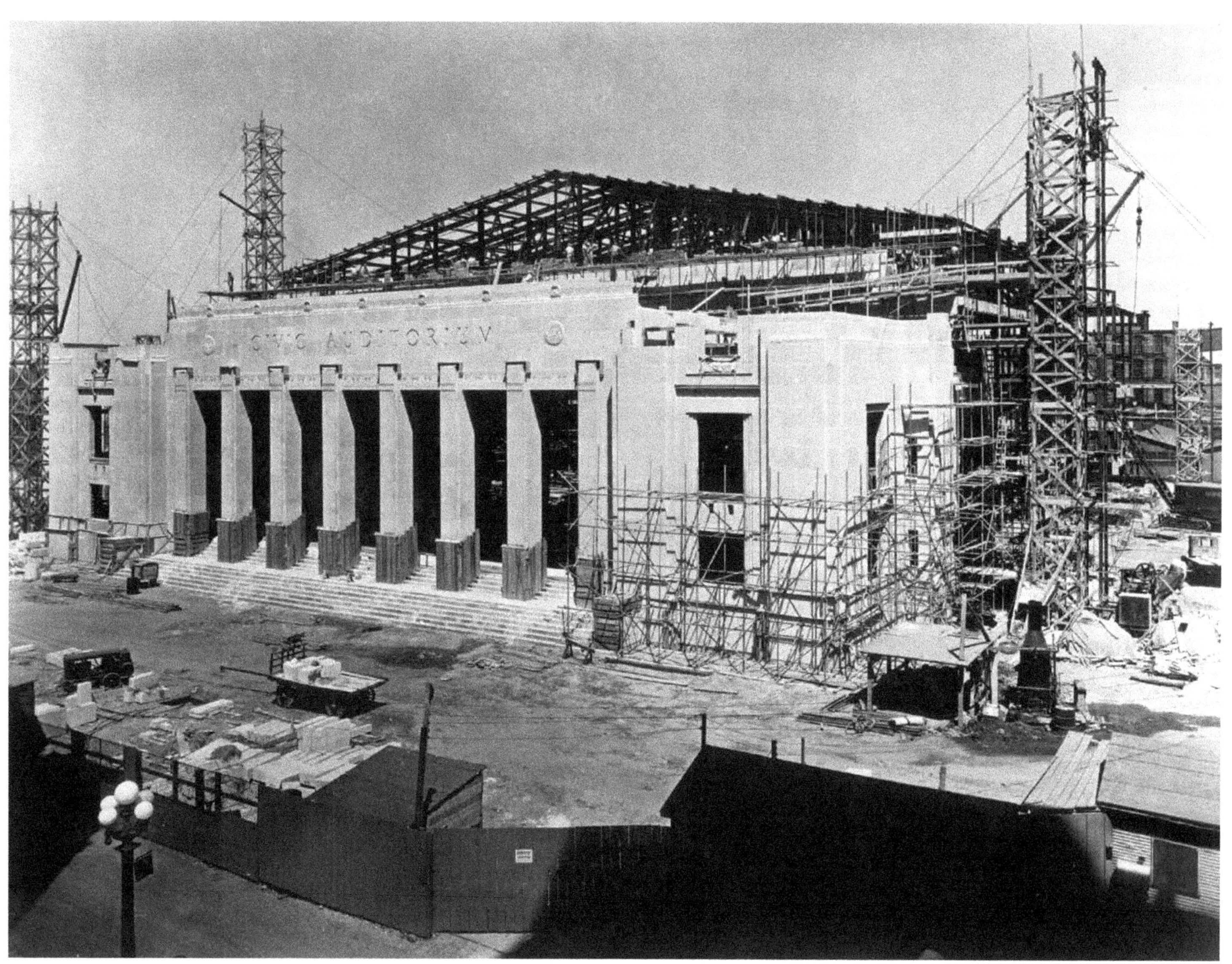

Funds for the Civic Auditorium were raised from a city bond issue that passed in 1932. Scrip laborers provided the manpower for construction. The auditorium was dedicated in 1933.

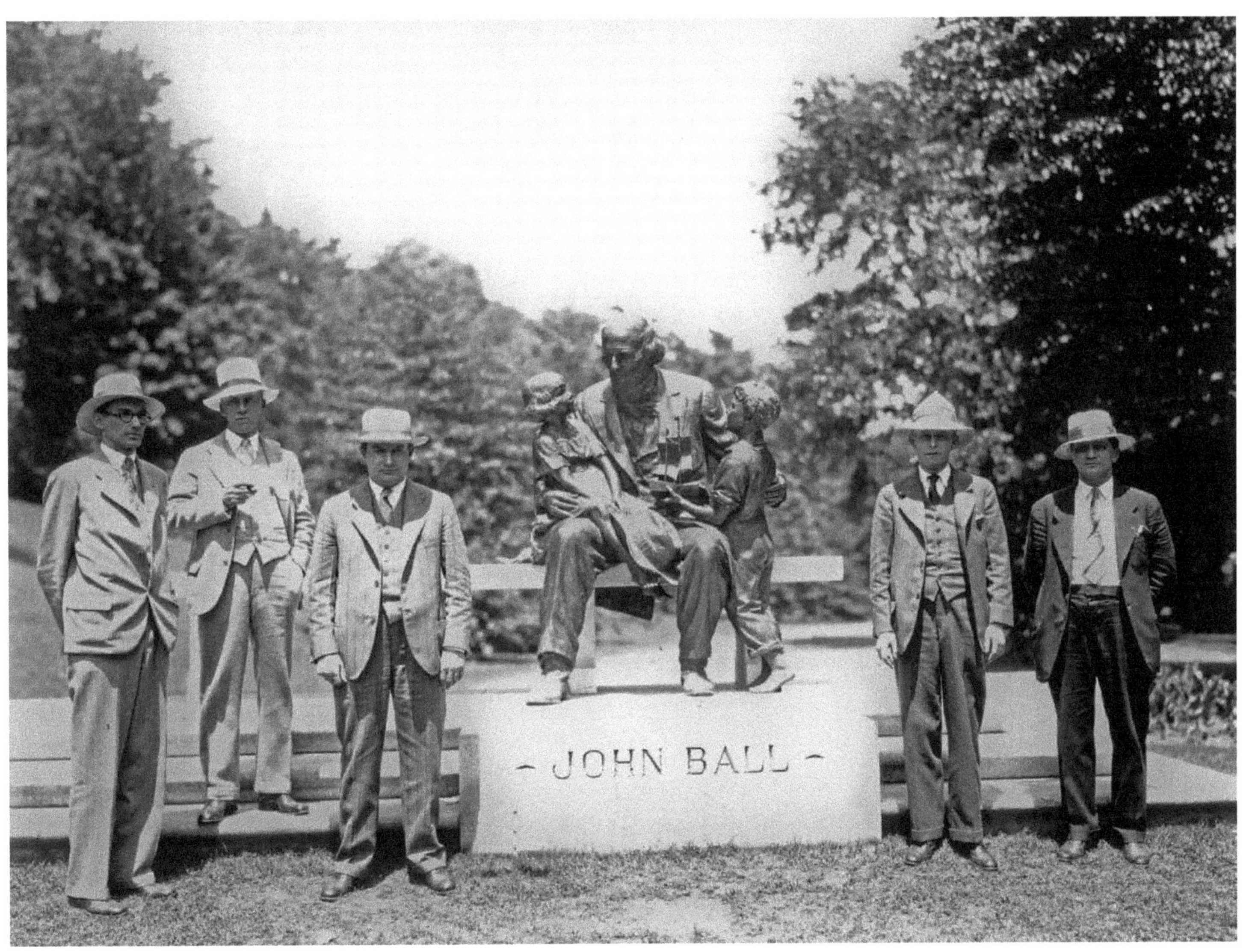

John Ball was a world traveler who came to Grand Rapids in 1836 as a land speculator. Ball left 40 acres to the city upon his death, which became John Ball Park and Zoo. This monument in tribute to Ball was based on a sketch by Gertrude Vande Mark, a local artist, and was sculptured by Pompeo Coppini in 1925.

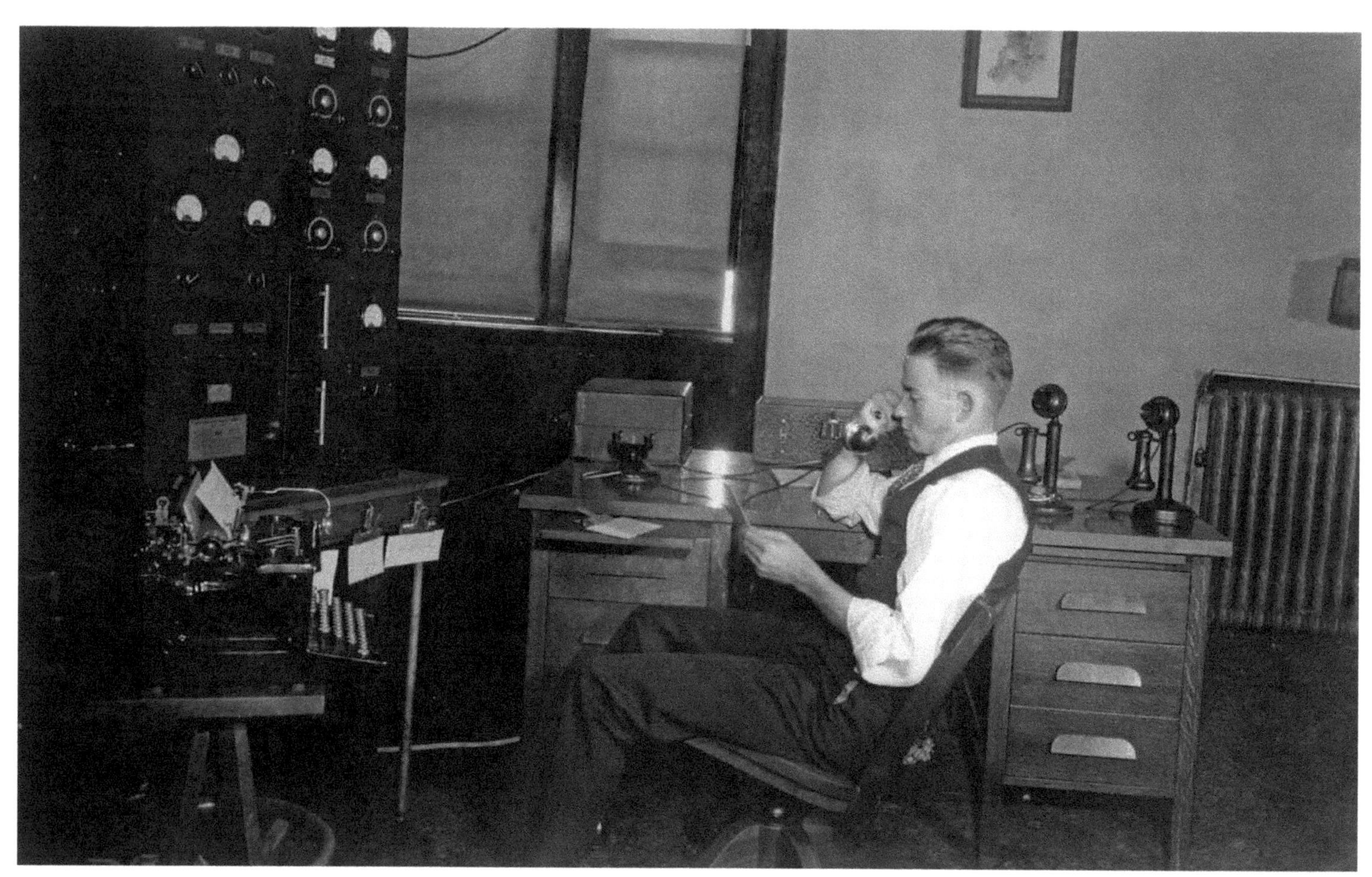

Keeping the peace, from the Grand Rapids Police Department Radio Room in 1932.

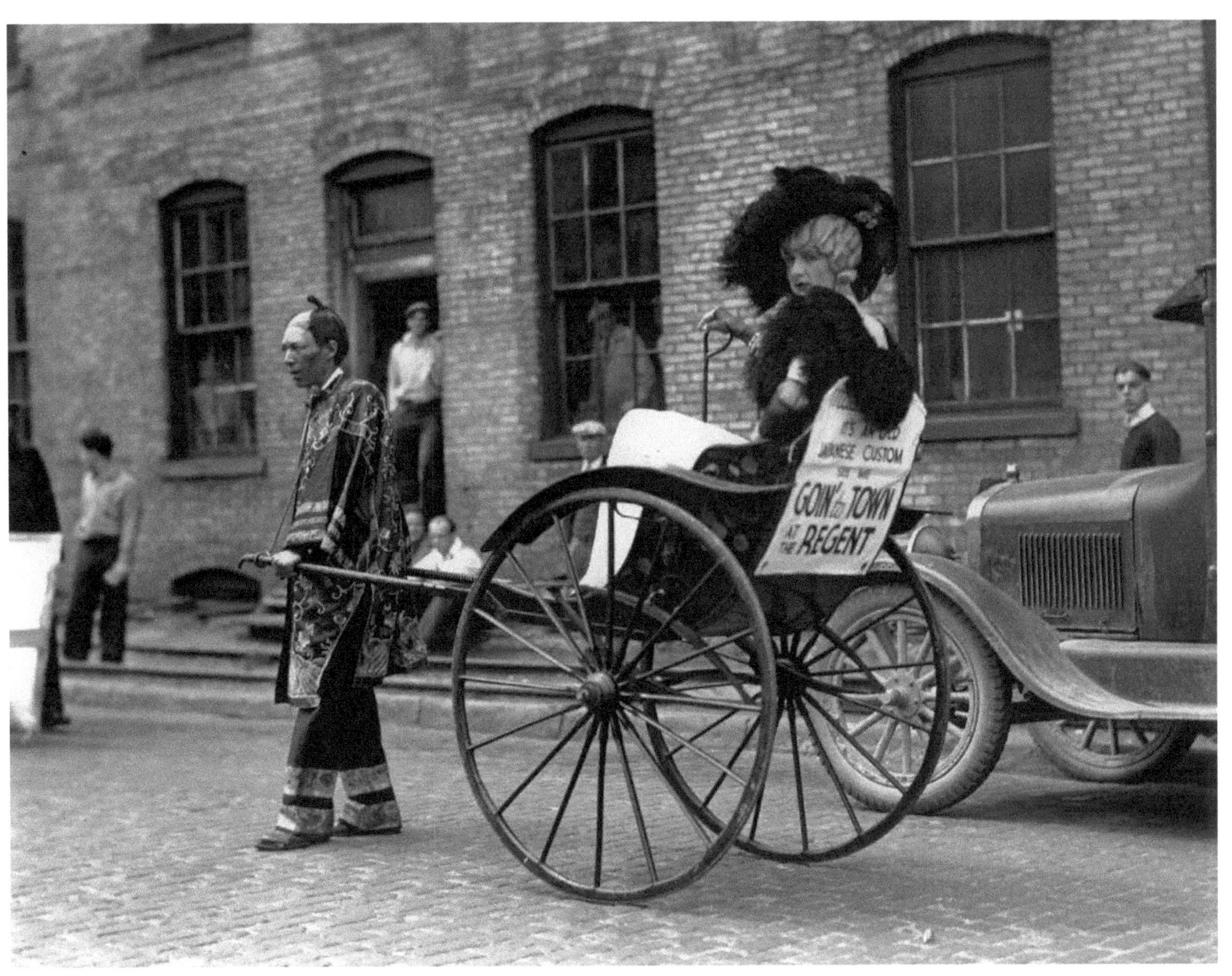

Promotion for the Mae West movie *Going to Town.* The film was being shown at the Regent Theater.

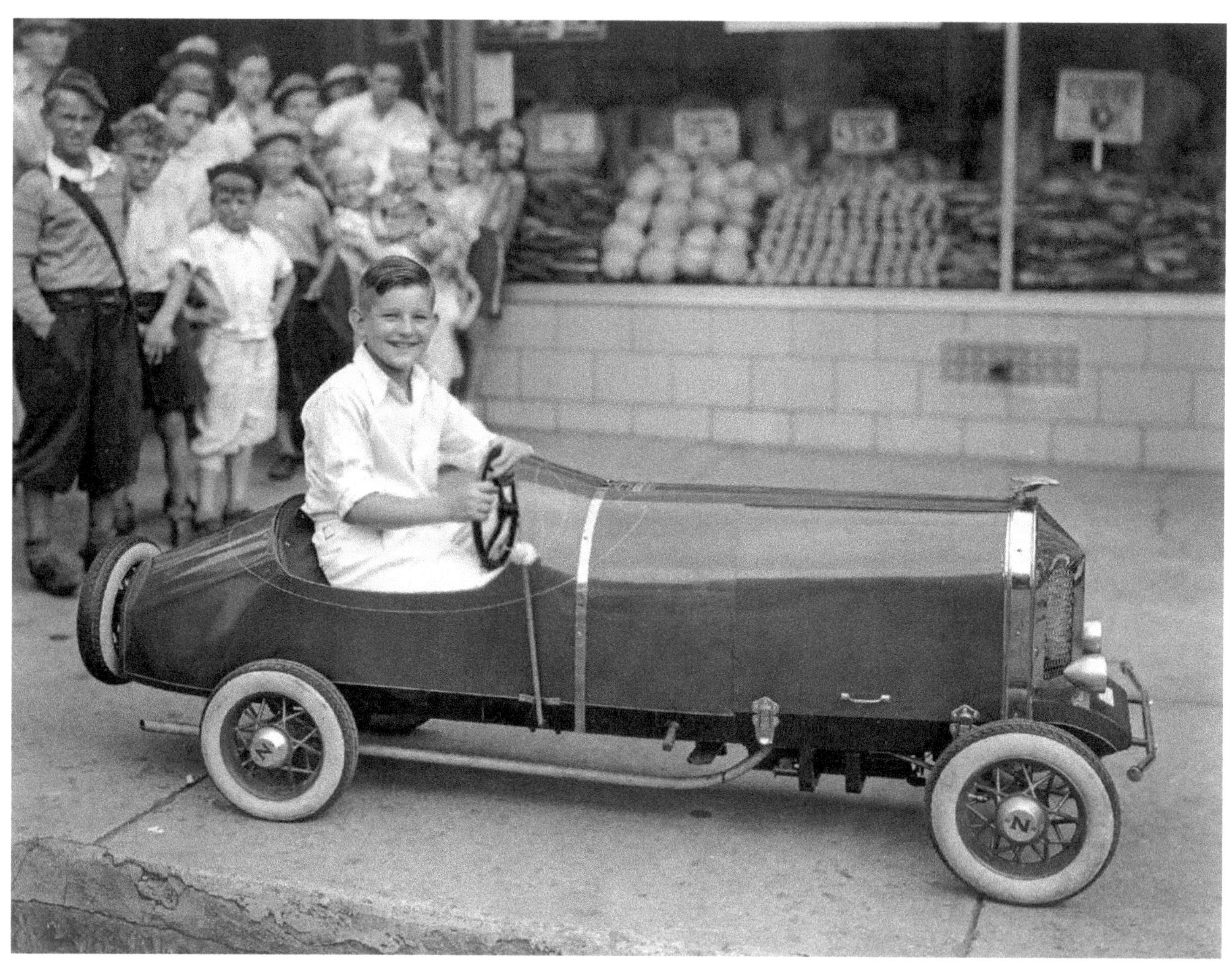

Which is shining brighter—the spiffy toy car or the young boy's smile?

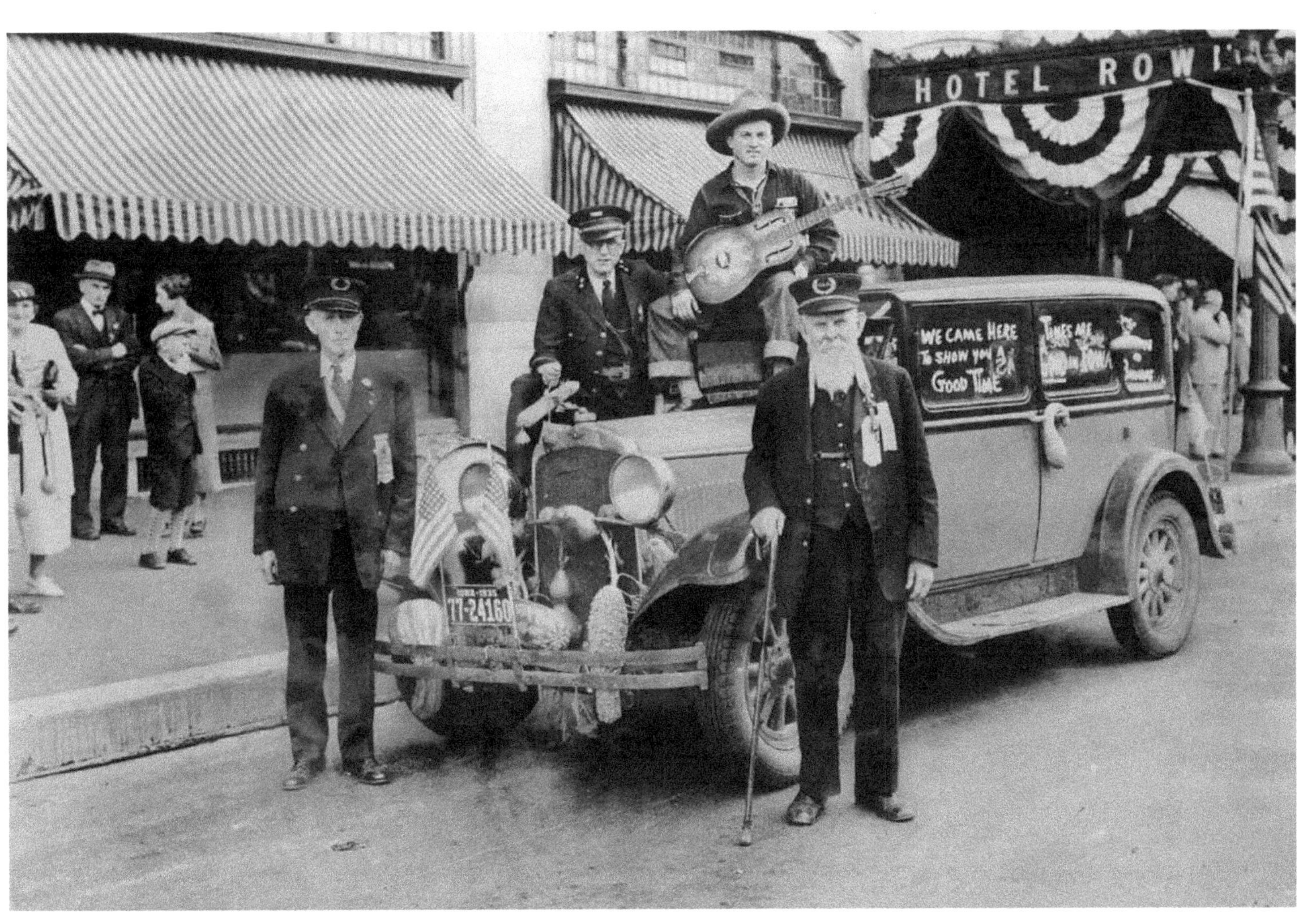

The Grand Army of the Republic (G.A.R.) Convention of 1935. These veterans traveled here from Iowa to take part in the festivities.

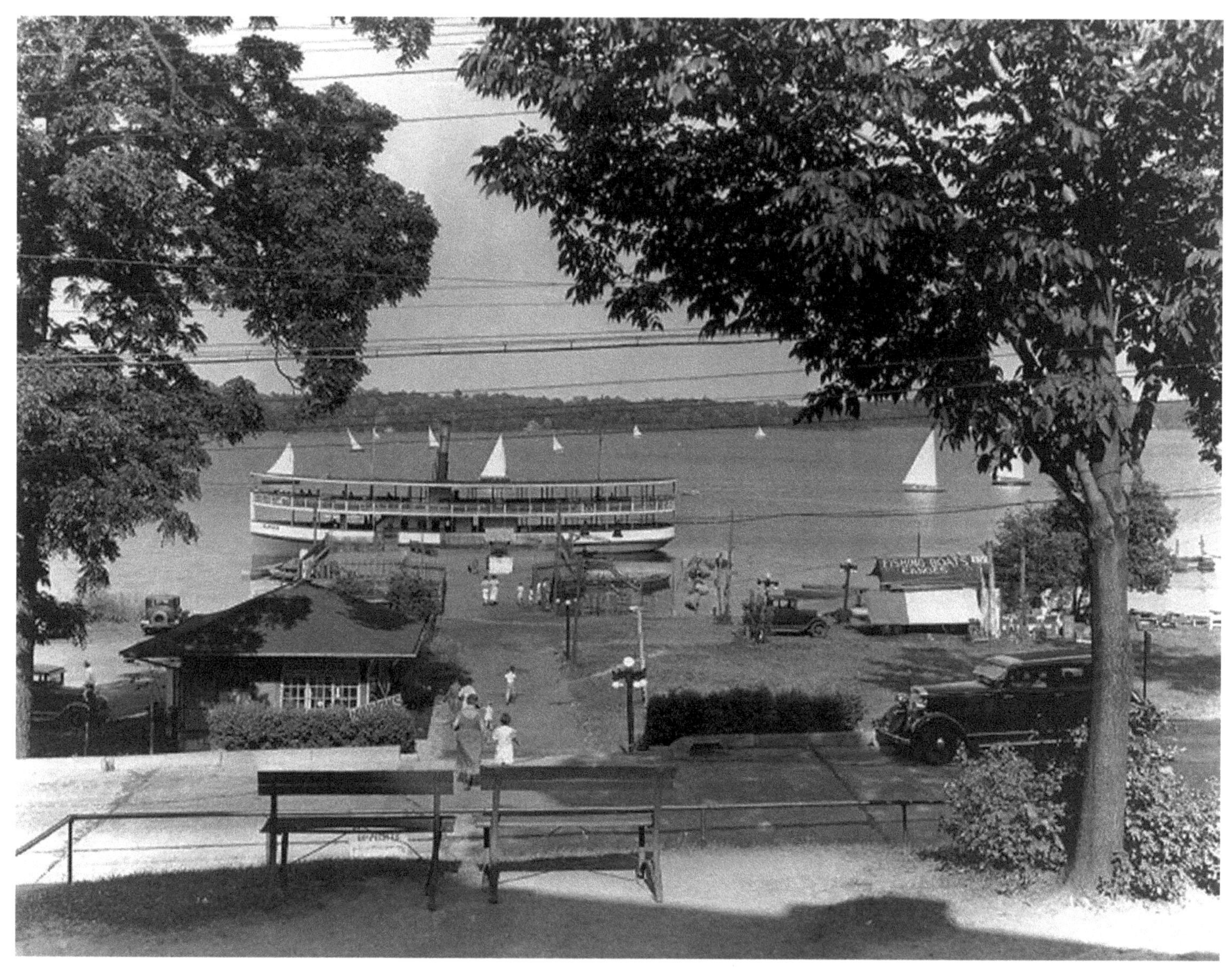

Ramona Park, at Reed's Lake.

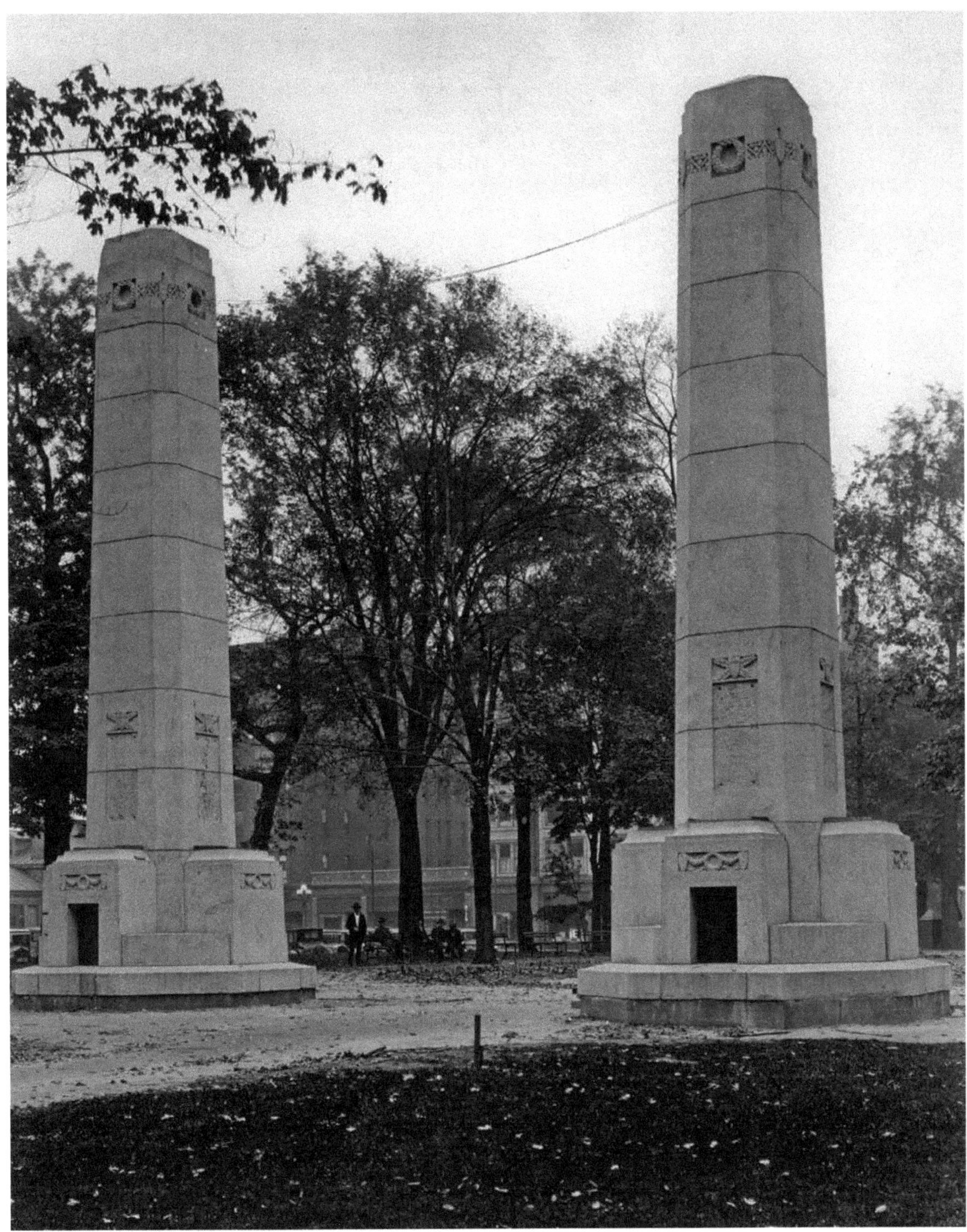

Inspired by Egyptian architecture, the Veteran's Memorial Pillars symbolize hope and freedom. The pillars were inscribed with the names of the dead from World War I. Later, the names of casualties from World War II and the Korean War were added.

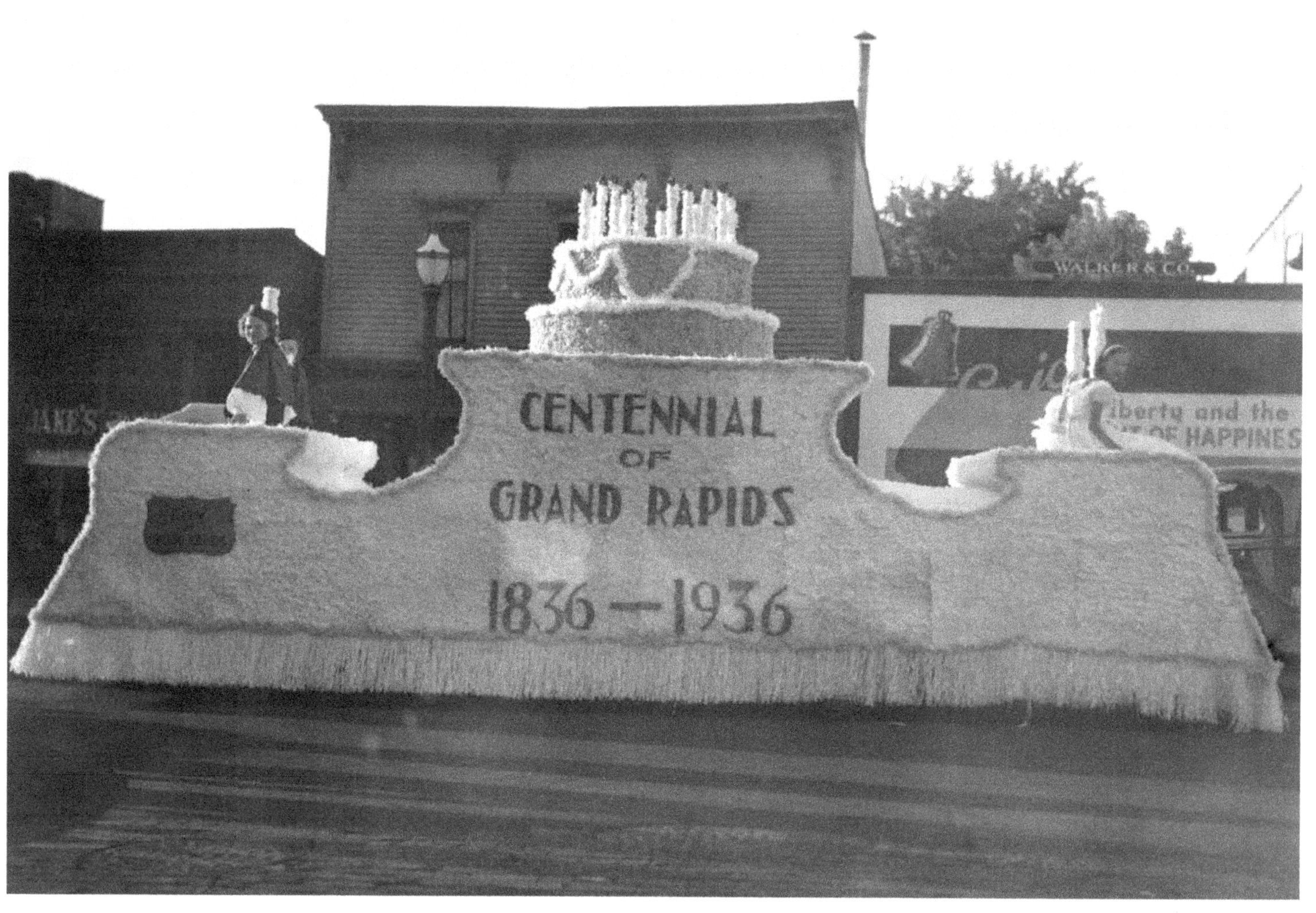

A float from the Grand Rapids Furniture Centennial Parade, which took place on July 7, 1936. The centennial commemorated the first furniture made commercially in Grand Rapids, which had taken place in 1836 in Deacon Haldane's workshop.

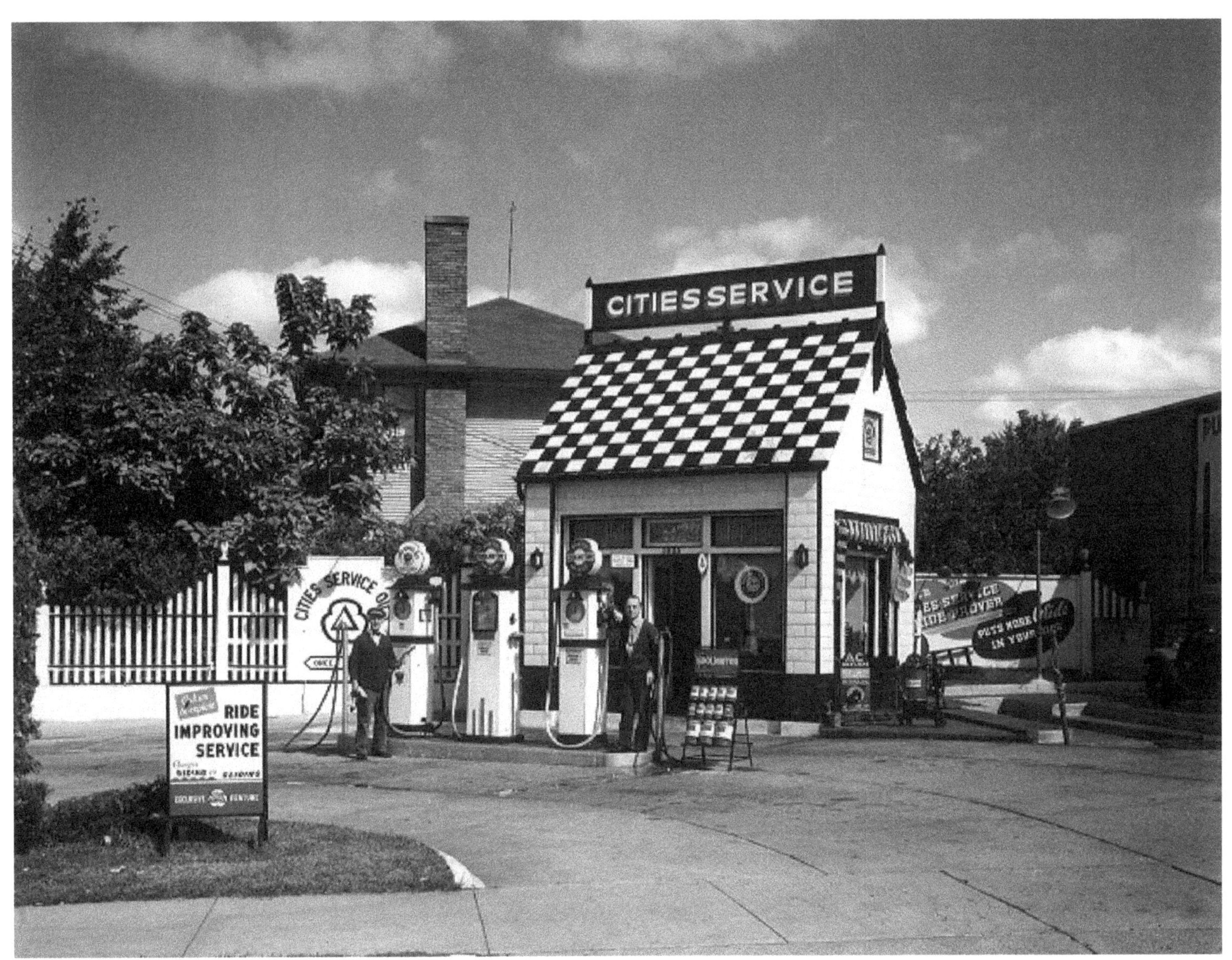

Cities Service gasoline station is open for business at Neland and Franklin SE.

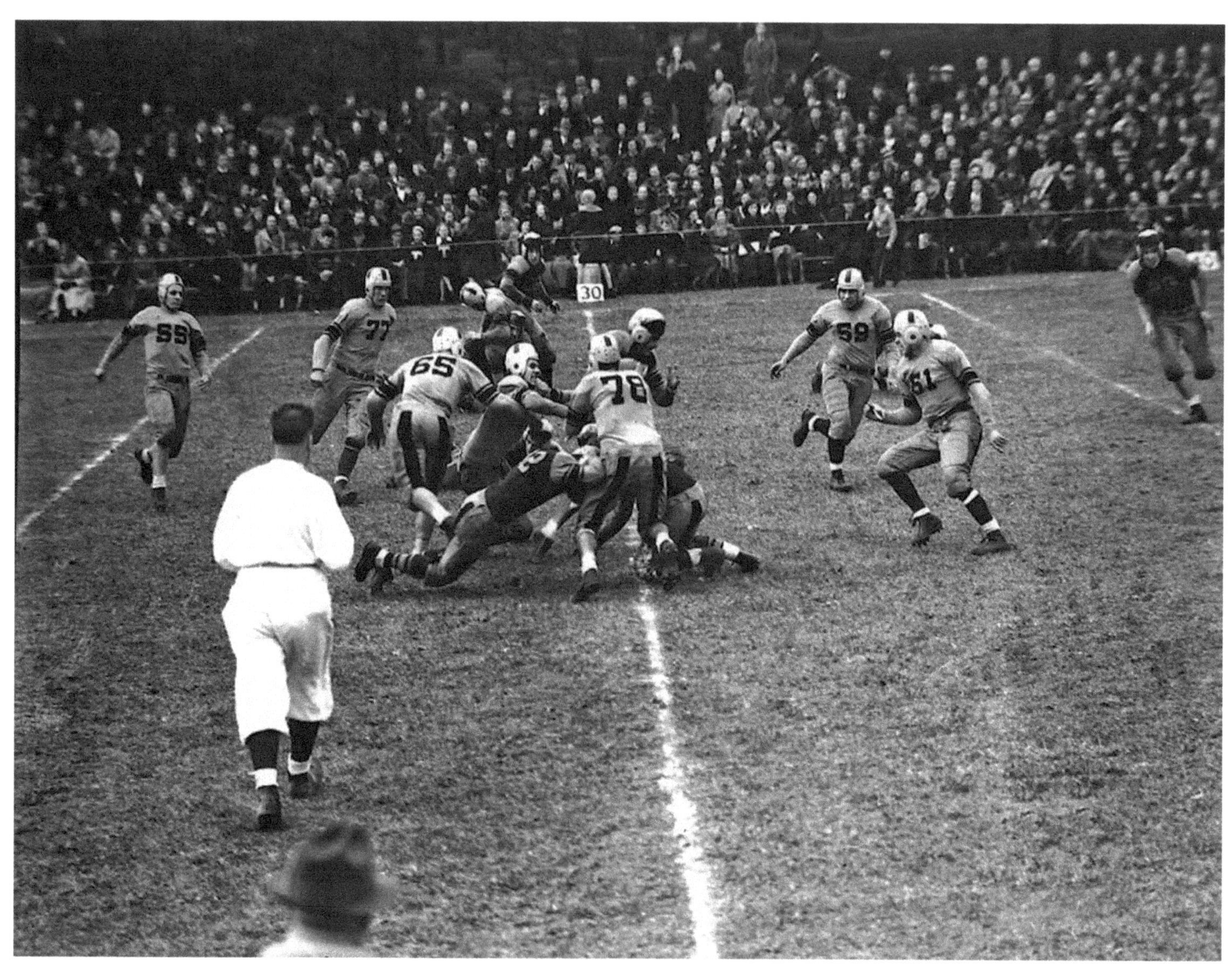

A Saturday afternoon football game between Central High School and Creston High School is in progress October 9, 1937. The game ended in a 6-6 tie.

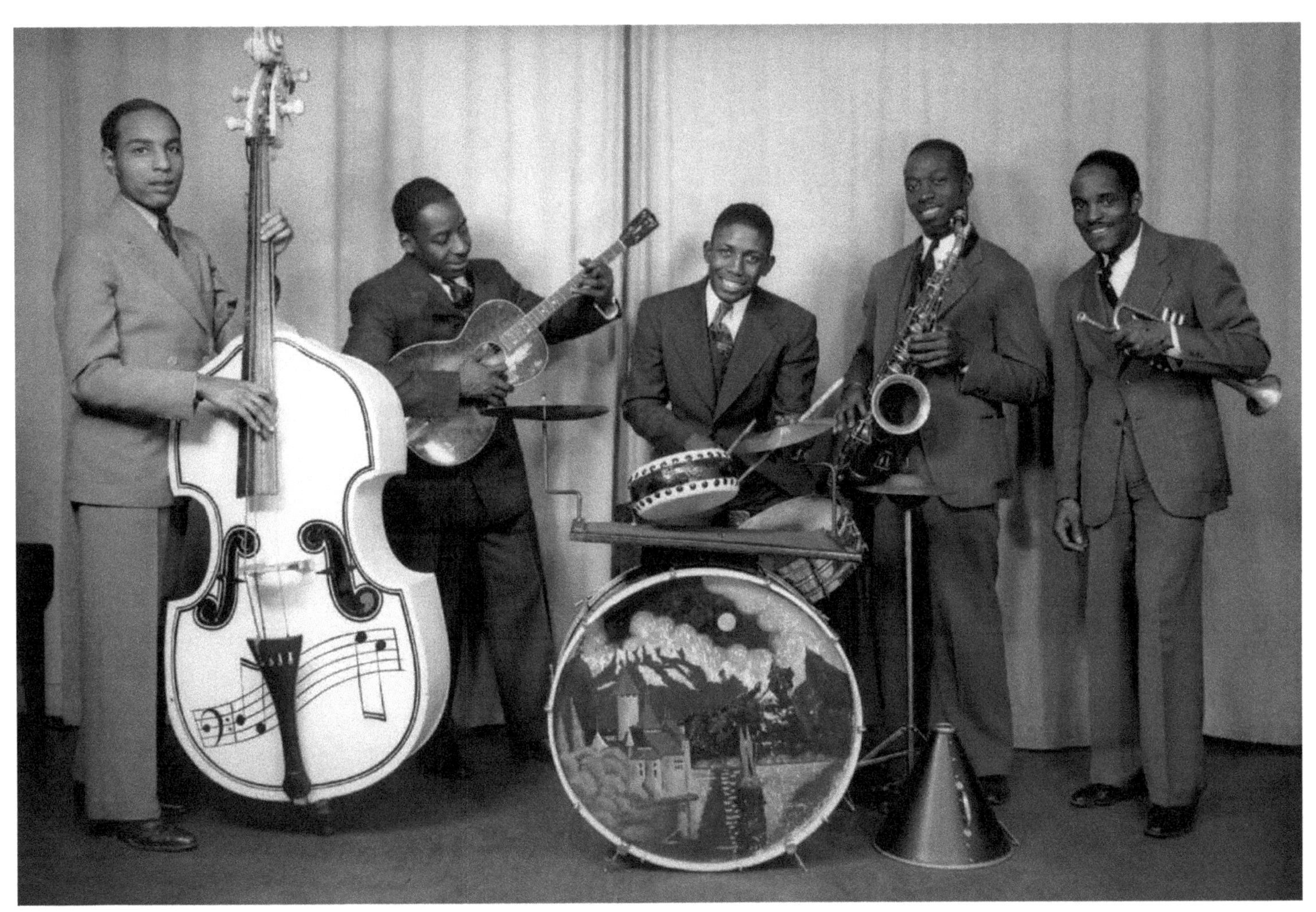

Five jazz band musicians pose for a publicity shot.

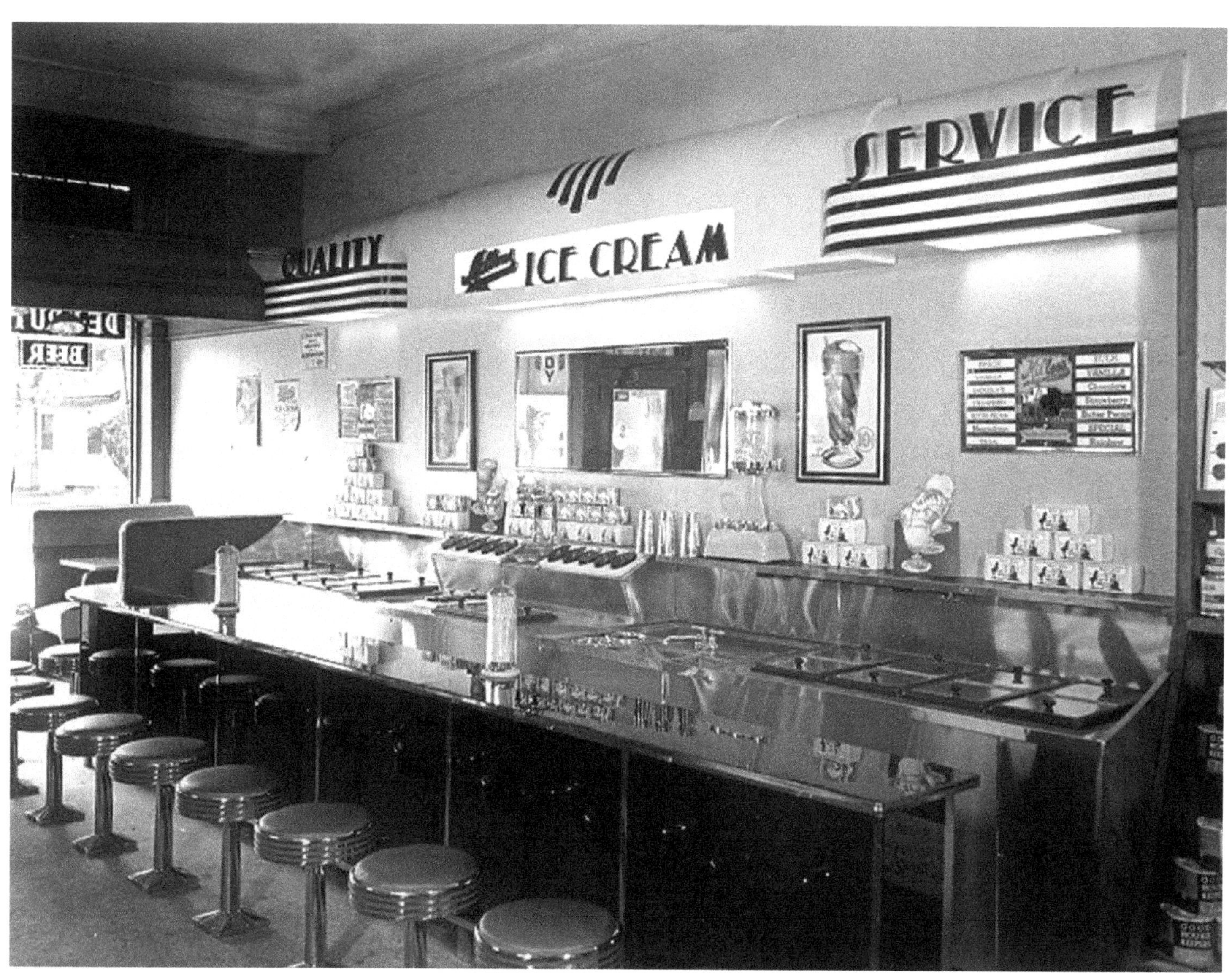

The soda fountain at DeKruil Drug Store, located at 944 Grandville Avenue SW. Anyone up for a malt?

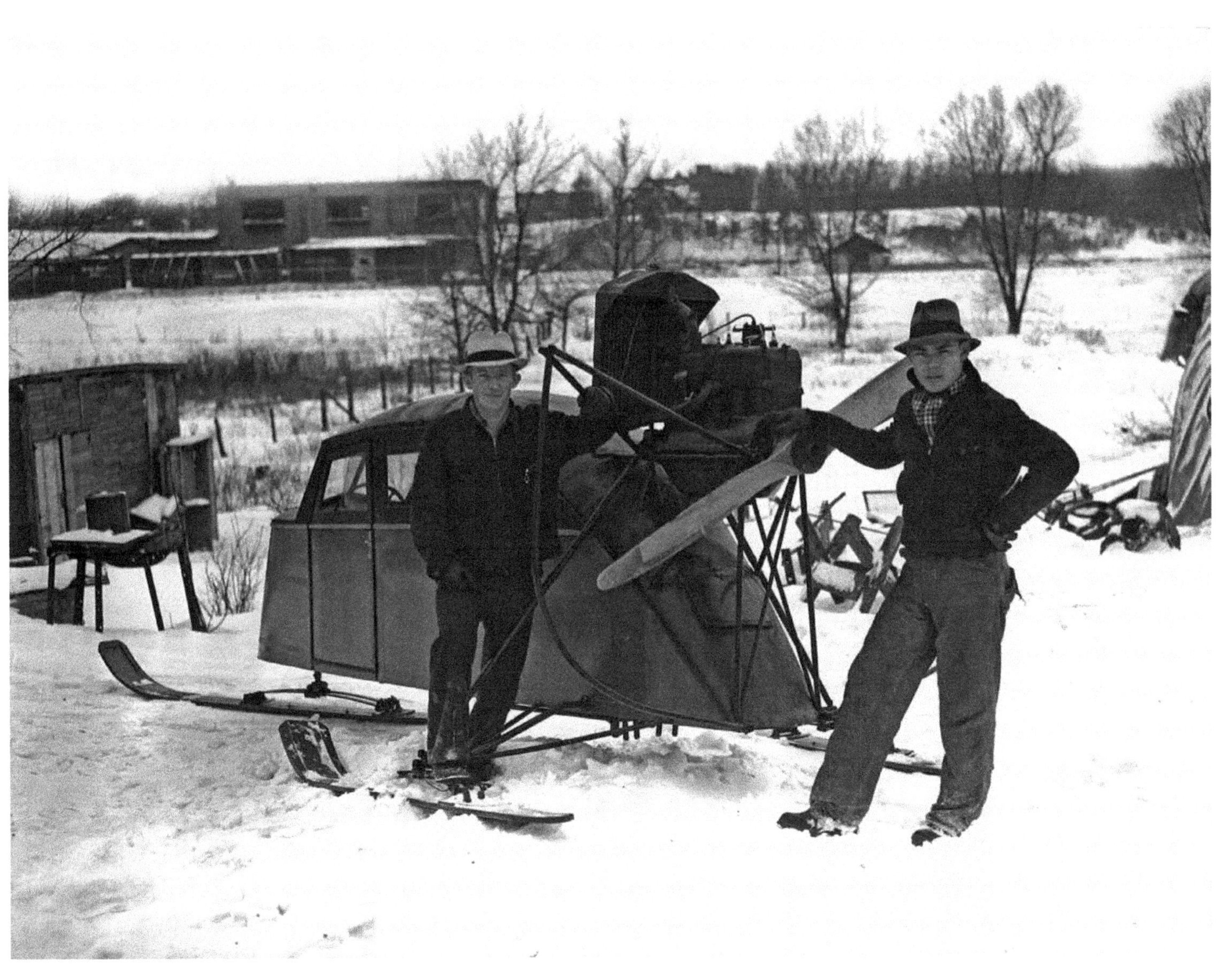

This "snow sedan" or "aero sled" was built by four young men, Alex, Water, and George Adastick, and Joe Svoboda. It was powered by a four-cylinder automobile motor equipped with a two-blade propeller. The body was made from aircraft plywood and seated two persons. The machine ran on three runners, or skis, about six feet long.

The F. W. Woolworth Co. dimestore was located at 169 Monroe, at the corner of Pearl Street.

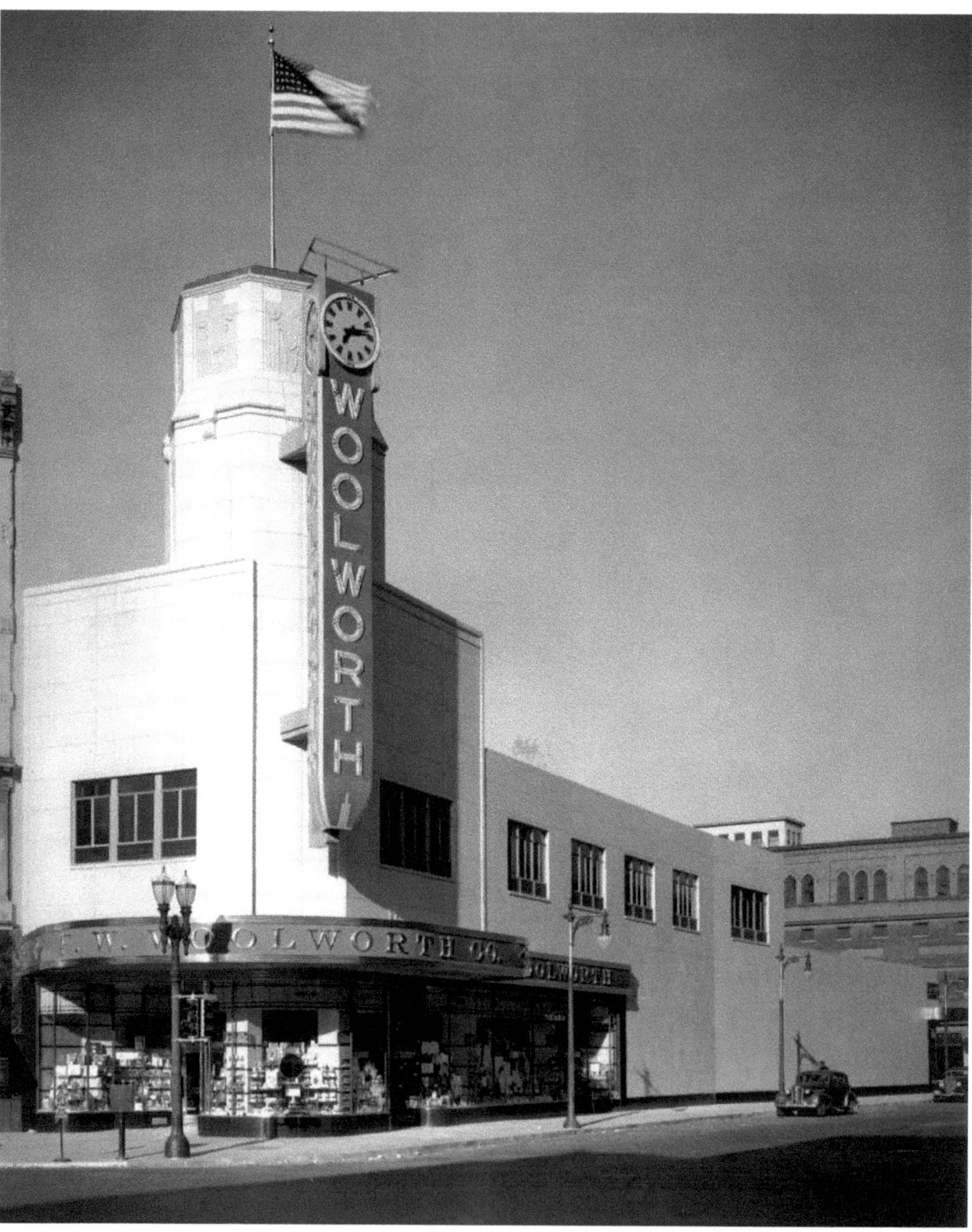

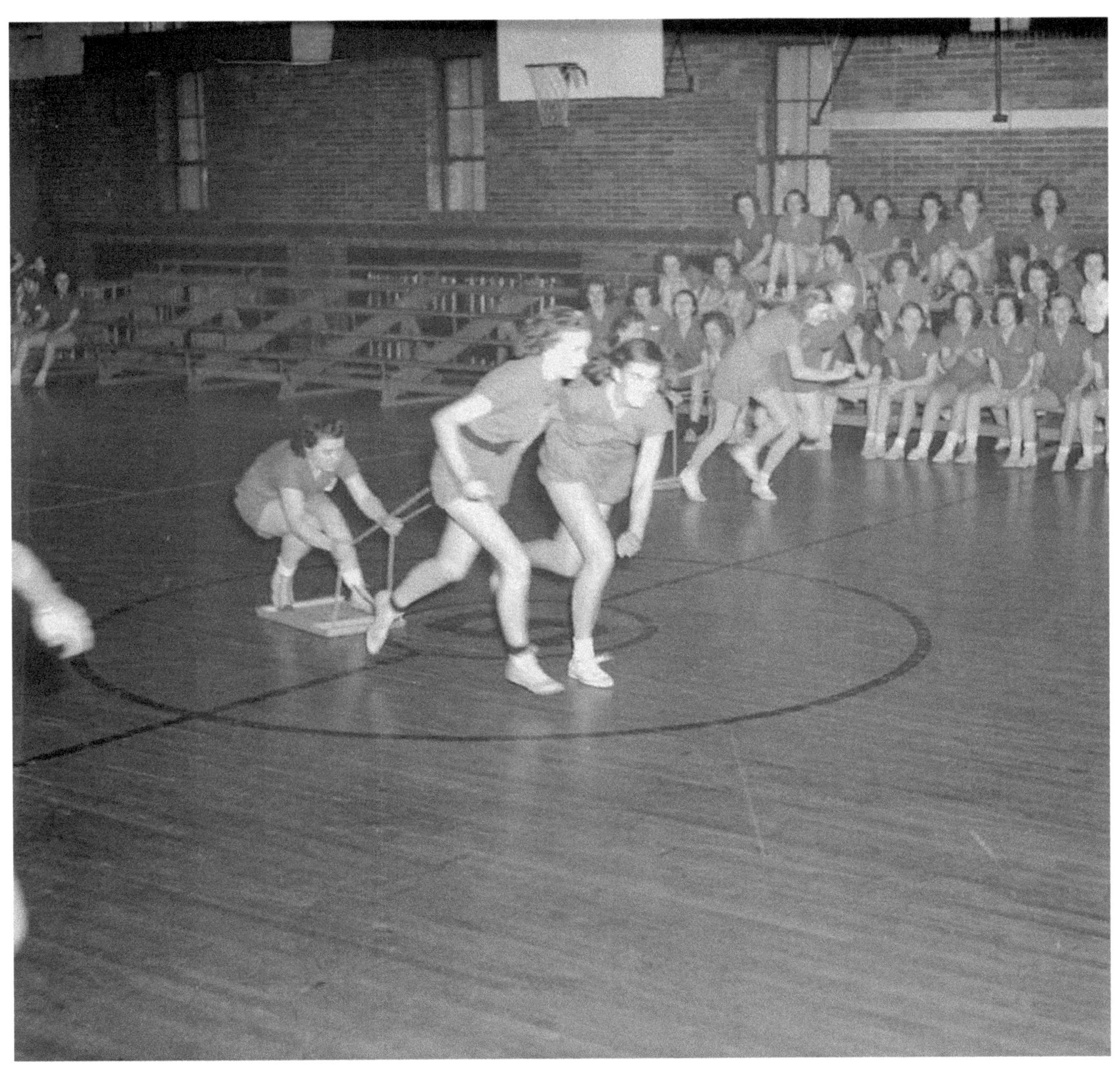

A diversified curriculum that included physical education was growing in importance at area high schools.

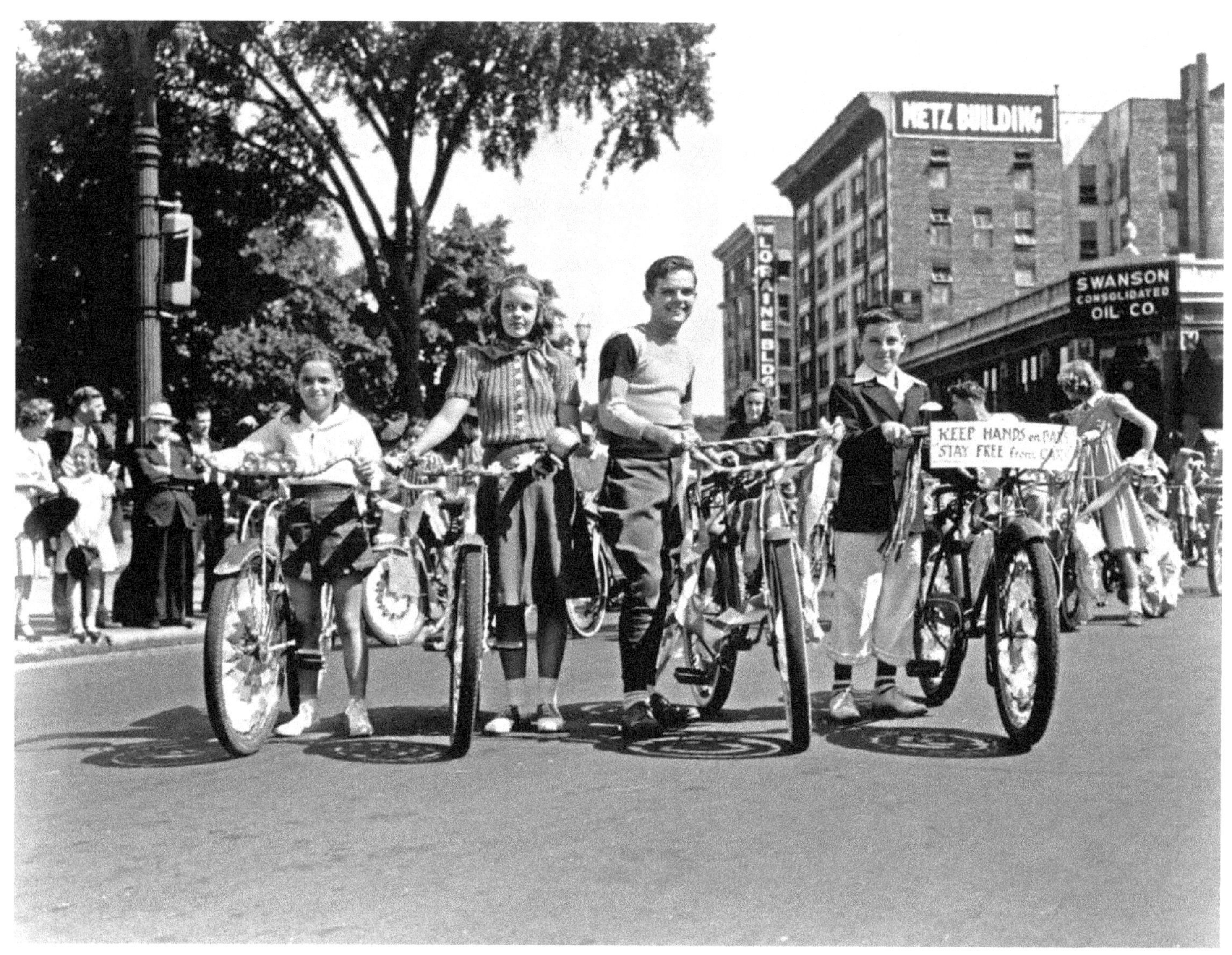

More than 200 children joined the Bike Safety Club parade on September 6, 1939.

World War II and Beyond

(1940–1969)

Before the start of World War II, future President of the United States Gerald R. Ford had finished high school as a local football star. After attending law school at the University of Michigan, he transferred to Yale to finish his law degree. He would go on to serve in World War II with the U.S. Navy.

Grand Rapids showed its patriotism during World War II in many ways. Women went to work at the steel plants, to offset a labor shortage created as men left for the frontlines overseas. Well-known furniture companies were converted to factories to support the war effort. Abbott and Costello, Bing Crosby, and Bob Hope were among the celebrities who made brief visits to the Furniture City to bolster morale. The nation celebrated victories and mourned the loss of loved ones.

During the war, citizens still found time for some fun. The All American Girls Baseball League found its way to West Michigan in these years, and Grand Rapids was one of only ten cities to have its own team—the Chicks. The team won the titles of Play-Off Champion and League Champion.

As soldiers returned home following the war, many women left their jobs to return to family life. An intense housing shortage unfolded, which gave rise to tents, Quonset huts, and prefab houses as temporary shelter for some families. In the years ahead, Grand Rapids would return to peacetime prosperity and be well-noted for downtown shopping. Families could also visit the Civic Auditorium to watch a play or go dancing, or go to the Speedrome to watch car races.

Over the years, Harry S Truman, John F. Kennedy, and Richard M. Nixon all made stops in Grand Rapids during their presidential campaigns. Since its charter back in 1850, Grand Rapids had aged. A period of controversial urban renewal began in the 1960s. Many historic buildings were destroyed in the name of progress, including Old City Hall. In their place arose Interstate highways, parking lots, and automobile traffic.

To symbolize the rebirth of the city and its dedication to the arts, Alexander Calder was asked to create a unique piece of art in 1969. The dedication of his abstract *LaGrand Vitesse* took place on June 14.

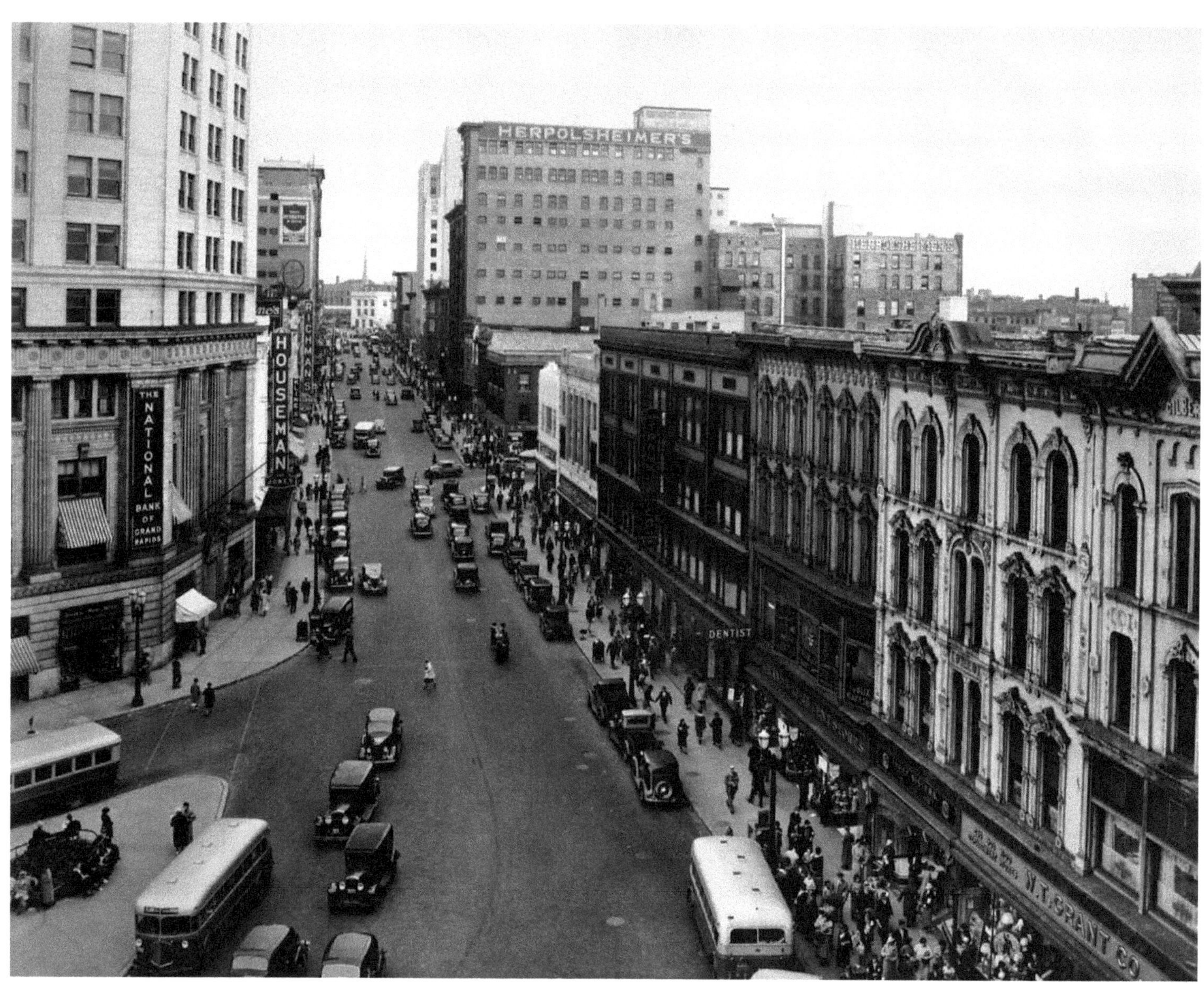

Monroe Avenue SE from Campau Square.

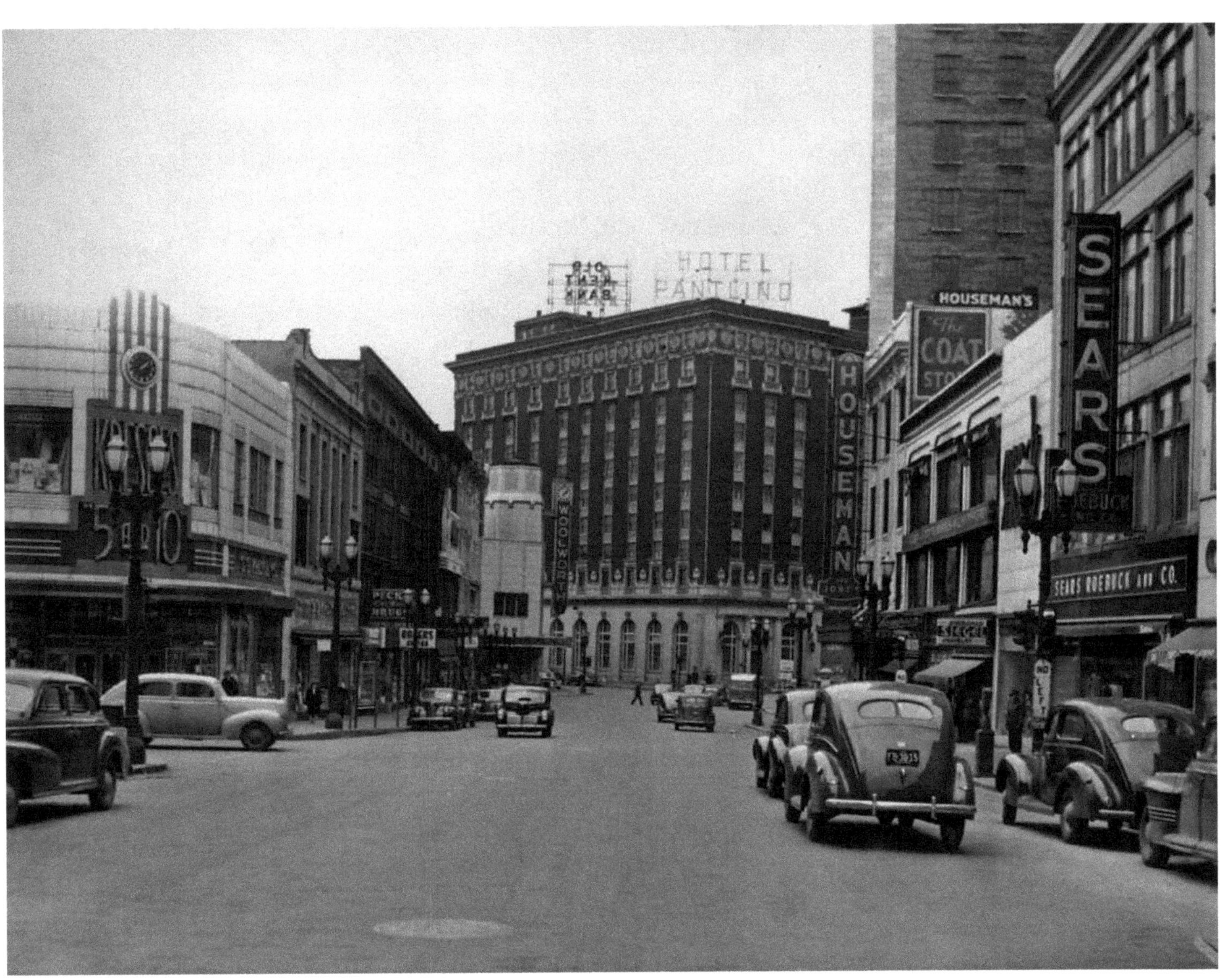

Monroe Avenue NW facing the Pantlind Hotel in the background. Kresge's Five and Dime is on the left, and Sears, Siegel and Houseman's are on the right.

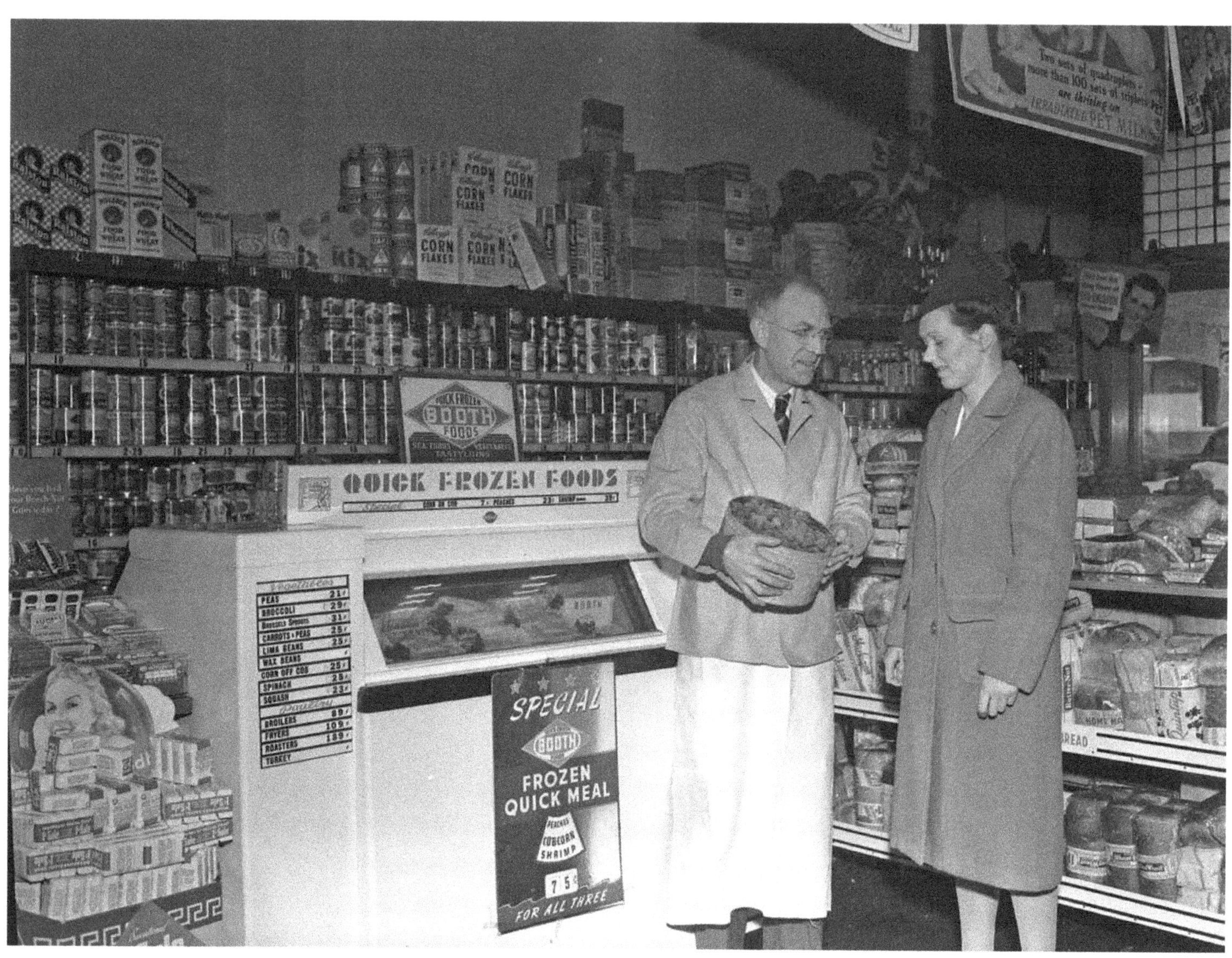

Interior view of Luidberg's Grocery Store, where "corn off cob" is a quarter, and Woodbury soap is on sale for a penny.

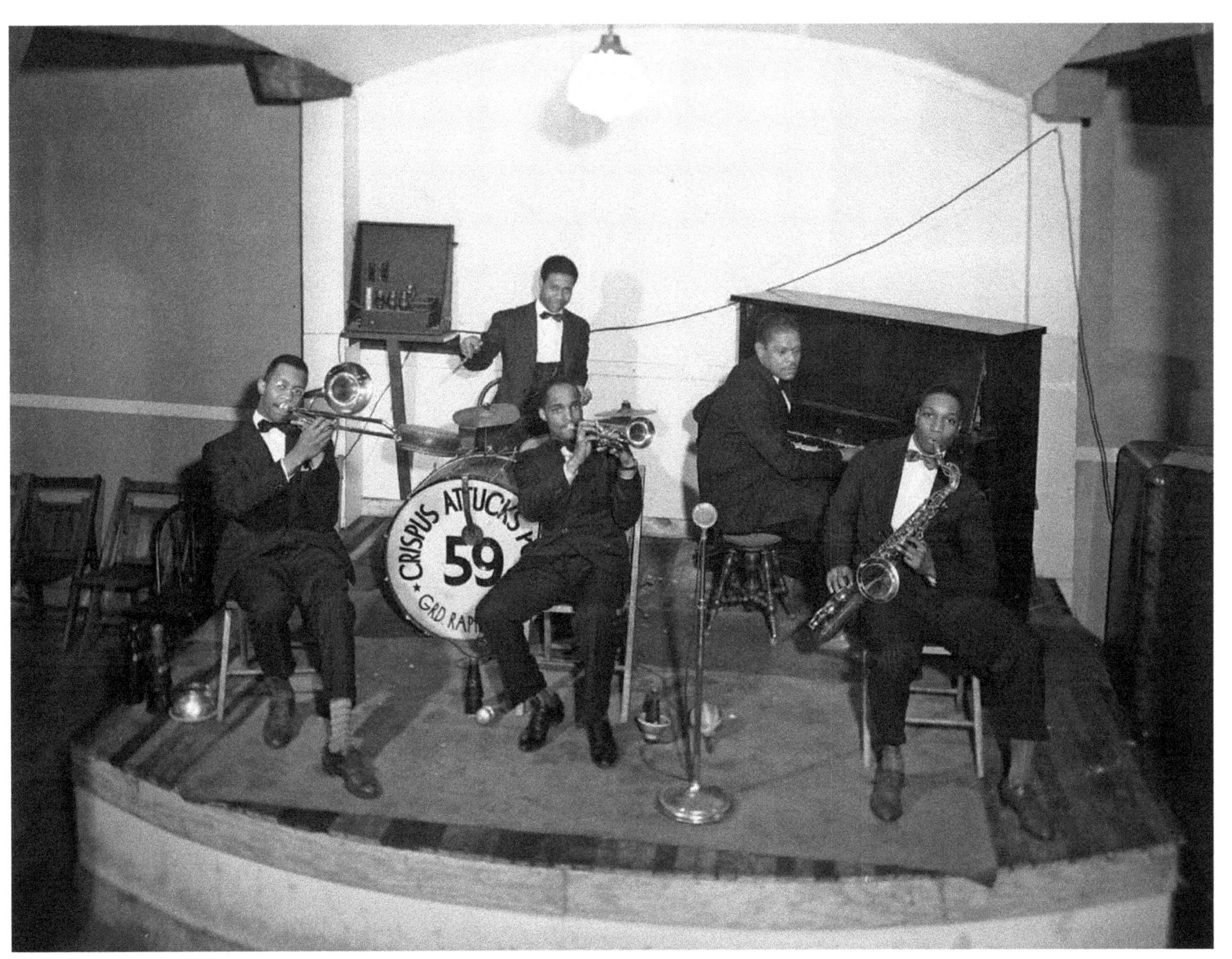

A concert is underway at the Crispus Attucks Post of the American Legion, located at 245 Commerce SW.

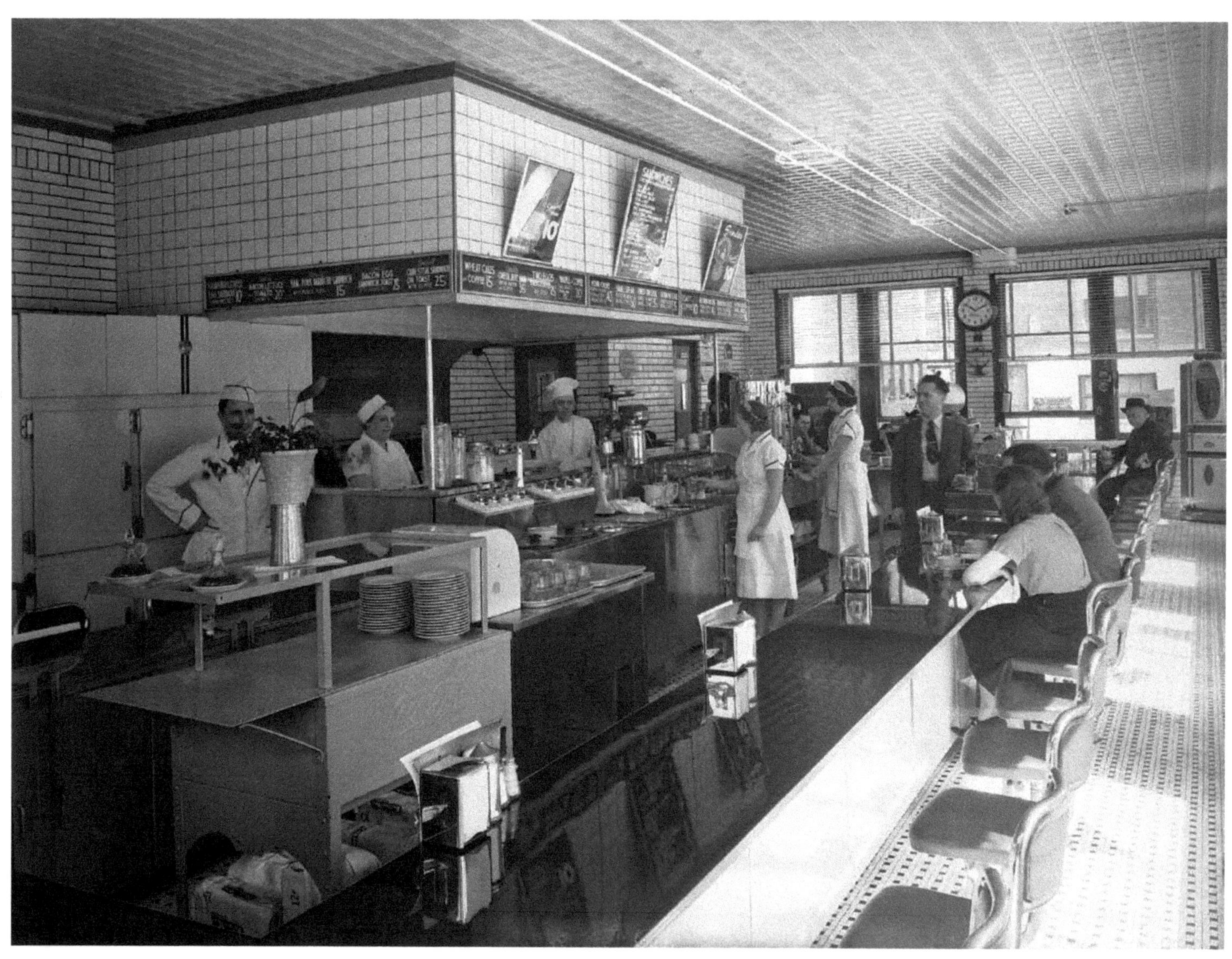

Inside the Banquet Bar-B-Q restaurant, located at 33 Sheldon NE, specials of the day include a bacon, lettuce, and tomato sandwich for twenty cents.

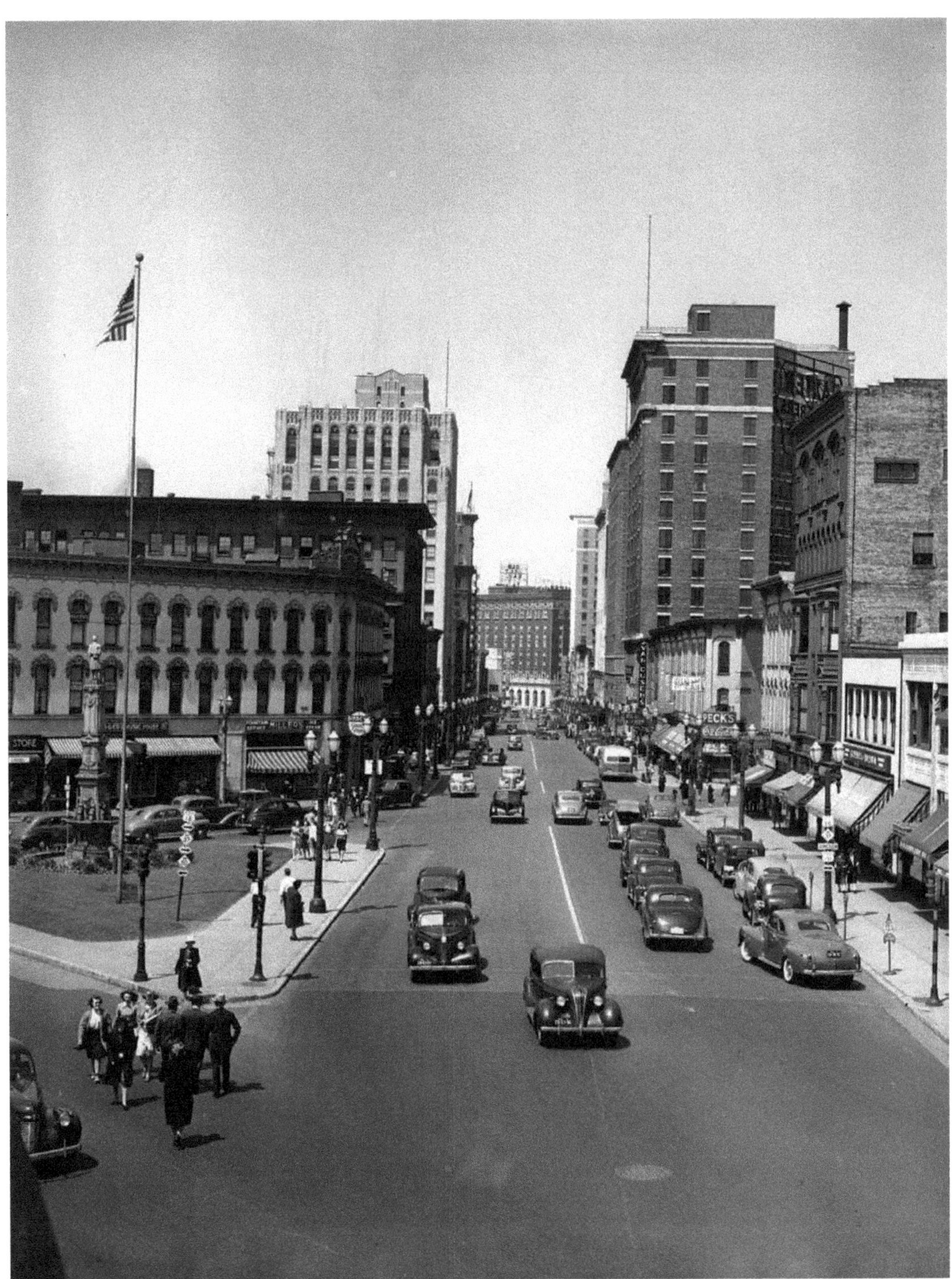

Monroe Avenue as it appeared in 1941. The Civil War Monument is visible to the left.

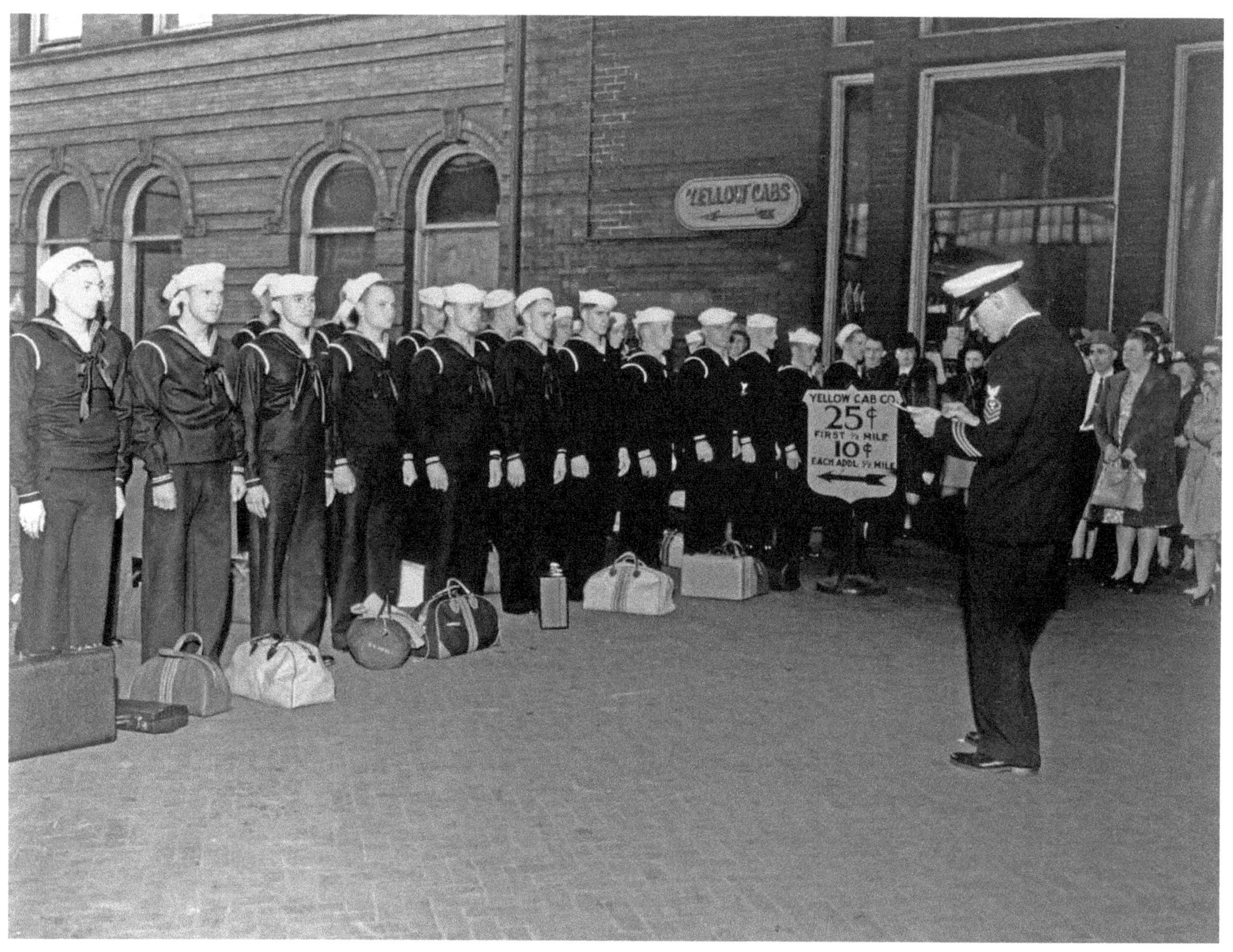

Naval Reservists stand at attention outside Union Station, awaiting their seat assignments.

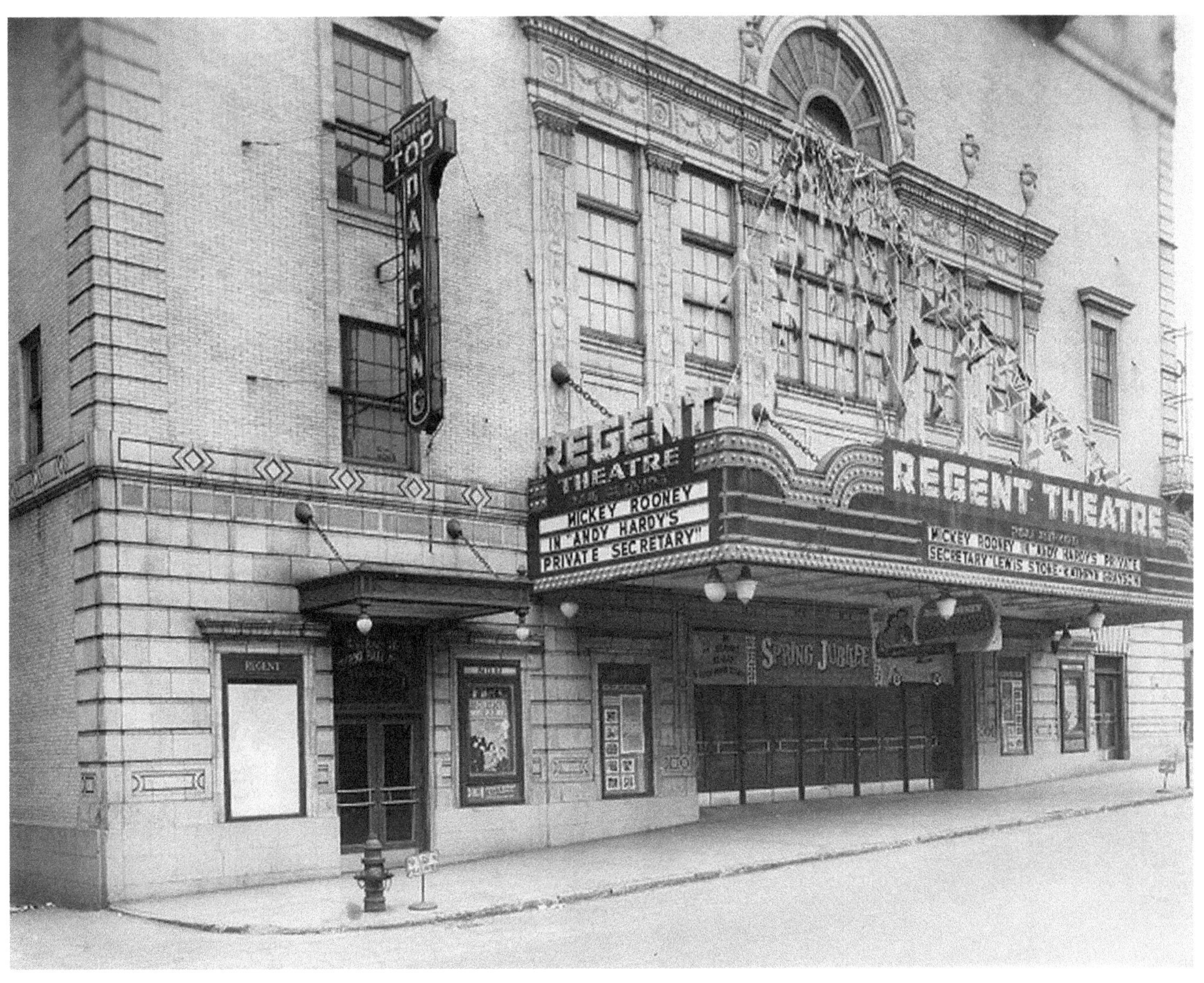

In 1941, Mickey Rooney stars in *Andy Hardy's Private Secretary* playing at the Regent Theatre. The lavishly appointed theater opened in 1923 boasting a rooftop garden for dancing.

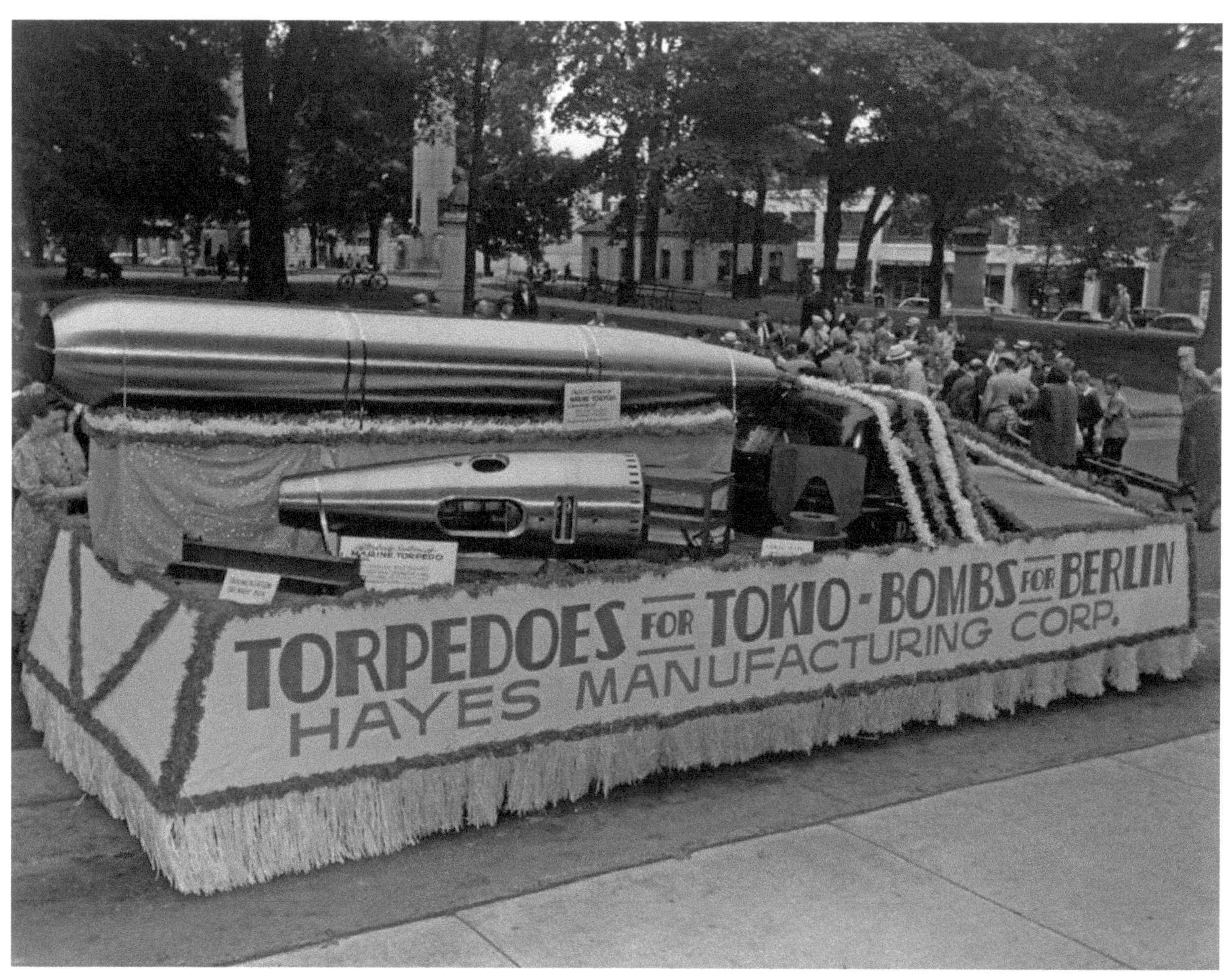

In a parade featuring locally made war products, this float represents Hayes Manufacturing. On display are a marine torpedo, a fragmentation grenade box, and a torpedo tail fin.

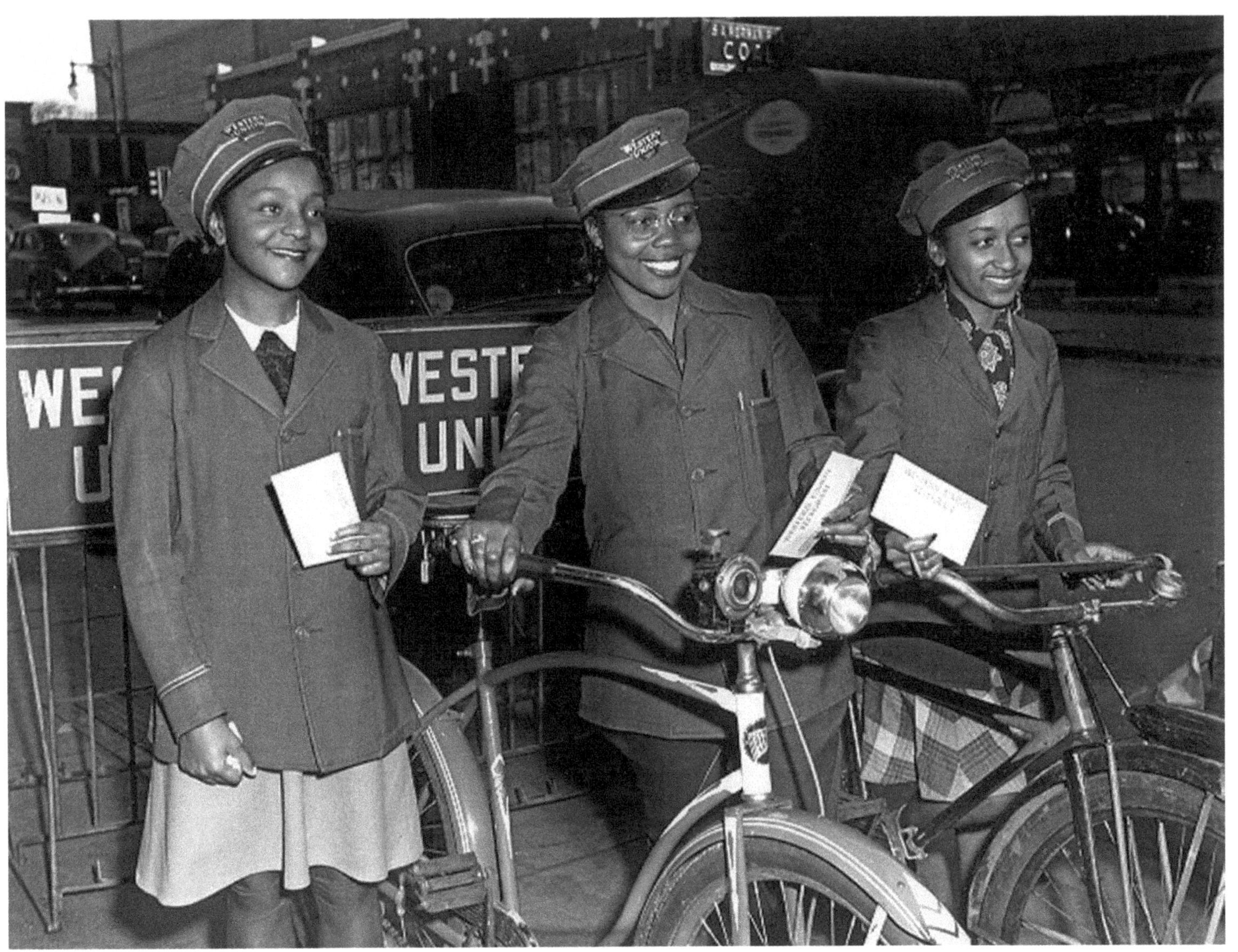

During World War II, girls were now able to work jobs previously held only by boys. These Western Union messengers are Earlene Robey, Marjorie Sam, and Doris Leah.

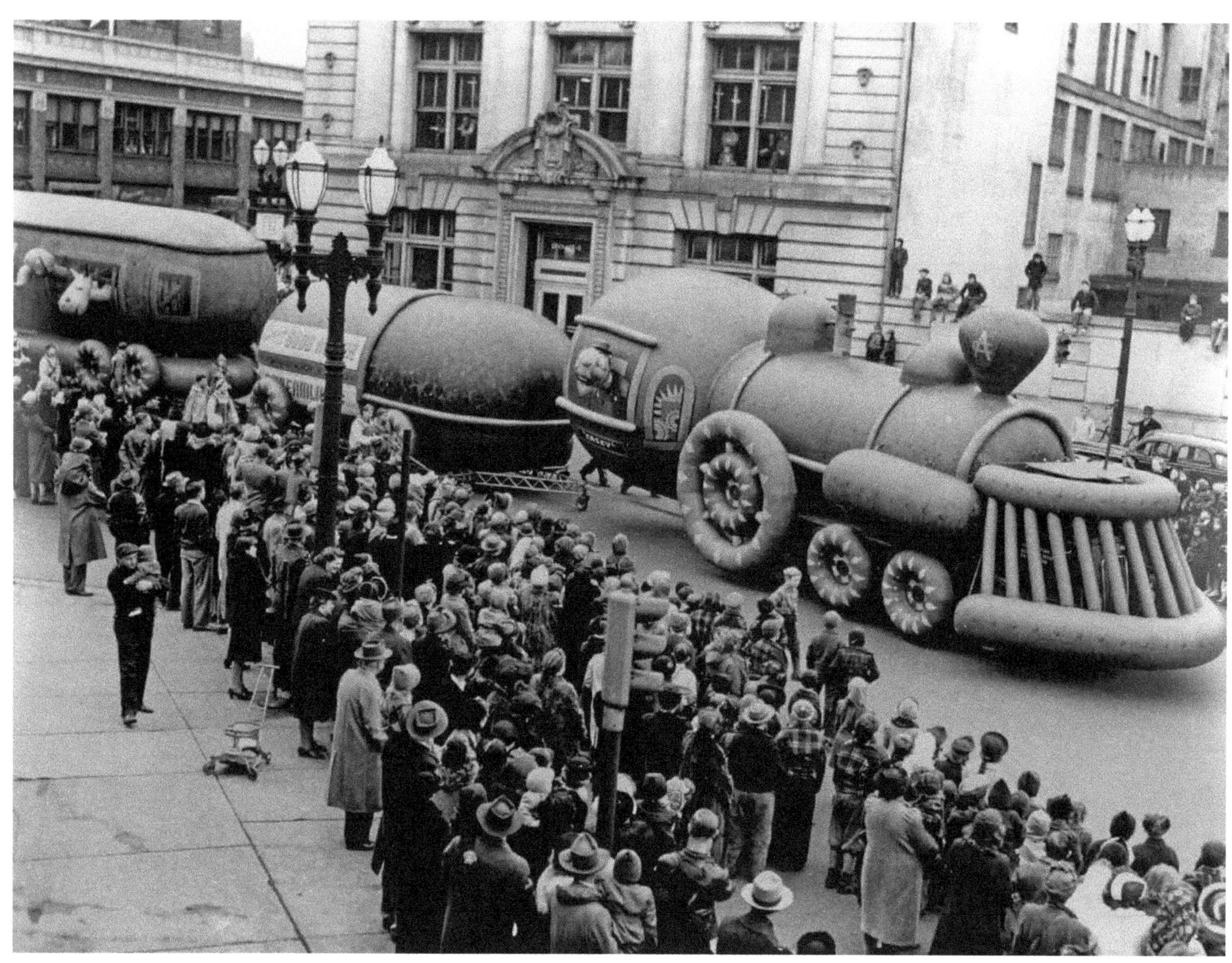

Children of all ages attended the annual Santa Claus parade sponsored by Wurzburg's Department Store.

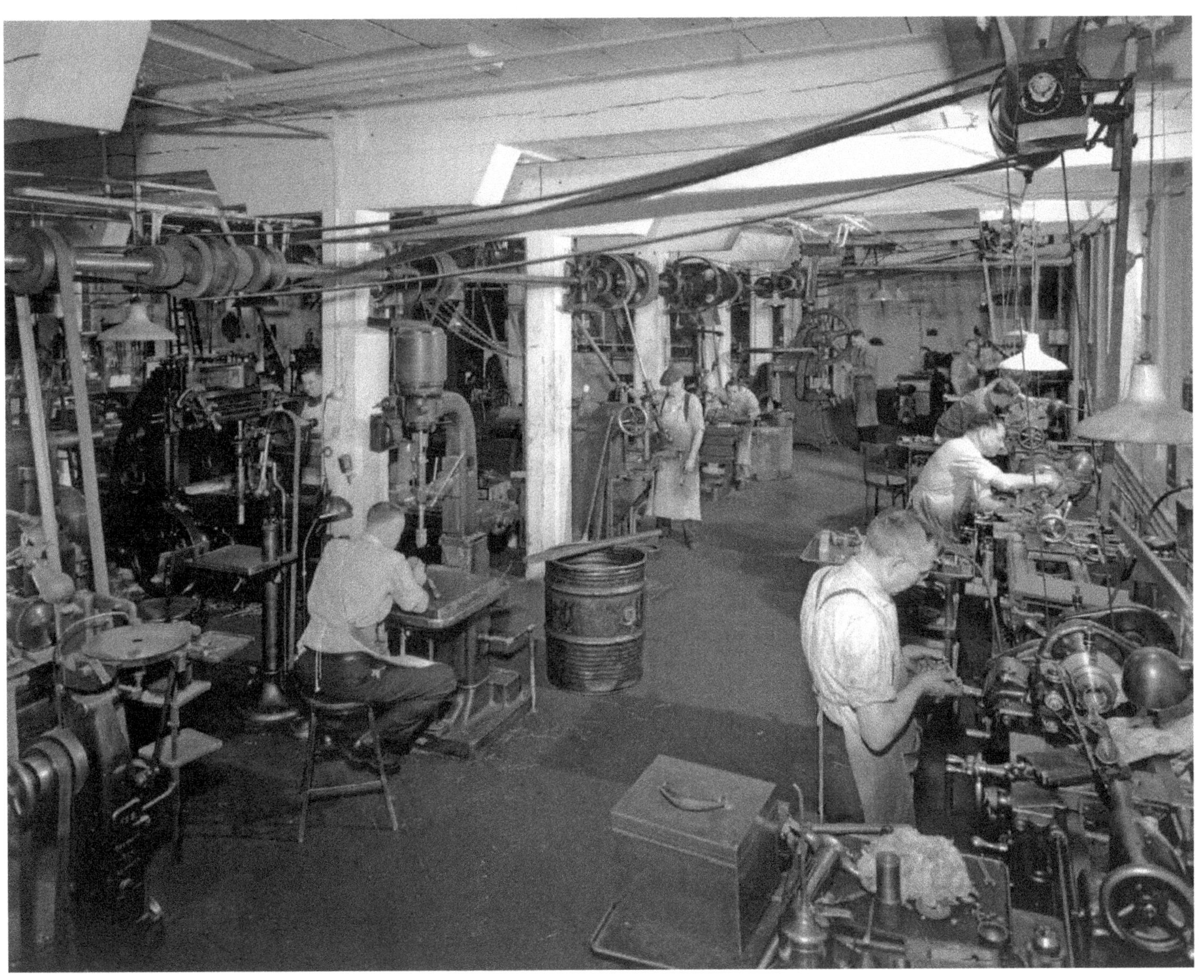

An interior view of the Bissell Carpet Sweeper factory, located at 210-218 Erie NW. Bissell began in 1876 and is still helping keep America clean.

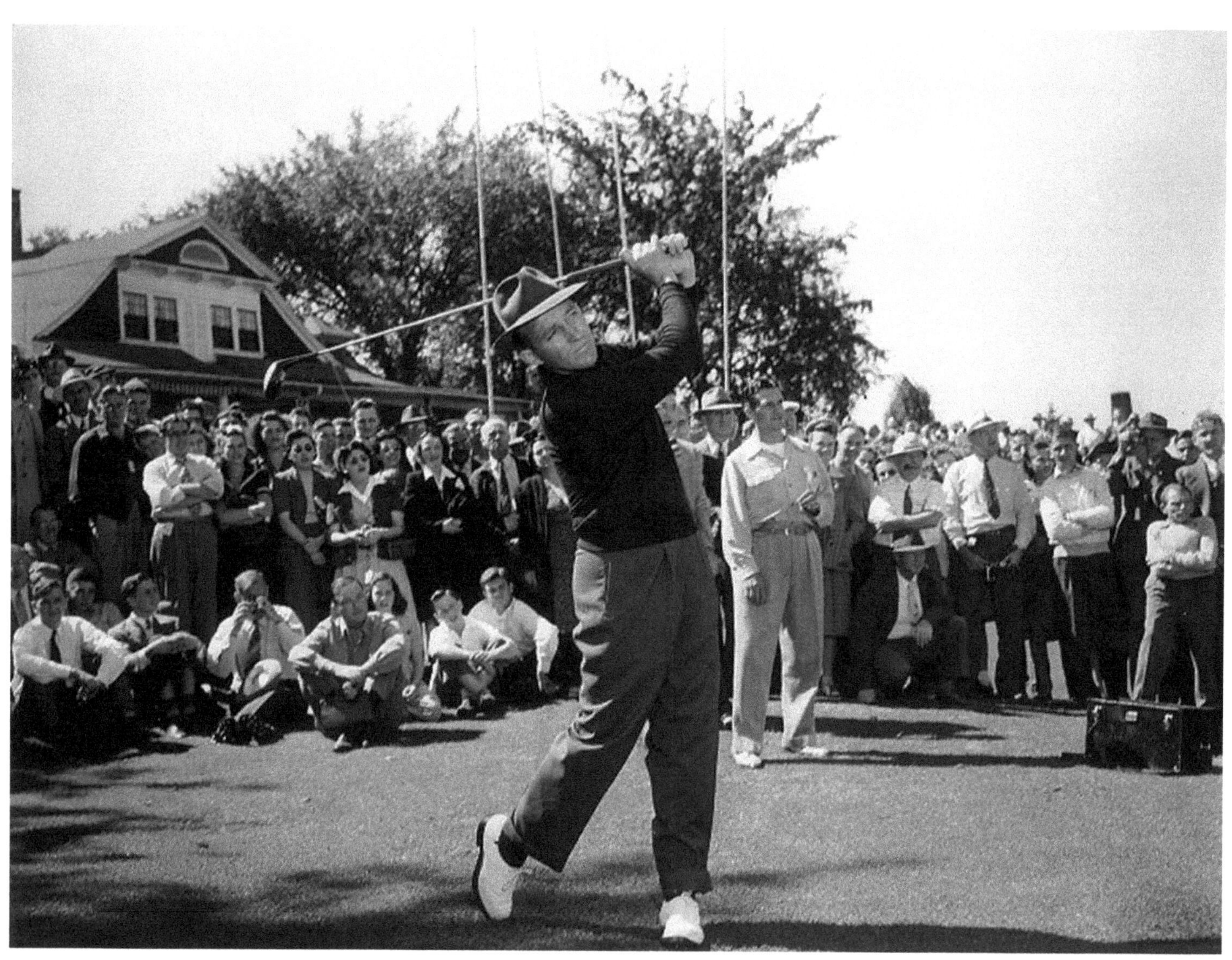

Bing Crosby takes a swing while golfing at the Kent Country Club. Crosby was playing in a benefit for the USO and Red Cross.

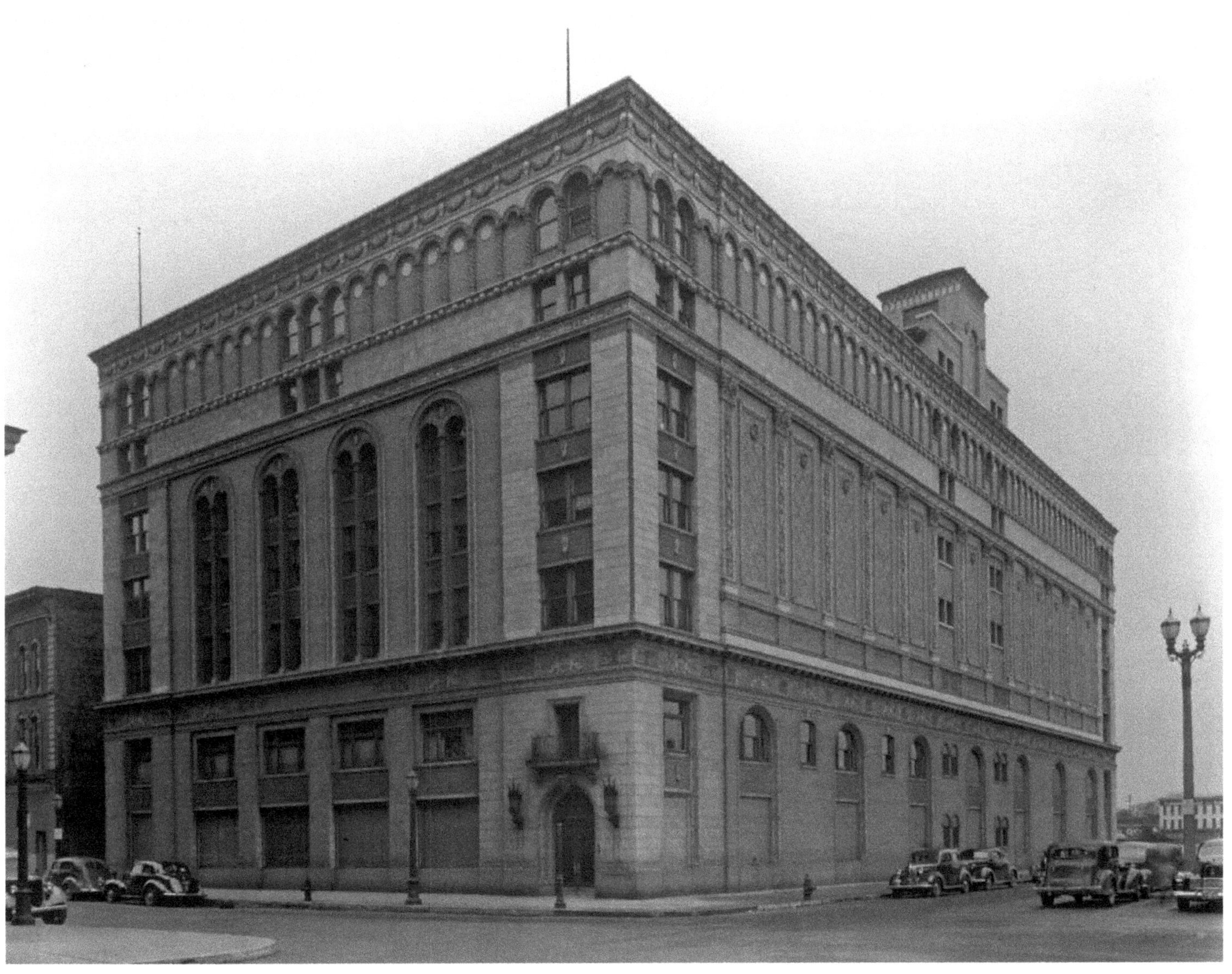

Several buildings, including the Pantlind Hotel, Civic Auditorium, and the Fine Arts Building, were converted during World War II into barracks, mess halls, classrooms, offices, and officer's quarters for the Weather Training School of the Army Air Forces Technical Training Command. Classes began in January 1943. By September, the school had closed.

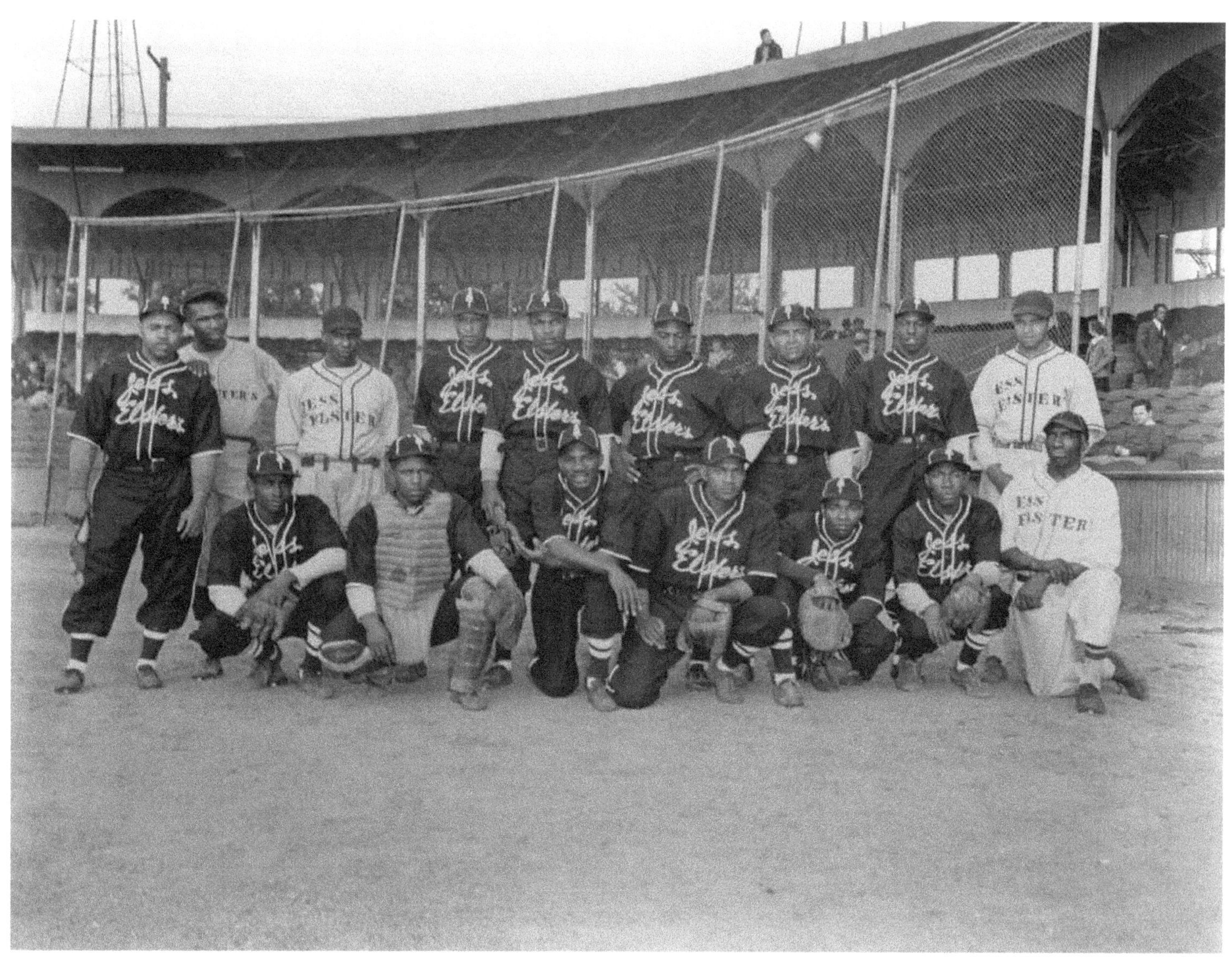

Jess Elster and his team, the Colored Athletics.

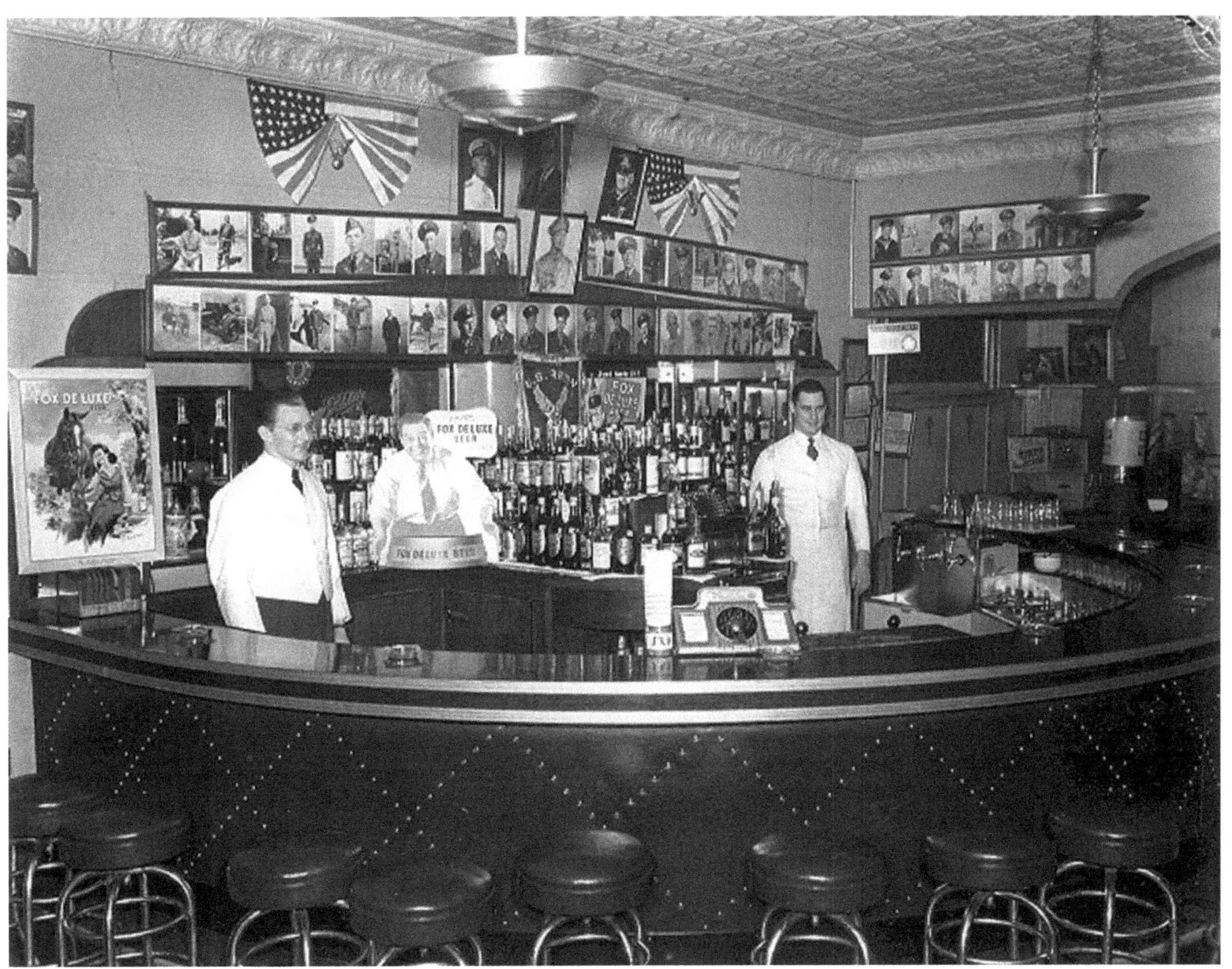

Brothers George (left) and John (right) Broekema, owners of the Silver Cloud Tavern, are shown honoring local soldiers and promoting Fox Deluxe Beer.

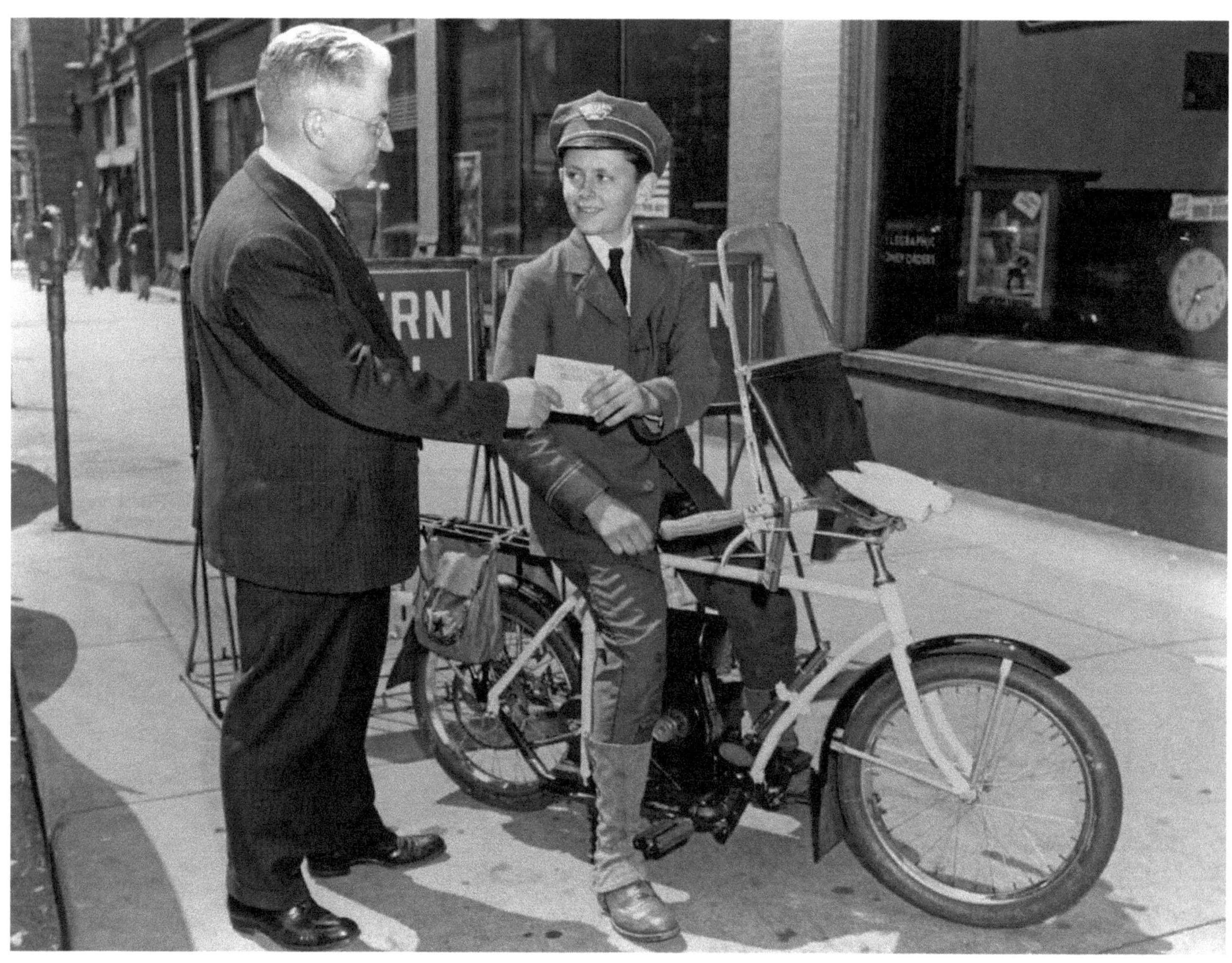

Harold Foote, with his motorized bicycle, prepares to deliver a Western Union telegram being given to him by C. E. Carpenter.

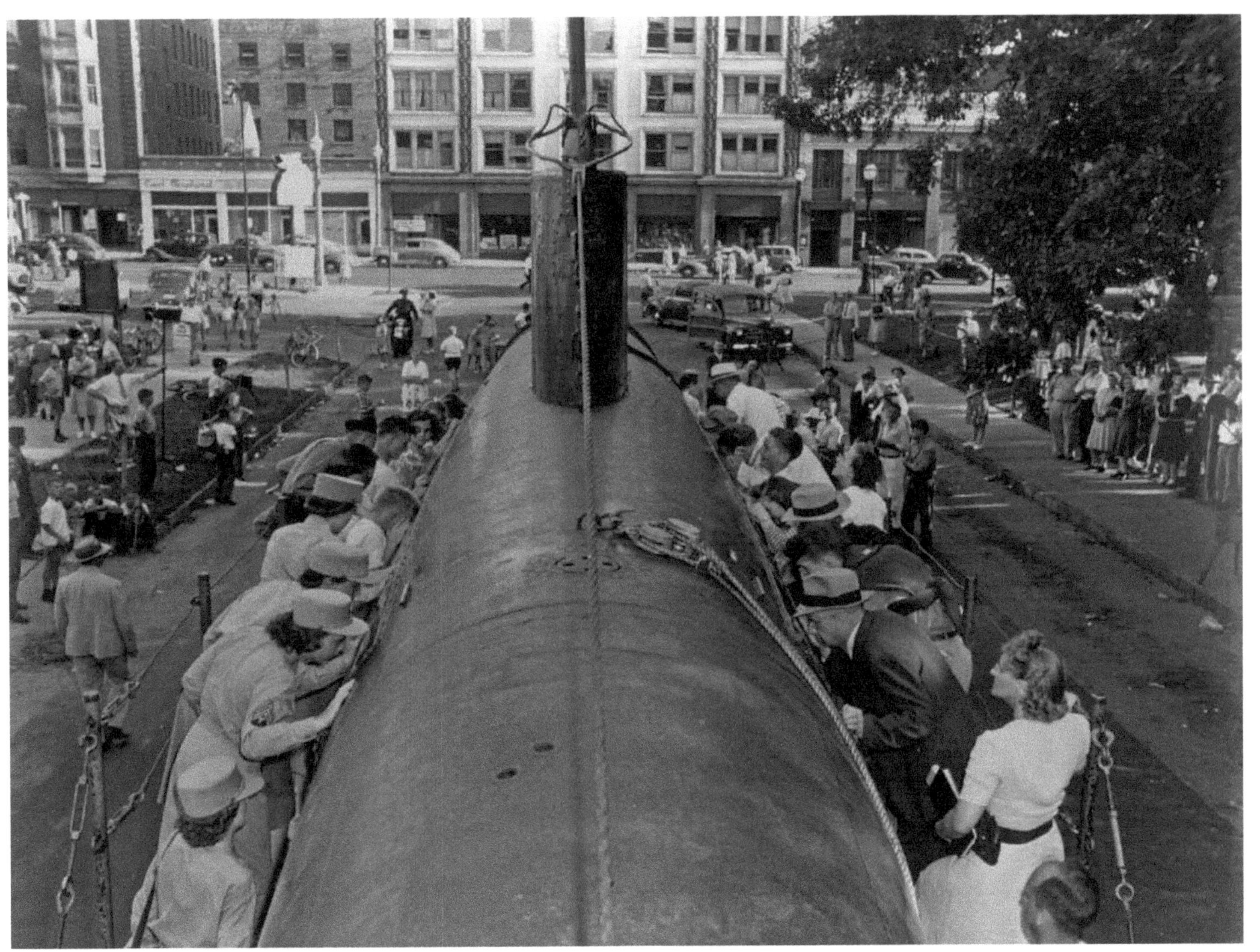

As it toured the nation, this Japanese two-man submarine, captured at Pearl Harbor, helped raise funds for the war effort.

As an inspector for the Robert W. Irwin Company, Clara Bush made sure stocks were produced to specific standards. Bush sought work with the company after her brother was killed in action in the South Pacific.

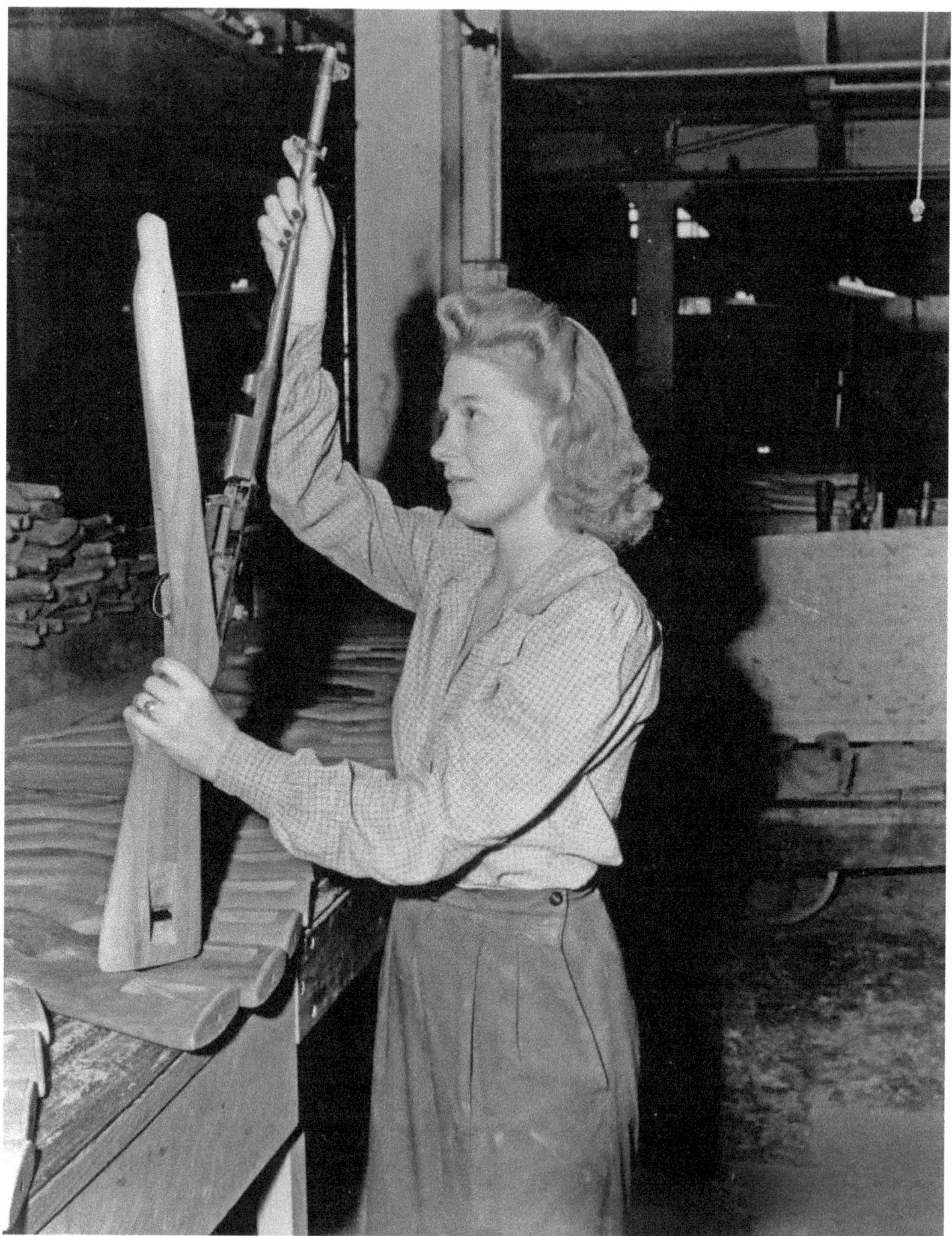

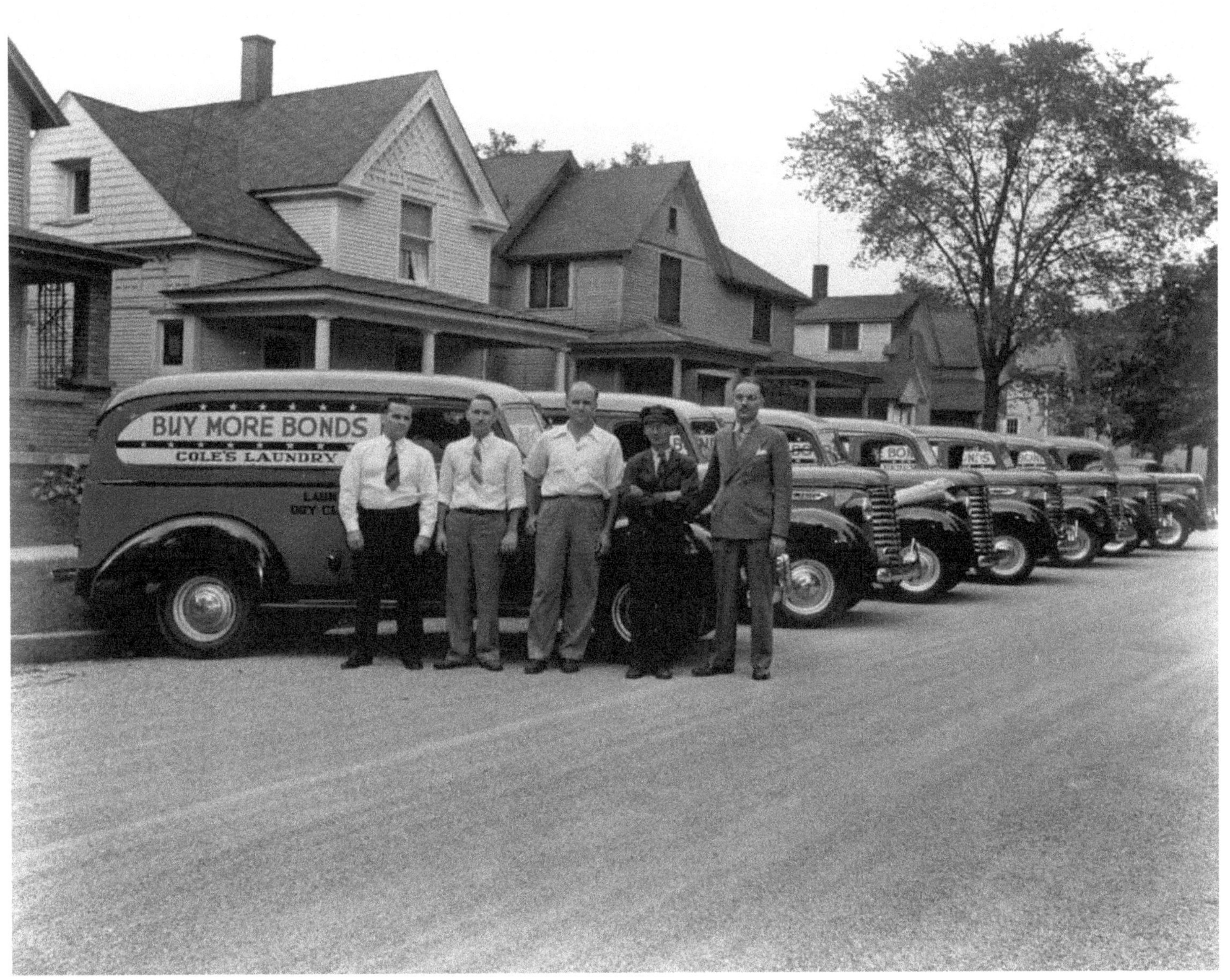

Cole's Laundry contributed to the war bond effort by advertising war bond sales on their delivery trucks.

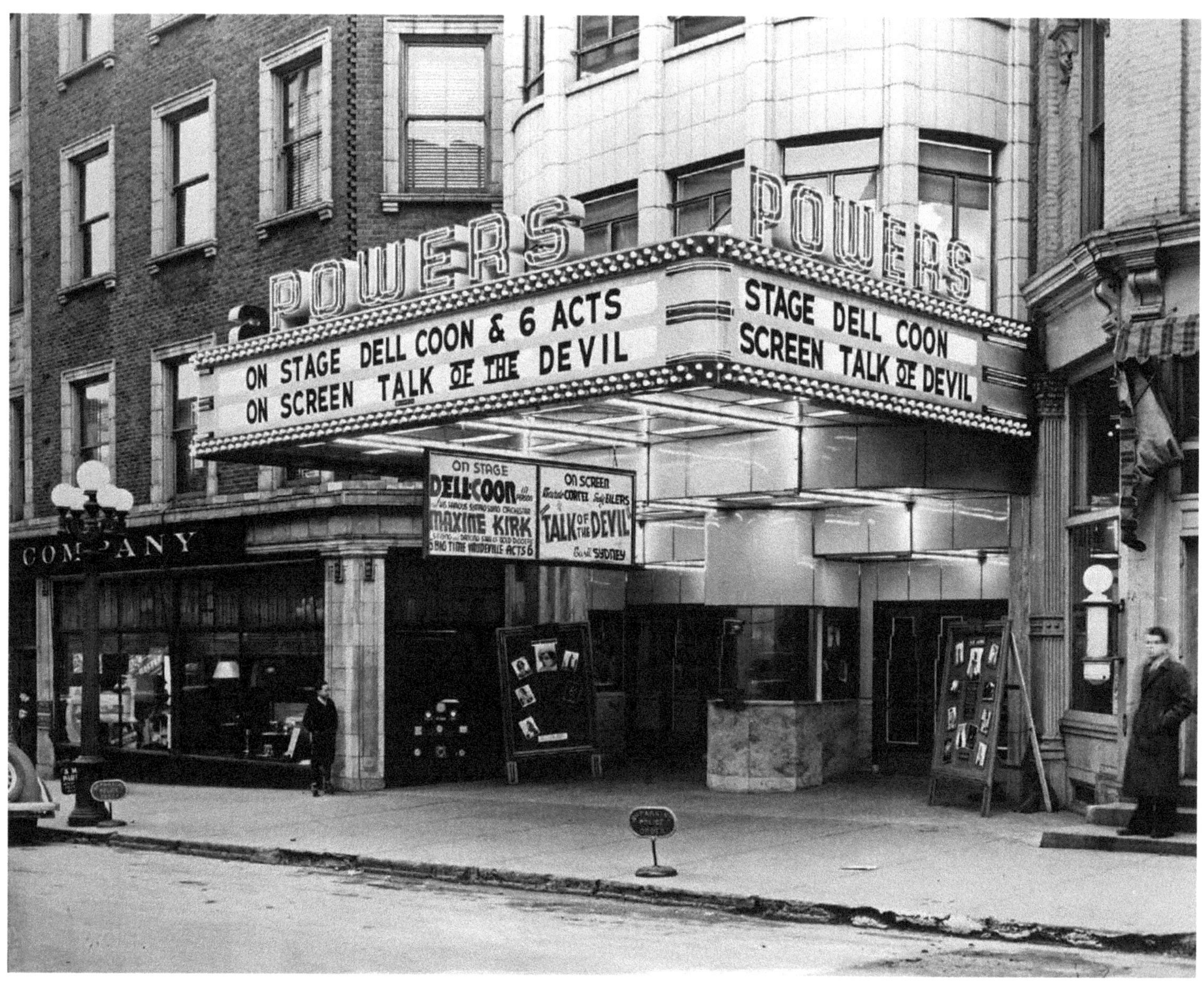

Now showing at the Powers Theater... *Talk of the Devil.*

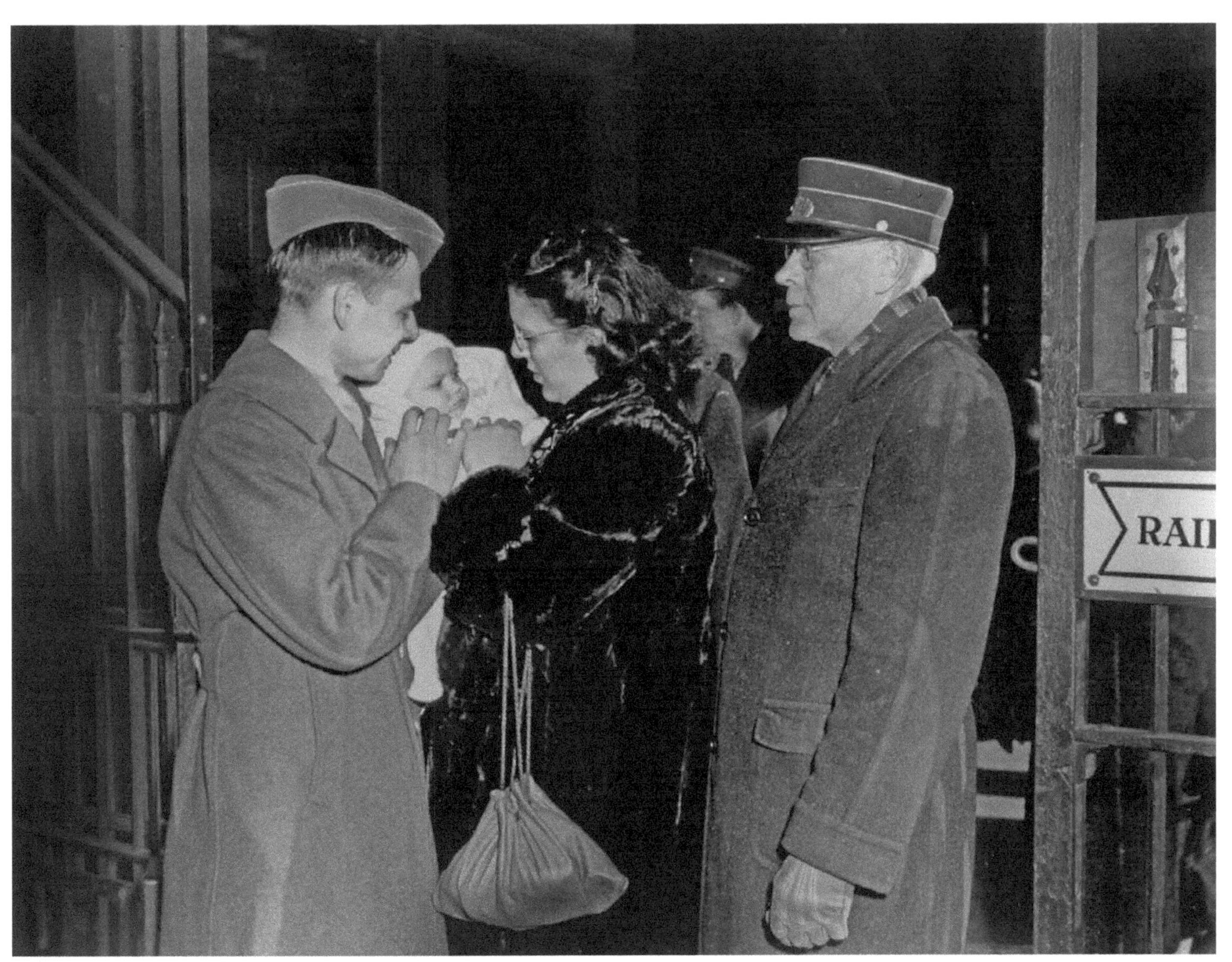

An officer says good-bye before heading to the trains and off to war.

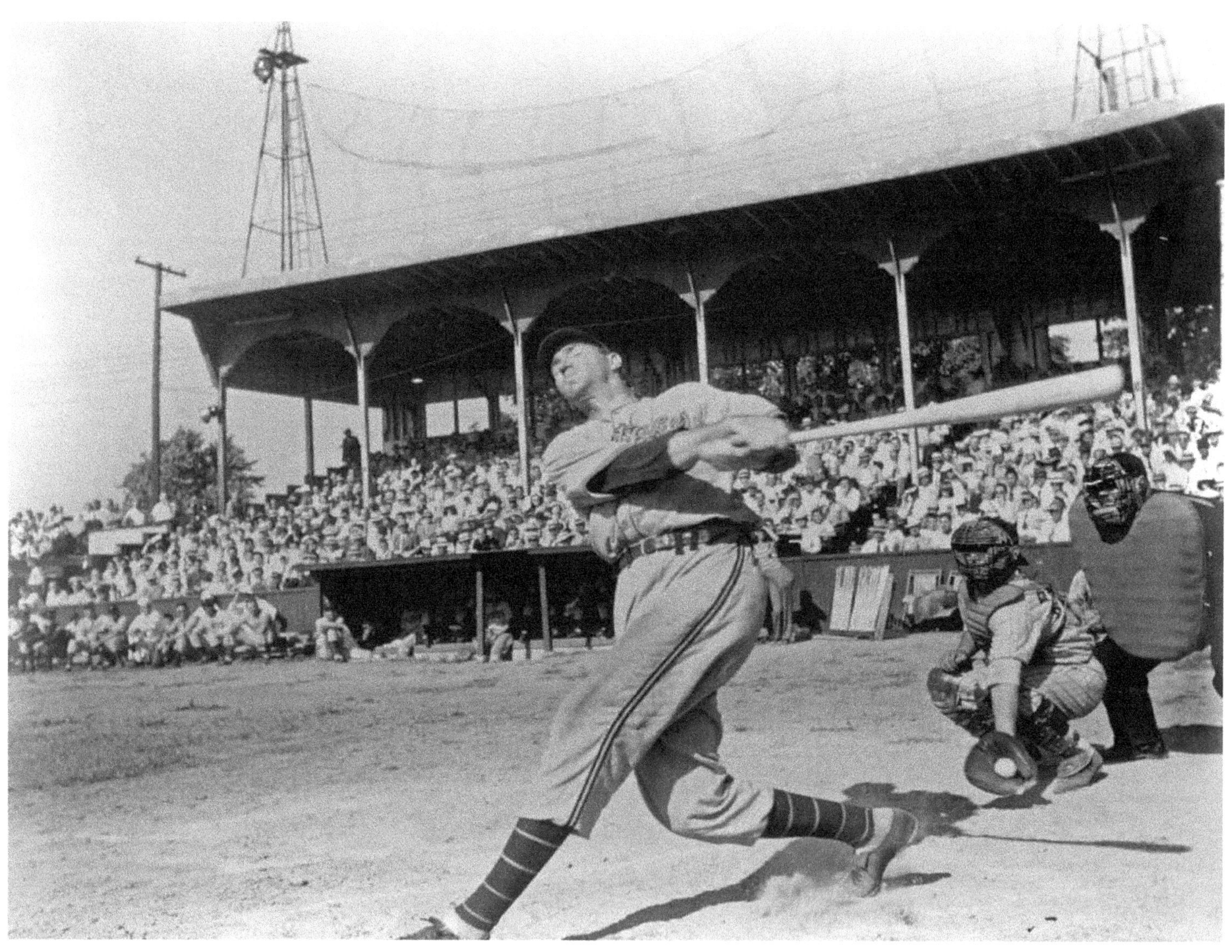

Strike! Lynwood Thomas "Schoolboy" Row, a Detroit Tiger before the draft, swings and misses as he plays with the Great Lakes Naval Station team against the Grand Rapids All-Stars.

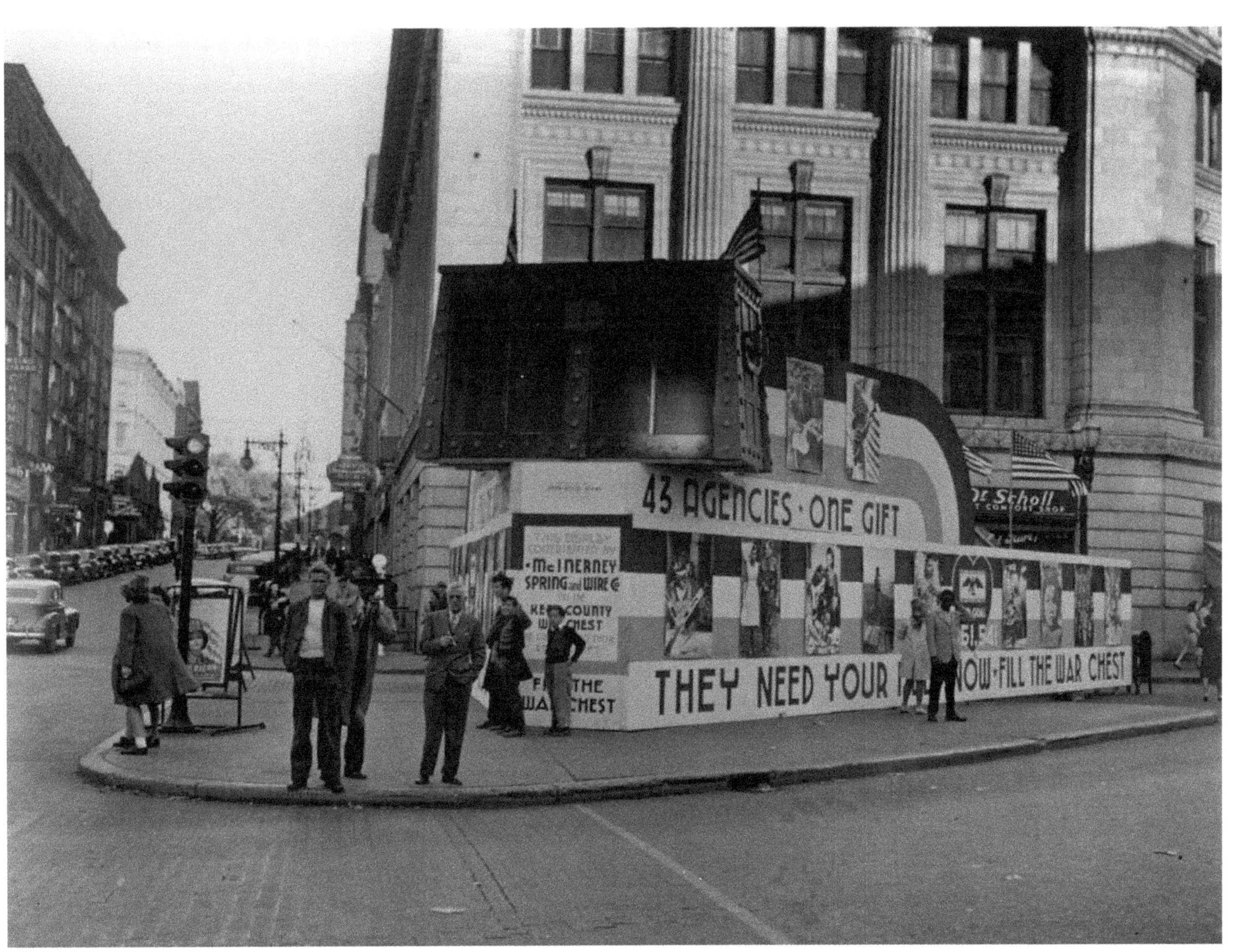

Fill the War Chest! The giant war chest on display at the McKay Tower recorded a goal of $851,541 for support of the war effort.

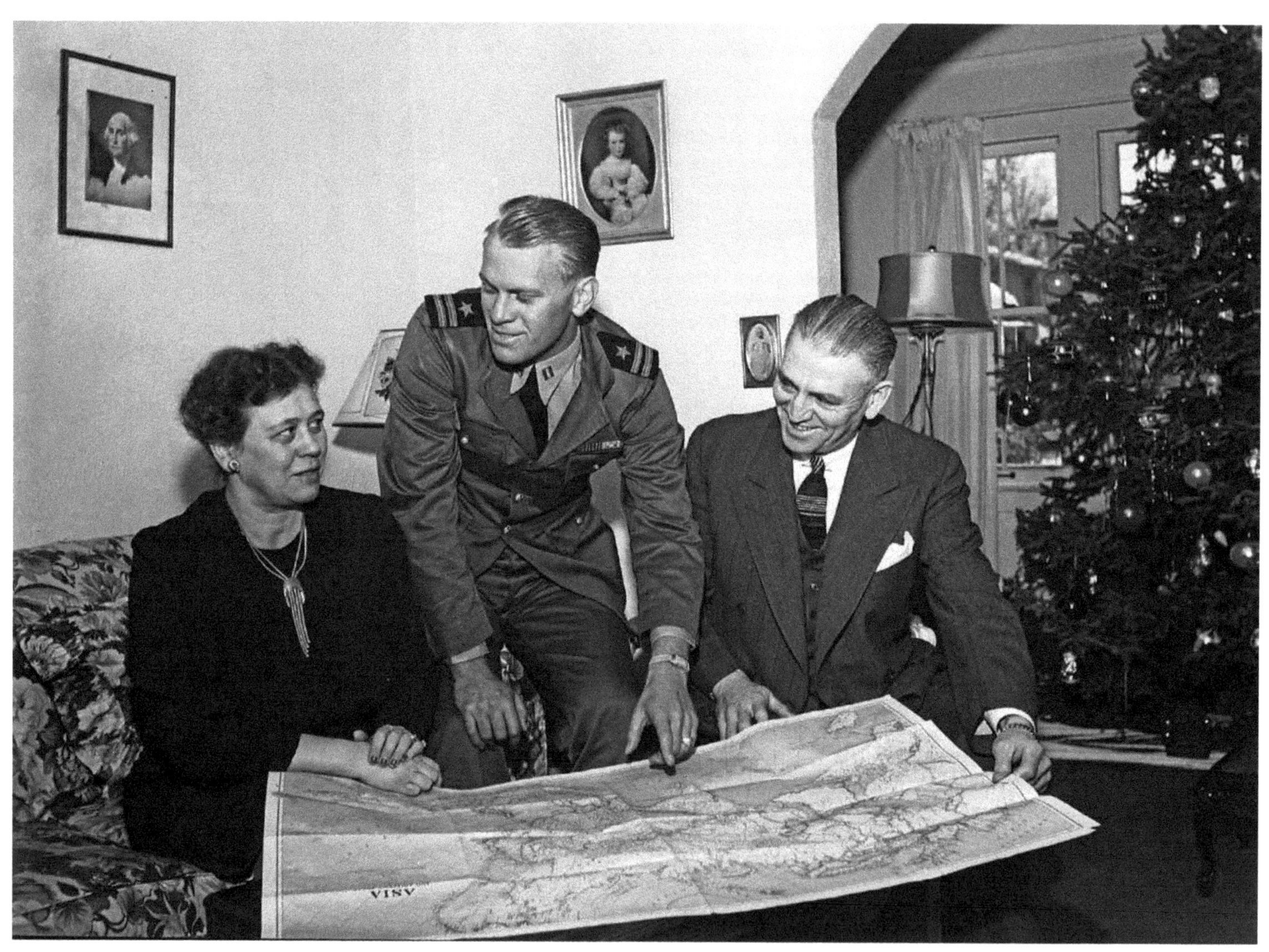

Lieutenant Gerald R. Ford visits his parents while en route to Washington, D.C., after serving in the South Pacific as an assistant navigation officer on a light aircraft carrier.

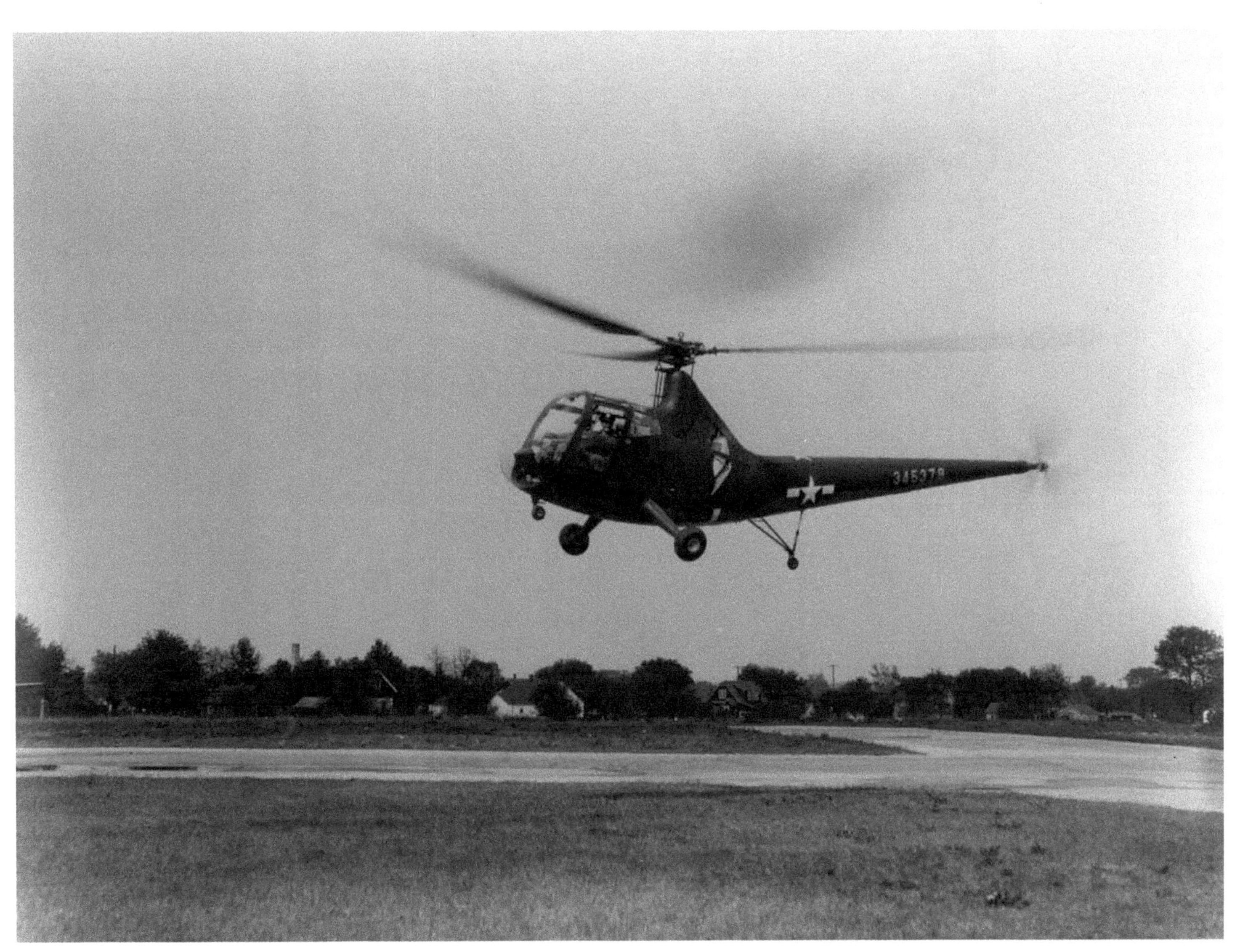

A Nash-Kelvinator manufactured R6 helicopter lands at the Kent County Airport.

The *Grand Rapids Herald* newsboys enjoy the Derby Racer at Ramona Park.

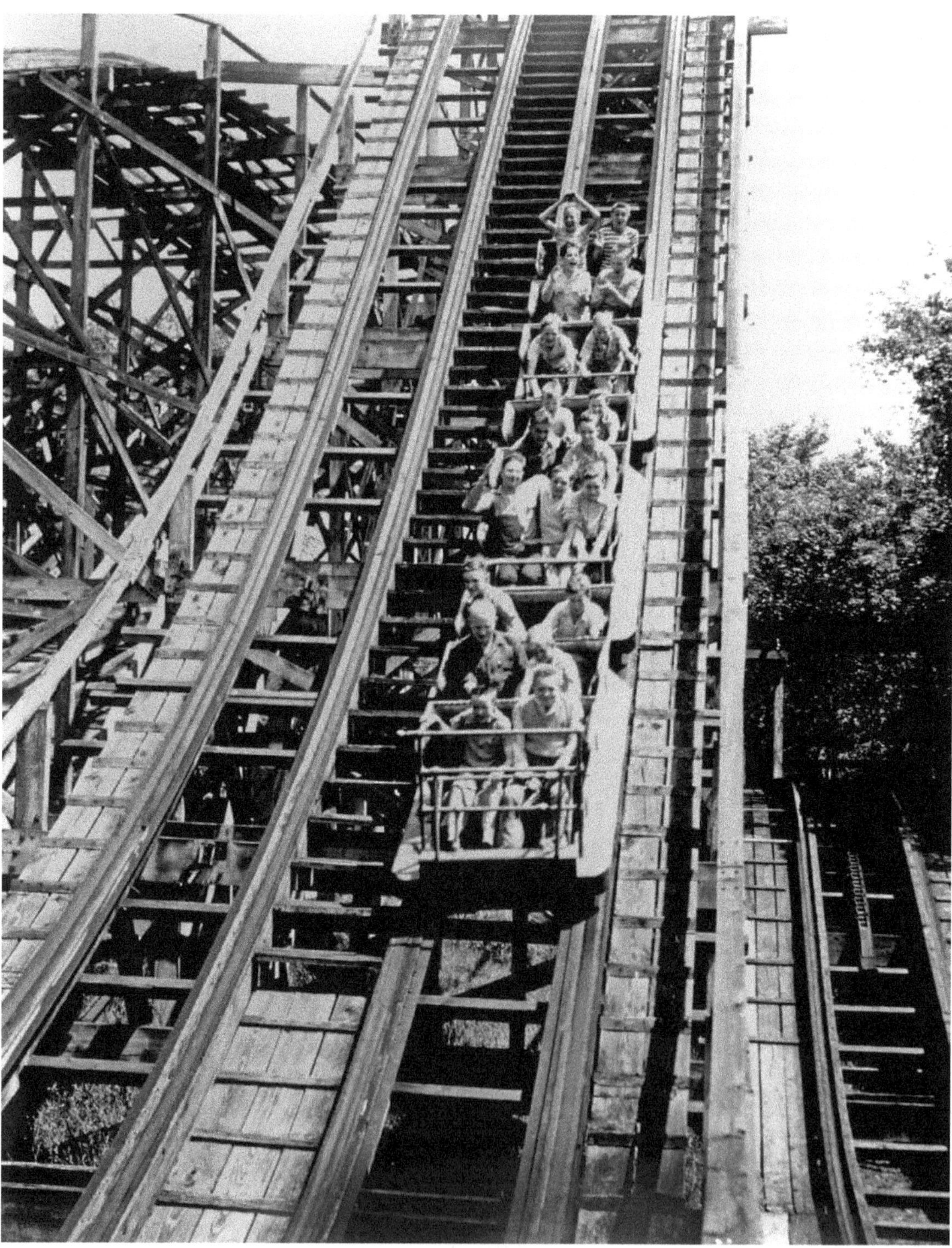

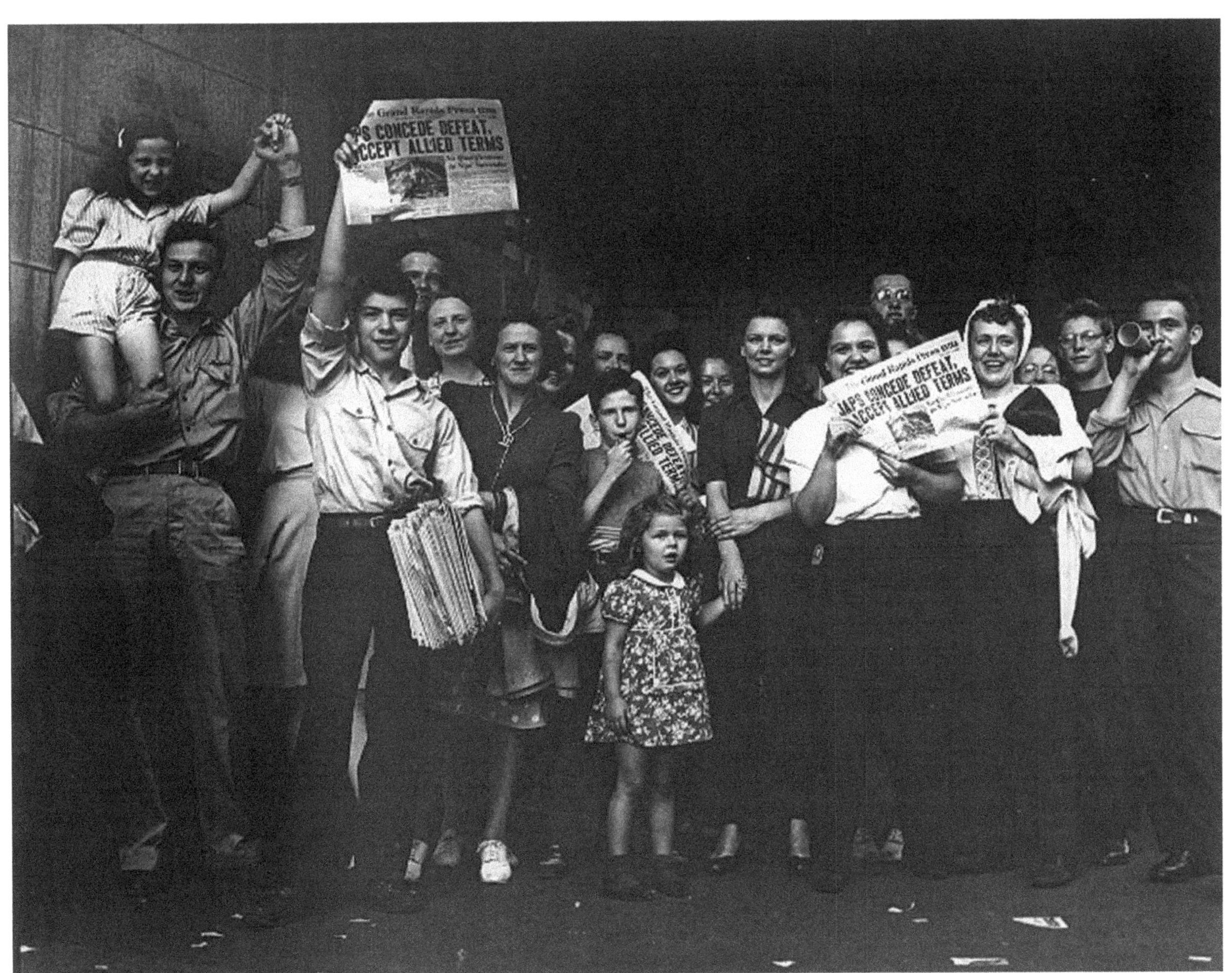

"Victory Over Japan!" Grand Rapids citizens celebrate the news.

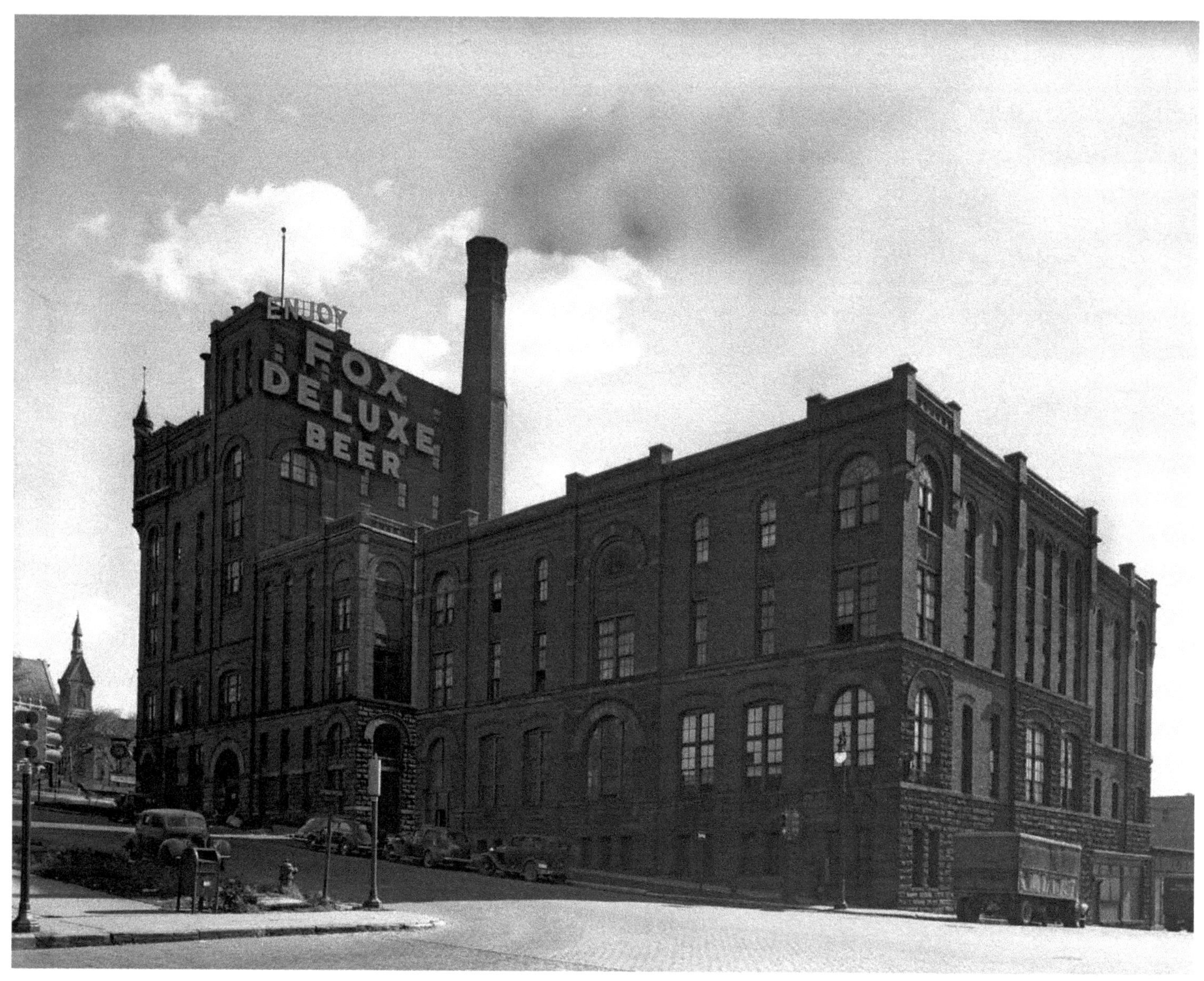

Fox Brewing Company, located at 26 Michigan NE, was in business from 1940 to 1951.

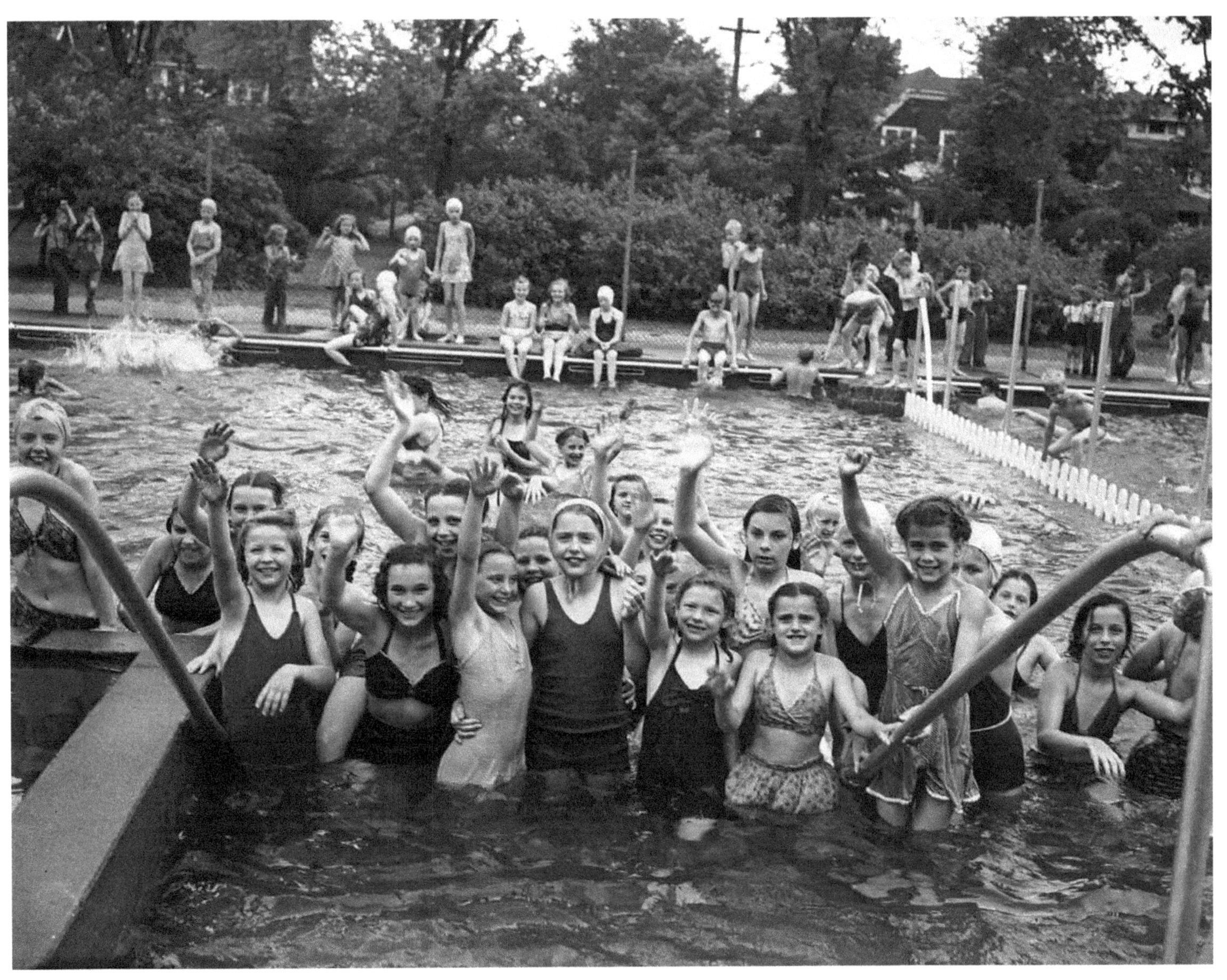

Swimmers at Franklin Park, now Martin Luther King Park, enjoy a cool dip. The city acquired the land in 1911.

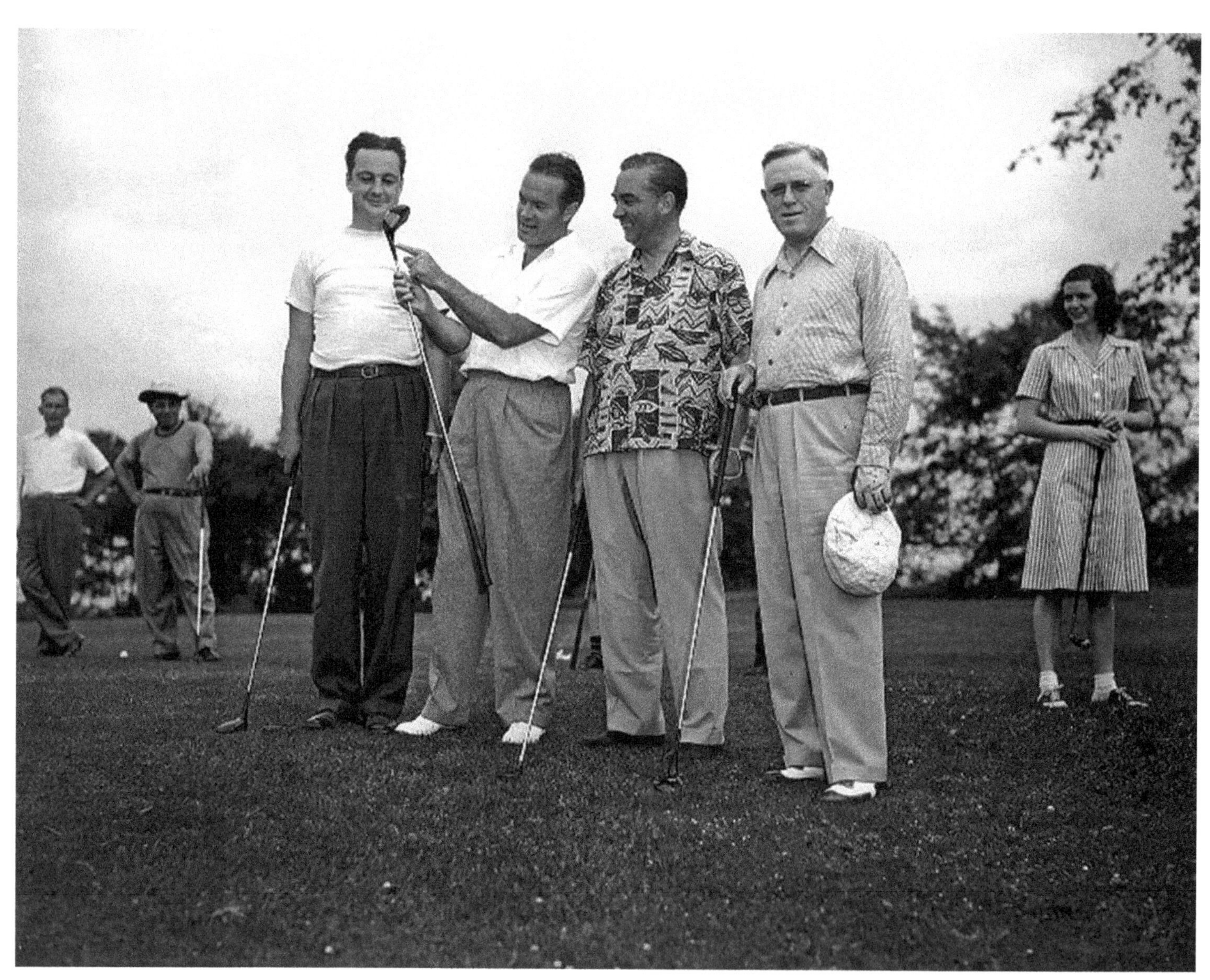

Bob Hope and friends examine Hope's golf club during an outing at Blythfield Country Club.

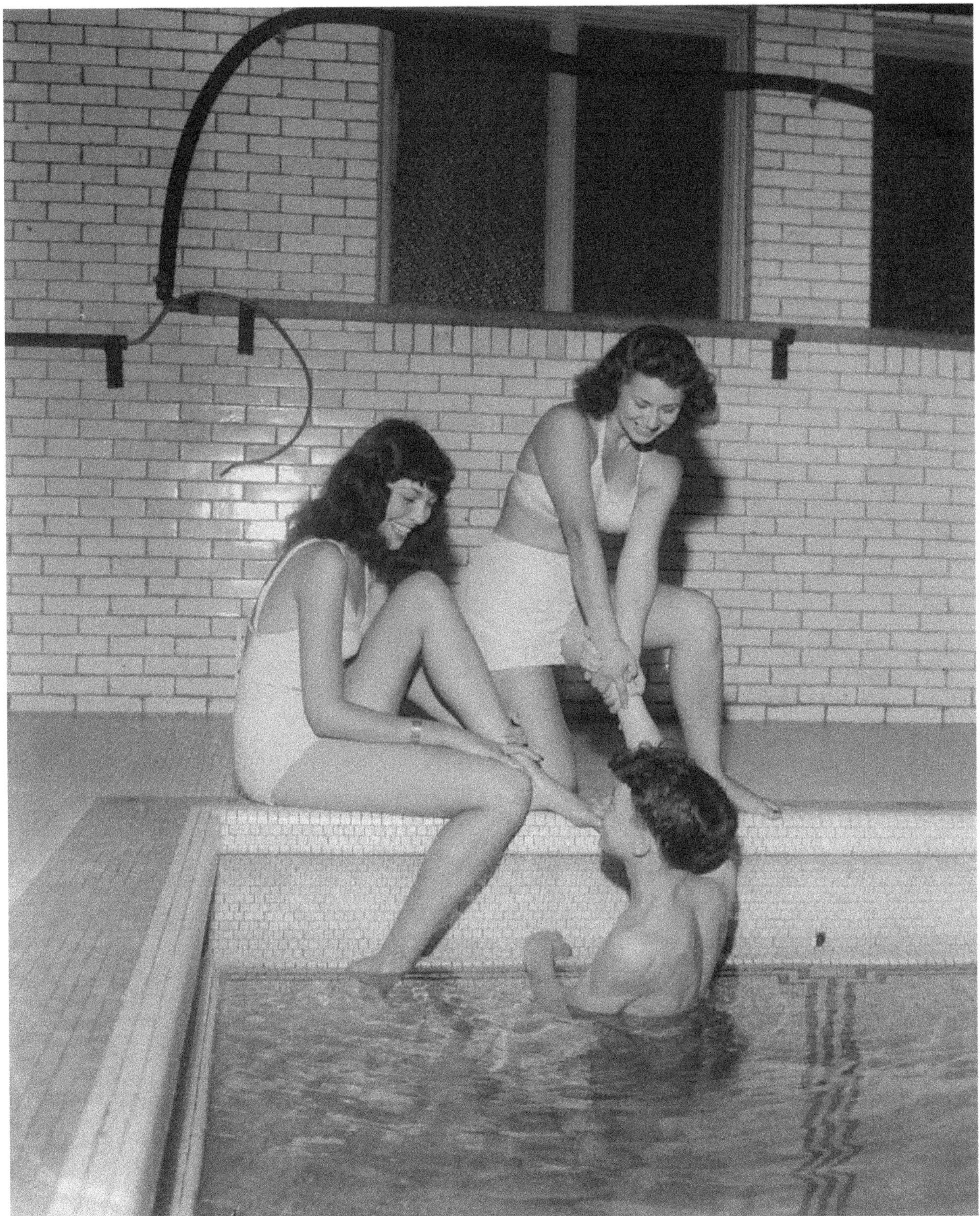

Several times during the summer, Club Co-ed members met at the YMCA for a Saturday night filled with activities. Offered were swimming, dancing to an orchestra, or participating in a variety of games. Harold Fortier is shown here coaxing Shirley Tweddale and Kay Romine into the pool.

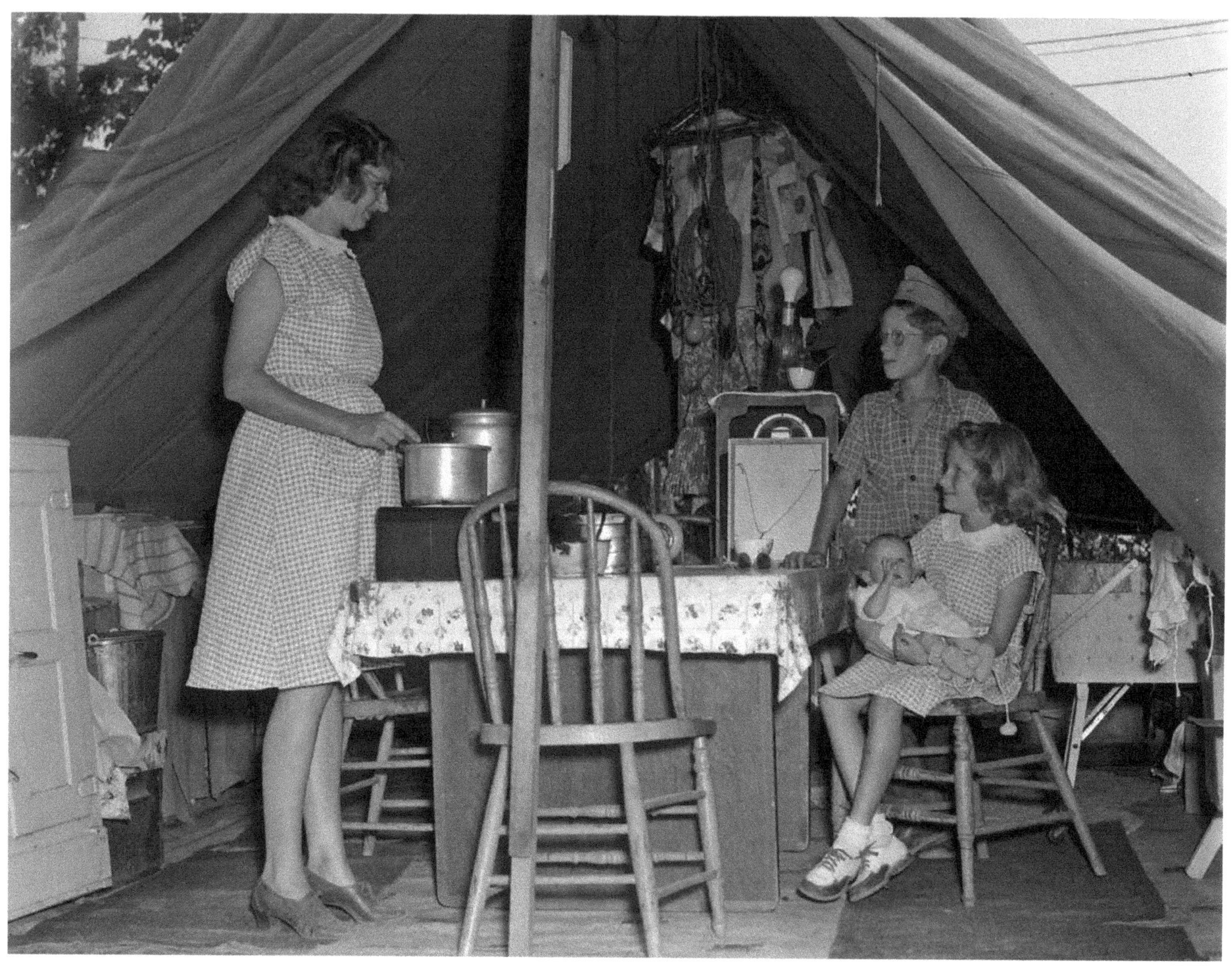

After World War II, there was a housing shortage in the area. This family made the best of it in a tent at the Garden Trailer Coach Park in Cutlerville.

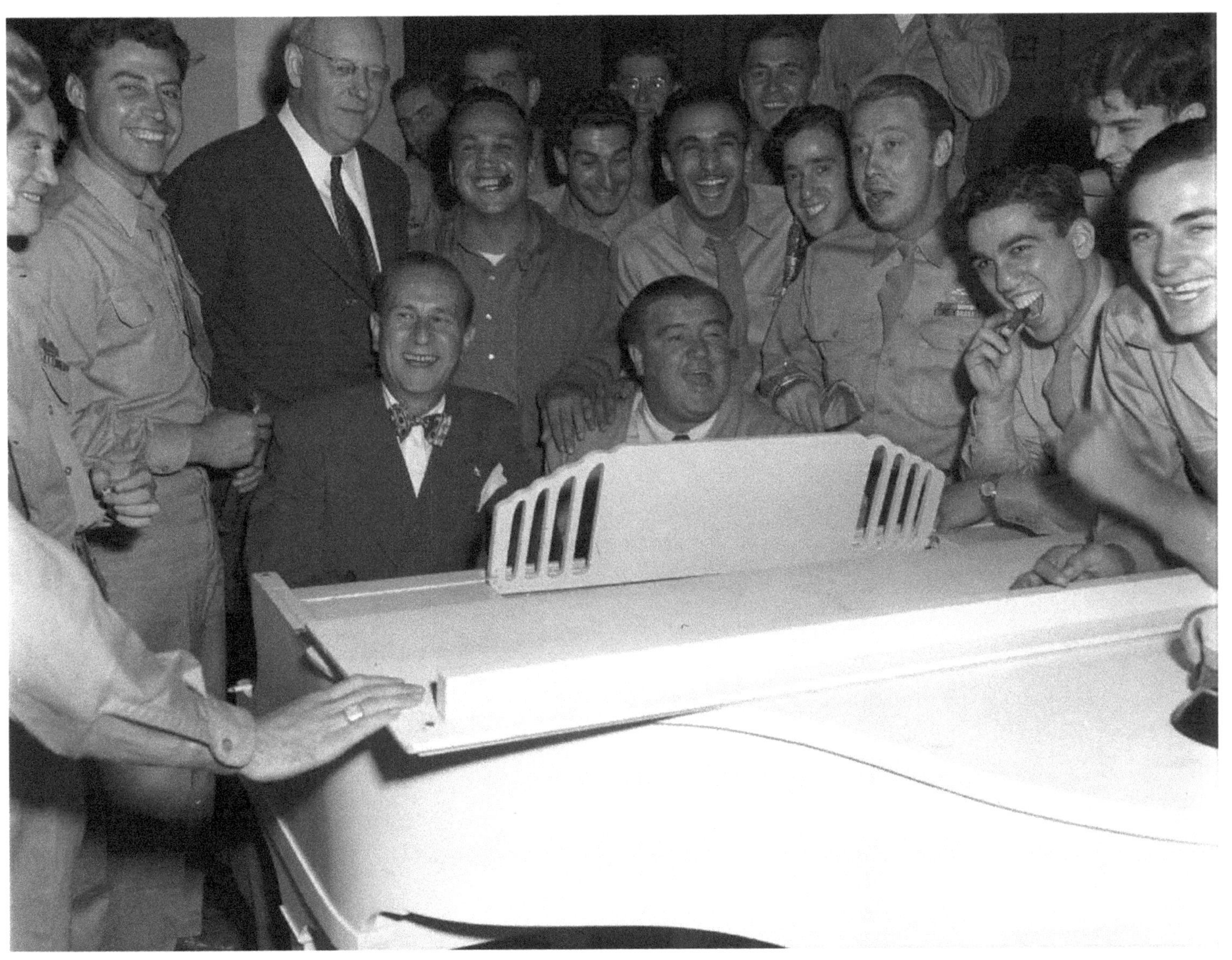

The Kiwanis Club hosted a dinner for wounded soldiers from the Percy Jones General Hospital at the Pantlind Hotel. Bud Abbott and Lou Costello provided the uproarishly funny entertainment.

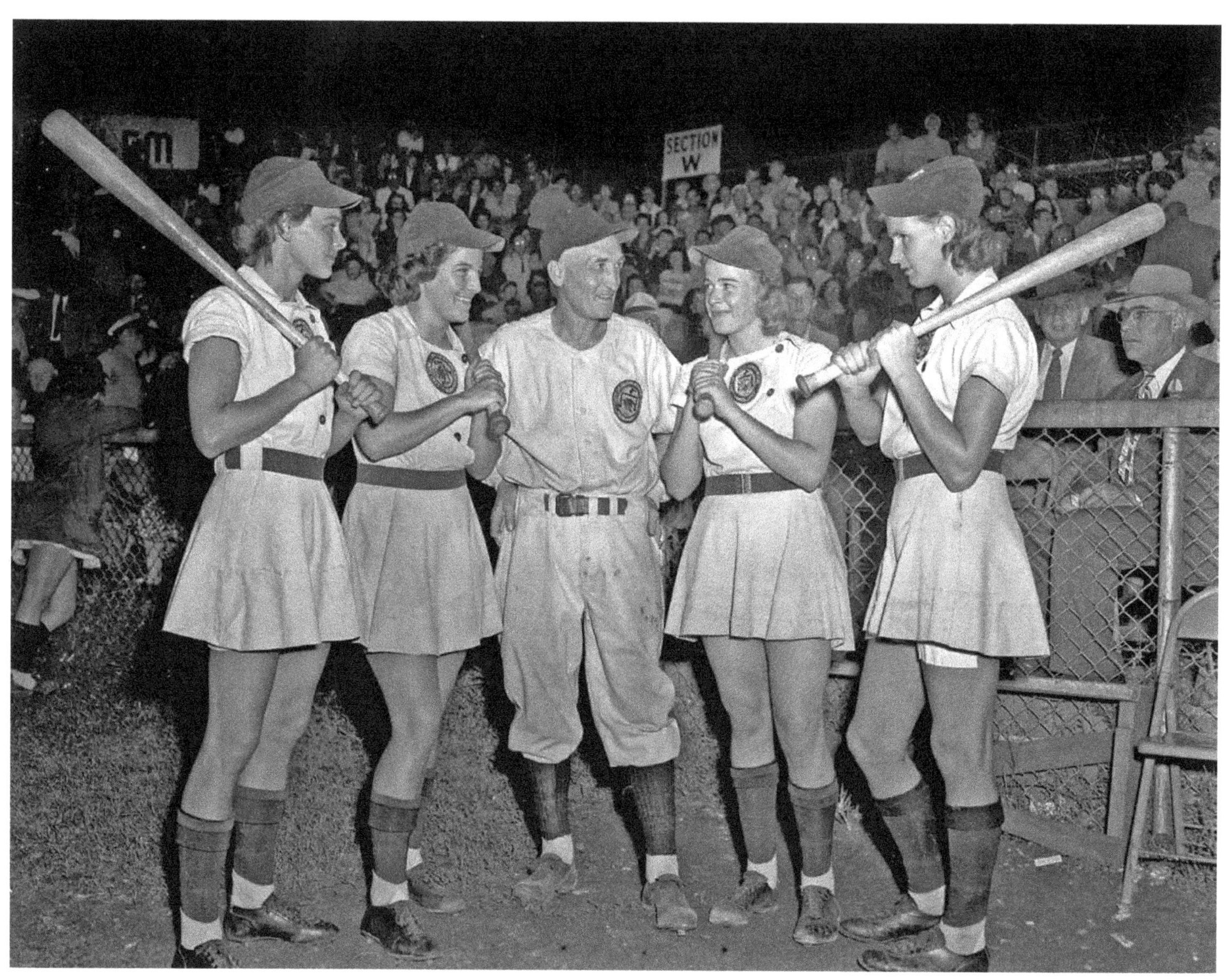

The Grand Rapids Chicks and their manager during the second playoff game versus South Bend.

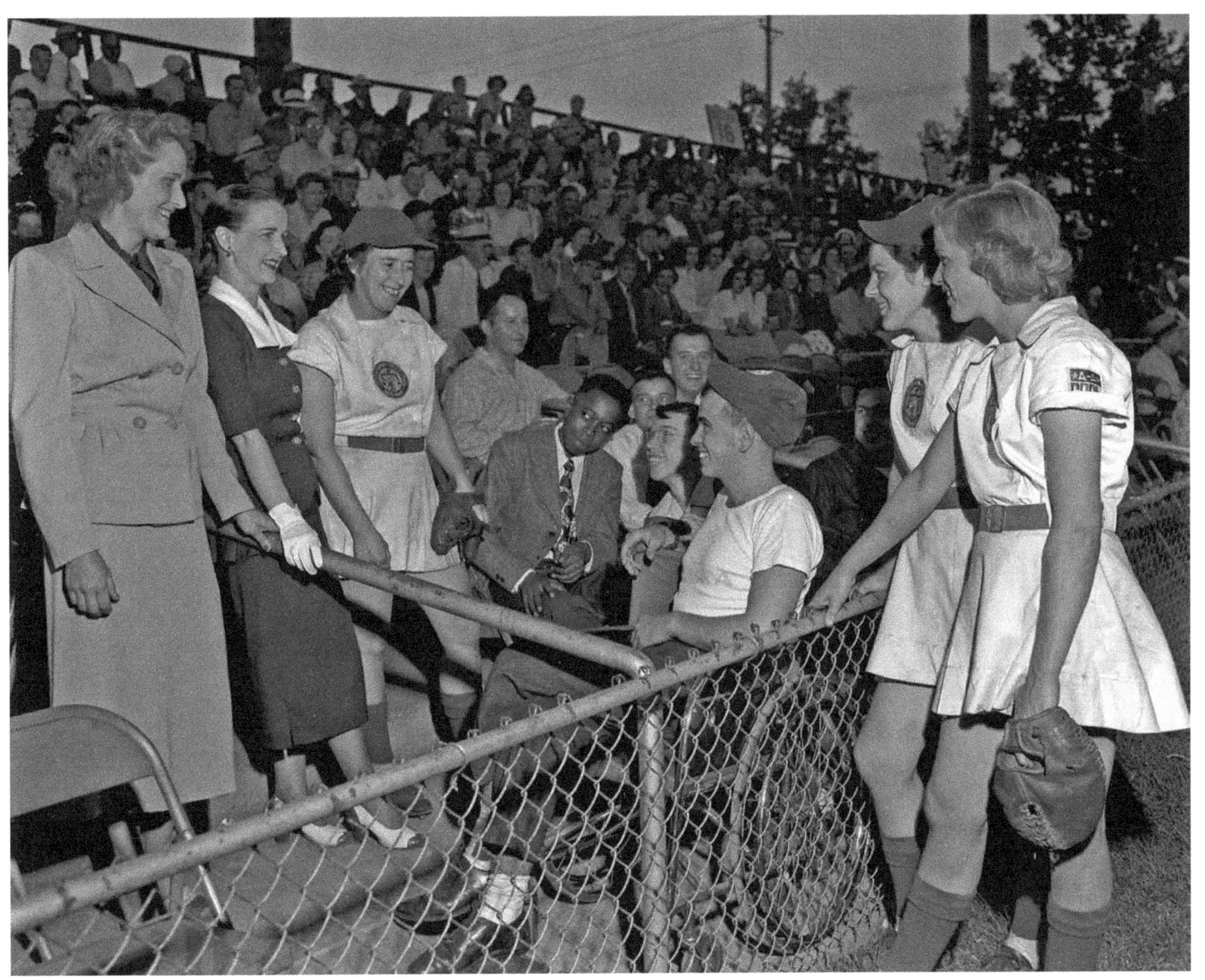

Grand Rapids Chicks players visit with patients from the Mary Free Bed Guild.

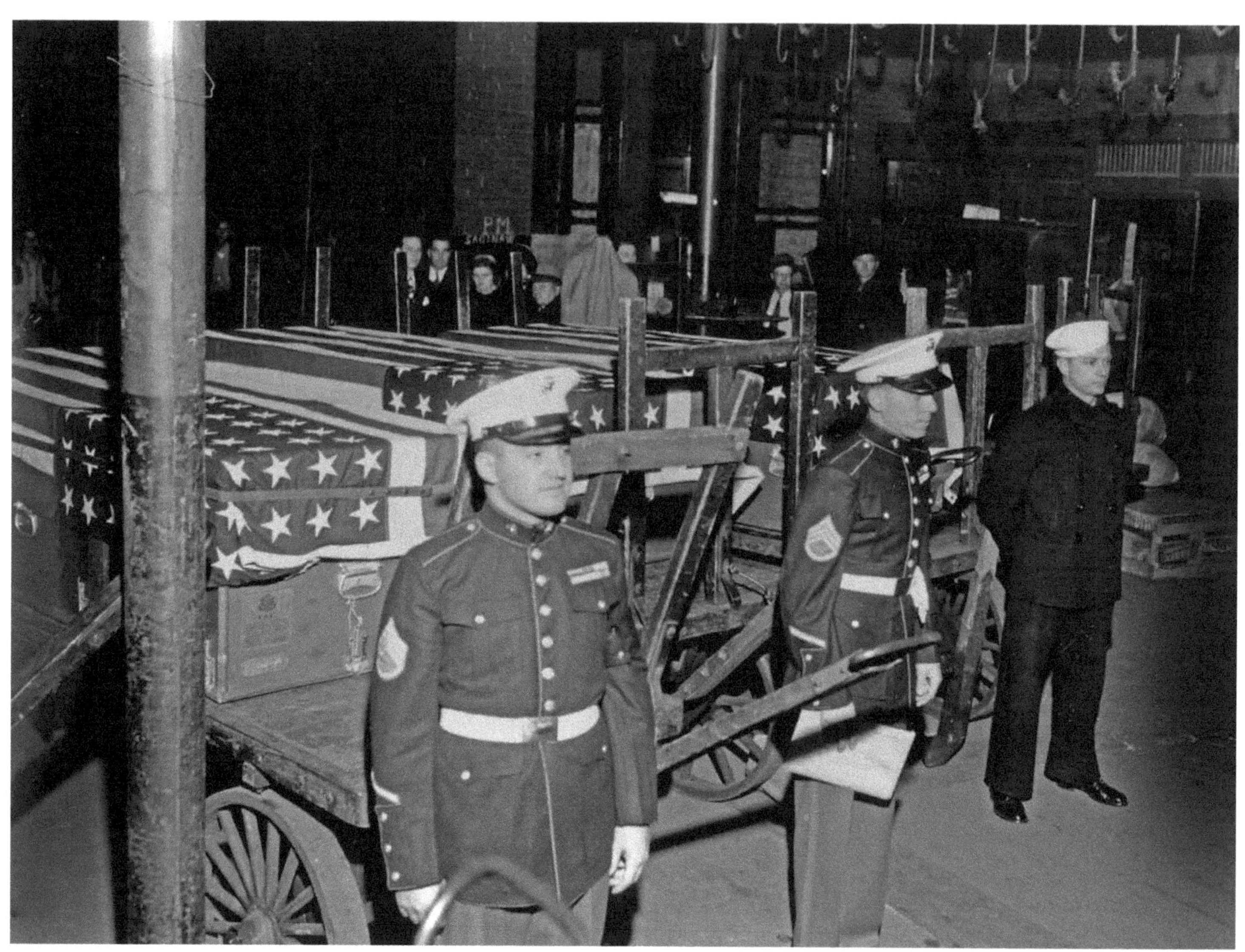

Fallen heroes are quietly returned to their hometowns by the military.

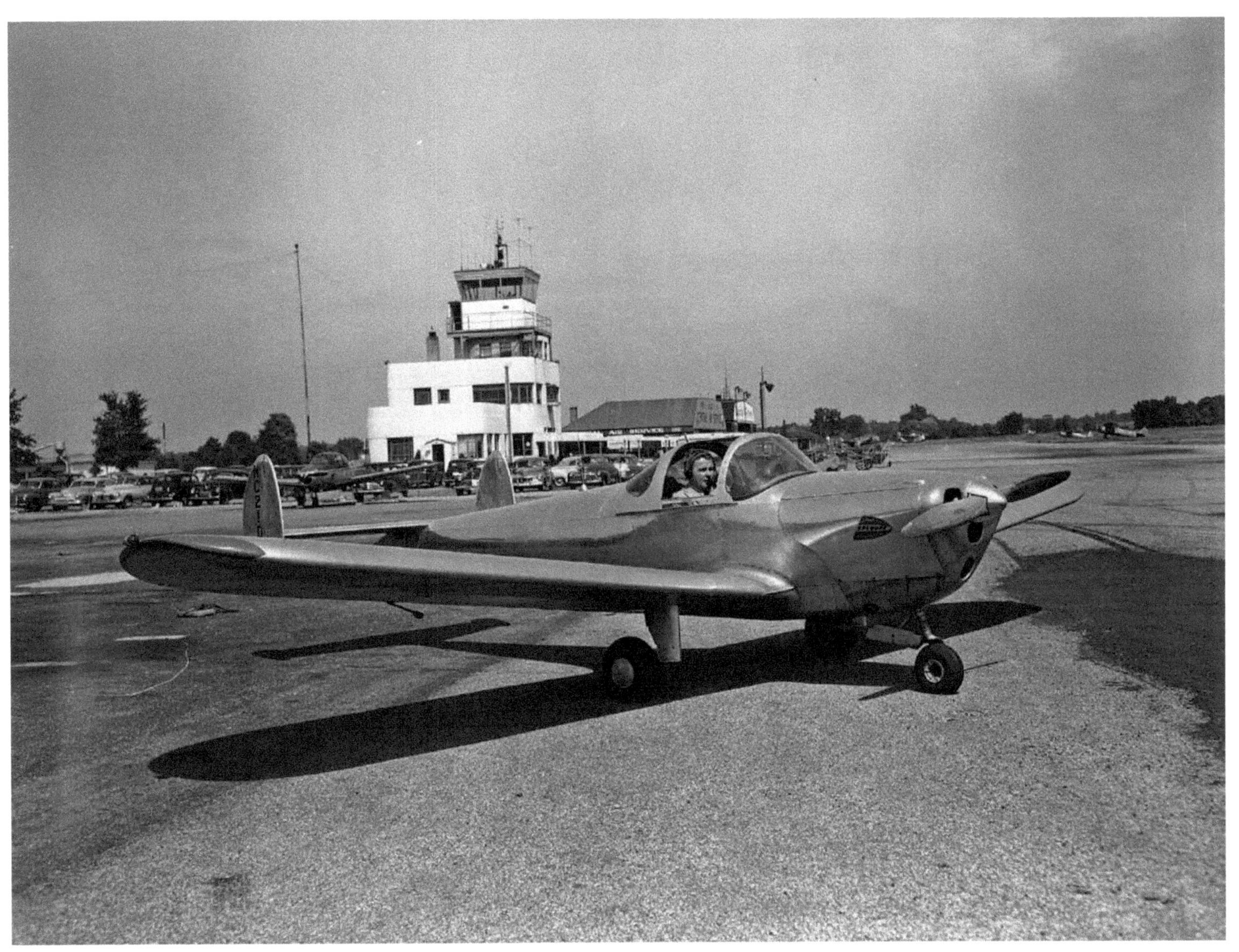

The single-engine private plane *Ercoupe* rests on the tarmac at the Kent County Airport on Madison Avenue SE, today known as Roger B. Chaffee Boulevard.

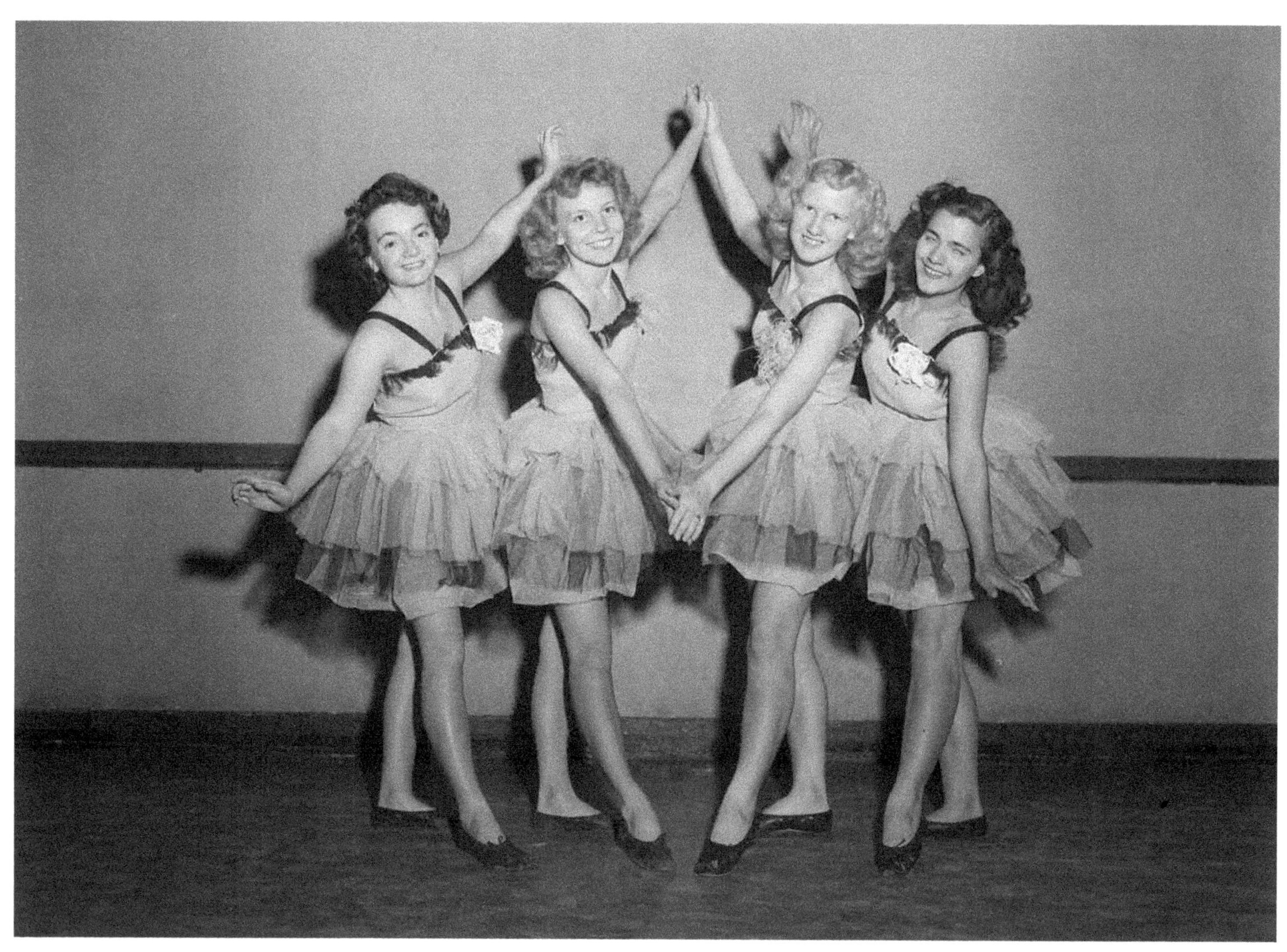

The Kelloggsville Kadettes rehearse before their show. Members are Mary Ann Stickney, Barbara Bronkema, Doris Thayer, and Eleanor Nelson.

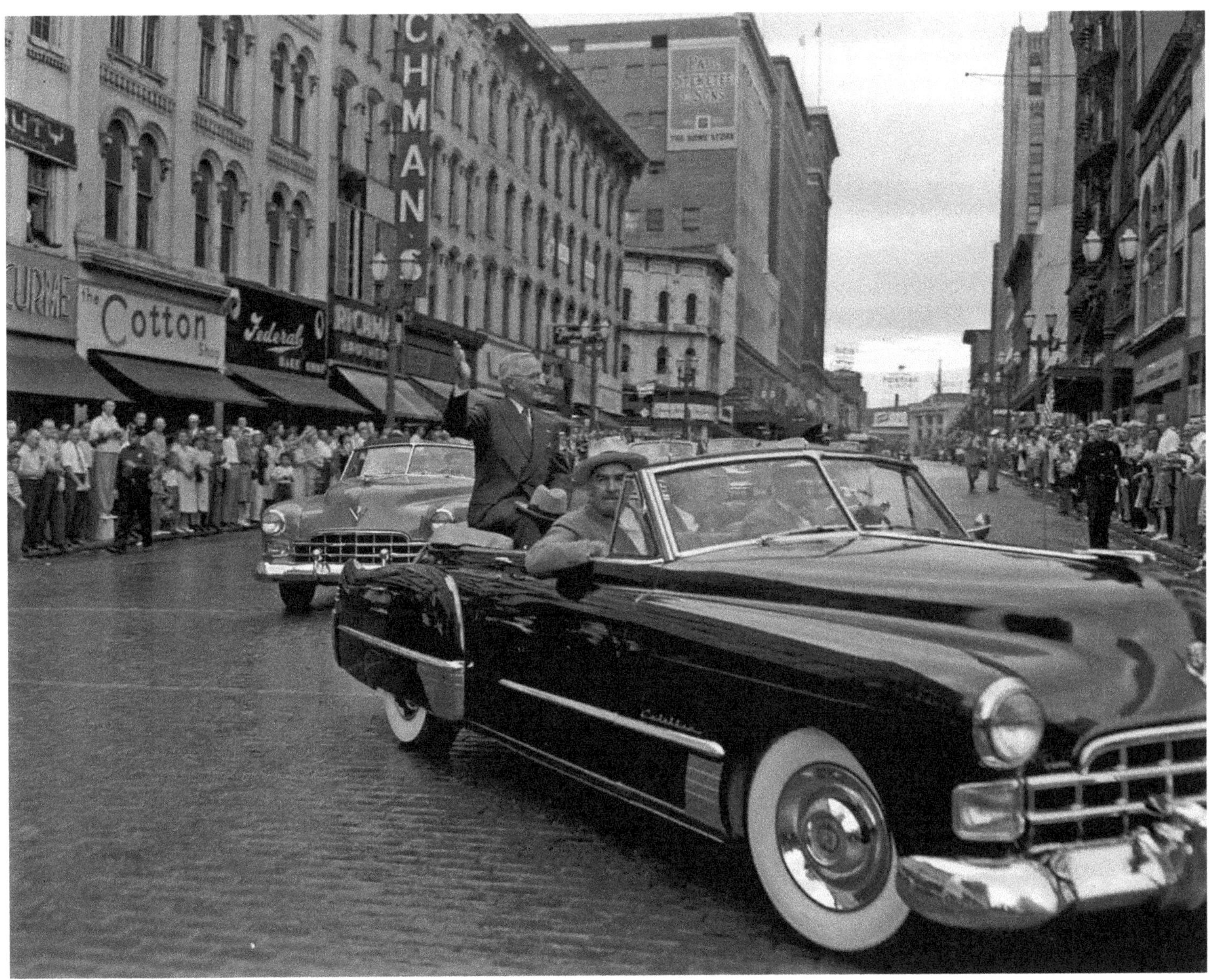

President Harry S. Truman visited Grand Rapids on September 6, 1948. There were approximately 20,000 people in attendance for the parade. Following the parade, Truman gave a brief speech to kick off his reelection campaign.

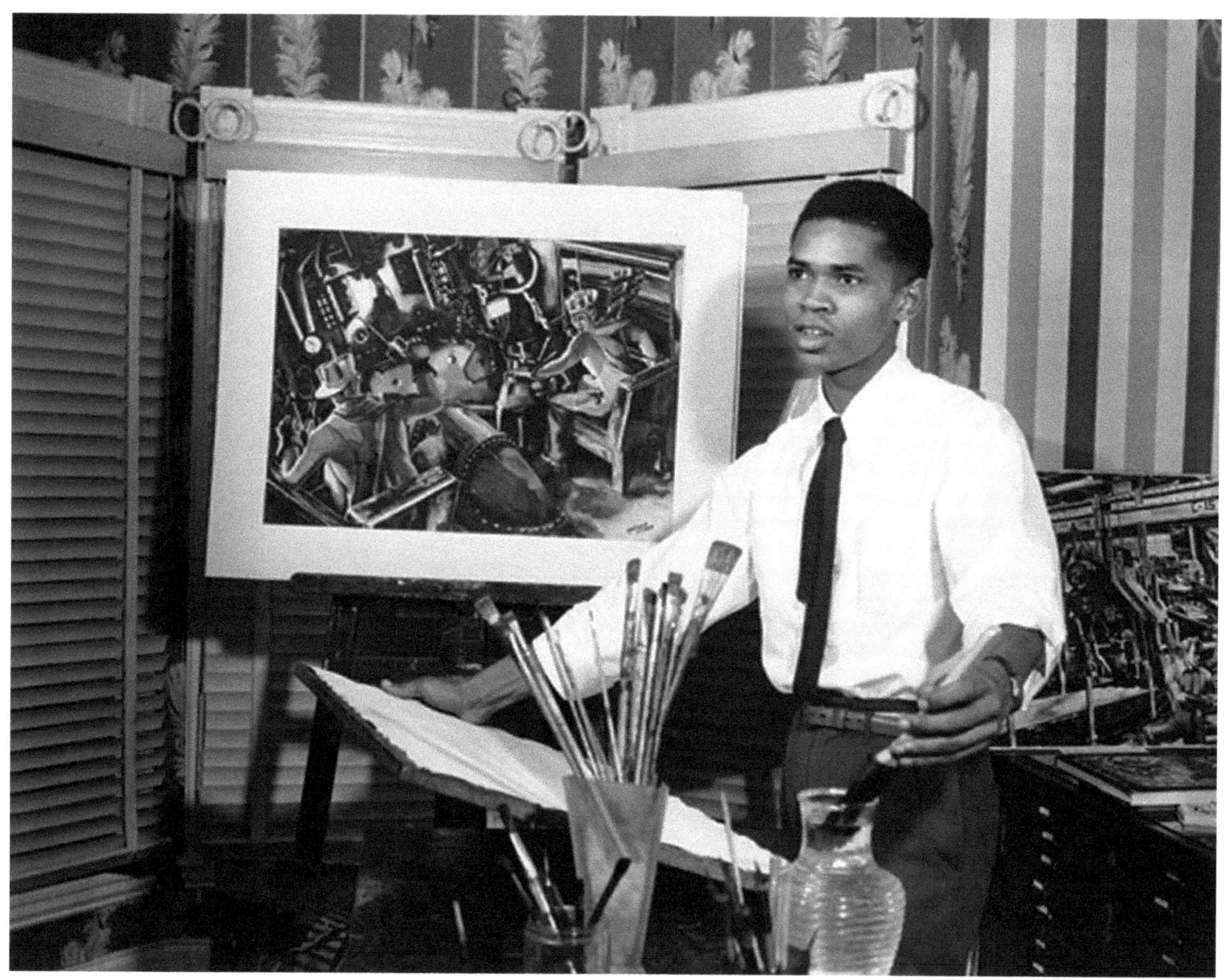

Award-winning Grand Rapids artist William Randolph (Randy) Brown was born in Louisiana and moved to Grand Rapids as a young boy. In 1946, Brown held his first one-man show at the Grand Rapids Art Gallery. He received Honorable Mention in the Grand Rapids National Annual Exhibition of Negro Artists and Sculptors in 1951. Brown likes to paint marine and industrial scenes and landscapes.

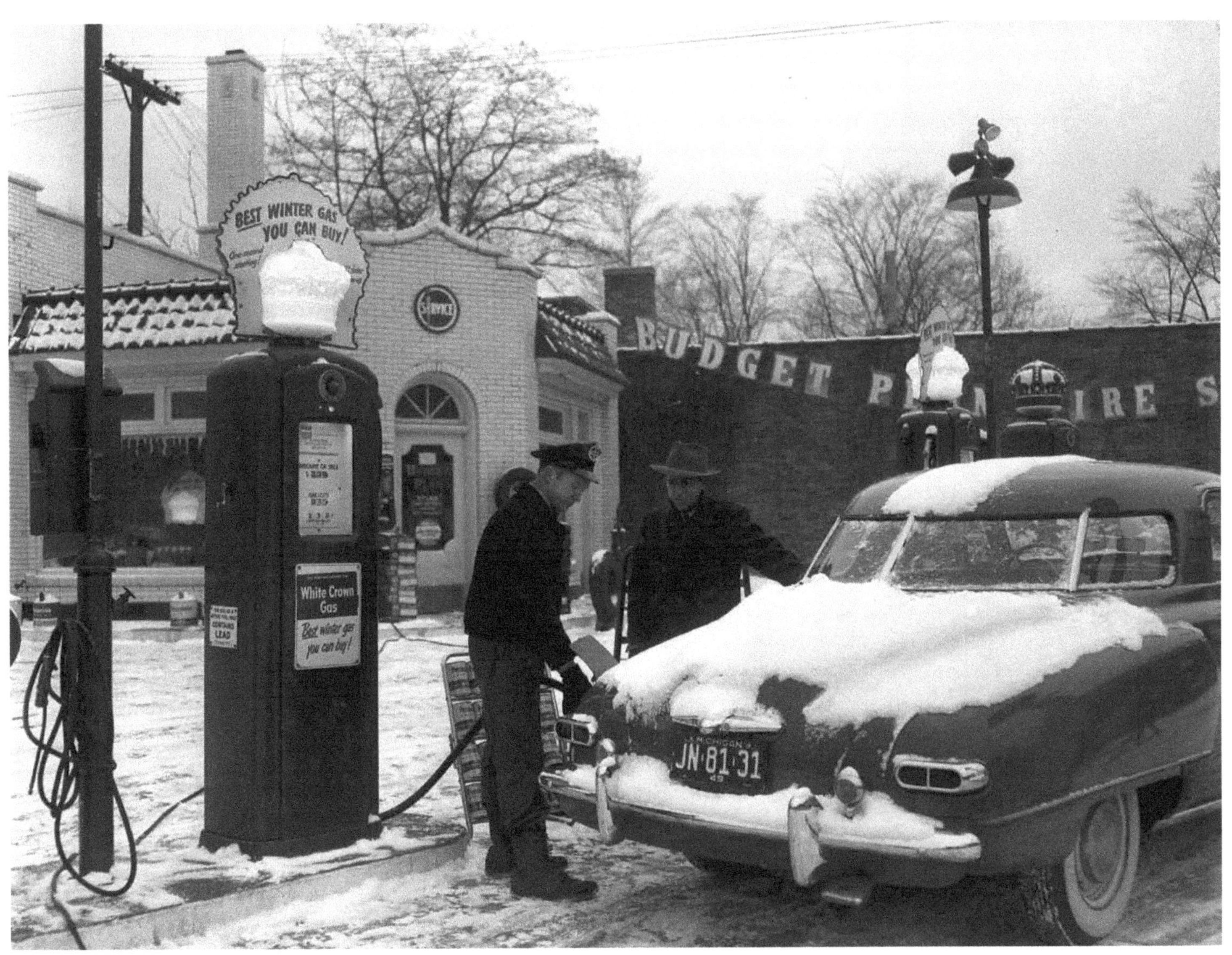

Remember the days of full-service gas stations? A station attendant pumps gas at Gietzen's Super Service Station, at 1412 Robinson Road SE, around 1949.

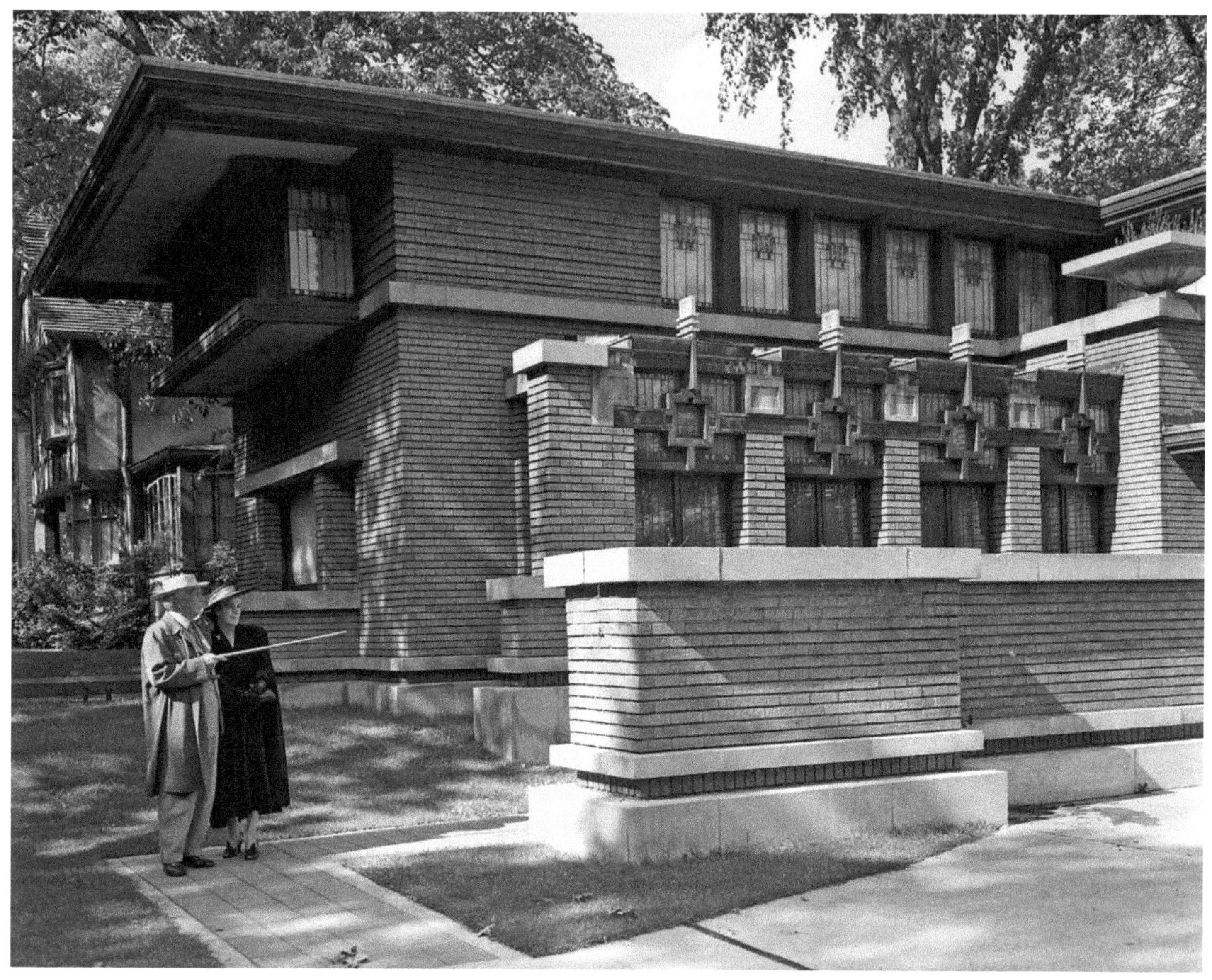

Frank Lloyd Wright points out features of the Meyer May House for his wife, Olgivanna. The house is located at Madison and Logan. In 1985, Steelcase furniture manufacturing purchased the home and did a complete renovation. In 1987, the home was opened to visitors.

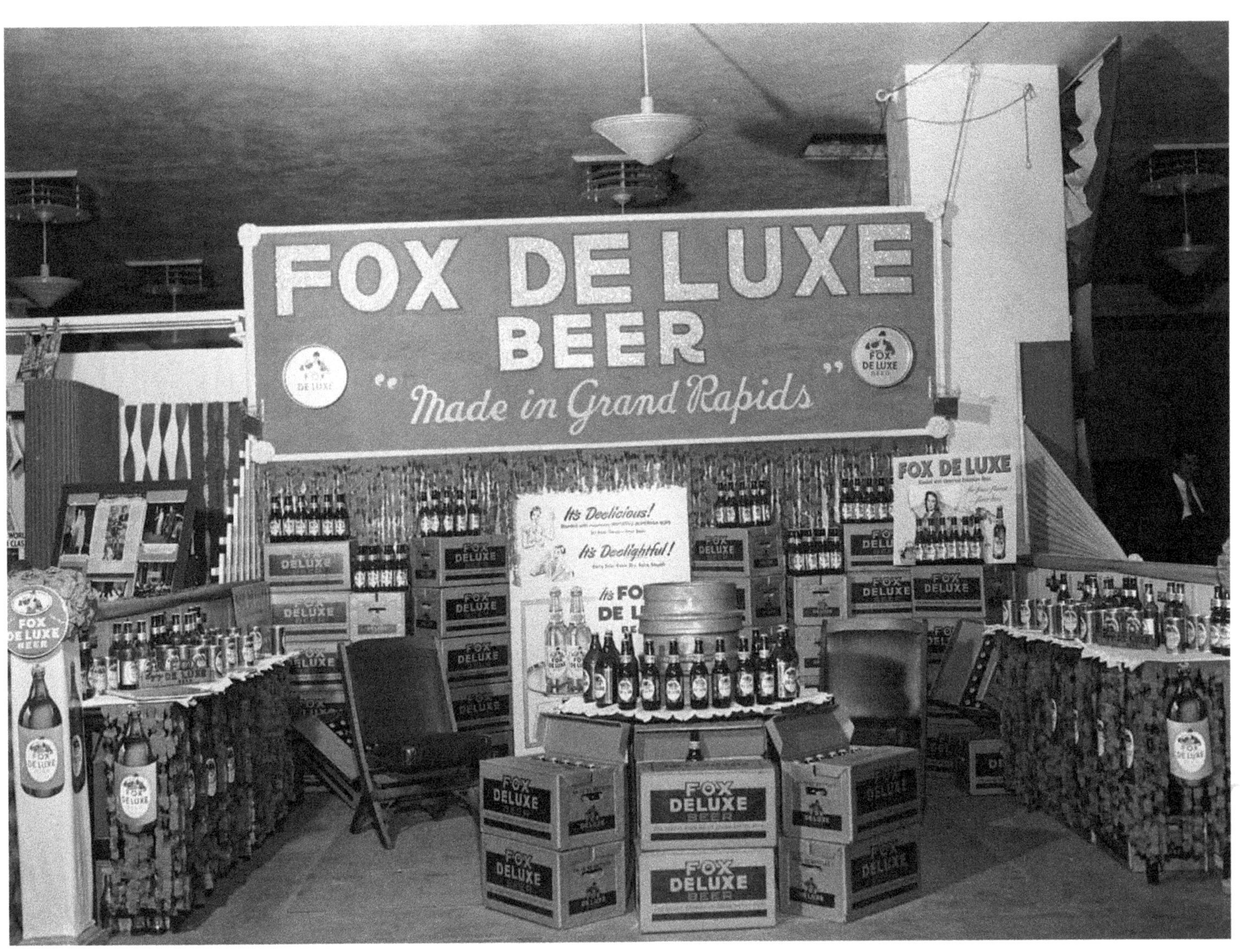

A display booth at "Grand Rapids on Parade" showcases Fox Deluxe Brewing Company.

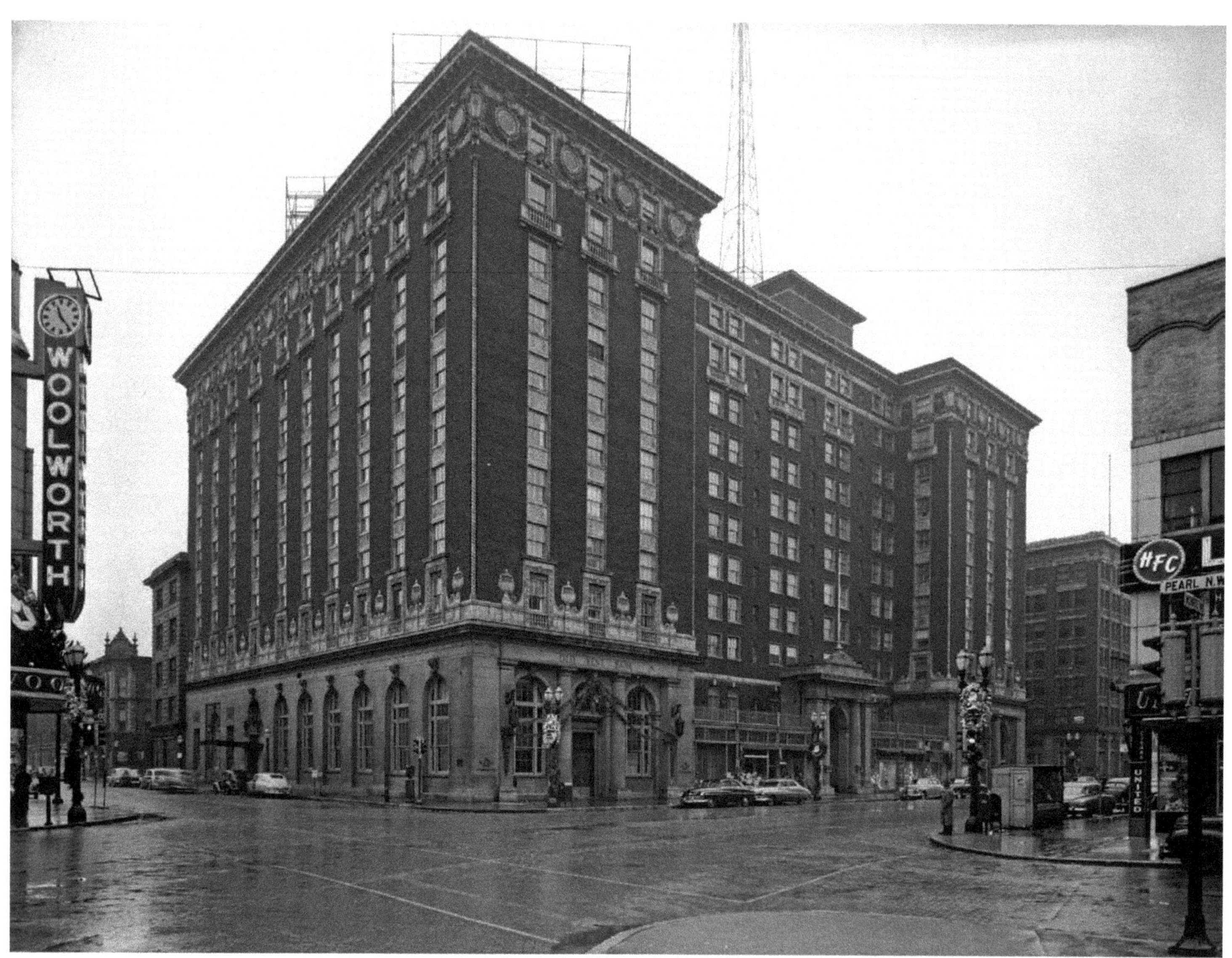

The Pantlind Hotel, now known as the Amway Grand Plaza Hotel.

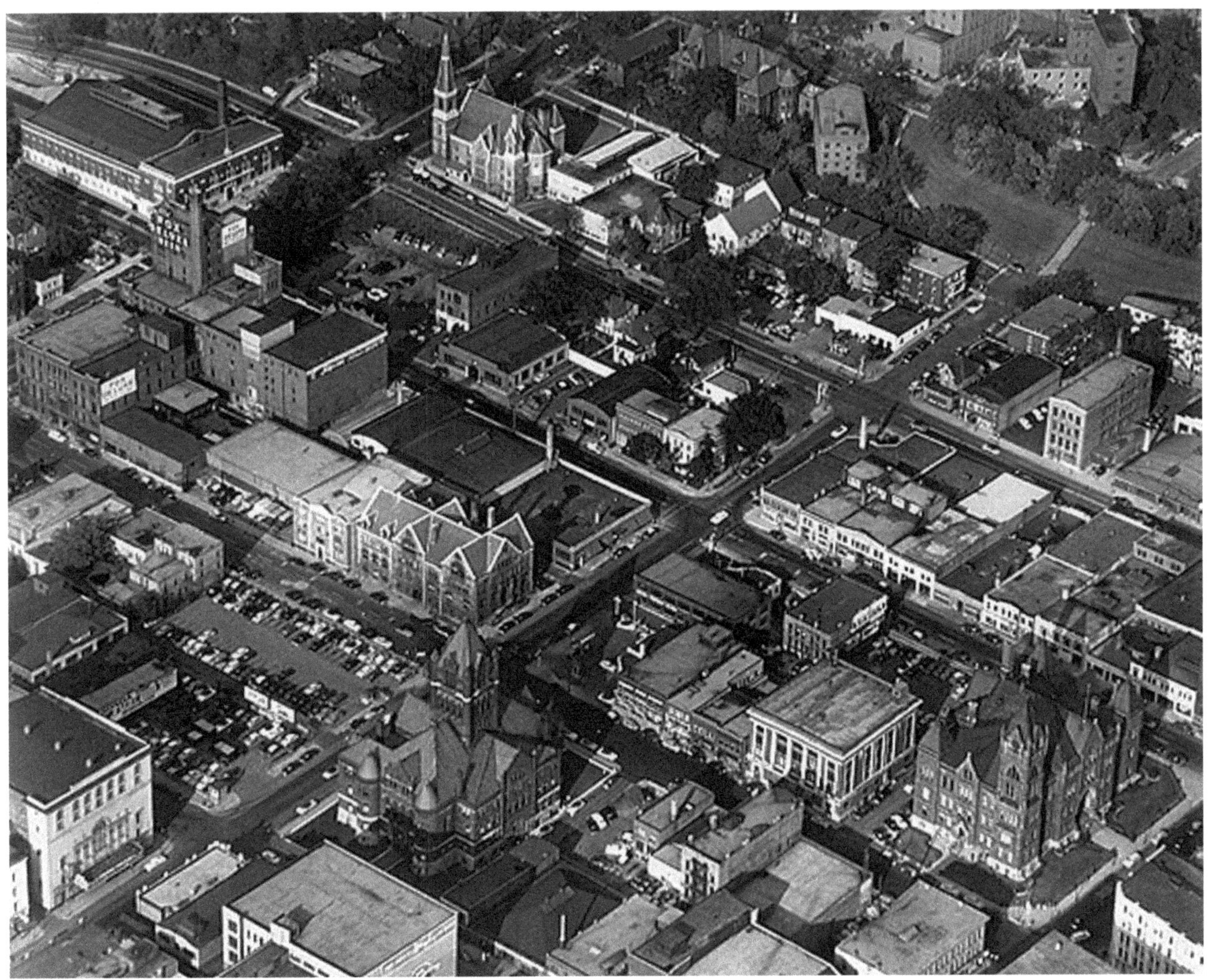

Before the expressways came through, an aerial view of Grand Rapids shows how downtown looked, from Lyon to Michigan, Bond to Bostwick, and South Ottawa to North. Buildings include Old City Hall, Old Kent County Building, Old Police Station, Regent Theater, Fox Brewery, Immanuel Lutheran Church, and Butterworth Hospital.

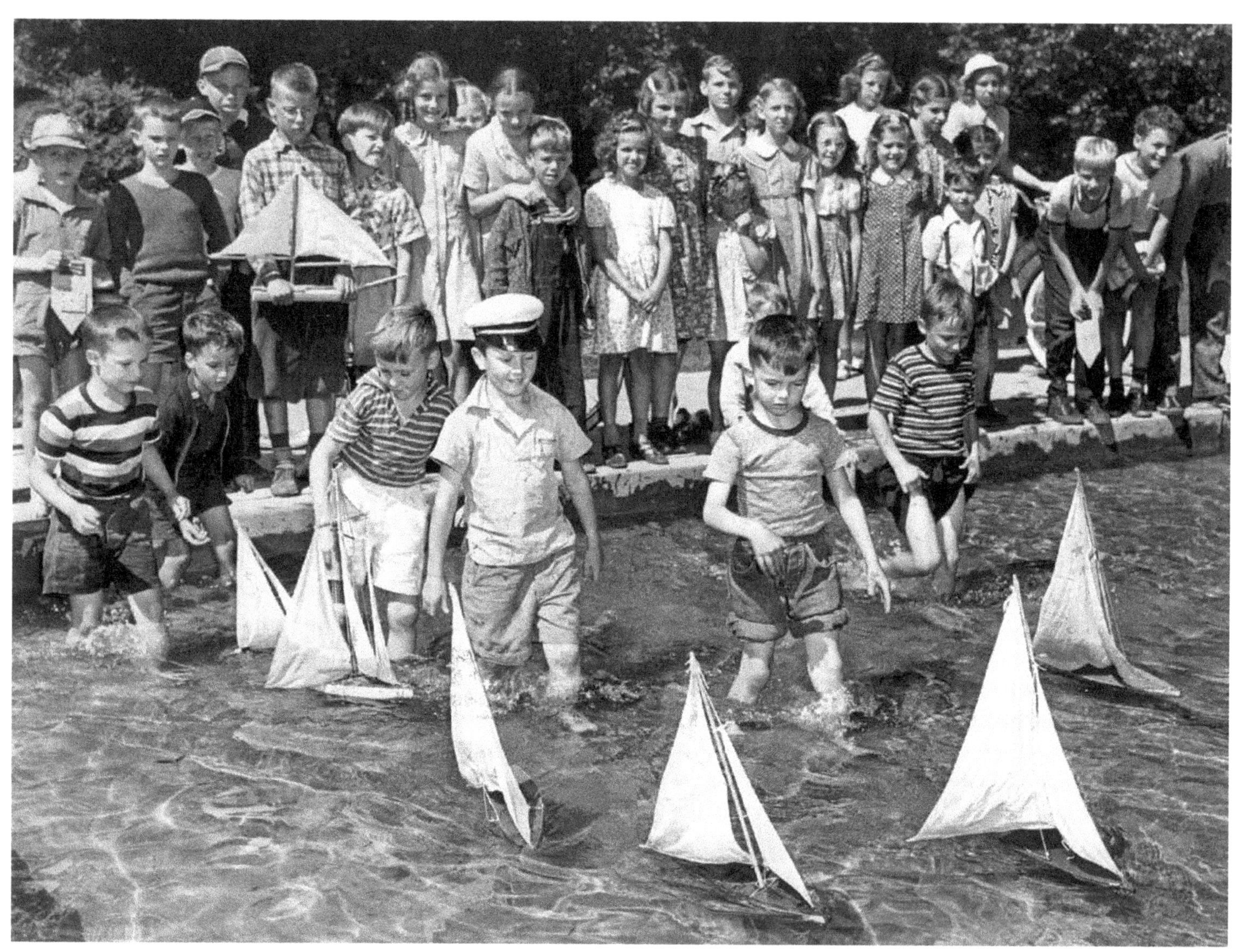

Children sail their toy sailboats at Wilcox Park.

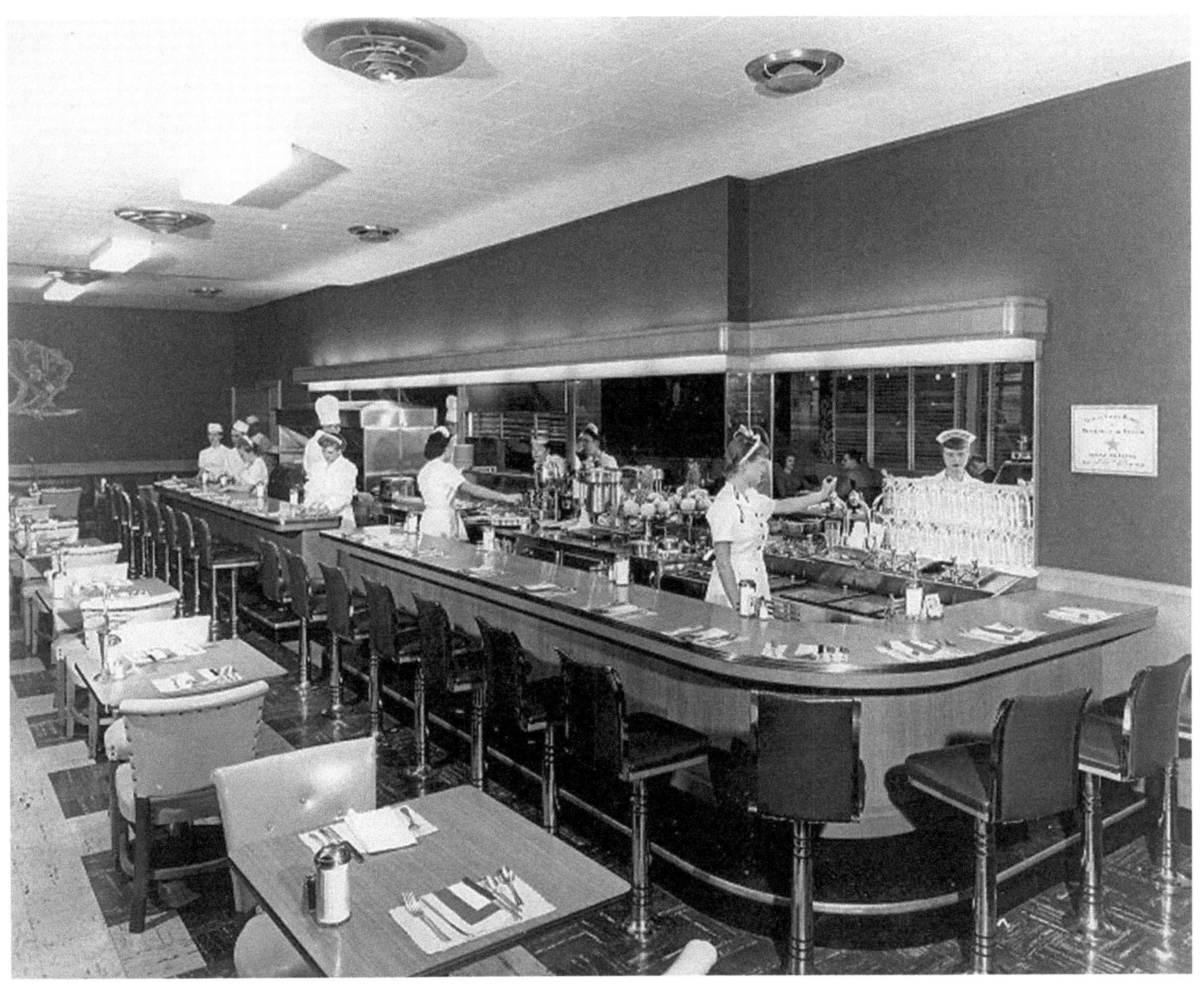

Interior view of the Rowe Hotel Coffee Shop.

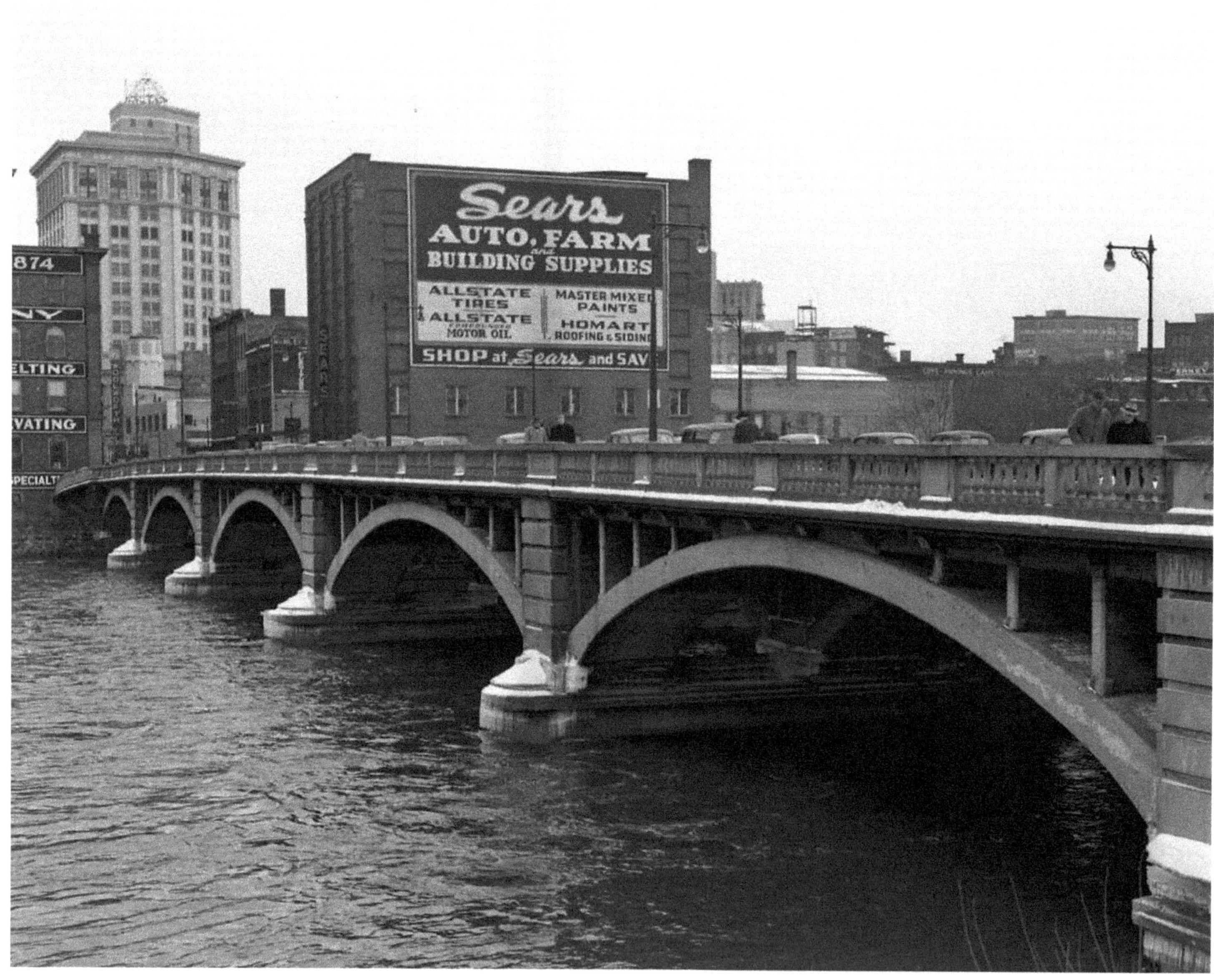

Pearl Street Bridge, completed in 1922, spans the Grand River.

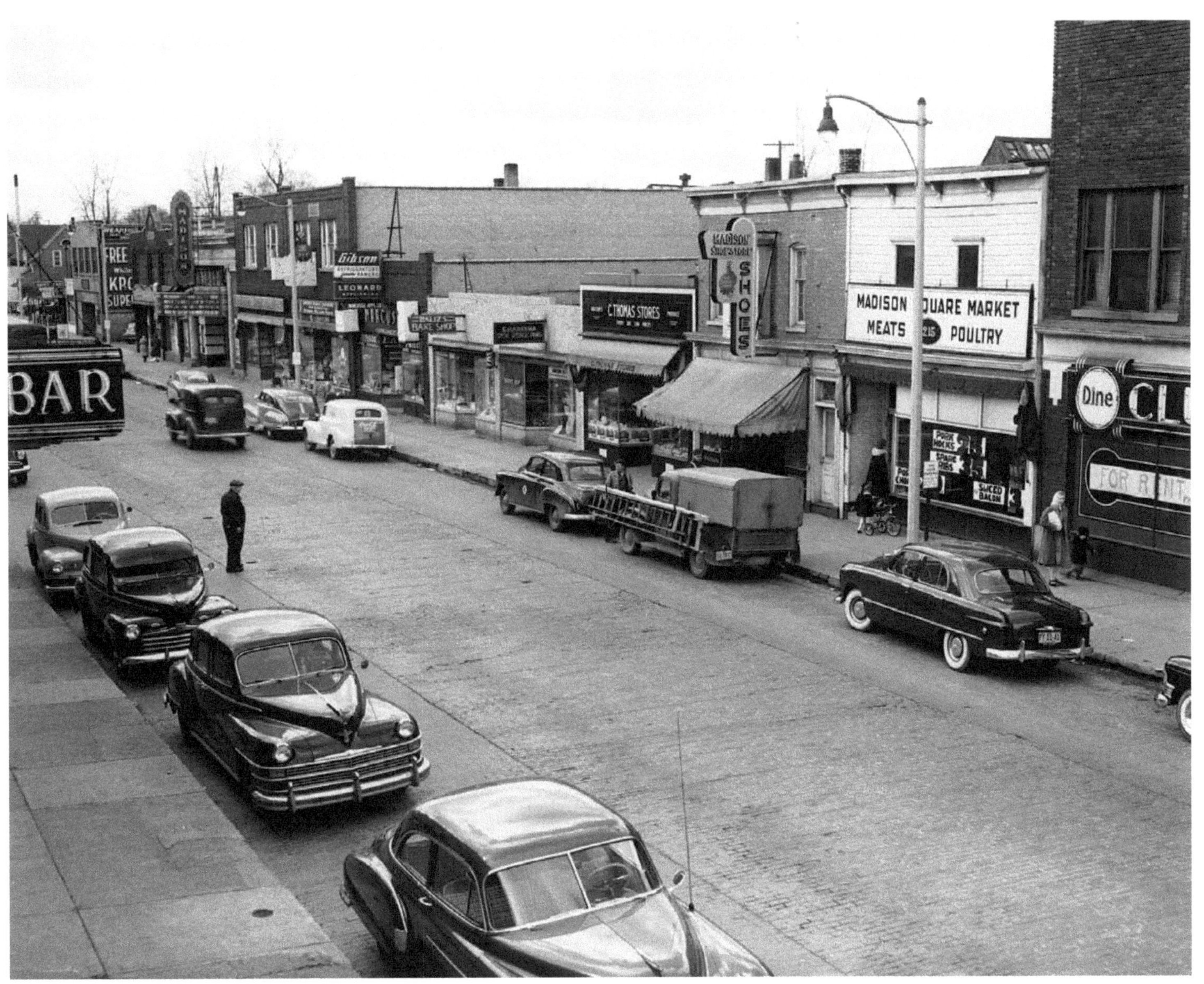

Madison Square, as it appeared in 1950.

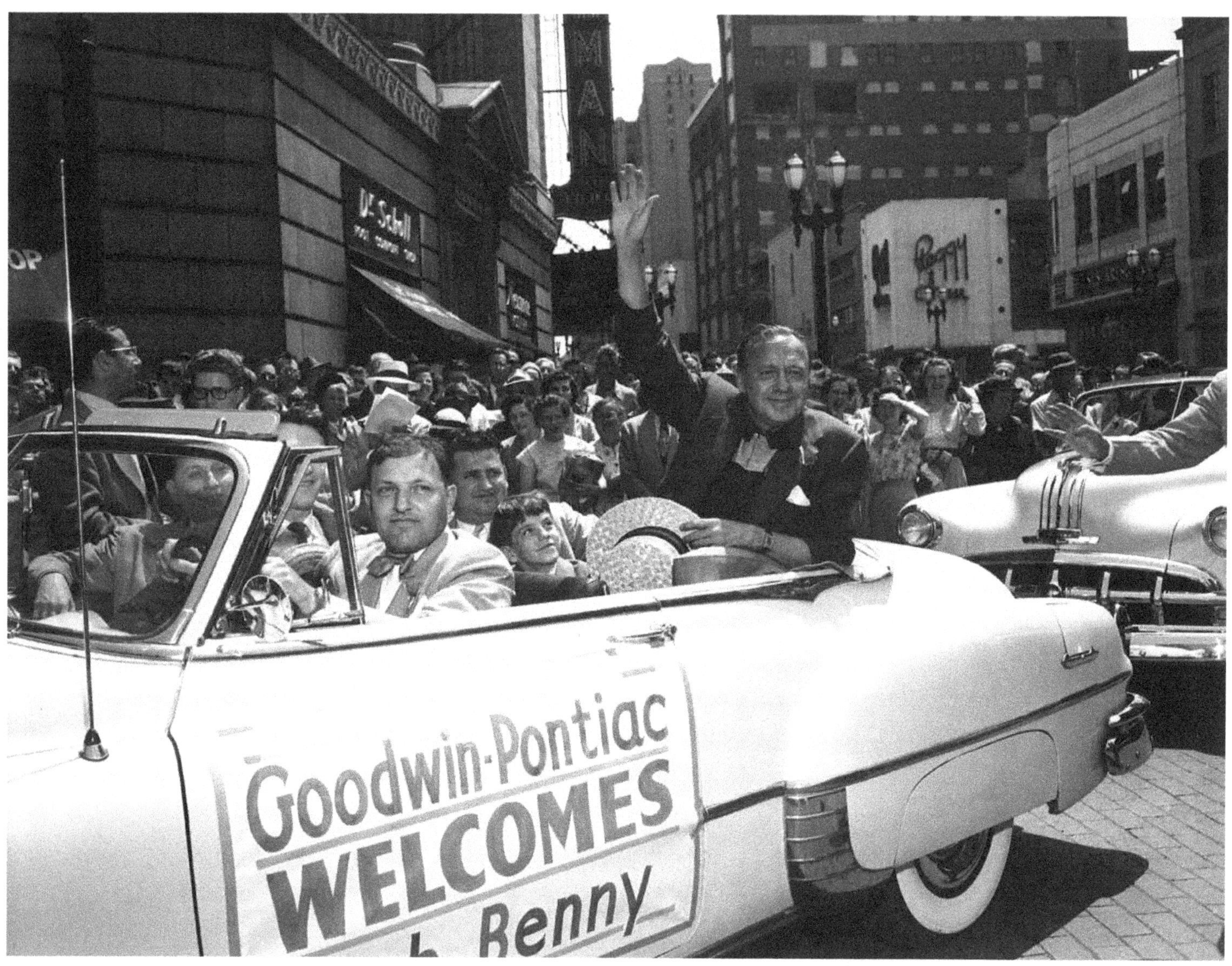

Jack Benny, radio and television star, is welcomed during the Liberty Bell Parade. The parade and ringing of the Liberty Bell replica signified the opening of the local Independence Savings Bond Drive by the United States Treasury Department.

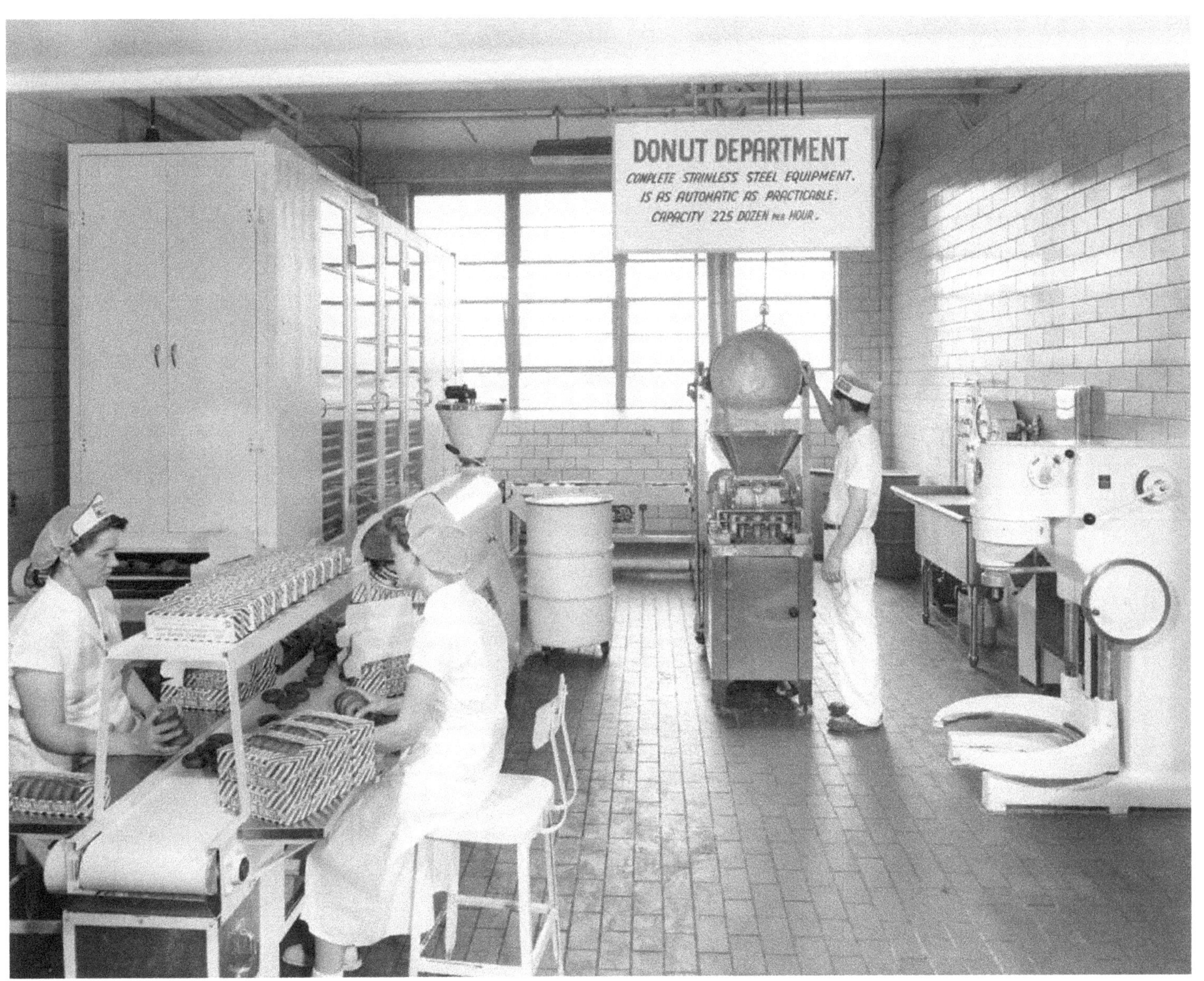

At the Michigan Bakeries, 1325 Edna SE, the latest in 1950s doughnut technology can yield 225 dozen per hour.

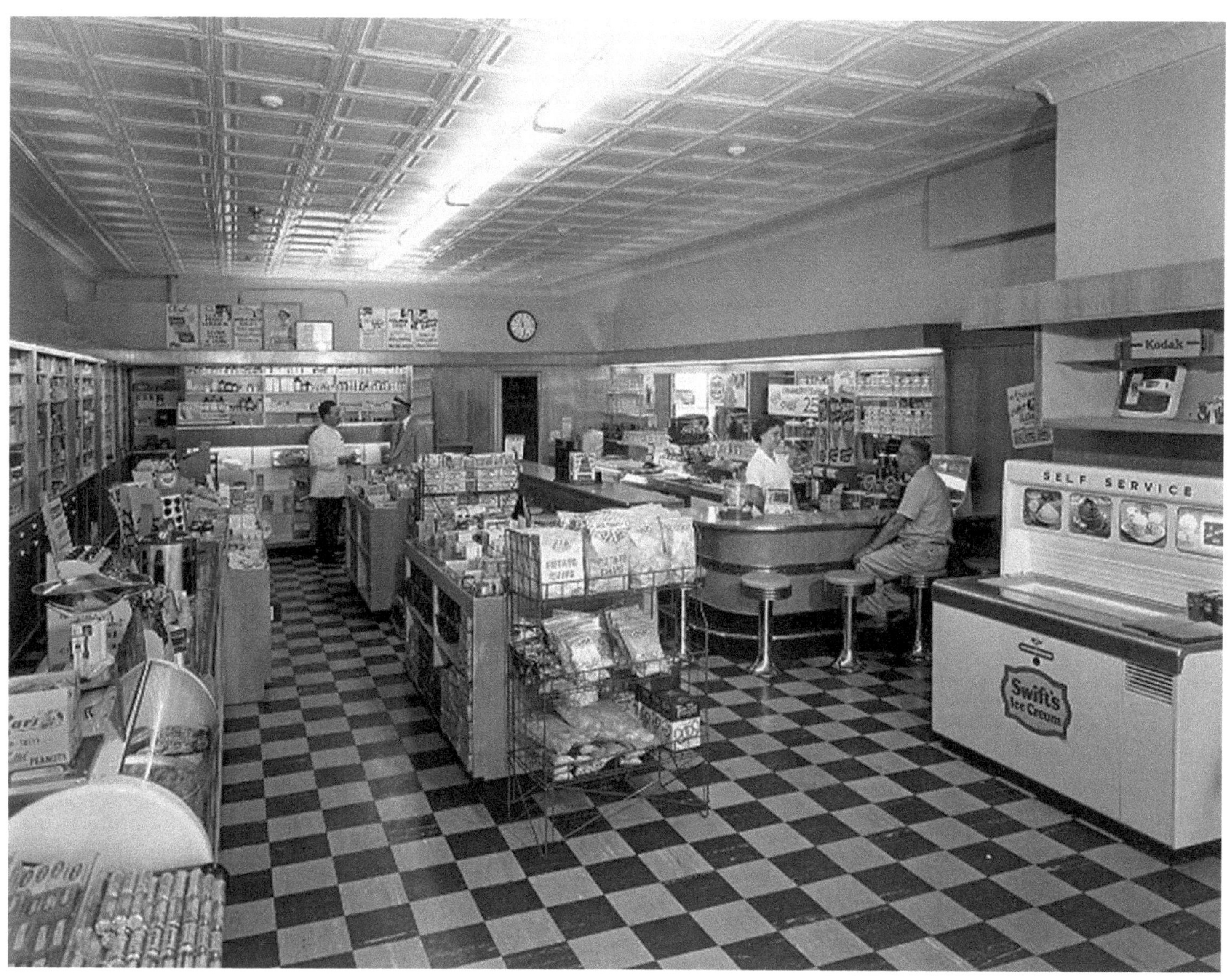

Interior view of Skripka's Drug Store, at 748 Leonard Street NW.

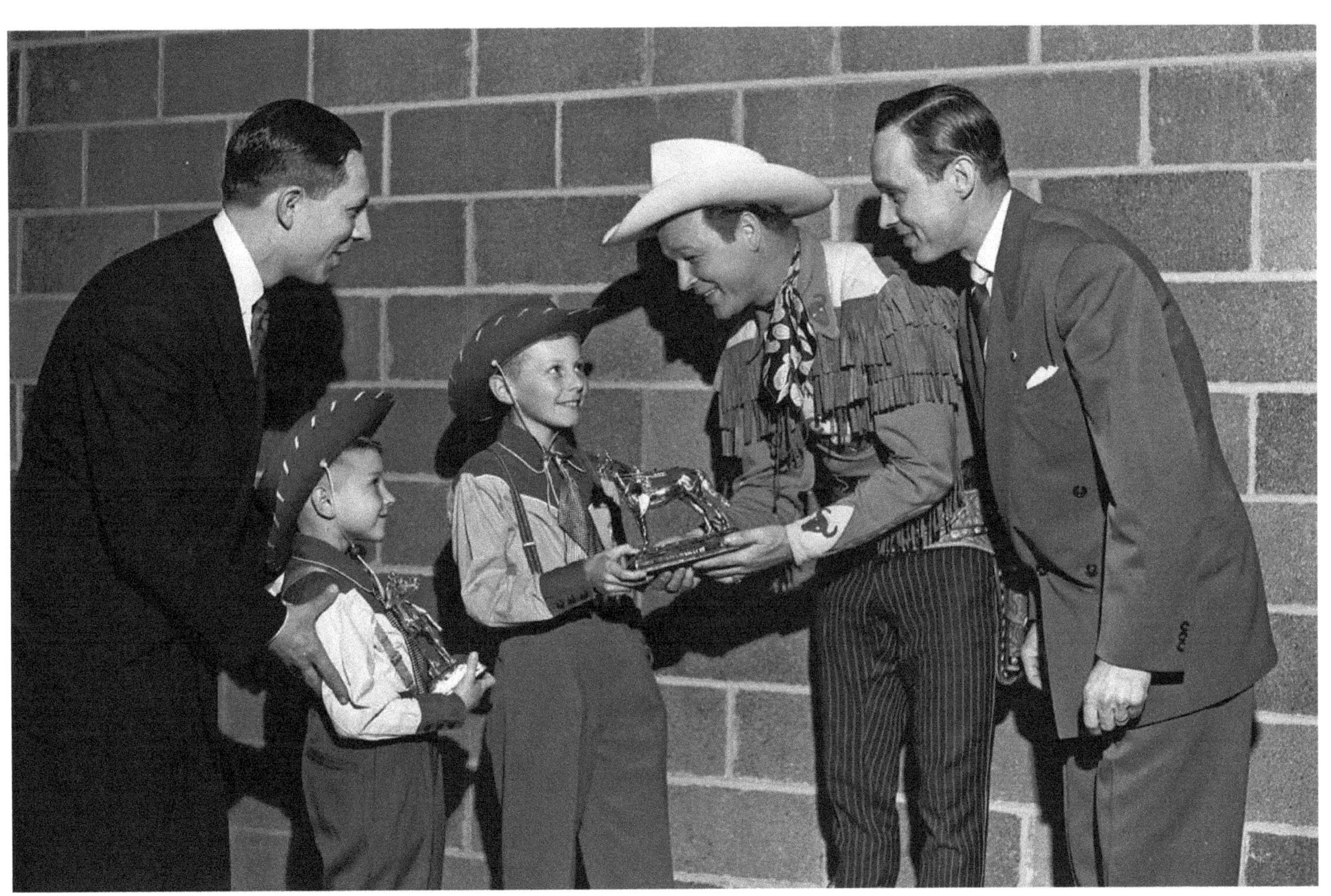

Winning prizes and meeting your favorite cowboy—a priceless experience for a youngster. Roy Rogers visits Wurzburg's Department Store in 1950.

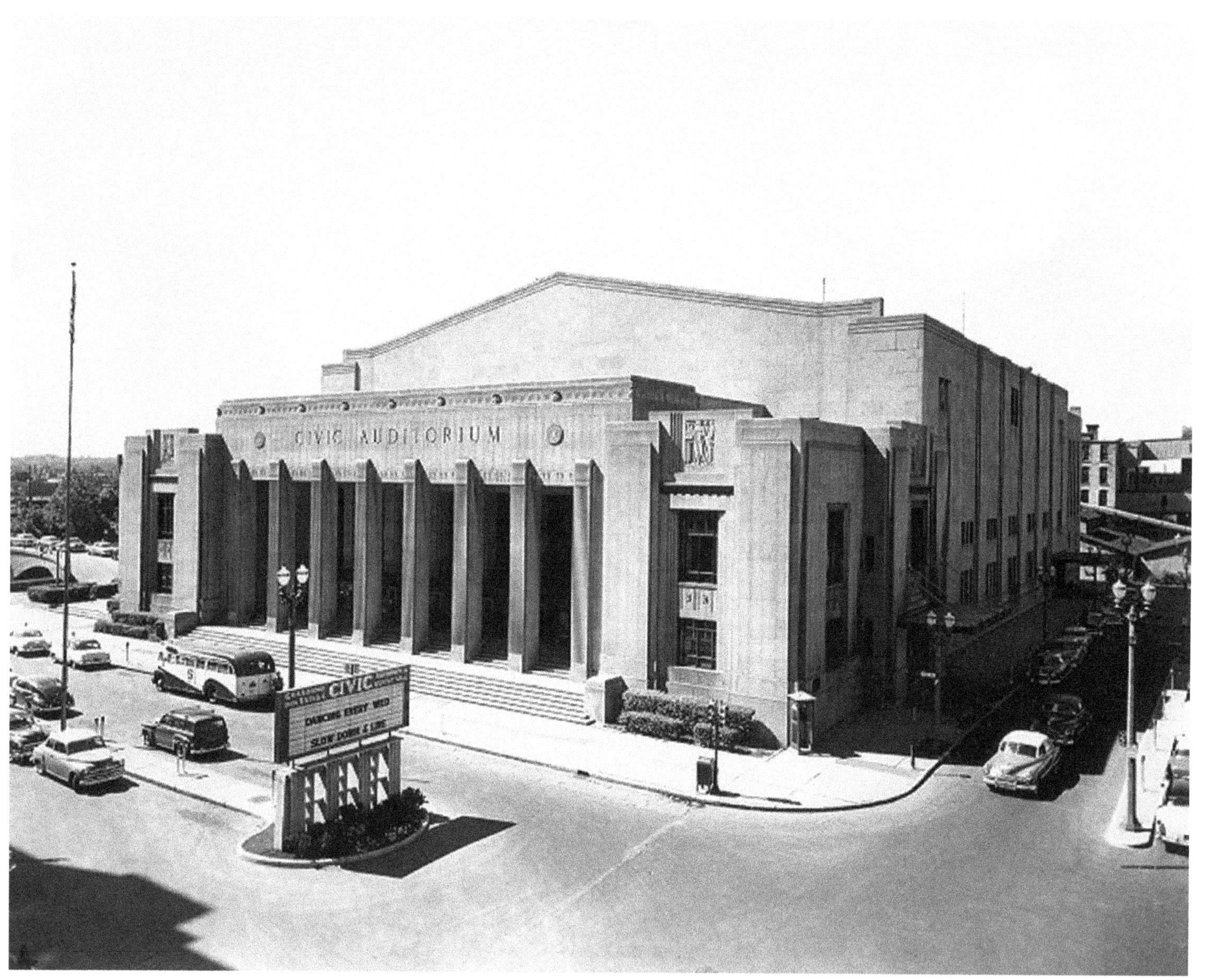

A 1950s bird's-eye view of the Civic Auditorium.

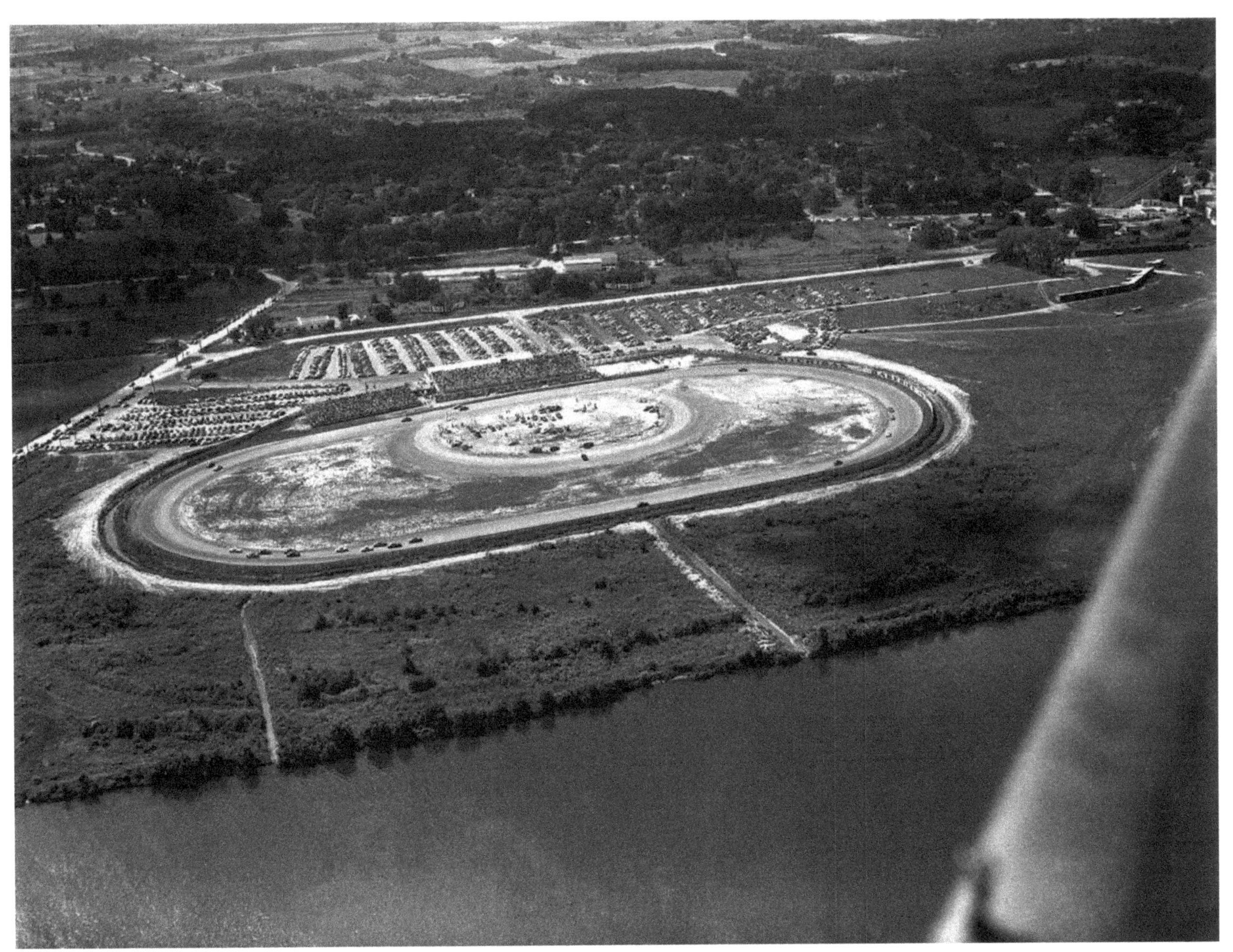

The Speedrome opened with its first race on May 28, 1950.

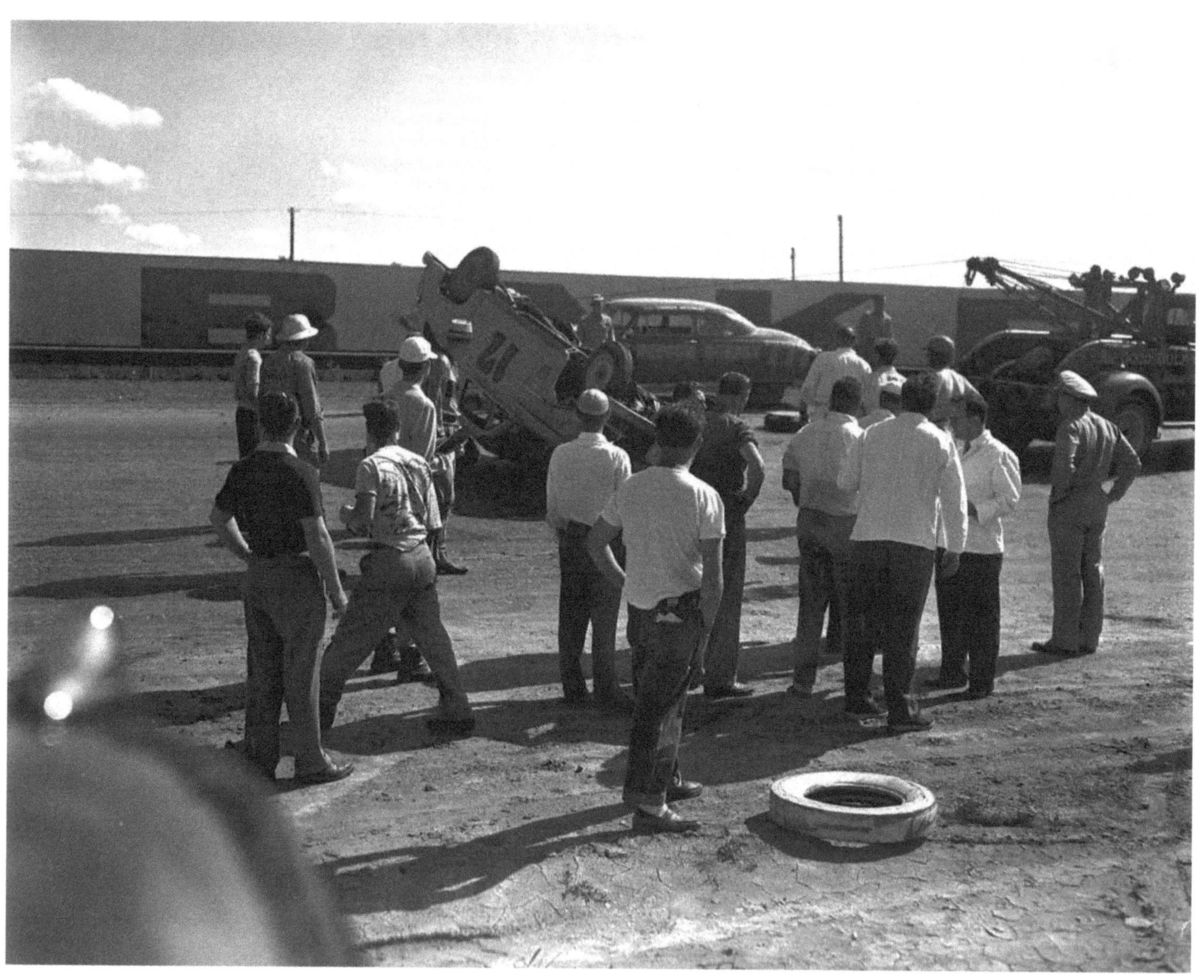

The caution flag is out, following this accident at the Speedrome.

Monroe Avenue, showing the Morton House and Steketee's Department Store.

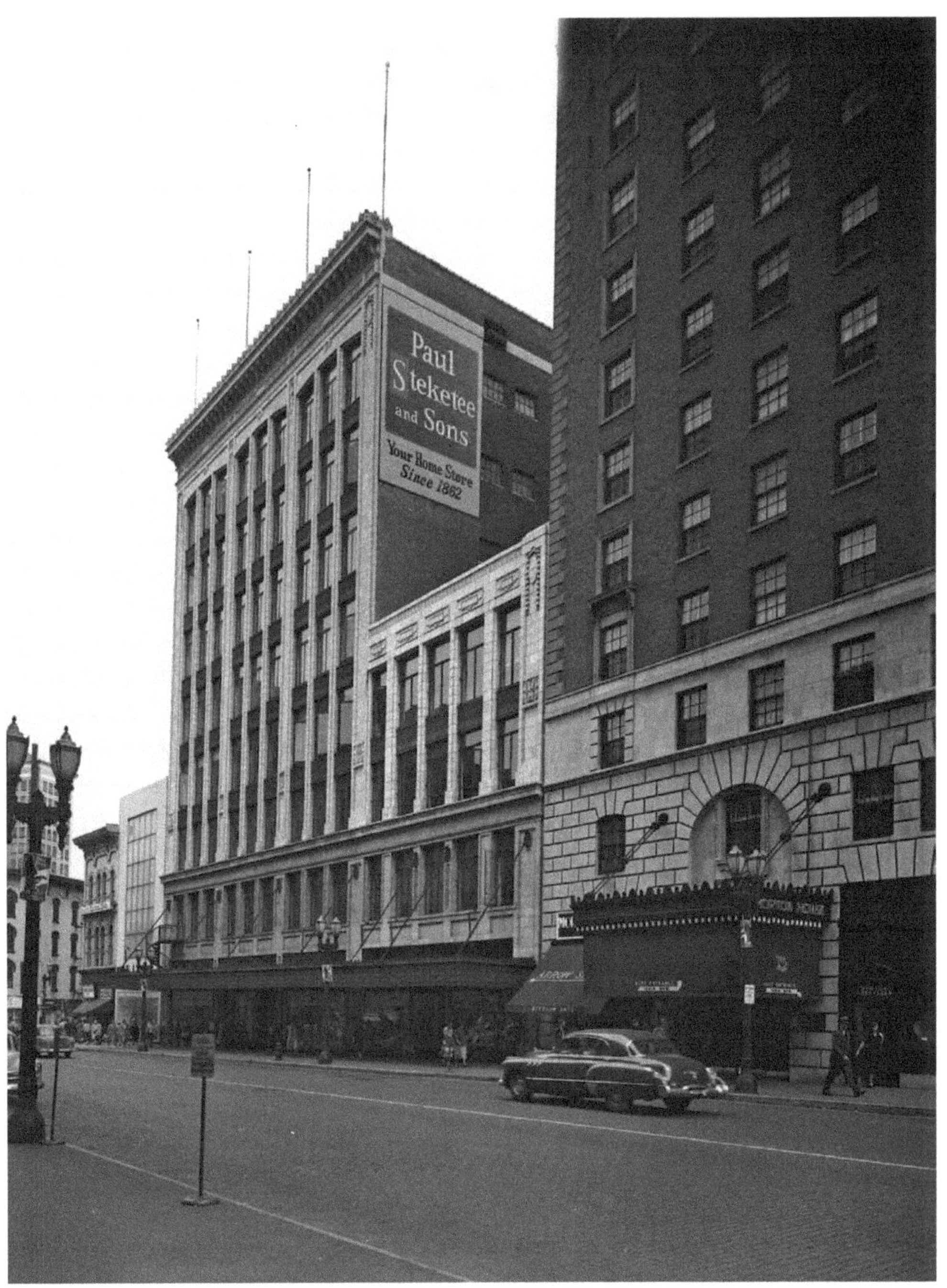

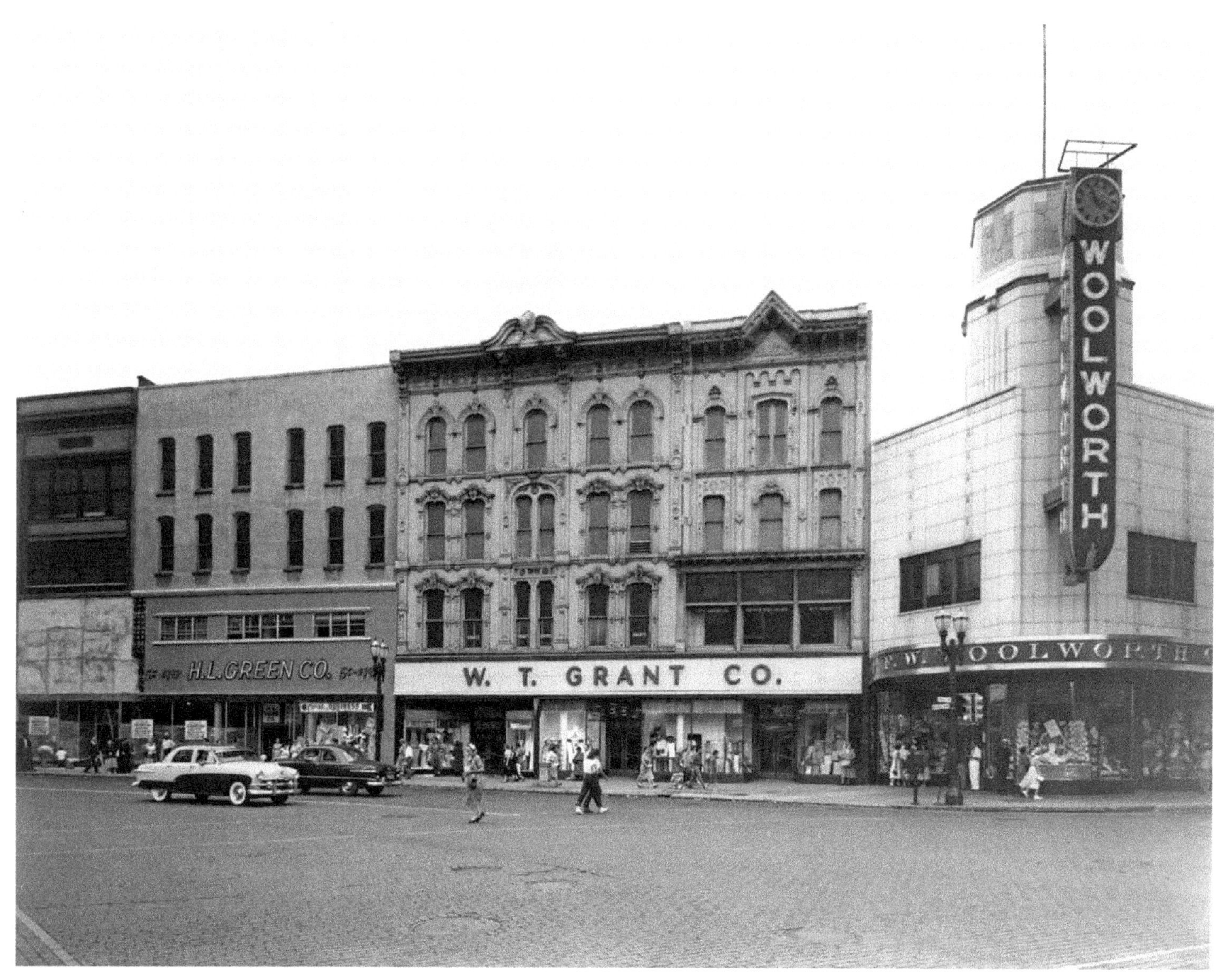

The dimestore block in Campau Square is busy with shoppers here in the 1950s. Open for business are the W. T. Grant Company, F. W. Woolworth's, and the H. L. Green Company.

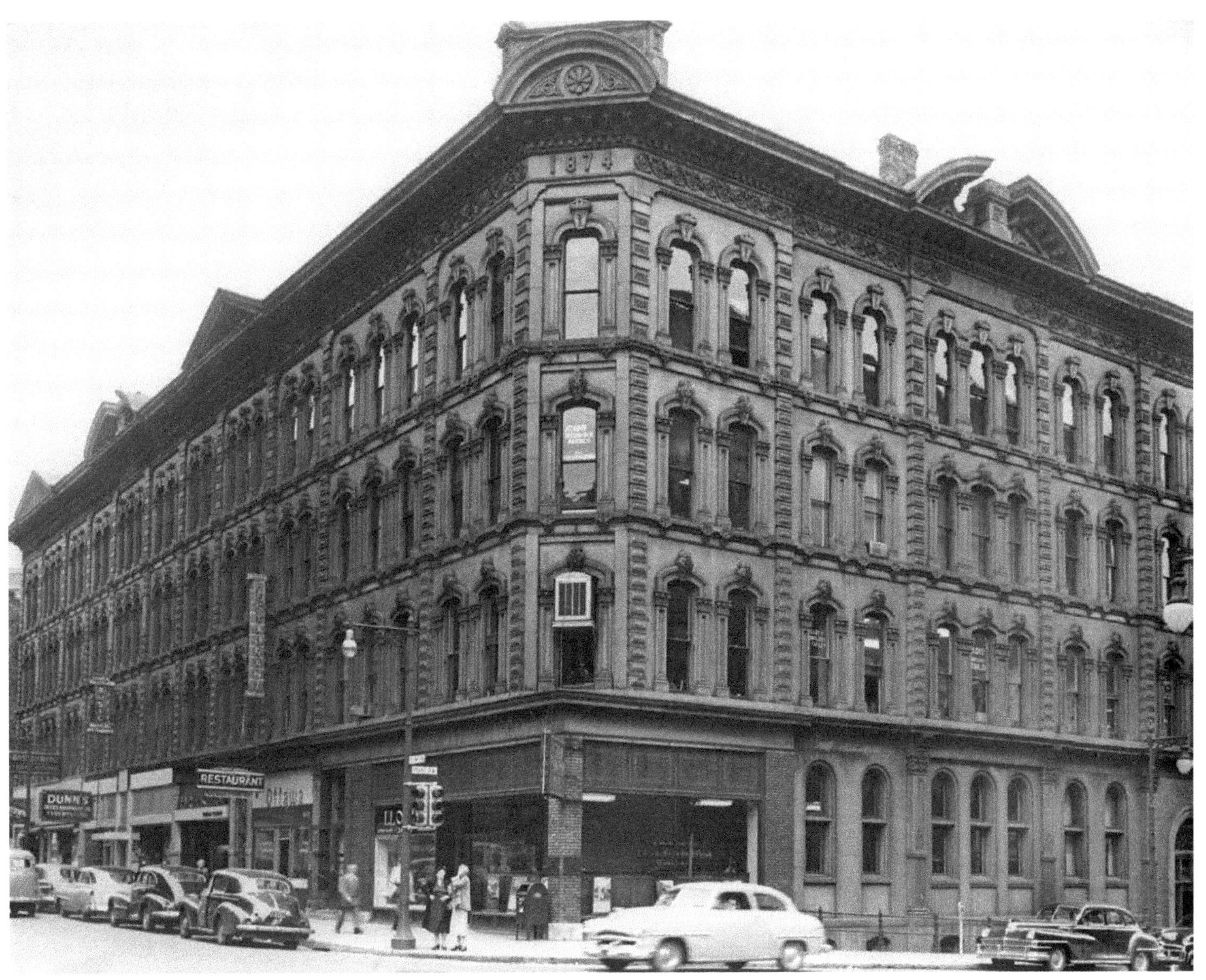

The Ledyard Building, built in 1874 and shown here in the 1950s, stands at the corner of Pearl and Ottawa streets. The historic edifice was renovated in 2007.

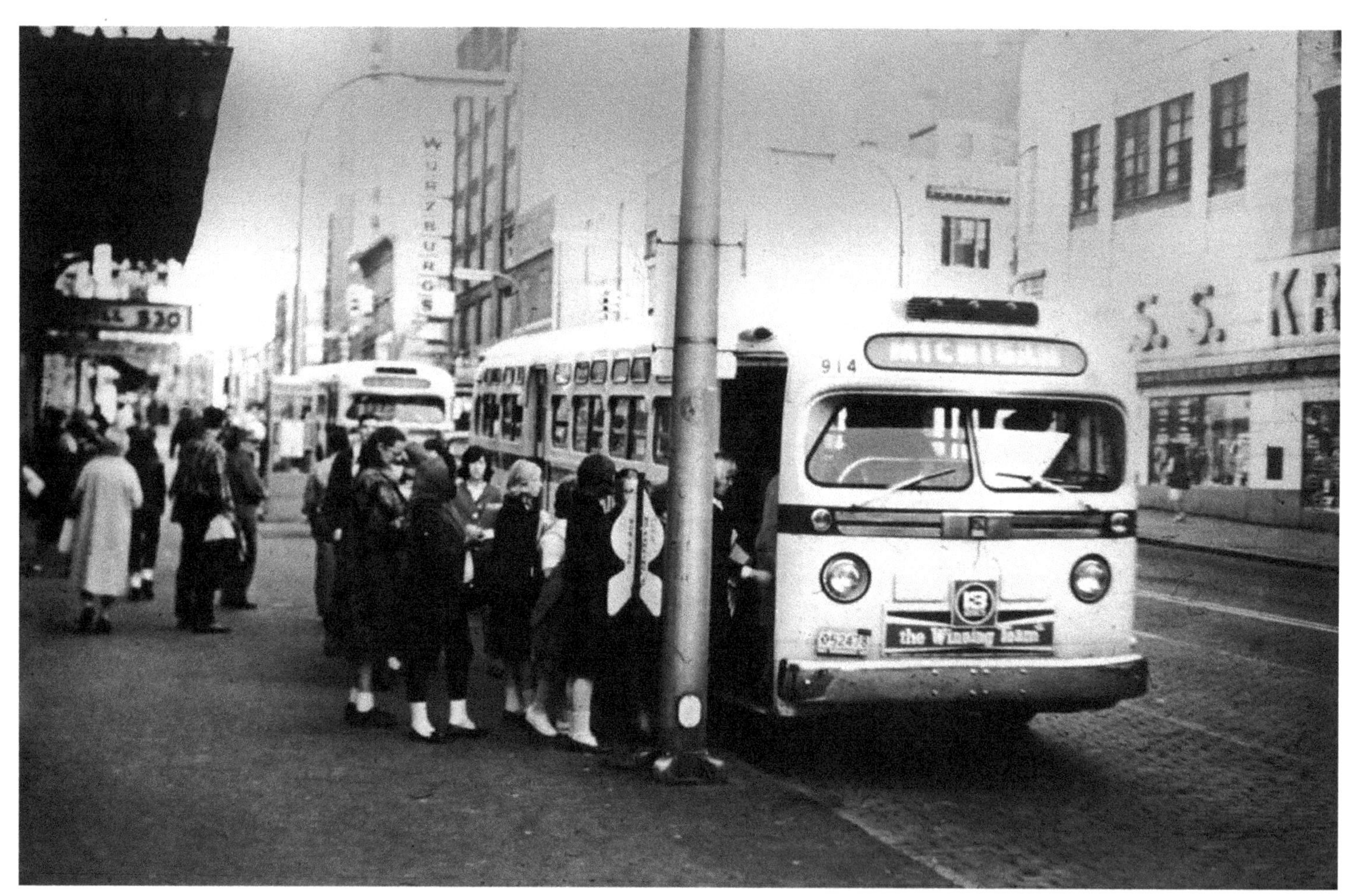

Young women catch the bus after spending the afternoon downtown.

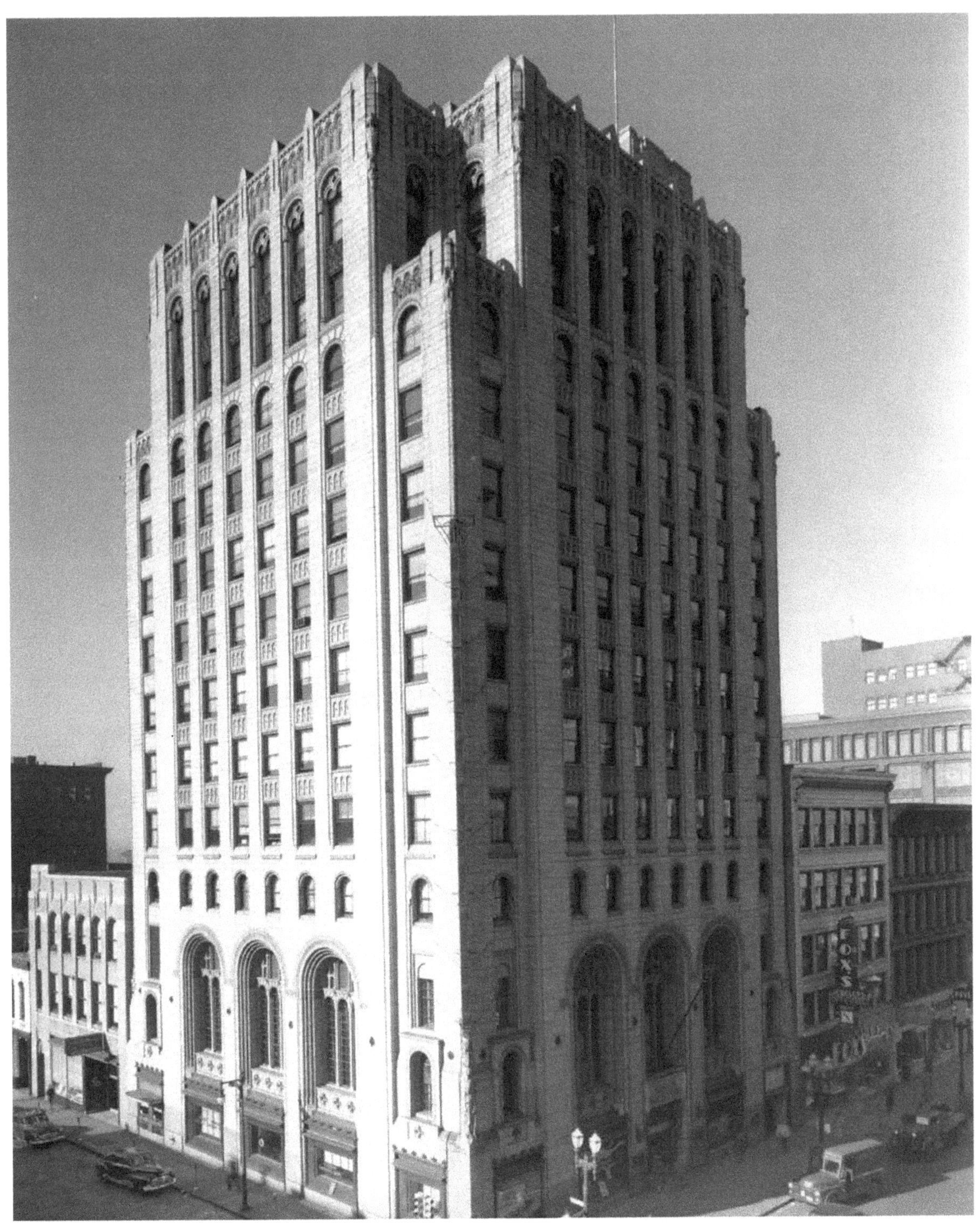

The Michigan National Bank was formed in December 1940 when Howard J. Stoddard consolidated six Michigan banks: the First National Bank and Trust Company of Grand Rapids, First National Trust and Savings Bank of Port Huron, Lansing National Bank, Battle Creek's Security National Bank, National Bank of Saginaw, and First National Bank of Marshall. The bank purchased and absorbed the National Bank of Flint in 1942.

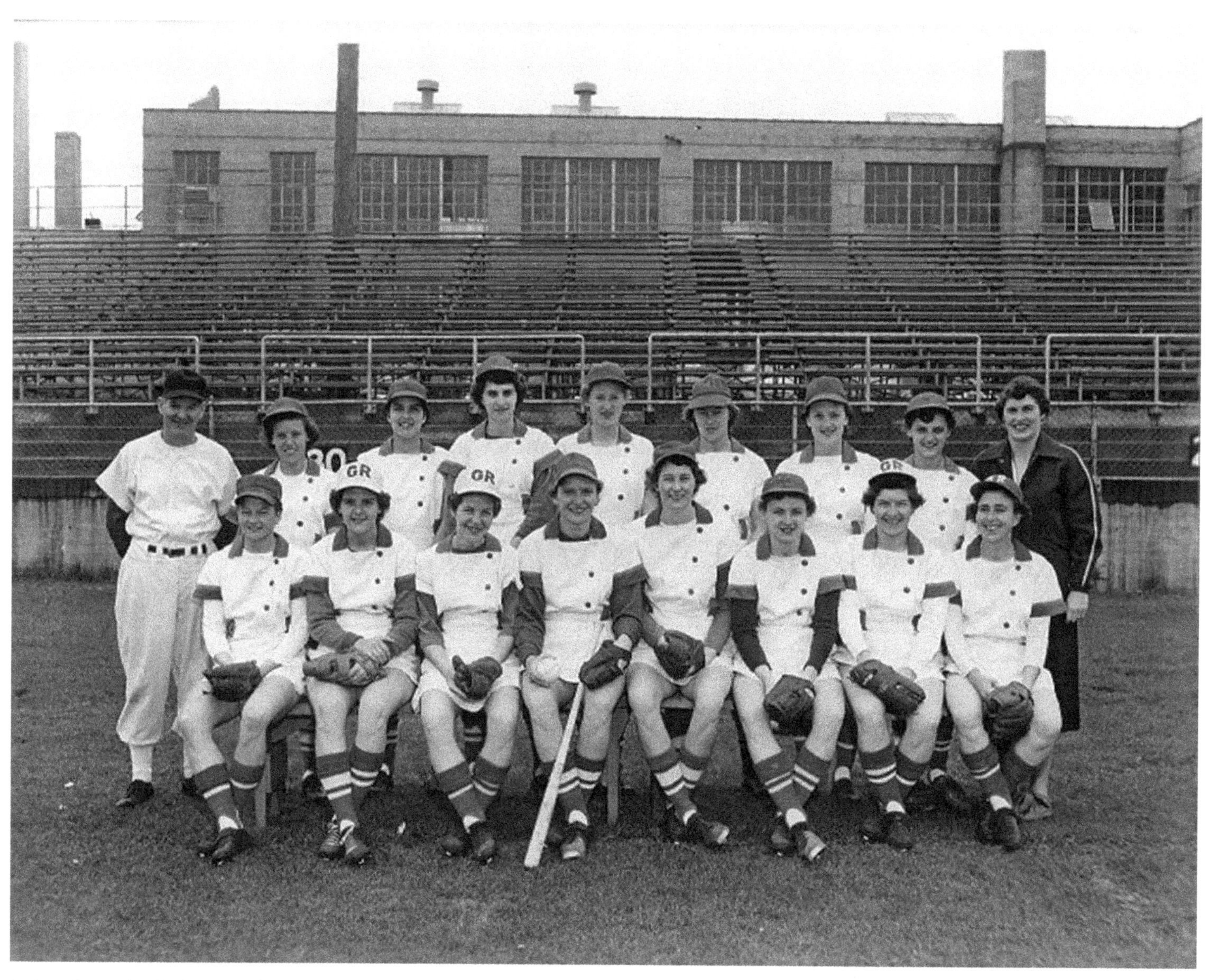

A Grand Rapids Chicks team photo.

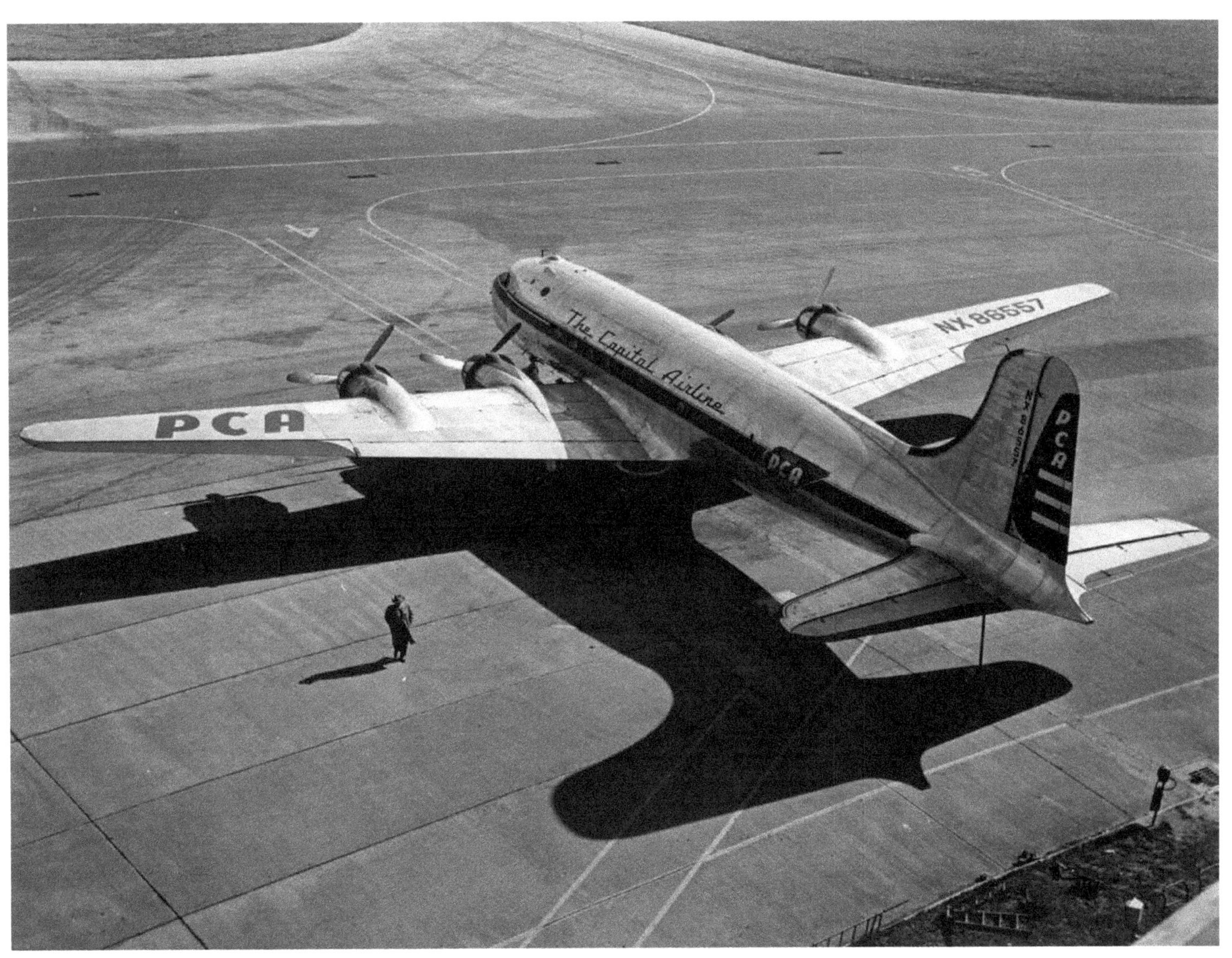

Capital Airlines, also known as Pennsylvania Central Airlines, inaugurated 4-engine passenger service in Grand Rapids in August 1952. The airline had a fleet of 25 of these planes.

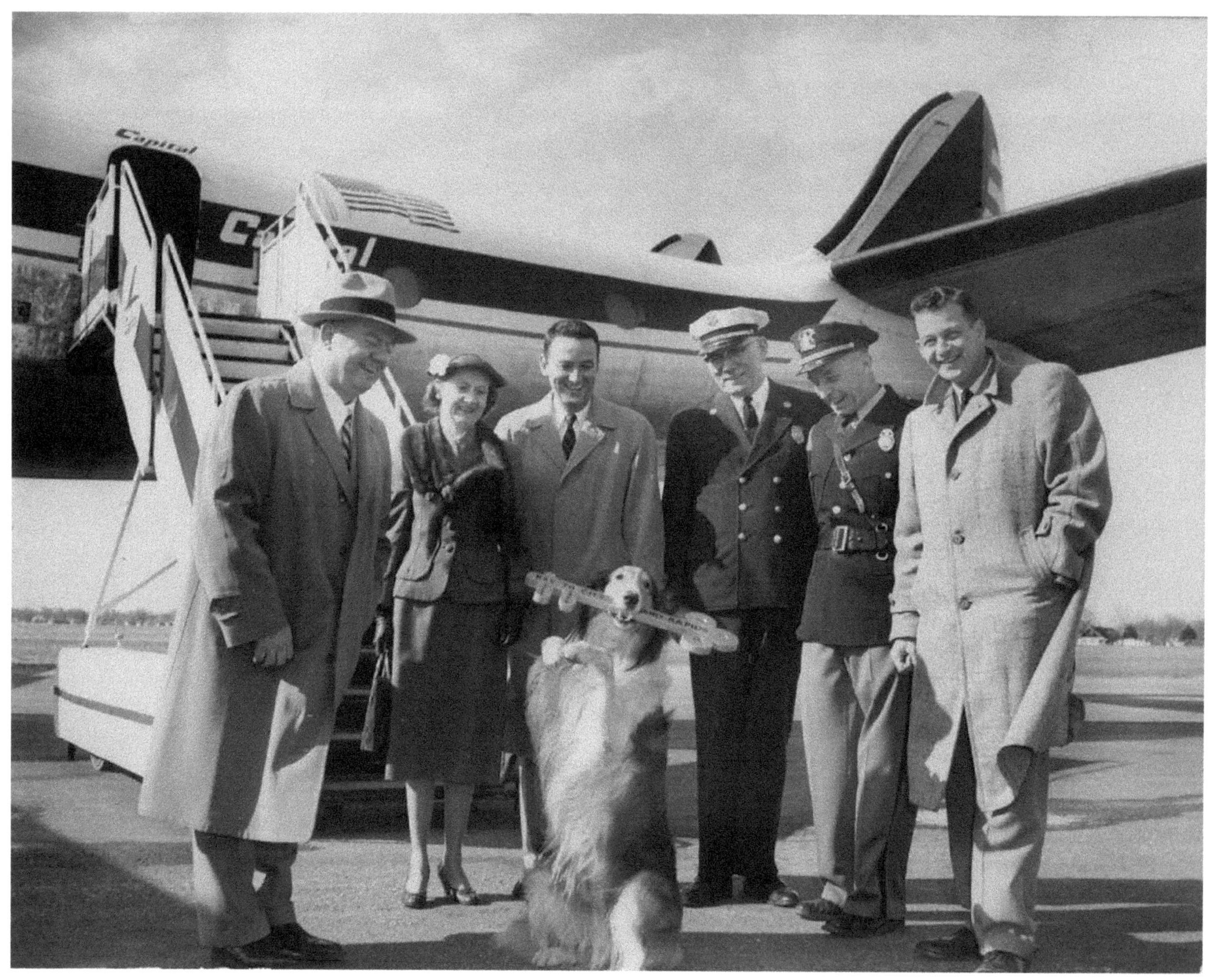

Celebrity canine Lassie receives the key to the city.

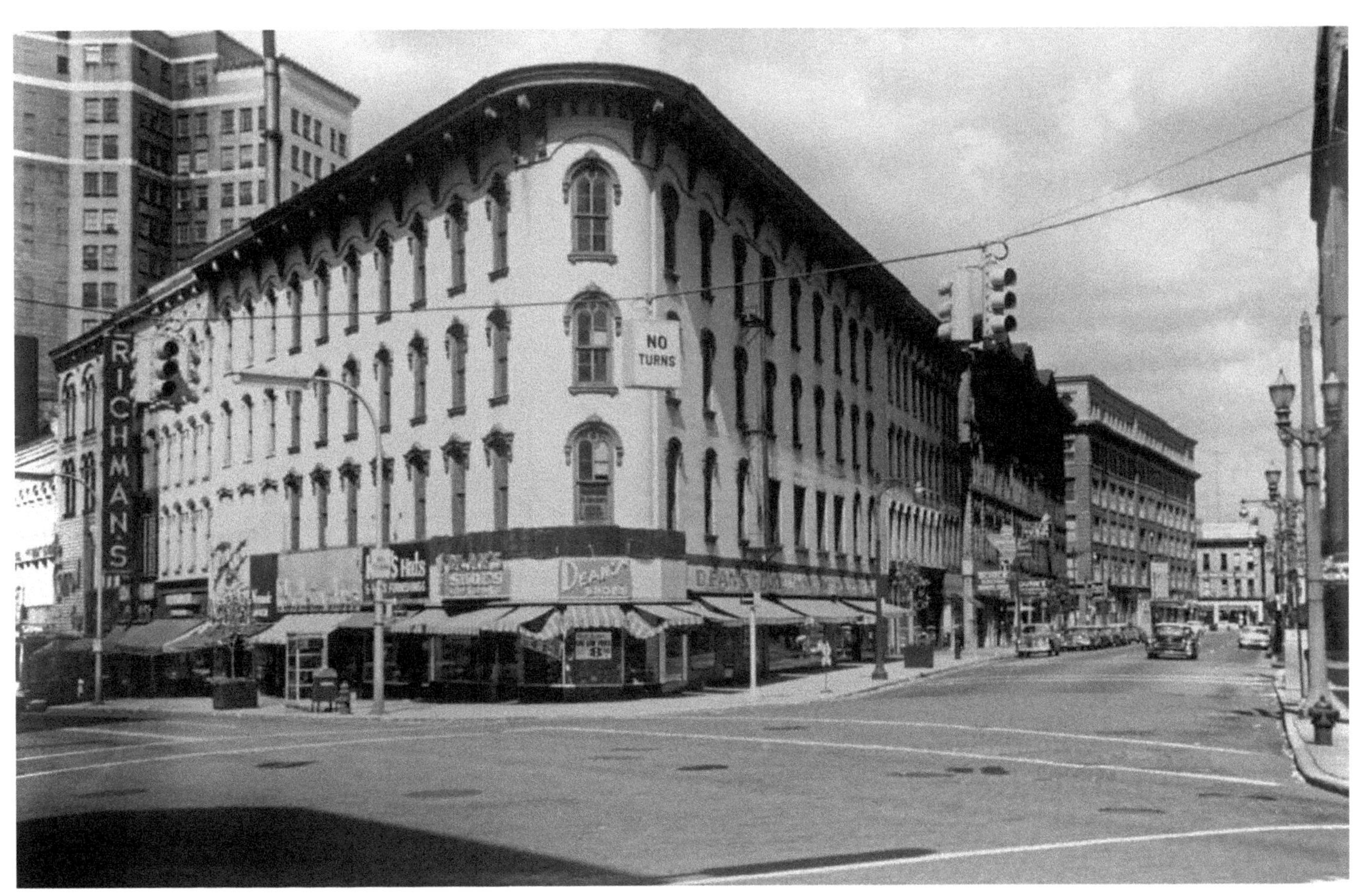

Shops at Monroe and Ottawa.

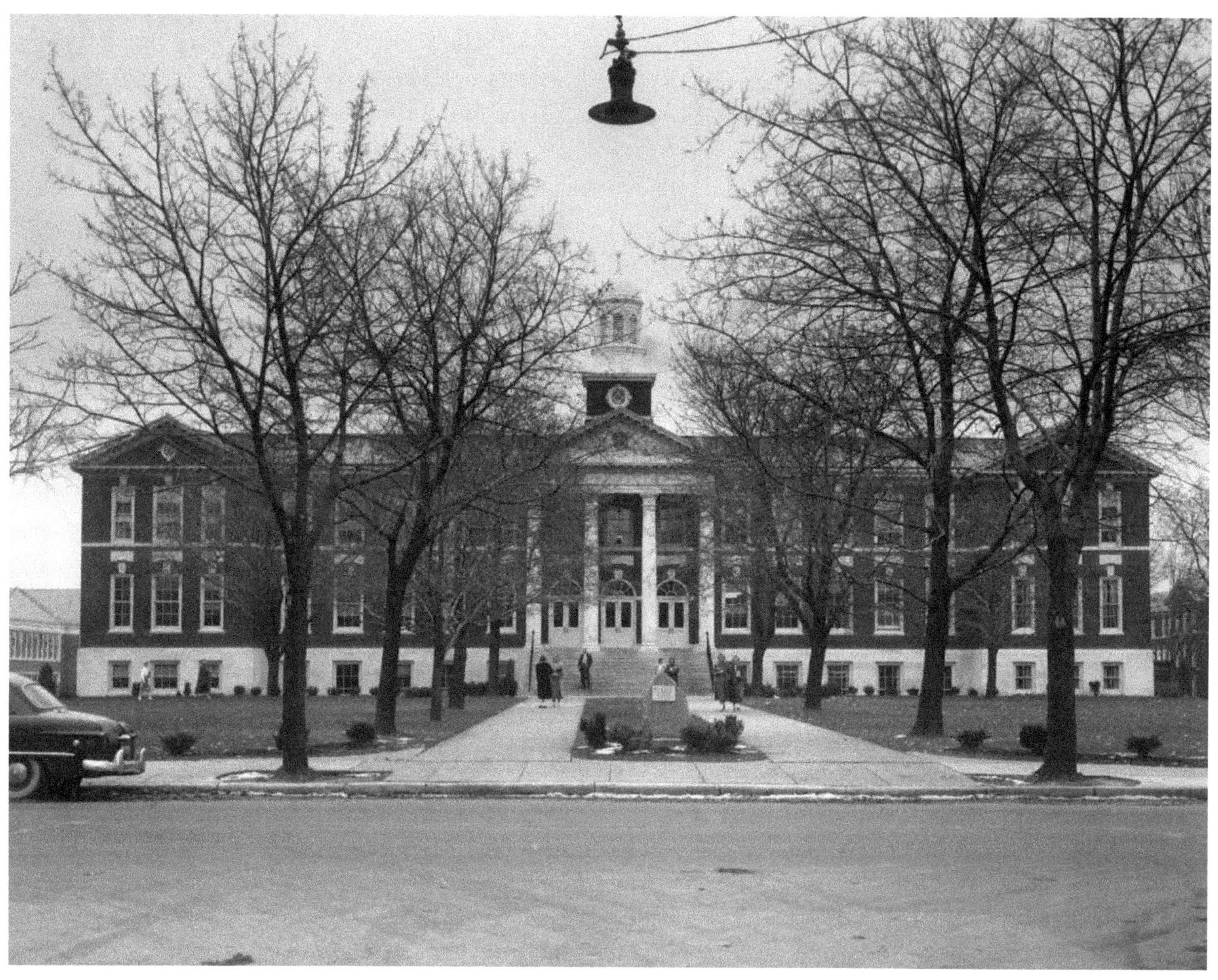

The Calvin College Administration Building on Franklin. Today it houses the Grand Rapids Public Schools administrative offices.

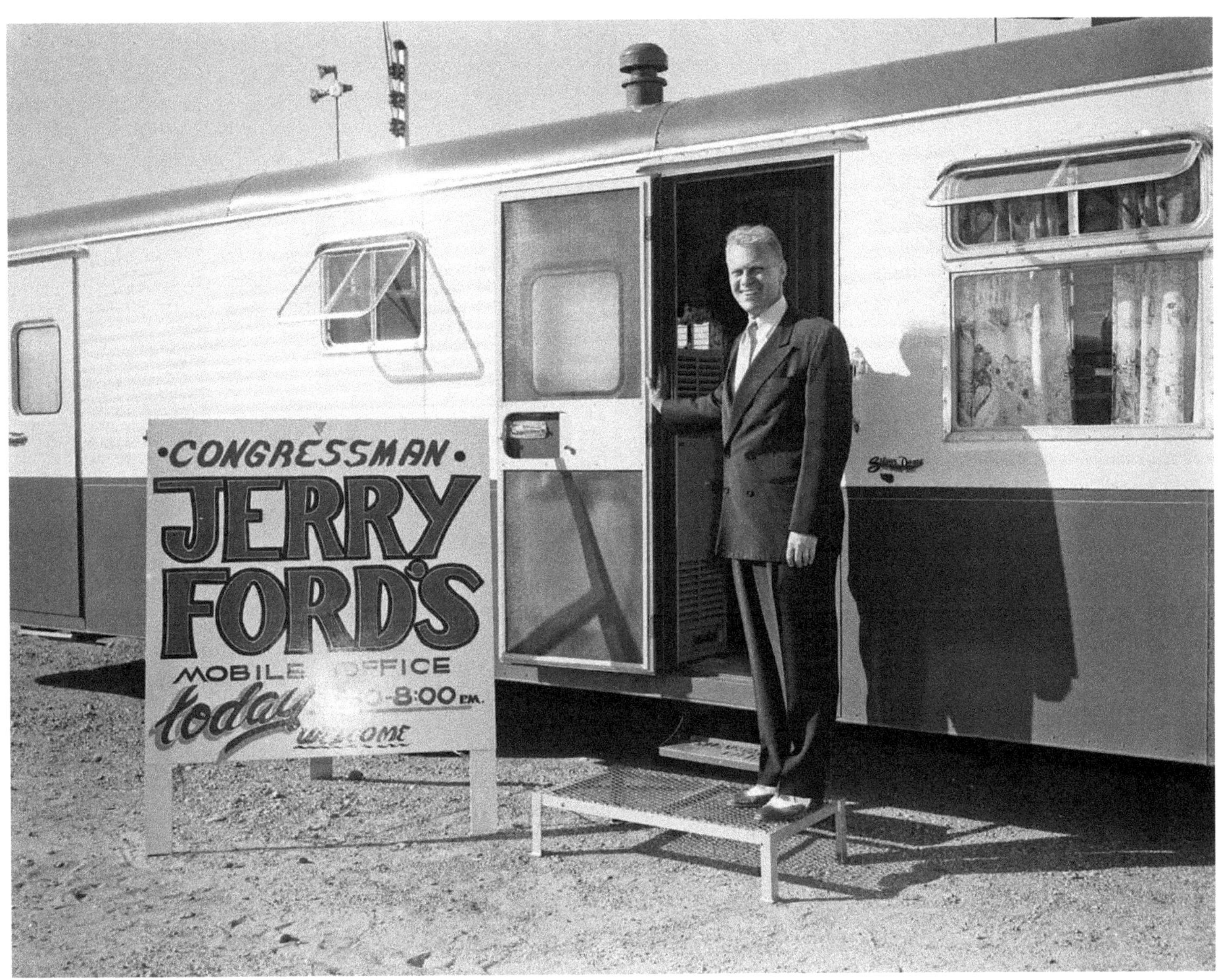

Where it all began. Gerald R. "Jerry" Ford runs for Congress.

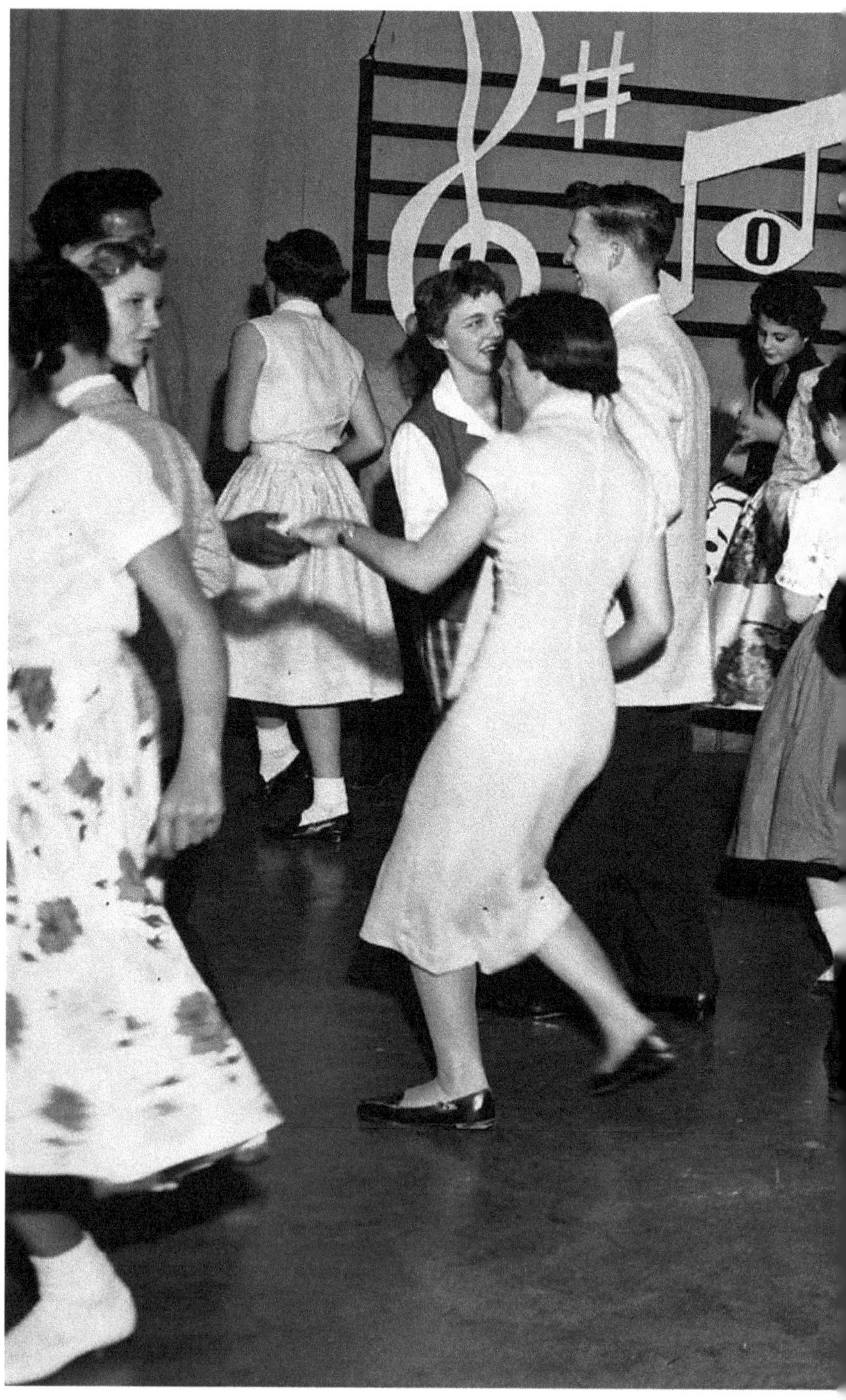

Grand Rapids' own American Bandstand—WOOD-TV's *Bop Hop.*

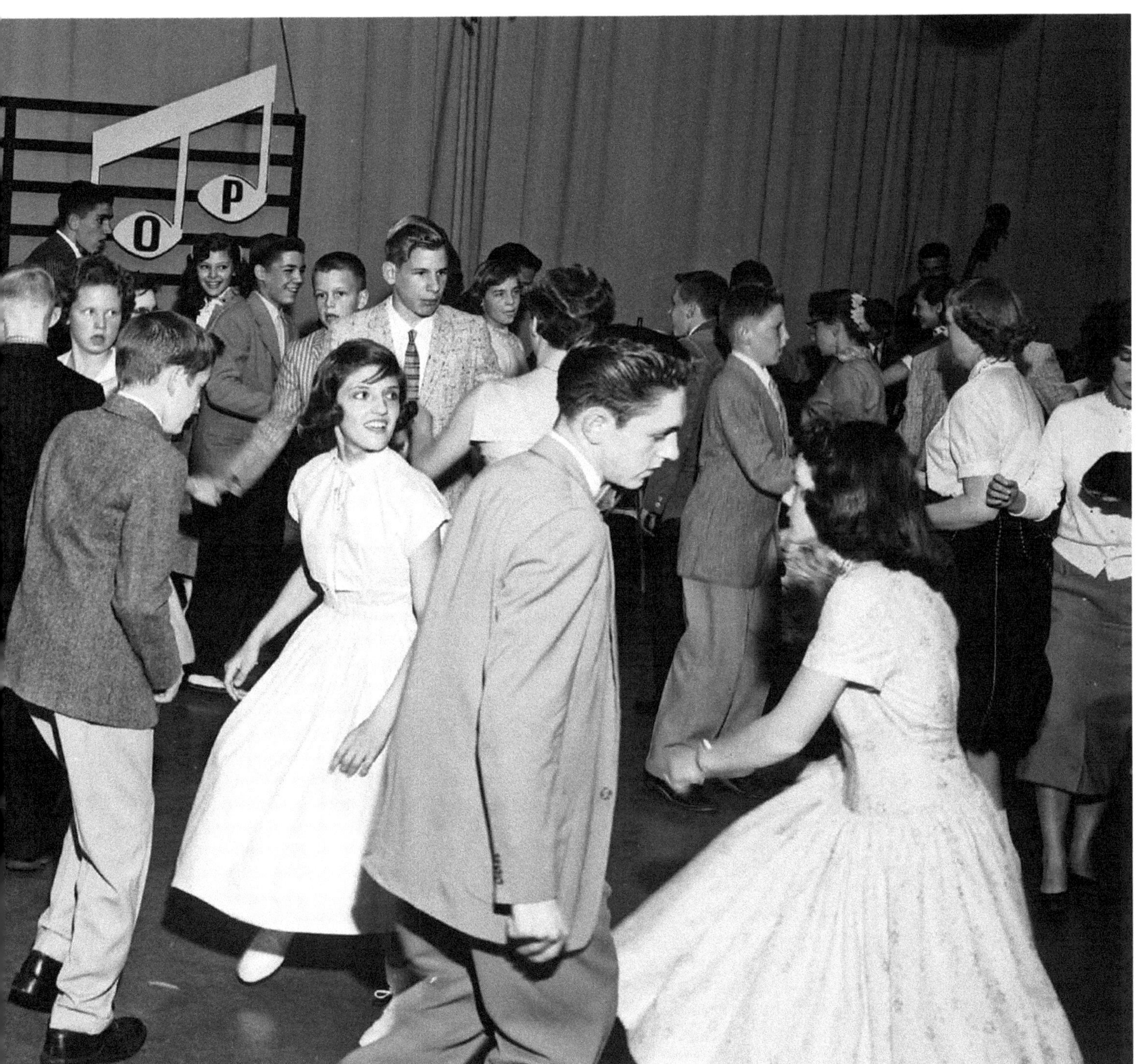
O
P

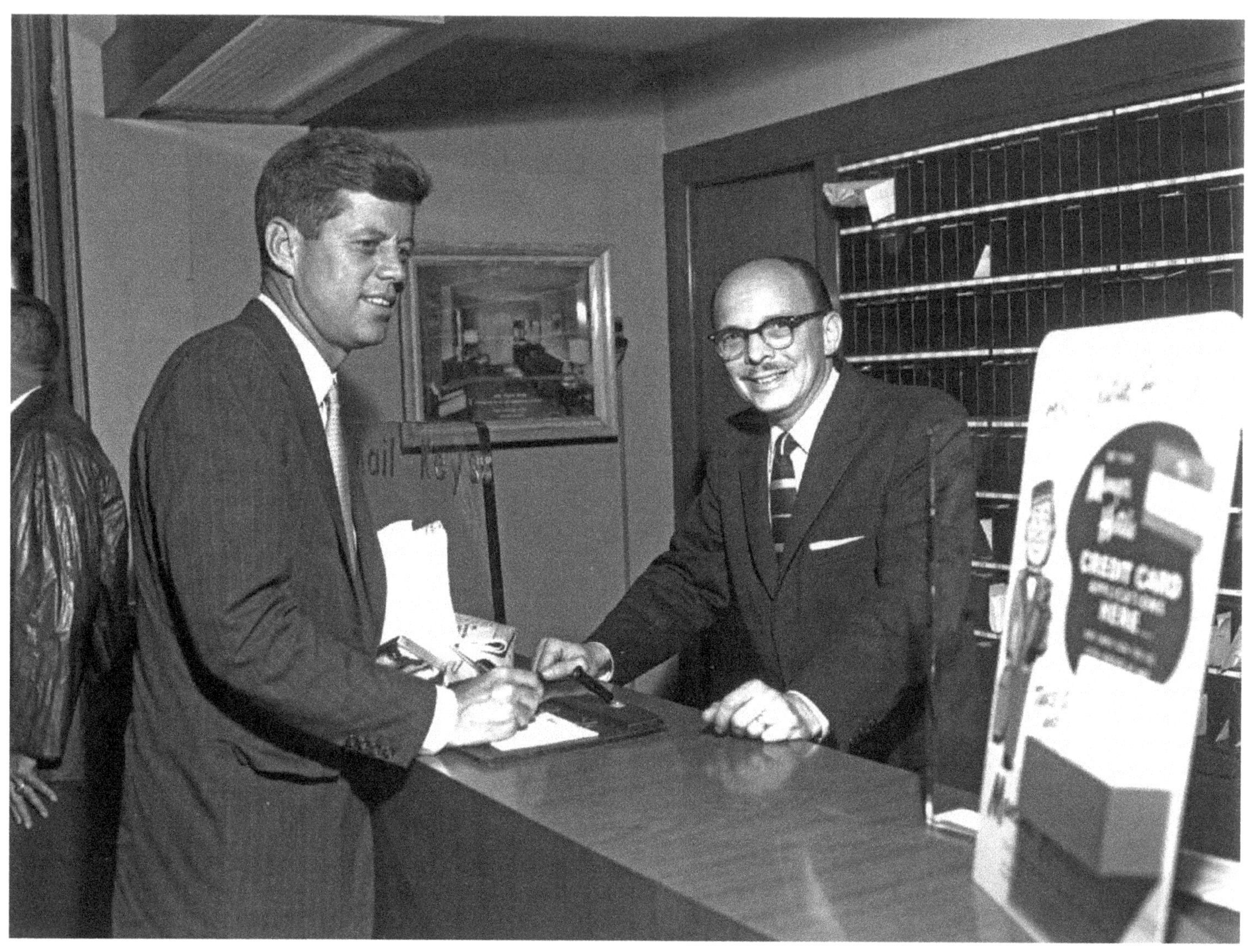

John F. Kennedy registers at the Manager Hotel in Grand Rapids on September 17, 1958.

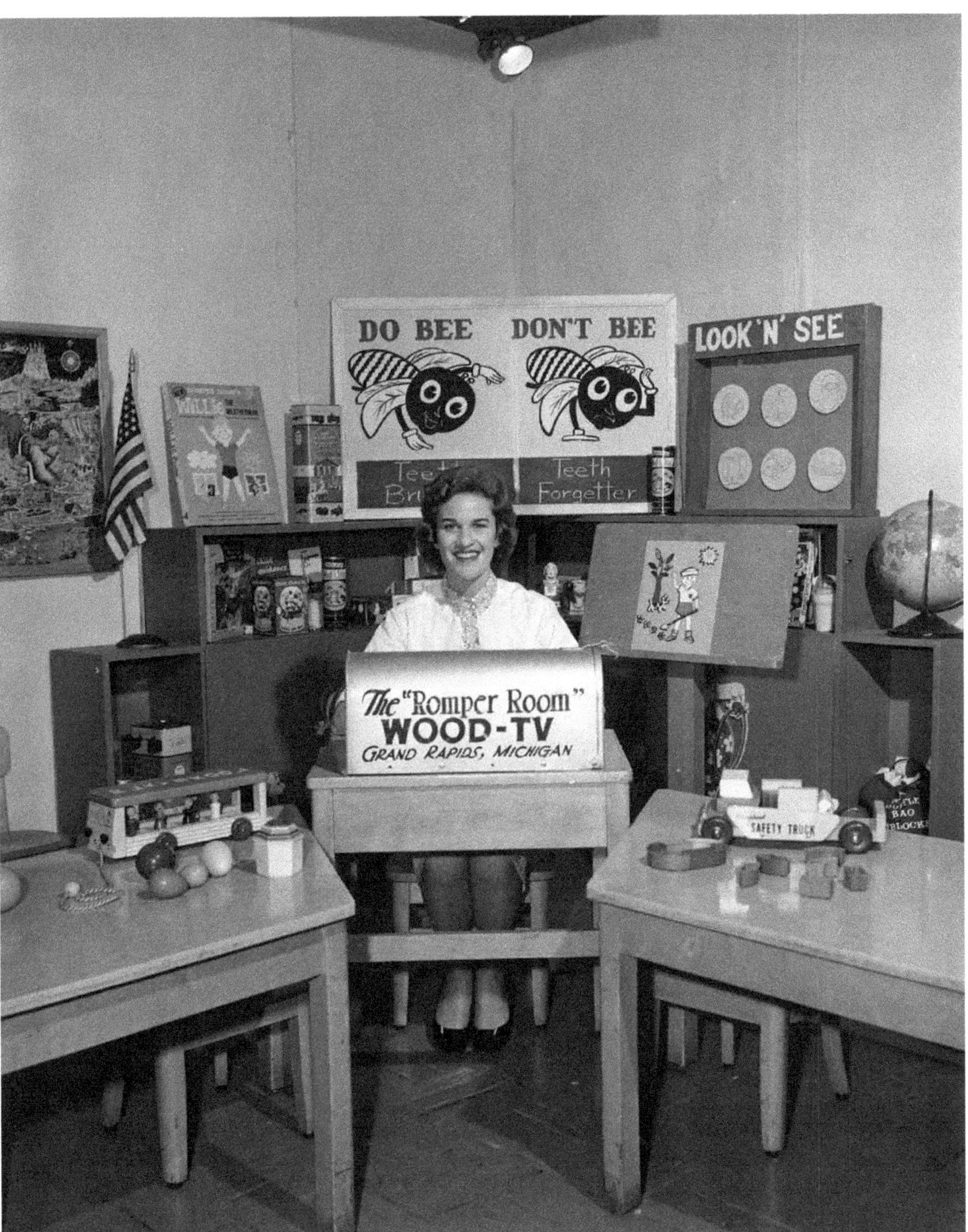

Miss Jean Gordon of WOOD-TV's *Romper Room*. The television show was popular with young children.

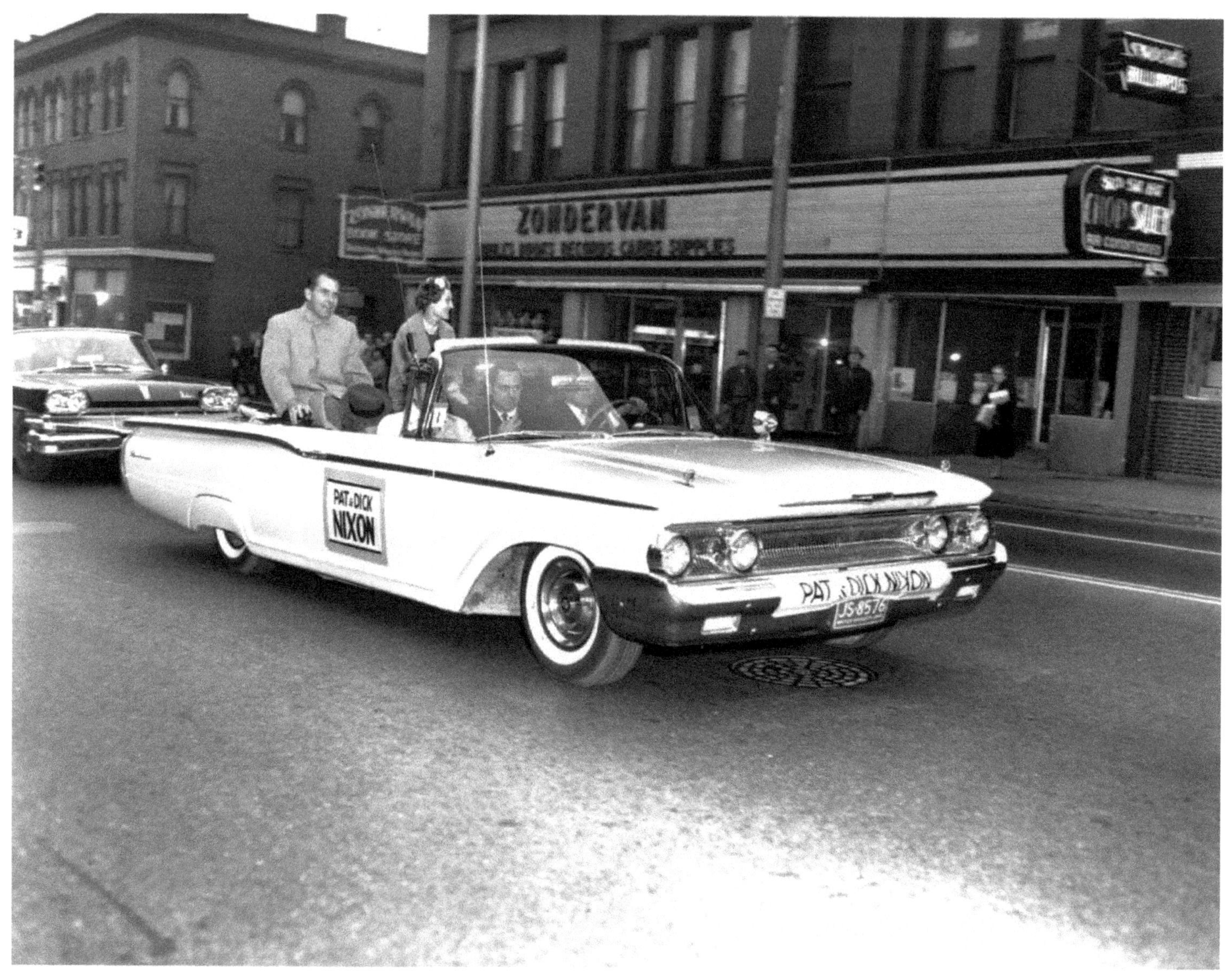

GOP presidential candidate Richard Nixon and wife Pat highlight a parade that drew 72,000 people to Grand Rapids on October 27, 1960. Nixon was unsuccessful in this election but went on to win the Presidency in 1968 and 1972.

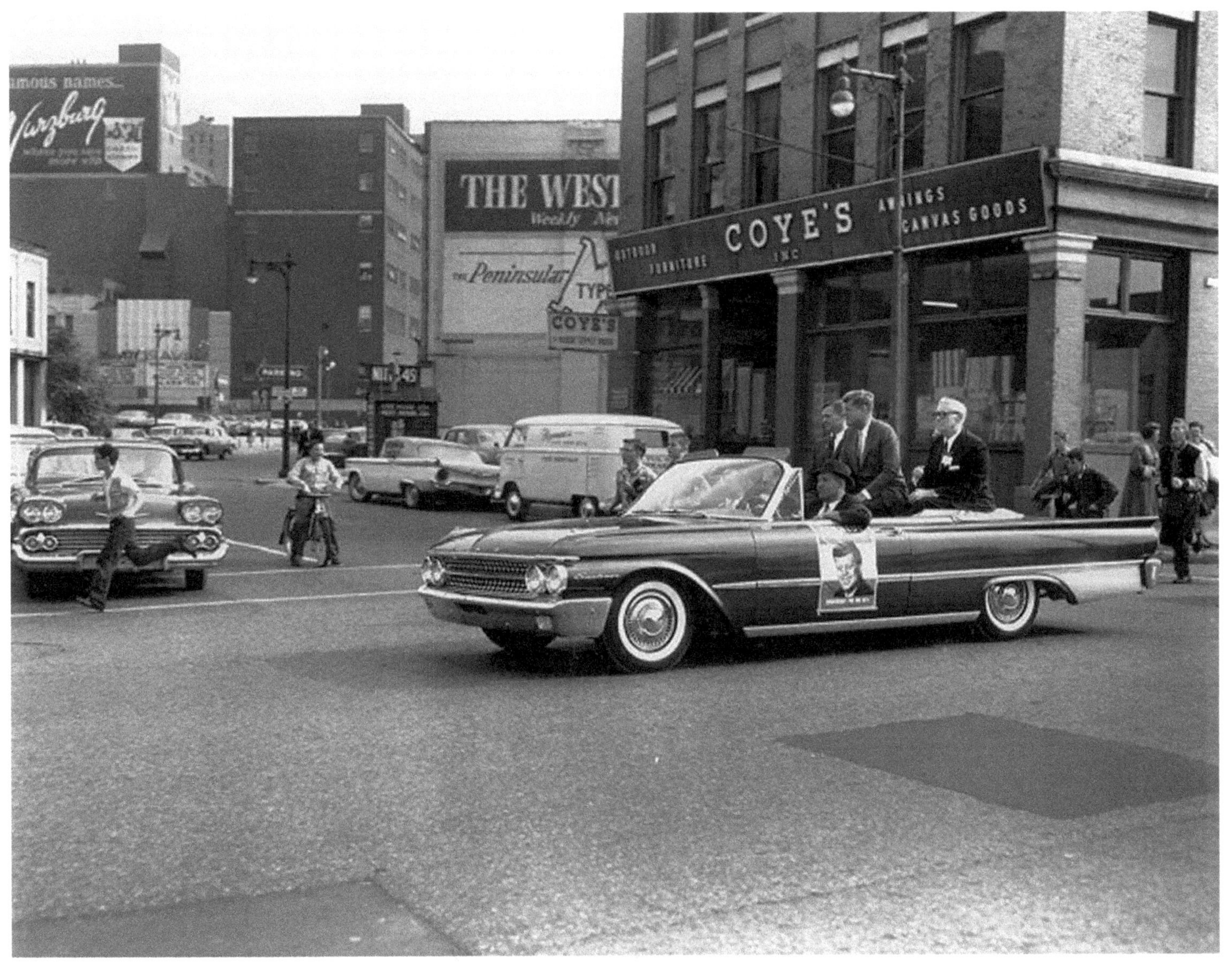

John F. Kennedy parades through downtown Grand Rapids during his 1960 presidential campaign. Kennedy served as President from 1961 until he was assassinated on November 22, 1963.

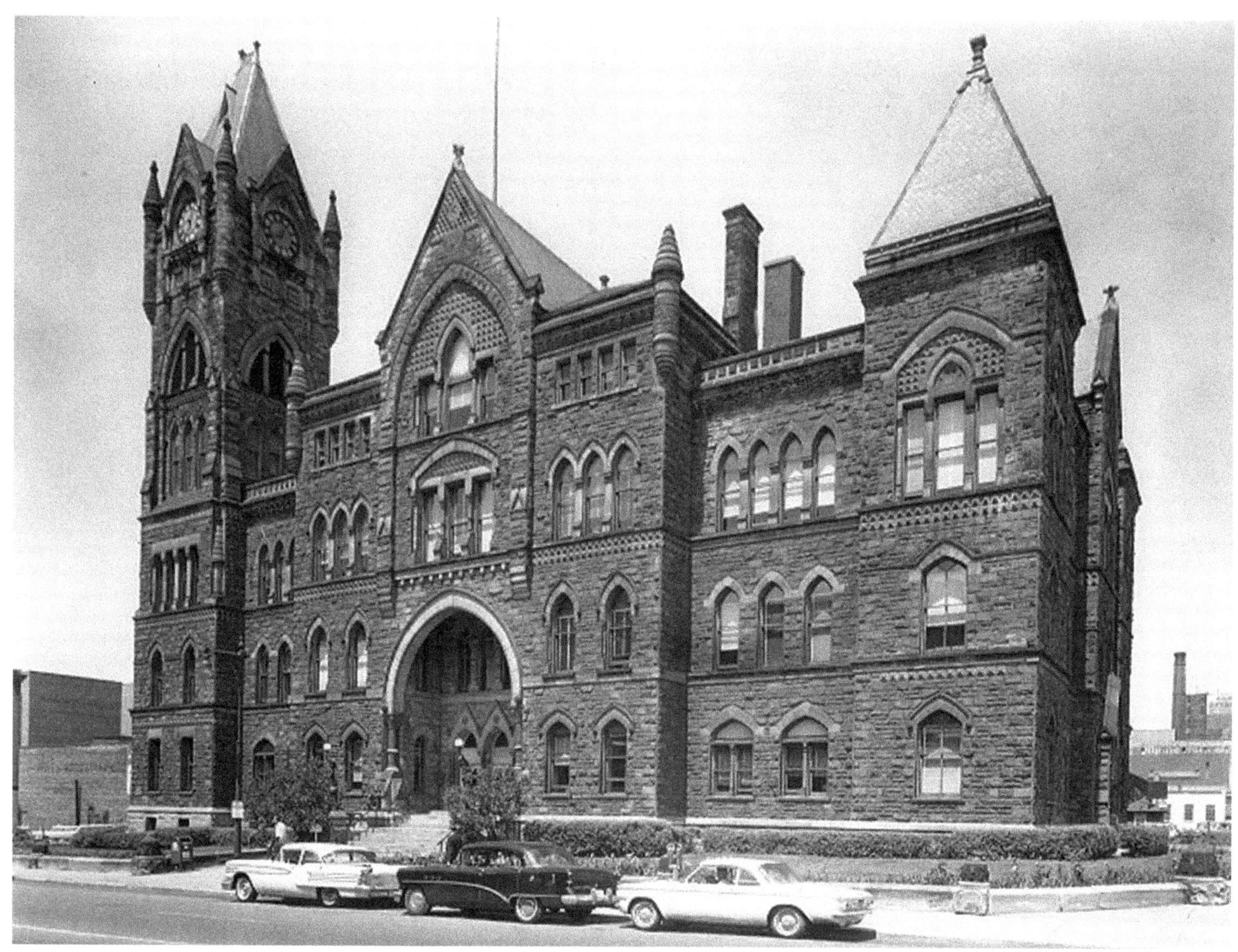

Construction of old City Hall was completed in 1888. It was located on Lyon, between Ottawa and Ionia, and became the subject of much controversy during the urban renewal movement of the 1960s. The stately edifice did not survive.

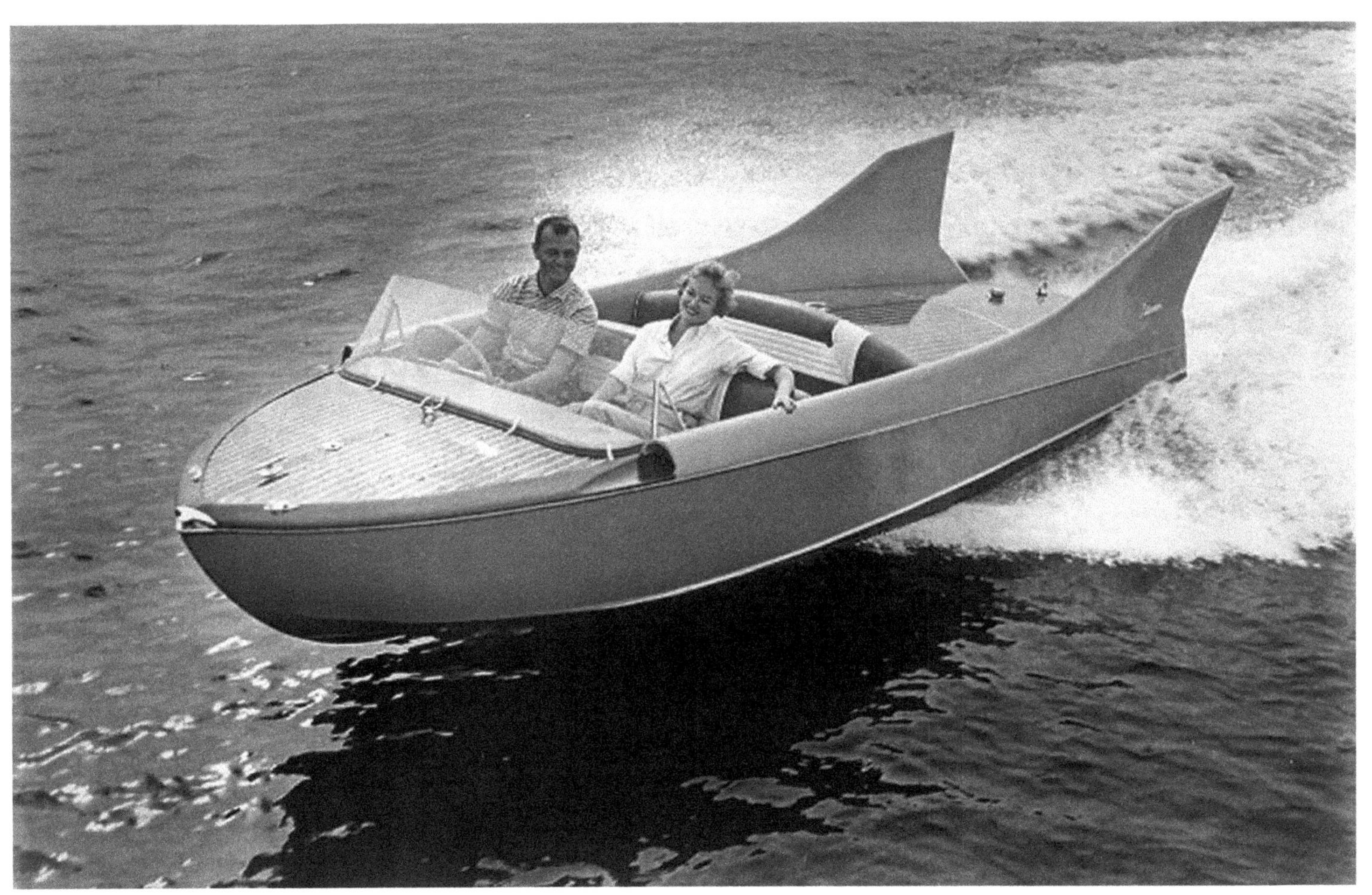

The all-marine plywood *Patrician* runabout, manufactured by Ancarrow Marine, takes a couple out for an enjoyable ride on Reed's Lake.

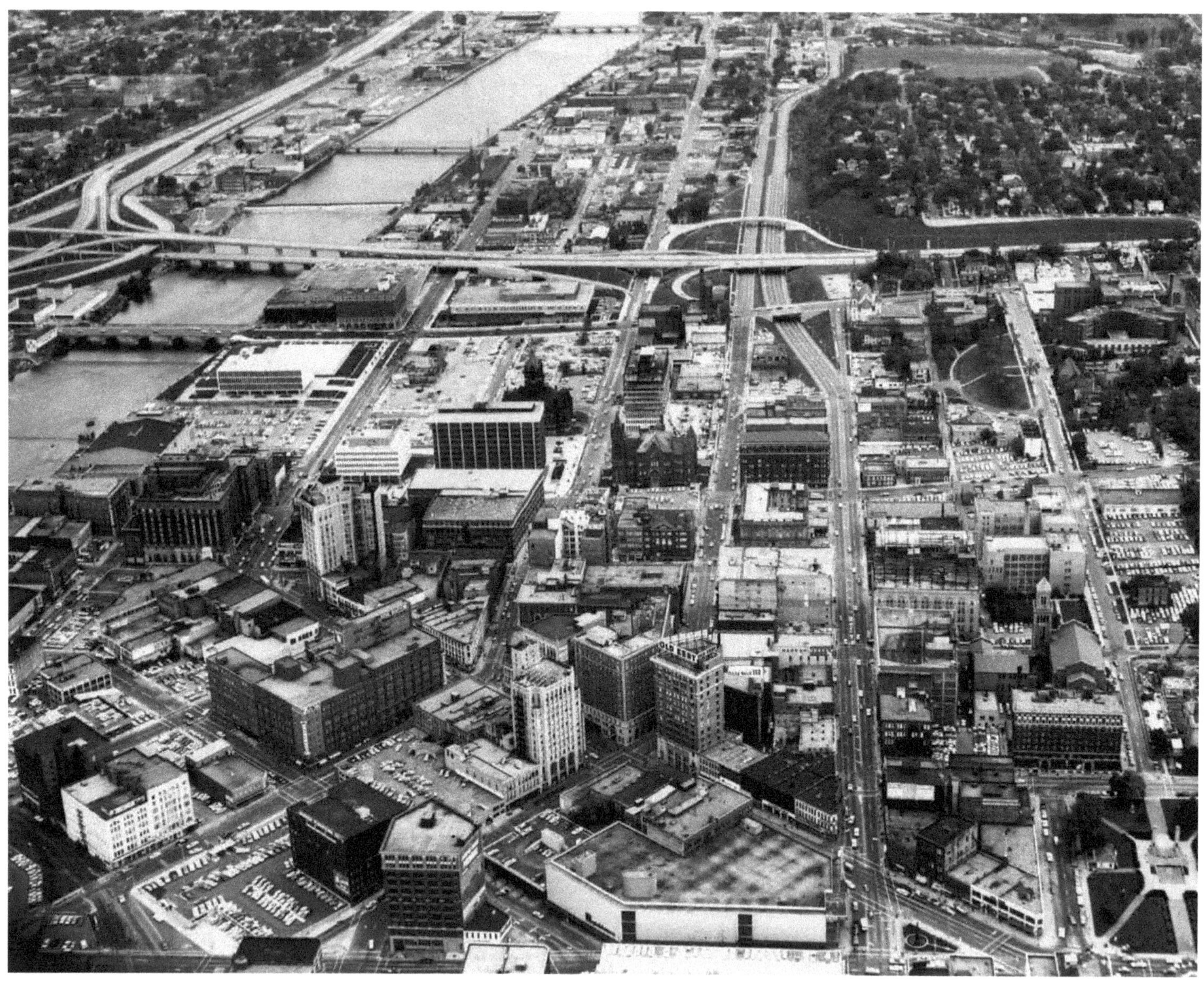

Aerial view of downtown Grand Rapids in 1966. The influence of the automobile, the interstate highway system, and urban renewal is evident, but many of the historic buildings remain standing.

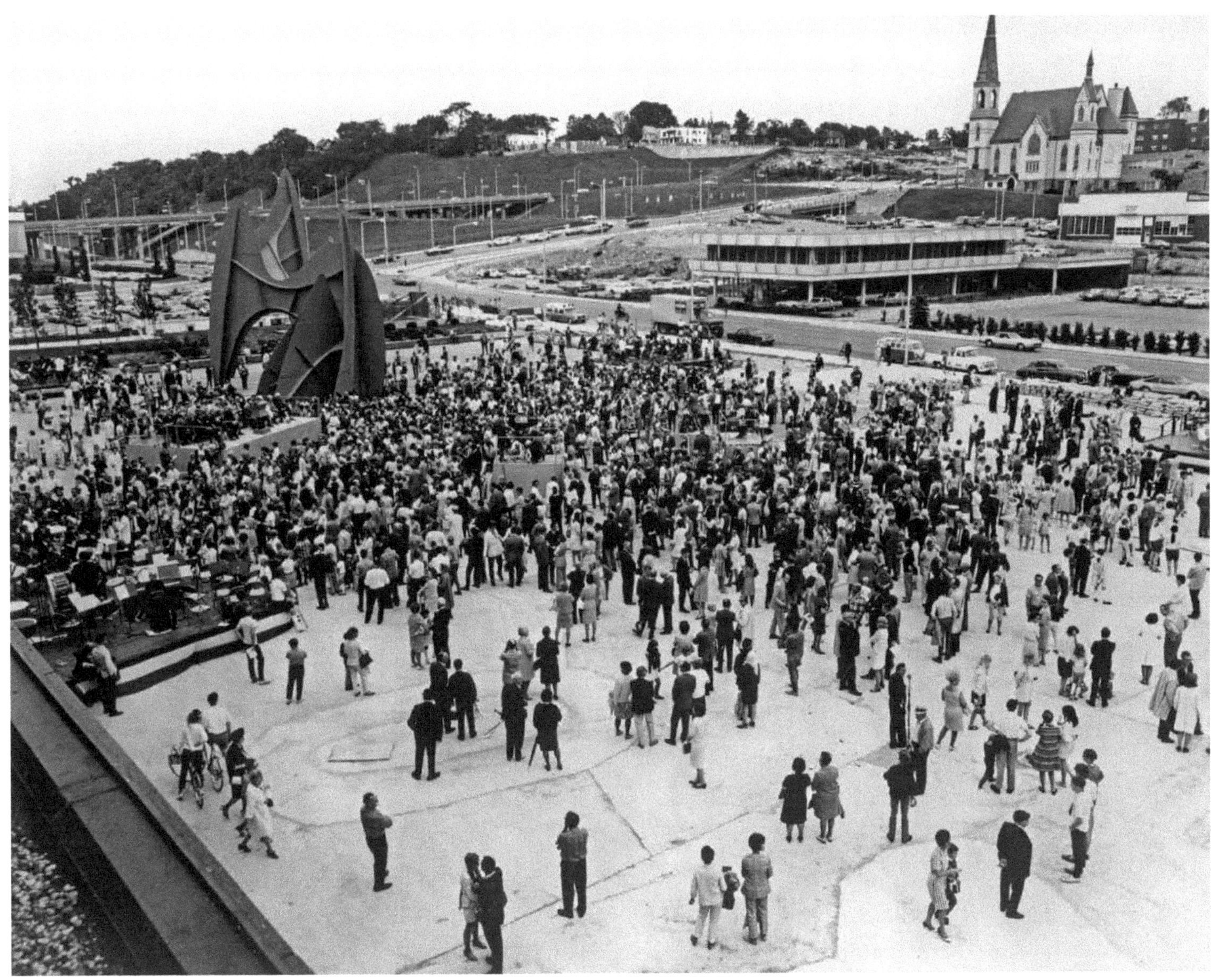

Dedication of *LaGrand Vitesse* by Alexander Calder on June 14, 1969. This was the first sculpture partly funded by the National Endowment for the Arts through the "Works of Art in Public Places" program.

Notes on the Photographs

These notes, listed by page number, attempt to include all aspects known of the photographs. Each of the photographs is identified by the page number, photograph's title or description, photographer and collection, archive, and call or box number when applicable. Although every attempt was made to collect all available data, in some cases complete data was unavailable due to the age and condition of some of the photographs and records.

II **Harvesting and Cutting Logs**
Grand Rapids Public Library
54-18-10

VI **W. H. Barrett**
Grand Rapids Public Library
54-44-12

X **Reed's Lake**
Grand Rapids Public Library
33-12-46.3662

2 **Sixth Street Hill View**
Grand Rapids Public Library
33-12-52.776

3 **Lyon Street**
Grand Rapids Public Library
33-12-52.a588

4 **The L. Jenison**
Grand Rapids Public Library
54-44-12.1662

5 **Wolverine Fire Company**
Grand Rapids Public Library
33-12-41.a430

6 **St. Mark's Episcopal Church**
Grand Rapids Public Library
54-43-11

7 **North Ionia School**
Grand Rapids Public Library
33-12-49

8 **Reed's Lake Street Railway Company**
Grand Rapids Public Library
33-12-51.1942

9 **First Police Headquarters**
Grand Rapids Public Library
33-12-41.1941

10 **C. Kusterer's Lager Beer and Kusterer's Cooper Shop**
Grand Rapids Public Library
54-17-11.1.95

11 **Post Office**
Grand Rapids Public Library
333-12-43.a435

12 **First O-Wash-Ta-Nong Club House**
Grand Rapids Public Library
54-20-30

13 **A Sewing Class**
Grand Rapids Public Library
54-44-24.nn

14 **Sweet's Hotel**
Grand Rapids Public Library
91.1128

15 **Local Football Team**
Grand Rapids Public Library
54-9-5.258

16 **Station and Streetcar Barns**
Grand Rapids Public Library
54-7-12.1.48

17 **First Union Station**
Grand Rapids Public Library
54-45-34.131

18 **Wood and Iron Spans of the Train Shed**
Grand Rapids Public Library
54-45-34.4444

19 **The Grand Steamboat**
Grand Rapids Public Library
54-44-12.936

20 **Pulling Wagons**
Grand Rapids Public Library
54-46-12 assylum

21 **West Bridge Street at Scribner**
Grand Rapids Public Library
91-2-9.96-71.nn

22 **Engine House #6**
Grand Rapids Public Library
54-8-14.2291

24 **Concert at John Ball Park**
Grand Rapids Public Library
54-15-21.30

25 **Wholesale Markets**
Grand Rapids Public Library
54-7-4.4b.86

26 **Ponds at John Ball Park**
Grand Rapids Public Library
54-15-22

27 **Monroe Avenue**
Grand Rapids Public Library
33-12-41

28 **Hooper Blacksmith Shop**
Grand Rapids Public Library
33-12-52.a585

29 **Lumberjacks**
Grand Rapids Public Library
54-18-2.3828

30 **Berkey & Gay Furniture Company Plant #1**
Grand Rapids Public Library
54-4-36

31 **Furniture City Barge**
Grand Rapids Public Library
54-46-12

32 **Widdicomb Furniture Company**
Grand Rapids Public Library
54-48-2.33

33 **R. W. Irwin-Phoenix Furniture Company**
Grand Rapids Public Library
84-17-10.1290

34 **Crescent Street at Kent Street**
Grand Rapids Public Library
91-1-17

35 **Winter Sleigh Ride**
Grand Rapids Public Library
122-23.3578

36 **City Mission and O.K. Laundry**
Grand Rapids Public Library
33-12-52.a587

37 **Island Park**
Grand Rapids Public Library
54-7-4.7.1426

38 **Electric Streetcars**
Grand Rapids Public Library
54-44-21.2619

40 **North Park Pavilion**
Grand Rapids Public Library
54-20-16

41 **Flood of March 1904**
Grand Rapids Public Library
66-1-4.848

42 **Flood of March 1904 #2**
Grand Rapids Public Library
66-1-4.859

43 **Ryerson Public Library**
Grand Rapids Public Library
54-11-6.2597

44 **Mail Carrier**
Grand Rapids Public Library
185-2-36.1646

45 **First Curling Club**
Grand Rapids Public Library
54-7-26.2485

46 **Soda Fountain at West's Drug Store**
Grand Rapids Public Library
69-1-25.25.922

47 **Homecoming Celebration in 1910**
Grand Rapids Public Library
54-11-13.2

48 **Horse-drawn Float**
Grand Rapids Public Library
54-11-13.1

49 **The County Building**
Grand Rapids Public Library
66-1-3.821

50 **Bus Line**
Grand Rapids Public Library
54-5-28.10

52 **Ada Covered Bridge**
Grand Rapids Public Library
43-2-2.423

53 **Streetcars and Automobile**
Grand Rapids Public Library
54-44-21.3030

54 **Police Department**
Grand Rapids Public Library
54-41-15.278

55 **Austin Automobile Company**
Grand Rapids Public Library
143-2.nn

56 **Streetcar on a Snowy Day**
Grand Rapids Public Library
54-44-21.2512

57 **Women's Suffrage Campaign Headquarters**
Grand Rapids Public Library
54-48-8.1545

58 **Killinger's Instrument Repair Shop**
Grand Rapids Public Library
54-17-7

59 **Silver Foam Beer**
Grand Rapids Public Library
54-10-20.2227

60 **Wolverine Brass Works Building**
Grand Rapids Public Library
54-48-7.39

61 **Grand Rapids Airplane Company**
Grand Rapids Public Library
84-21-6.3666

62 **Grand Rapids Airplane Company**
Grand Rapids Public Library
84-21-7.1557

64 **The YMCA**
Grand Rapids Public Library
54-48-14.204

65 **Harry Houdini**
Grand Rapids Public Library
43-1-7.315.nn

66 **School Equipment Company Basketball Team**
Grand Rapids Public Library
54-48-14.4075

67 **The Ramona Steamship**
Grand Rapids Public Library
43-2-1.370

68 **Elks Parade**
Grand Rapids Public Library
54-7-47.4

70 **Grand Rapids Herald Delivery Truck**
Grand Rapids Public Library
54-10-29

71 **Automobile vs. Streetcar**
Grand Rapids Public Library
54-44-21.2662

72 **Saint Mary's Hospital**
Grand Rapids Public Library
54-43-12.nn

73 **The Hart Plate Mirror Company**
Grand Rapids Public Library
54-48-14.4072

74 **League of Women Voters**
Grand Rapids Public Library
141-0-17.4364

75 **Robert W. Irwin Furniture Factory**
Grand Rapids Public Library
84-21-11a.nn

76 **Supporting Prohibition**
Grand Rapids Public Library
101-1-17.2431

77 **Post Office Explosion**
Grand Rapids Public Library
43-1-4.904

78 **Grand Rapids Fire Department**
Grand Rapids Public Library
43-1-4.185.902

80 **Two "Polar Bears"**
Grand Rapids Public Library
43-1-1.37.879

81 **Veterans Parade**
Grand Rapids Public Library
54-46-4.18

82 **Ford-Stout Airplane Miss Grand Rapids**
Grand Rapids Public Library
43-1-1.877

83 **Grand Rapids Girl Scouts**
Grand Rapids Public Library
43-1-3.135.nn

84 **Officer John J. Lemke**
Grand Rapids Public Library
43-2-3.476.3365

85 **Monroe Avenue at Division**
Grand Rapids Public Library
43-231.387.724

86 **Grand Rapids National Bank**
Grand Rapids Public Library
54-6-4.25.1395

87 **Furniture Capital Air Service and Kohler Air**
Grand Rapids Public Library
46.3271

88 **Leonard Street Produce Market**
Grand Rapids Public Library
54-7-4.1423

89 **Wingear Furniture Store**
Grand Rapids Public Library
43-2-2.413

90 **Second Congregational Church**
Grand Rapids Public Library
43-2-2.450

91 **Infant Clinics**
Grand Rapids Public Library
141-10-14.nn

92 **Civil War Monument**
Grand Rapids Public Library
43-1-6.265.nn

93 **Jefferson Avenue Toward Fulton Street**
Grand Rapids Public Library
33-12-52.a583

94 **Script Workers**
Grand Rapids Public Library
67-2-10

95 **Script Workers #2**
Grand Rapids Public Library
67-2-11

96 **Script Workers #3**
Grand Rapids Public Library
67-2-12

97 **Script Workers #4**
Grand Rapids Public Library
67-2-13

98 **DeVaux Automobile**
Grand Rapids Public Library
125-934-2.nn

99 **Script Workers #5**
Grand Rapids Public Library
67-2-8.26

100 **Blodgett Hospital**
Grand Rapids Public Library
125-931.132

101 United Suburban Railway Bus Line
Grand Rapids Public Library
54-5-28.13699

102 Script Workers #6
Grand Rapids Public Library
67-2-6.2

103 Snow Removal
Grand Rapids Public Library
67-2-6.6

104 Civic Auditorium
Grand Rapids Public Library
67-2-13.1714

105 John Ball
Grand Rapids Public Library
54-15-18

106 Radio Room
Grand Rapids Public Library
43-2-3

107 Movie Promotion
Grand Rapids Public Library
125.r35021.4

108 Boy and Toy Car
Grand Rapids Public Library'
125.r35200

109 Grand Army of the Republic Convention
Grand Rapids Public Library
54-46-4.16

110 Ramona Park
Grand Rapids Public Library
125.c031719.2

111 Veteran's Memorial Pillars
Grand Rapids Public Library
43-1-6

112 Float in Furniture Centennial Parade
Grand Rapids Public Library
125.r36750.5

113 Gasoline Station
Grand Rapids Public Library
125.o1084

114 Football Game
Grand Rapids Public Library
125.h005651.11

115 Five Jazz Band
Grand Rapids Public Library
125.12057.3

116 Soda Fountain at Drug Store
Grand Rapids Public Library
125.o2524

117 Aero Sled
Grand Rapids Public Library
125.h015561.2

118 F. W. Woolworth Co.
Grand Rapids Public Library
125.e2676.1

119 Physical Education
Grand Rapids Public Library
125.h016045.1

120 Bike Safety Club
Grand Rapids Public Library
125.h001346.2

122 Monroe Avenue
Grand Rapids Public Library
54-19-36.45.130

123 Pantlind Hotel
Grand Rapids Public Library
54-19-36.2493

124 Luidberg's Grocery Store
Grand Rapids Public Library
125.h010512

125 Crispus Attucks Post of the American Legion
Grand Rapids Public Library
125.c038112a

126 Banquet Bar-B-Q Restaurant
Grand Rapids Public Library
125.h000749.2

127 Monroe Avenue #2
Grand Rapids Public Library
125.h015315.2

128 Naval Reservist
Grand Rapids Public Library
125.h011923.3

129 Regent Theatre
Grand Rapids Public Library
125.2140

130 Hayes Manufacturing Float
Grand Rapids Public Library
125.c016620

131 Western Union Messengers
Grand Rapids Public Library
125.h018524.2

132 Annual Santa Claus Parade
Grand Rapids Public Library
125.h014601.2

133 Bissell Carpet Sweeper Factory
Grand Rapids Public Library
125.e0213.3

134 Bing Crosby
Grand Rapids Public Library
125.h003965.6

135 Fine Arts Building
Grand Rapids Public Library
125.h005360.2

136 Jess Elster and Team
Grand Rapids Public Library
125.018447.1

137 Silver Cloud Tavern
Grand Rapids Public Library
125.c004556.6

138 Harold Foote and C. E. Carpenter
Grand Rapids Public Library
125.h018525.1

139 Japanese Two-Man Submarine
Grand Rapids Public Library
125.h009046.4

140 Clara Bush
Grand Rapids Public Library
125.h014177.1

141 Cole's Laundry
Grand Rapids Public Library
125.h003439

142 Powers Theatre
Grand Rapids Public Library
125.c043686.5

143 Military Officer and Family
Grand Rapids Public Library
125.h017666

144 Lynwood Thomas "Schoolboy" Row
Grand Rapids Public Library
125.h000890.2

145 Giant War Chest
Grand Rapids Public Library
125.h018271

146 Lieutenant Gerald R. Ford
Grand Rapids Public Library
125.h018271

147 R6 Helicopter
Grand Rapids Public Library
125.h007753.2

148 Derby Racer
Grand Rapids Public Library
125.h012045.3

149 Victory over Japan
Grand Rapids Public Library
125.h018093.9

150 Fox Brewing Company
Grand Rapids Public Library
125.e077.3

151 Swimmers at Franklin Park
Grand Rapids Public Library
125.h006057.3

152 Bob Hope and Friends
Grand Rapids Public Library
125.h008279.5

153 Co-ed Members at the YMCA
Grand Rapids Public Library
125.h003365.1

154 Housing Shortage
Grand Rapids Public Library
125.h003989.1

155 Kiwanis Club
Grand Rapids Public Library
125.h019655.4

156 The Grand Rapids Chicks
Grand Rapids Public Library
125.h006950.3

157 The Grand Rapids Chicks #2
Grand Rapids Public Library
125.h006972.2

158 Fallen Heroes
Grand Rapids Public Library
125.h018032.4

159 Ercoupe
Grand Rapids Public Library
125.h019830.1

160 Kelloggsville Kadettes
Grand Rapids Public Library
125.h009570.1

161 President Harry S. Truman
Grand Rapids Public Library
125.h017460.21

162 William Randolph Brown
Grand Rapids Public Library
125.h002059.1

163 Gietzen's Super Service Station
Grand Rapids Public Library
125.c035149.1

164 Frank Lloyd Wright and Wife
Grand Rapids Public Library
125.h020152.1

165 Fox Deluxe Brewing Company
Grand Rapids Public Library
125.c011323

166 The Pantlind Hotel #2
Grand Rapids Public Library
125.e1887.1

167 Downtown Grand Rapids
Grand Rapids Public Library
54-12-1

168 Wilcox Park
Grand Rapids Public Library
46-21c-45.nn

169 Rowe Hotel Coffee Shop
Grand Rapids Public Library
125.e2172

170 Pearl Street Bridge
Grand Rapids Public Library
125.h001990.9

171 Madison Square
Grand Rapids Public Library
125.h010575.4

172 Jack Benny
Grand Rapids Public Library
125.h010253.3

173 Michigan Bakeries
Grand Rapids Public Library
125.e1541.1

174 Skripka's Drug Store
Grand Rapids Public Library
125.e2326

175 Roy Rogers
Grand Rapids Public Library
125.c042954.3

176 Civic Auditorium
Grand Rapids Public Library
54-47-1.3727

177 The Speedrome
Grand Rapids Public Library
125.c035001.13

178 Caution Flag at the Speedrome
Grand Rapids Public Library
125.c035001.5

179 Morton House and Steketee's Department Store
Grand Rapids Public Library
125.c026764

180 Dimestore Block
Grand Rapids Public Library
125.e1020

181 The Ledyard Building
Grand Rapids Public Library
54-17-20.nn

182 Catching the Bus
Grand Rapids Public Library
46-23a-5

183 Michigan National Bank
Grand Rapids Public Library
125.e1661

184 The Grand Rapids Chicks #3
Grand Rapids Public Library
125.c013159.4

185 Capital Airlines
Grand Rapids Public Library
54-4-3

186 Canine Lassie
Grand Rapids Public Library
26-19-1.1.nn

187 Monroe and Ottawa
Grand Rapids Public Library
33-12-52.a597

188 Calvin College Administration Building
Grand Rapids Public Library
125-933.21.nn

189 Gerald R. "Jerry" Ford
Grand Rapids Public Library
125.c011251.1

190 WOOD TV's Bop Hop
Grand Rapids Public Library
125.c038106.1

192 John F. Kennedy
Grand Rapids Public Library
125.c012579

193 Miss Jean Gordon
Grand Rapids Public Library
125.c038110.1

194 Richard Nixon and Wife Pat
Grand Rapids Public Library
125.c010010.3

195 John F. Kennedy #2
Grand Rapids Public Library
125.c010009.1

196 Old City Hall
Grand Rapids Public Library
326.3481

197 The Patrician Runabout
Grand Rapids Public Library
54-5-8.1

198 Downtown Grand Rapids #2
Grand Rapids Public Library
125-934-37.3958

199 LaGrand Vitesse Dedication
Grand Rapids Public Library
1-5-2.5

HISTORIC PHOTOS OF GRAND RAPIDS

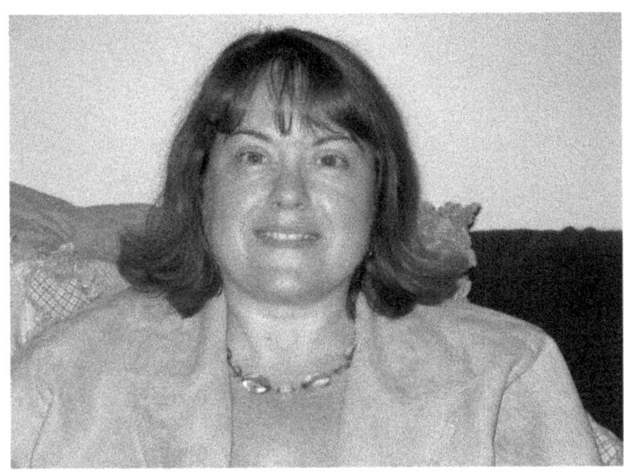

Karolee R. Hazlewood was born and raised in Michigan, living in various cities in the Upper and Lower Peninsulas.

She has worked in the Grand Rapids History and Special Collections Department of the Grand Rapids Public Library for nearly 14 years, and has developed a fondness for Grand Rapids and its rich history.

Karolee's many interests include reading, flea markets, and camping with her family.

What began as a fur-trading post grew into the second-largest city in Michigan, a center for industry and the arts. As "Furniture Capital of the World" and an All-American City three times, Grand Rapids has a fascinating past. *Historic Photos of Grand Rapids* explores that past in images depicting a range of subjects, including the furniture industry, the Flood of 1904, recreational activities, the Pantlind Hotel, the original Ada Covered Bridge spanning the Thornapple River, civic celebrations, a 1941 Monroe Avenue, the 1889 County Building, and countless others.

These striking black-and-white images are the pride of the Grand Rapids Public Library's History and Special Collections Department. Come take a tour through the pages of *Historic Photos of Grand Rapids* and discover the charm of bygone eras, the fortitude of the city's pioneers, and the richness of the old city.

WWW.TURNERPUBLISHING.COM

www.ingramcontent.com/pod-product-compliance
Lightning Source LLC
LaVergne TN
LVHW060604110826
845154LV00003B/35
* 9 7 8 1 6 8 4 4 2 0 2 8 5 *